OXFORD COGNITIVE SCIENCE SERIES

SEEING REASON

OXFORD COGNITIVE SCIENCE SERIES

General Editors
MARTIN DAVIES, JAMES HIGGINBOTHAM, PHILIP JOHNSON-LAIRD,
CHRISTOPHER PEACOCKE, KIM PLUNKETT

Published in the series

Concepts: Where Cognitive Science Went Wrong
Jerry A. Fodor

Context and Content
Robert C. Stalnaker

Mindreading
Stephen Stich and Shaun Nichols

Face and Mind: The Science of Face Perception
Andy Young

Reference and Consciousness
John Campbell

SEEING REASON

Image and Language in Learning to Think

KEITH STENNING

OXFORD

UNIVERSITY PRESS

OXFORD

UNIVERSITY PRESS

Great Clarendon Street, Oxford OX2 6DP

Oxford University Press is a department of the University of Oxford
It furthers the University's objective of excellence in research, scholarship,
and education by publishing worldwide in

Oxford New York

Auckland Bangkok Buenos Aires Cape Town Chennai
Dar es Salaam Delhi Hong Kong Istanbul Karachi Kolkata
Kuala Lumpur Madrid Melbourne Mexico City Mumbai Nairobi
São Paulo Shanghai Singapore Taipei Tokyo Toronto

Oxford is a registered trade mark of Oxford University Press
in the UK and in certain other countries

Published in the United States
by Oxford University Press Inc., New York

© Oxford University Press 2002

The moral rights of the author have been asserted

Database right Oxford University Press (maker)

First published 2002

British Library Cataloguing in Publication Data

Data available

Library of Congress Cataloging in Publication Data

Data available

ISBN 0–19–850773–9
ISBN 0–19–850774–7 (pbk.)
1 3 5 7 9 10 8 6 4 2

Typeset by The Author
Printed in Great Britain
on acid-free paper by
Biddles Ltd.,
Guildford & King's Lynn

Preface

Prefaces are puzzling. It is conventional in prefaces to credit colleagues as the origins of one's true ideas, and to disavow their responsibility for the howlers. This practice assumes at least that one knows which are which. I do not need to spell out the paradox, or its ramifications for the author's responsibilities to his readers. I hasten to assure the reader that though I have strong general grounds for believing that some of the ideas set forth here are false, I have removed all the particular ideas which I believe to be false, to the best of my abilities. For those which remain, I take full responsibility for them being here wheresoever they may have come from.

I would feel this paradox of the attribution of credit and blame even more acutely if it had not been my universal experience that it is ideas that own people rather than people who own ideas. Sometimes when you are in in the grip of an idea it is possible to identify who else it owns in your acquaintance, and sometimes even who it owned first, and who was instrumental in its coming to have its hold over you. This is indeed an intimate relation and a source of pleasure and gratitude. But we have so little choice in these matters, and no choice at all other than extreme gratefulness to colleagues for all the gripping ones—whether they turn out true or false in our own interpretations.

This book grew out of the work of the Graphics and Language Working Group of the Human Communication Research Centre (HCRC), over the past 10 years. The Graphics and Language Working Group included, at various times, Richard Cox, Judith Good, Corin Gurr, Robert Inder, John Lee, Padraic Monaghan, Irene Neilson, Jon Oberlander, Richard Tobin, and Peter Yule. It has been a privilege to work in this group. Without such a varied range of insight a research programme like this would have been unthinkable. If I have not recorded in the text particular acknowledgement for particular contributions, then that is only because the frequency of acknowledgement would have made the text unreadable. In many ways, a jointly authored work would have better reflected credit, but this book is not intended to represent the whole work of the group—only a single strand. The 'we' that recurs so frequently throughout should be taken as referring to members of this group rather than being the authorial plural. The best guide to who did what is the author lists of the associated publications, a good sample of which are in the bibliography. Needless to say, they would all write very different books.

HCRC is an interdisciplinary research centre which was funded by the Economic and Social Research Council (UK) (ESRC) and which began life in 1989. I am grateful to the ESRC for making much of the work reported possible. The Council's long-term commitment to interdisciplinary research enabled us to maintain momentum and direction across the fields of study in a way that short-term grants would have made impossible. Other funders include the Joint Councils' Initiative in Cognitive Science and HCI, the Engineering and Physical Sciences Research Council (EPSRC), NATO, and the McDonnell Foundation of St. Louis. Finally, I must thank the ESRC once again for granting me a Research Fellowship (R 000271074) without which this would probably never have reached the page.

Without John Etchemendy and Jon Barwise's generous support (and that of other members of the Hyperproof team), the empirical programme would have been hugely depleted. They had the not inconsiderable courage to expose their software and their teaching to the electron microscope of behavioural analysis; they went to the lengths of teaching a 'control course' which they would not otherwise have had to teach so that we could obtain more insightful comparisons; they modified the HP software so that we could log student activity 6000 miles away; and they tolerated us under their feet with a thousand naive questions and ten thousand data files. I only regret that Jon will not get to read the setting of this study in its larger context.

The chapter on conditional reasoning reports work that is very much a joint effort with Michiel van Lambalgen. Michiel, a logician, asked me what would be a suitable area in which to get to grips with some cognitively oriented research which used the techniques of the psychology laboratory. His question came at a time when I had become interested in researching an area I had taught for many years—Wason's four-card task. Without Michiel's intervention this work would not have got underway, and without his time, energy, and insight (to say nothing of his speed up the learning curve) I would never have come to see how the study of conditional reasoning complements the other work reported here. Magda Osman gave us lots of help and insightful criticism with the observational work.

I thank the Center for the Study of Language and Information (CSLI) at Stanford for hosting a research visit which made writing possible, and the Stanford students who took the course 'Seeing Reason' and helped me eliminate at least some obscurities. Patrick Scotto DiLuzio gave me particularly insightful feedback on Chapter 2.

Several colleagues, in particular, Rick Alterman, John Lee, and Padraic Monaghan, have read the whole or parts of the book and it has benefited greatly from their comments. Christopher Peacocke made insightful editorial comments which materially improved the book.

Without the time and patience of the several hundred students who submitted themselves as part of their classes to the strange tasks in the various experiments and observations reported here, there would have been no book. It was often a source of frustration to me that I could not explain the purpose of our work to them more adequately, either for lack of their time, or for lack of my understanding. Some of them may now get a chance to read the considered outcome, and be reassured that their investment of time and effort has benefited subsequent classes.

Finally, I must thank Lynn and Nye for tolerating the authorial moods with good grace. Living with someone else's book must rank high amongst tests of patience. And Fingal Brown, for putting in almost as many hours as I did at the desk.

July 2002   K. S.

Contents

. . . .

To Caroline and Dave

1 Swallowing squiggles—the internalization of formalisms

What difference does it make whether information is presented in words or in diagrams? Diagrams, and philosophical puzzlement about their meaning, have been with us at least since classical Greece. But the sudden expansion of computer display facilities has been one of the driving forces behind recent interest in this question. A pandora's box of 'multimeejah' has burst upon the computer user, with mixed results for his or her consumption of information, and the issues, both practical and theoretical have been taken up by researchers in a range of disciplines. Having to instruct machines how to process diagrams has been wonderfully revealing of how practically significant these philosophical puzzles turn out to be.

Both the theoretical and the practical concerns demand a theory of human information consumption—a theory which can tell us which picture is worth which ten thousand words, for whom, doing what task, with what background skill and knowledge. This theory must explain the similarities and differences between diagrammatic and linguistic representation systems.

Cognitive science was founded above all on the study of the structure of natural language. It was this focus which enabled the different disciplines concerned (artificial intelligence, computer science, linguistics, philosophy, psychology, . . .) to see a common focus camouflaged in a jungle of methods. But when the research this book reports began around 1990, the methods for studying natural language syntax and semantics had barely been applied to any representations other than artificial and natural languages. This provoked the question whether we could use the insights of natural language semantics to investigate the properties of images, and to compare them with language?

This is of course an exaggeration of the neglect. Chandrasekaran *et al.* present a useful sample of the narrow thread of interest in diagrams before this time along with some contemporary papers. But it is exaggeration in the service of truth. The vast majority of concern with semantics had been with language, and the vast majority of concern with imagery had been in terms of the imagery debate which was focused on the nature of internal mental representation (Block 1981). The longevity of that debate is testimony to the inaccessibility of these theoretical entities. Far less attention had been paid to the readily accessible external representations on paper and screen and their relations to mental processes.

Could we develop a theory of the cognitive effects of the modality of information presentation which went all the way from the semantic fundamentals to the impact on communication and thought? There are always a thousand excuses for stopping short of studying thinking, but once questions are defined by *comparison* of modalities of presentation, then it is much harder to sidestep these issues.

At the outset, as always with semantic studies, the focus was heavily on the banal. Diagrams consisting of a pair of circles proved quite sufficiently challenging without considering technicolour moving images. Two Euler's circles are to diagrams what Tarski's 'Snow is white' is to sentences—the bare bleached bones of representations— but quite sufficiently rich to cause lots of trouble. Starting here with simplest cases tends to be acceptable to logician or philosopher, but lest psychologists desert, I promise to show that the semantic theory that results has real measurable behavioural consequences for the mental processes of students using multimedia interactive learning environments during real college courses on reasoning.

It was a piece of extreme good fortune, born partly of necessity and certainly of convenience, that led us to investigate the cognitive impact of diagrams on *learning*, and especially on learning logic in our own classrooms. We could have chosen (and have in other studies) to explore the use of diagrams in practice (software engineering, for example) rather than in learning. Even within learning, plenty of topics further from the study of communication and reasoning than elementary logic are available.

Getting farther from our own classrooms and from the teaching of the analyst's own logical tools might have fitted in better at the surface level with demands for ecological validity. But ecology demands a deep understanding of the environment, and it was lucky that we did choose to study the learning of reasoning. Without a grasp of the ecology of the classroom built up over years, it would have been much harder to get to grips with the data of learning. And learning turns out to be fundamental for understanding modality differences in communication.

So the research came to be at least as much about the discourse of learning (and in particular learning to reason and communicate) as it is about the different impact of images and language. If one wants a theory that can go all the way from semantic fundamentals to impact on communication and thinking, then that places heavy demands on understanding precisely *what* has to be learned, the practices in which learning can be observed, the conceptual starting point of the students, and what changes when teaching and learning are both effective. Somewhat to our surprise, the research increasingly developed a focus on a theory of educational communication.

Educational communication is well known to be a hard case. Teacher and student are under no illusion that success is assured. Both know at the outset that they do not speak the same language about the topic at hand. If their communication succeeds, then they emerge with a newly mutual language. Hard cases may make bad law, but they stretch theories, and theories of communication need some stretching if they are to deal with the communication of new concepts. A theory of human communication that cannot explain how concepts are communicated is hardly worthy of the name.

The learning of elementary logic taught with and without diagrammatic aids will seem a highly specialized arena for developing a theory of representational behaviour. And so it is—a microcosm. How should we think of this microcosm so that we can generalize from it? Elementary logic teaching as studied here uses various formalisms— artificial languages, diagrammatic systems and natural language itself. At one superficial level of understanding, these formalisms—the famous Ps and Qs we learn to mind—just are the novel subject matter of logic. But they make a pretty odd subject matter, and indeed a search amongst them for subject matter quickly reveals that it is difficult to find any novel topic. Logic is about reasoning, and if students could not reason, they would not be in logic class. In fact, if logic is merely minding Ps and Qs, then students' native reasoning might better keep them out of logic class altogether.

Topics with these two characteristics—they use novel formalisms and they make explicit something already implicitly known—are actually widespread in the curriculum. The most obvious examples—the two that loom largest for the greatest number of students—are learning to write one's native language and learning mathematics. Both are closely related to logic. When children are taught to write, what they learn is to formalize their own behaviour—to transcribe their own speech. In learning, the child internalizes a formalism—'swallows the squiggles'. Doing so brings about widespread changes in the child's language itself, what the child can do with it, and the child's social competences. Talk of formalisms in this book is to be construed in this broad sense in which writing is a formalism. In fact the formalisms of logic are best seen as extensions of the formalisms of orthography.

Thinking of learning as the incorporation of formalisms opens up many questions about learning. What has to be there already? How is the new formalism 'attached' to what is there? How does this change the repertoire of the student? If learning to write is learning a formalism for speech, how are we to think of the acquisition of speech? Some of these questions were, of course, first made famous by Vygotsky (1978 translation) in revolutionary Russia. What follows here should be seen as an attempt to bring to bear a modern understanding of representational systems on some problems that Vygotsky would have found familiar.

Although in the twentieth, the uses of logic may have given the appearance that it belongs as a part of mathematics or computer science, logic's origins are as a theory of the adversarial communication that is the business of courtroom and parliament. Reasserting these origins makes it clear that logic is dialogical and dramatic. Learning logic is swallowing squiggles, but squiggles that formalize social relations of cooperation and competition. Here is the basis of a theory of communication which can explain how communication is an essentially social activity however much cognitive apparatus is required to engage in it; and can even go on to explain why talking to oneself can be so rewarding. Along with the squiggles, a community is internalized.

For this traditional founding of communication on logic to work, the modern technical expansion of logic plays a vital part. The lessons learned in logic through analysing the foundations of mathematics cannot be left behind. The most important of these many modern understandings of representation systems, one that needs much more extensive application in cognitive science, is that faced with an argument, there are always many systems in which to interpret it, and the resulting representations can be viewed system-externally as well as system-internally. Cognitive science has so far been dominated by theories which portray mental processes as system-internal reasoning—in single grammars, logics, expert systems or whatever. One of the most useful lessons of comparing diagrammatic with sentential modalities is that there are many distinct systems of representation, and a substantial part of human reasoning is choosing, or constructing, or finding a system, and an interpretation in which to solve the problem. As a slogan: *people reason by finding a representation in which the problem is trivial to solve. If they can't find one, they give up.*

This slogan is over-dramatized, but not much. Sustained intra-systemic reasoning is rather rare outside a few arcane professional practices. The literature on problem solving is all about finding good representations often for problems deliberately concocted to suggest bad ones. However, from a computational point of view, this slogan is deeply paradoxical. Computing over representation systems to find one that makes the particular problem tractable—however could one do that? How could one know that the reasoning was tractable within a system, without actually solving the problem first? And the range of possible representations is so utterly vast, how is this landscape structured that we can search it? One of the empirical findings of the research reported here is that people appear to have a variety of contrasting ways of going about this search. Study of these differences is a promising way into the field empirically.

The technical understanding of the distinction between object-level (intra-systemic) and meta-level (extra-systemic) phenomena is crucial for understanding human communication, reasoning and learning as computation. Focusing on modality differences forces us to think about choices between systems because diagrams and sentences just look so different. As long as the different systems are all sentential languages, or even all semantic interpretations of the same sentential language, then it is too easy to elide system-external reasoning about which system to adopt with system-internal reasoning to solve the problem.

Another barrier to psychologists' applying the relevant lessons of modern logic to understanding human reasoning has been the issue about how form is related to content. Formalisms may make it easier to understand computation, but they pose, particularly transparently, deep problems about how content attaches to form. Even as formal understandings of logic and computation have reached new heights of sophistication, psychological acceptance of their relevance to understanding human reasoning has reached a new trough. Psychologists frequently assert that we reason in virtue of content, believing this to be an alternative to reasoning in virtue of form, and that logic is of no help in guiding our researches into the processes involved.

Two examples among many will suffice for to give a taste of how these ideas are made concrete. In the narrow field of the psychology of deductive reasoning, the two main theories (mental models theory) and mental logic theory see the central issue as the nature of the mental representation system in which we reason. Mental models theory claims that its representations are 'semantic' in some way that the representations of mental logics are not. As we shall see (in Chapter 4), simple logical analysis shows that the systems proposed by the two theories are indistinguishable for the kind of evidence provided. Every particular theory of processing formulated in one framework can be emulated in the other. The issue of how either formalism attaches to the content it encodes is essentially the same issue for both theories. If one is 'semantic' in whatever sense is intended, then the other can be semantic in the same sense. How can theories address the attachment of content to form? In Chapter 6 we again will see mental models theory failing to address the reasoner's problem of choosing between the many alternative interpretations of the task and materials in Wason's selection task. Ironically, despite mental models theory's rejection of logic as a basis for explaining human reasoning, it adopts a single narrow logical interpretation of Wason's materials as a competence model for assessing subjects' reasoning. Psychology needs a modern logical appreciation of object and meta levels, and to take the process of interpretation seriously as a real mental process.

A second example is the claim of the 'evolutionary psychologists' that human reasoning is conducted by many special innate modules. This sweeping assertion is founded on an analysis of the difference in undergraduate students' performance on Wason's (1968) selection task, and in particular on the observation that this task is easier when reasoning about 'social contract exchanges' than about descriptive regularities. In Chapter 6 we shall see how a slight inspection of the semantics of the conditional shows that these two kinds of rules present tasks of very different complexity in Wason's setting. Whatever our Pleistocene ancestors used to get up to, present-day undergraduates show the kind of behaviour one would expect from the complexity profile of these tasks. What is more, the evolutionary psychologist's 'cheating-detector' widgets, under any reasonable specification, ought to be able to perform the task with descriptive conditionals. This reanalysis suggests something like the opposite evolutionary story— that communication in general intentionally interpreted representation systems must have preceded 'social contractual exchange'.

One of the goals of this book, then, is to propose a quite different and much more intimate and multifaceted relation between logic and psychology in the study of cognitive processes, especially of reasoning and communication. Our focus on learning and teaching formalisms gives new perspectives on the issues: it proposes that much human reasoning is meta-reasoning about representation systems; that there are many possible relations between logical description and mental process with many different causal involvements for a particular logical analysis; that psychology should often be about how systems are implemented in minds; that affect plays a critical role in implementing reasoning; and that logic is the fundamental mathematics of information systems, so that ignoring logical analyses when doing empirical analyses of behaviour is usually a poor strategy.

With the goal of understanding how formalisms figure in human social and mental processes we are turned back on classical issues about meaning but in the new guise of questions about how representation systems are implemented in minds. Here there is some advantage in starting with cases in which the formalism starts life outside the student's mind (in the textbook) and winds up inside, after successful learning. This Vygotskyan perspective on formalisms as cognitive technologies, contrasts with the naturalistic perspective that sees formalisms as analysing systems which exist already in human nature—logic as the laws of thought (or grammar, or whatever).

Our proposal is not that the technological view replace the naturalistic. Understanding human reasoning demands both perspectives, and some clarity about their relations. Not just any formalism can be internalized, and the process of internalization has to connect it to what is there already. Psychological theory needs to explain how form is found in content, both on the ephemeral level of the problem at hand, and in the longer term processes of learning new formal systems. If we think of reasoning as always conducted within one system of representation, then these processes of finding form are mysterious. But if we realize how much of human reasoning is settling on a system to reason within, then this provides the framework we need to study them.

If in the course of research it was surprising how prominent the discourse of education became, it was an even greater surprise to me in the writing of this book how questions about the relation between cognition and emotion ended up centre stage. Emotion figures in the classical psychological literature on reasoning as an interference with the orderly operation of cognition. Our resuscitation of an older social role for logic in communication shows how inadequate this interference model proves for emotion. On the view that emerges, logic plays its part as a criterion for alignment between interpretations, especially in adversarial communication, when meanings are least clear and passions most inflamed. The resulting theory sees communication as the articulation of feelings through the development of representations and interpretations of them. But it also sees affect as the source of many abstract concepts, and comes to the view that our affective structure should be seen as implementing our cognitive systems. The final chapter makes some speculative proposals about these relationships to social understandings of communication.

Having entered the maze with a question about diagrams and sentences, we exit with a reorganized framework for relating the cognitive, the social and the affective phenomena of communication and reasoning. Only within such a framework are the detailed questions answerable about which diagram is worth which ten thousand words and when a diagram is not worth the paper it is drawn on. The journey in between cuts across the fields of research as conventionally constituted. This makes it hard to do justice to any of them. We must crave the reader's indulgence. Our only excuse is that something from all of these fields turns out to be required to answer the questions at hand, and the act of attempting to find an overall map of how the fields contribute to the answer forces reappraisals of each contribution. Perhaps the unsatisfactoriness of our efforts will goad the experts to propose alternative solutions?

The book aspires to be readable without a technical grasp of each field, especially of logic. It is the very elementary concepts that are critical, and every attempt has been made to explain them in the text. From experience, the problems of this interdisciplinary approach are far more to do with preconceptions (often deeply held) about what other disciplines claim, than about the technicality of the concepts. Above all we must crave the readers' suspension of these preconceptions. Some particular clashes between the usage of different fields are highlighted in the text.

Although the aim is a cognitive theory, our course is never far from some intensely practical issues in education. The teaching of general reasoning and communication skills has been repeatedly identified under slightly different terminology and different guises as a contemporary problem in many countries around the world. In Scotland, the talk is of 'core skills'; in England of 'key skills'; in the USA of 'critical thinking' and 'enquiry'. In Asia there is a belief that there must be some conflict between asian social structures based on the seeking of consensus, and the development of the skills of conducting controversy. And so on.

On all sides the cry goes up of crises in the teaching of these elusive topics. Whether we are doing any worse than any previous generation of educators in teaching thinking skills is far from clear. What is clear is that our cultures have decided that these skills should be taught to a far wider range of students than the small elites who used to be deemed sufficient. The demands of our workplace environments for thinking skills is becoming ever more intense, with resulting calls for 'lifelong learning'. The sheer growth and differentiation of technical knowledge also emphasizes the problems of transferring learning across domains, and of communication between experts, and between experts and public.

The reader should be warned that a single answer to the question of how best to teach reasoning and thinking skills is not forthcoming here. The main empirical investigations presented are studies of the teaching and learning of some component reasoning skills, at a certain level to a certain kind of student. They do at least provide evidence, that teaching these essentially ancient topics formally *can* improve general reasoning skills—a claim widely dismissed on rather little evidence in recent times. But not just any formal teaching will do, and it is not intended to dismiss informal methods merely because we do not explore them here. We do not intend to denigrate other methods, nor to claim these specific methods will work without adaptation for students in general.

I hope a much more important contribution of this work to the educational debate is a theoretical understanding of what these mysterious skills are; of some of the mechanisms that are involved in the transfer of general reasoning skills from domain to domain; and of their relation to our value systems. What is it that we learn when we learn to reason, to communicate and to think? What is it that is in common, despite all the differences, across domains of knowledge? In what sense is logic universal, and in what sense is it extremely local? Where does its authority originate?

In our intensely specialized educational (and, for that matter, research) system these conceptual answers are of some importance. The days when logic could get away with establishing its relevance by simple imperialism are long gone. Logic is a special science. Its subject matter is the understanding of representation systems and their deployment in reasoning. As society simultaneously differentiates and globalizes, reasoning and communication across divides become an ever larger part of our gross national product. Logic is a special science, but one which everyone needs to apply. There cannot be one answer about how to teach such skills to the whole range of students for the whole range of purposes they need them. But knowing something more about what constitutes these skills is a prerequisite for tailoring teaching methods to context.

In Chapter 2 we begin by laying out a theory of the commonalities and distinguishing characteristics of sentential and diagrammatic representation systems. We propose that graphical presentations need to be more finely classified in order to make progress on our question about when they make reasoning easier. In fact some graphical systems are 'just like' sentential systems. We propose a terminology in which only 'directly interpreted' graphics are considered to be diagrams. This reclassification, like many theoretically motivated ones, does some violence to everyday usage, but gains something in insight. It enables an explanation of the ways that systems get their significance and how that determines their tractability for reasoning. This analysis focuses attention on the differences in the expression of abstraction which are the key to empirical investigations.

As they stand, the proposals are purely conceptual, but we need to connect them to the empirical phenomena of human reasoning. Chapter 3 finds a place to evaluate the theory empirically in a study of the impact of teaching elementary reasoning skills using a multi-media computing environment called Hyperproof. This study vindicates logic teaching's ability to improve general reasoning skills, but its most striking results are the exposure of *differences* in students' reasoning styles. These styles can be related directly to the contrasting semantics of the diagrammatic and sentential modalities described in the previous chapter. Analysis of the reasoning processes underlying these styles reveals much about the strategies and representations students develop.

Chapter 4 tests the generality of the Hyperproof findings by studying a microcosm of logic learning in the laboratory. Syllogisms have been a part of the curriculum since classical times. Diagrams have been used for teaching syllogisms since the eighteenth century. Syllogisms have been extensively studied by psychologists in search of 'the fundamental human deduction mechanism' since early last century. We apply semantic analysis to existing alternative theories of how naive students solve syllogisms without external representational aids, and question how distinct the theories are. We then look at some new data on students' learning to use alternative external representation systems. Here we can actually see differences in students' learning evidenced in their dialogues with their tutor. The results lead to a reappraisal of the way we attempted to connect semantic theory to behavioural prediction in Chapter 2. In learning new representation systems, it is not just expressiveness that affects reasoning, but also whether the constraints on expressiveness of weak systems are available to the learner.

Having presented some evidence that students do learn something in logic classes, Chapter 5 raises the question of how it can be possible even to think of *learning* logic. If logic is the fundamental pattern of thought, how can we learn it? Chapter 5 proposes a rational analysis of just what it is that students have to learn—an analysis which makes sense of their 'errors', and explains why learning logic is both possible and hard. We might summarize this analysis with the slogan: 'It's the discourse stupid'.

Chapter 5 goes on to present evidence for our rational analysis through an empirical study based on Grice's original observations, made as a teacher of logic, of students' quantifier inferences. The study focuses on the relation between students' naive interpretations of quantifiers, and their reasoning from those interpretations. The results reveal systematic and contrasting patterns of interpretation before students receive any logic instruction. These patterns can be thought of as reflecting alternative student models of communication, and can be related to the individual differences observed in earlier chapters.

A cognitive theory of the incorporation of formalisms needs to explain the process whereby content is encountered and provides cues to how to impose form, reason with it, and translate back into contentful response. Chapter 6 looks at the relation between form and content through three illustrations: conditional reasoning in Wason's selection task; analogical reasoning; and problems in word-meaning.

Wason's selection task involves seeking evidence for conditional rules, and has been one of the main sources of psychologists' arguments that logic is not an adequate basis for a theory of human deductive reasoning. It has also served as the foundation of a particular 'evolutionary psychology' which claims to be able to read the course of human evolution from these observations. We argue that semantic studies of the conditional provide a necessary basis for understanding the phenomena of Wason's task and for explaining how content is engaged in reasoning. Again, an alternative conceptual analysis highlights the relevance of new kinds of data, some of which is presented here, and throws doubt on the founding evidence of evolutionary psychology.

Analogical reasoning also poses the problem of imposing form on content—two 'contents' simultaneously. Founding a psychology of representation on a logical basis allows us to see analogical reasoning as the finding or construction of representation systems, and subsequently reasoning within them. This is another example of the need to observe the meta-level/object-level distinction in psychological analysis. Our further distinction between directly interpreted diagrams and indirectly interpreted sentential languages casts analogical reasoning as the operation of direct systems of representation (analogies) generally through indirect systems (languages). We propose that an important basis for much analogical reasoning is the affective structure we assign to narratives.

Thirdly, word-meaning is an obvious point at which content meets form. Under-standing logical semantics as a model for natural language requires that it is seen as a criterion for the mutual alignment of interpretations in communication, and that it applies at the fully contextualized level of the discourse of argument, rather than the synoptic level of the language's lexicon. We develop some of the consequences of this view by contrasting it with Lakoff's interpretation of 'cognitive semantics' and then by revisiting Wittgenstein's arguments about the meaning of the word 'game'. Both examples point to a role of affect in implementing word-meanings. These three cases—conditional reasoning, analogical reasoning, and word-meaning—illustrate something of what is involved in a cognitive theory of how form engages content.

Finally, Chapter 7 takes up questions about the relation between systems of represen-tation and their implementations in individuals and communities. The earlier chapters' consideration of formalisms and their engagement with content lead us to the 'argument' model of communication, founded on a traditional interpretation of logic. This model is shown to combine both essentially cognitive and essentially social elements, and is defended against some common misconceptions. But how, on this view, are systems of representation instrumental in communication and other mental processes?

Representations systems can be theorists tools for analysing nature, or can be 'tech-nologies' for thinking. Both these stances require integration in a cognitive theory of representation. They pose different problems for evolutionary accounts of how hu-mans came to be such a peculiar species which could theorize about its own behaviour and mental processes, and incorporate the resulting formalisms into its own mind's workings. We end with three illustrations of how our affective structure is the key to understanding how systems are implemented in human individuals and communities: from neuropsychology, from conditional reasoning again, and from the anthropological study of symbolism.

Our aim then is to restore to its central position in cognitive science, the study of representations systems and their implementations in minds and societies. To get the many relations between psychology and logic right requires that we take a much more abstract view of logical systems than is customary in psychology, and to combine that abstract understanding with a broadly based study of implementation. Only then can it be seen what part informational abstractions play in cognitive processes. Only then shall we be able to make sense of the different disciplines contributions to our understanding of minds.

2 Representation systems

2.1 Systematicity

The study of representation systems is conventionally introduced through artificial sentential languages, and their correspondences to natural languages. The goal of comparison of sentential languages with other systems means starting a little farther back, by describing representation systems only some of which will involve sentences. Here what is critical is the **systematic** nature of the representations. Starting from this far back focuses on commonalities between diagrams and sentences; later in the chapter we shall come to the differences which are so important for determining the consequences of choosing one modality or another.

Systems of representations are sets of objects (sentences, diagrams, films . . .) each of which stands for something else. These sets are often essentially infinite. What makes for **system** in these sets is that the representations bear relations to each other which correspond in useful ways to the relations between the situations they stand for. One of the surprises is that representation-to-representation relations are just as important in understanding systems as representation-to-represented ones.

So, to use an example which will become rather familiar to us throughout this book, the two Euler diagrams in Fig. 2.1 are topologically related to each other. Figure 2.1(a) is interpreted to mean that all A are B, and Fig. 2.1(b) that some A are B. As we shall see, the topological relations between the diagrams correspond to the relations in meaning between these two statements about the properties A and B.

By the same token, the sentences *All A are B* and *Some A are B* are representations drawn from a different system, and the relations between them as strings of symbols on the page bear systematic correspondences to the relations between their meanings.

With systematicity comes abstraction. We have to abstract what is *significant* about the diagrams in order to understand what is systematic about them. The reader is probably familiar enough with these or similar diagrams to make some intelligent guesses about what is significant about Fig. 2.1 and what is not. For example, moving the centres

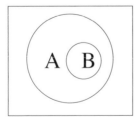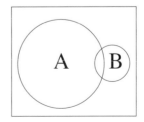

Fig. 2.1 Systematicity and representation: some changes in the surfaces of the representations are significant, some not.

of circles A and B apart in the one sub-diagram, transforms it by a potentially infinite sequence of steps into the other sub-diagram. Most of the diagrams along this infinite path are *in*significantly different from their neighbours in the sequence. But at one point there is a jump from something which means what the first sub-diagram means to something which means what the other one means. If we keep going, we will get to a second jump where a third diagram is created in which the circles have no intersection and which has a different significance—that no A are B. In the system of Euler diagrams which we will describe in detail presently, there are five significantly different arrangements of two circles inside a rectangular field (see Fig. 4.2).

Attention to this level of detail is certainly pedantic, but I hope to persuade the reader that it is necessary if we are to understand what is the same and what is different about diagrams and sentences, and ultimately how we learn from them. What we have described so far is absolutely in common between diagrams and sentences. Some changes to the letters in the sentences are significant and some are not. Letters can be progressively transformed into each other. Before moving on we should ask what our description of systematicity rules out as *non*-systematic?

What is it like to set up completely non-systematic representations? 'I declare that this key ring stands for the Brazilians winning the cup.' Sounds pretty unsystematic and it sounds like a representation. What can we do with it? Not much. I can perhaps use this representation to remind you of this event—a particular kind of flourish of the key ring might serve to taunt perhaps? But I cannot say anything about the event using this representation unless I build more into the system. I cannot, for example assert properties of the event without more system. Completely unsystematic representations are single pairings of representing thing and represented thing, but they are probably rather unusual in practice because they are of so little use.

People often set up small local representation systems—the re-enactment of a road accident by a witness using a keyring, a pen, and a paper clip arranged on a table is a classic example. These systems may be small, and highly arbitrary in the pairings of objects to represented objects, but they are highly systematic nonetheless. The key-ring is the bus, the paper clip is the pedestrian, and the pen is the traffic island, and the spatial relations between them represent the spatial relations of the scenario represented. It is the relational part that is systematic. It may be far from clear exactly what the 'grain' of the representation is—how large a movement of the clip is significant—but the relations are nevertheless highly systematic.

Consider another kind of example. A Rembrandt etching certainly represents something (perhaps it is a self-portrait), but it would take some work to establish that it does so in a systematic way. (So much the worse for our theory, you might say, but we are not making a value judgement—merely limiting our field). What we would have to establish about the etching to establish its systematicity would be to define changes in significance as we proceed to transform the etching, in the way we did with Fig. 2.1. The representation changes, and what it represents changes, but we would be in some trouble to define these changes systematically.

There is clearly some systematicity here. If the etching is distorted in various ways, then it represents something different. If we stretch Rembrandt's self-portrait sideways, then we might see it as representing a fatter Rembrandt, and so on. But it is far from clear where the boundaries of this system are. At one level, it is part of a highly general system of representative pictures. This is the level of the sharing of gross projective properties between picture and pictured. Cameras are built to ensure these correspondences for photographs. Artists exploit these correspondences, although with some latitude. But this general system falls far short of a well-specified system of significance for the representations involved, and captures little of what we intuitively take to be the meaningfulness of the etching. Does the etching represent a general man? Or a particular man? And what does the picture represent about the man? Our definition of significance was designed so that specification of a system required us to say what difference changes to the representation made to what the representation asserted. Here, there is some system but it is unclear what system, and there may be many overlapping possible systems, only partially specified.

An art critic, interested in a much more narrowly defined system than the general representational one (perhaps Dutch Old Masters, or Rembrandt portraits), might hold out the hope of defining something about Rembrandt's style in terms of the possible transformations of the image. But notice that the kind of significance such analyses usually find is quite different than the one depending on general projective correspondences (Berger 1972).

Alternatively, two spies might establish a code reliant on systematic transformations of copies of the etching for communicating about military secrets. This code is likely to have nothing interesting to say about Rembrandt, but emphasizes the fact that it is specifying 'what the picture says' that is an essential ingredient in specifying system.

Were critic or spy to succeed they would have, *ex hypothesi*, established some systematicity. This makes the point that systematicity is not a physical property of the representation but always a property of its interpretation. To assert that Rembrandt's etching is not part of a single system of representation is only to assert that we have not deciphered or defined such a system. On some aesthetic theories, openness to multiple interpretations is an essential property of works of art and if this is right we should expect distinct limitations to the degree which seeking system will capture what the Rembrandt means. We may agree or differ about how systematic such art is, or about the level at which it is systematic, but that is another topic. We touch on this topic again in Chapters 6 and 7 in seeking an account of relations between cognition and emotion. Here the upshot is that the world is full of things which may serve as representations but which await systematic definition, and that definition may come in degrees, or not. Representations and the business of representation have to be studied through *systems* of representation, not by classifying the furniture of the universe into things that are and things that are not representations.

Empirical studies start from the other end. Their phenomena, like Rembrandt's etching, do not come with explicit specifications of significance. However, if they are to be studied as representation systems the theorist must analyse them in terms of a system or systems. This is the most important limitation of our methods, and as such is the source of their power.

This way of approaching the definition of significance is adapted from Nelson Goodman's *The languages of art* (Goodman 1968), a source much to be recommended for pursuing the many issues which arise. But the reader should be warned that the terminology here is considerably changed in order to align more closely with contemporary usage. Goodman would not have called many of the systems of representation that we discuss here representations at all.

Here only a few observations about systematicity are appropriate. The Euler example might give the idea that it is the discreteness of the jumps in significance as we transform one diagram into another that makes the case systematic. But this would be a mistake. The very same physical diagram in Fig. 2.1 might be given a different systematic interpretation in which the significance of the same transformation is interpreted continuously. But this interpretation of the diagram could still, unlike what we know of our interpretation of Rembrandt's etching, be systematic. For example, suppose that Fig. 2.1 is actually composed of two architectural plans for a building. The distance between the centres of the circles may well now have the conventional continuous significance, indicating the relative and position of the two component circles of each. Now we can again say what changes in significance when a certain change occurs in the diagram, but now in a continuous interpretation.

Another mistake is to suppose that it is the preciseness of the description of changes in significance that makes a representation systematic. Our circles are elegantly circular, at least to the naked eye, but a rather rough hand drawn sketch could be used to make the same point, under both continuous and discrete interpretations. This serves as a reminder that representations are abstract ideal objects distinct from their token realizations on particular occasions. As an Euler diagram, the topological relations of the ideal diagram are what is significant. A rough sketch might make these a little indeterminate or ambiguous in some cases (perhaps one 'circle' might not quite close), but the range of significance would still be clear. In the architectural case, some grain is placed on the continuous interpretation of the relative positions of the circle centers by the roughness of the sketch. But again the range of significance is clear. After all, even our printed circles have imperfections and can only be measured to a granular accuracy. Rough sketches, in this respect, are just like noisy words—difficult to make out, but nevertheless part of a clear abstract system of significance. There are Euler sketches so rough that we might not be able to decide which topological relations they represent—or even whether they are sketches or coffee stains. But all this applies to token inscriptions of the best defined of mathematical languages. This is another property shared between diagrams and languages.

There are, of course, many intermediate cases between Euler's diagrams and Rembrandt's etchings in the degree of system we can specify for them. For example, imagine a Highway Code illustrated with photographs of traffic situations, appropriately captioned with descriptions such as 'Turning across oncoming traffic: give way!'. Here we might feel we can say enough about what is systematic about the photograph's significance to describe them as drawn from a systematic representation system, especially with the guidance of the captions. We know enough to know that the fact there is a newsagent's shop in the background is not intended to mean that giving way to oncoming traffic only applies in front of newsagent's shops. But we only know this because of how much we know about traffic and traffic regulations, not because of something we can see in the picture.

The issues that decide for us how to treat the Highway Code pictures as systematic will be such issues as whether competent readers classify them into the same categories, whether they agree which ones are too near borderlines to categorize easily, which borderlines they are judged to be near, etc., etc. These are just the same kinds of issues that decide us that inscriptions of a sentential language are systematically interpreted. The illustrations that are actually used in the Highway Code are highly schematized drawings which are well on the way to being diagrams. This is done to reduce the load on the interpreting reader by reducing the task of inferring which features of the illustrations are significant and which are 'mere detail'. As we shall see, the problems may be eased by being schematic, but they are by no means eliminated.

One of the commonest errors in understanding how diagrams achieve their significance is to assume that our access to the intended interpretations of diagrams is immediate and transparent. This is discussed in more detail later. Here, we just note that it is important to be able to stand back from even the most familiar cases of representation systems and remember how sophisticated we have become about distinguishing the significant from the insignificant. This point was brought home to the elementary school teacher who, after giving a lesson on triangles, with copious examples drawn on the board, found that the students had induced that triangles have to have one side horizontal—an accidentally true generalization about the examples chosen.

The implicitness of interpretation often proves a stumbling block for psychologists' understanding of formal accounts of significance. When semanticists talk of a system of representations they usually mean a system of representing objects along with an interpretation (i.e. a mapping from the representing to the represented objects). This interpretation is no more a psychological object than are the representing objects themselves. Semantics postpones the issue of what users *know* about systems of objects and their interpretation—how the system is mentally implemented and put into communicative practice in social settings. This postponement is crucial, but must not be forgotten if semantics is to function in cognitive theory.

Significance applies to sentential languages as representation systems in just the same way as to the diagram example. Taking the most atomic level first, we observe that letters (or speech sounds) as physical objects vary continuously in a large number of dimensions. We can imagine a sequence of transformations between an R and a B (or phonemes /p/ and /b/). We can appreciate that there will be items in this sequence that are hard to classify as one or the other. But we have a rather firm grasp of when we can discern which letter is which. At this atomic level, marks represent letters. Their significance lies entirely in their categorization as letters.

This is, of course, an oversimplification, but a useful one. Printed letters also vary in font and case. R, r and R represent the same letter, but different fonts, and fonts have systematic meanings, at least sometimes. The system of font and case significance overlies the fundamental system of significance for a printed natural language. It is additional, but it cannot be understood in isolation from the fundamental system of letter-types. Font and case are exceptions that support the general rule that the only significant thing about letters is what letter-type (a, b, . . . , z) they are.

There are also more molecular levels of significance in sentential languages. Words are defined by sequences of phonemes (or letters), and only some sequences correspond to any word. Similarly with sentences, only some sequences of words make sentences. The neatness of the stratification in sentential languages is distinctive, but not unique. Euler diagrams are also tratified to some extent. They have elements—frames, circles, annotations, labels, legends etc.—and some combinations of these elements are not significant e.g. two distinct circles with the same label, or a circle outside the frame. There

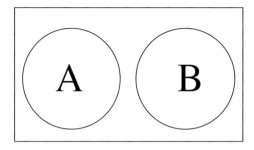

Fig. 2.2 A diagrammatic representation of the proposition that *No A are B*

are differences here, which we return to below, but first we stress the commonalities.

Just as with diagrams, changing the arrangement of the marks that make up the sentence on the page changes the significance in systematic ways. 'All A are B' can be transformed into 'All B are A' by moving the marks on the page, and the significance changes with the changes of representation. Just as with Euler, these changes of significance are abrupt, at least relative to some specified granularity. The exact length of white space between 'All' and 'B' is not significant, but there are boundaries which lead to abrupt changes.

To summarize this discussion of the 'roughness' of representations, representations have abstract categorizations, just as represented things do. The Euler diagram with circle A properly inside circle B is an abstract class of representation (quite apart from what it represents) which can be inscribed in indefinitely many token realizations or varying degrees of clarity. This is exactly analogous to the indefinitely many token realizations of this sentence.

Another property that diagrams and sentential languages share is that diagrams and sentences are both bearers of truth values—or to use a logical term, they both express propositions. It is true that, so far, the reader has not been given enough context to decide their content or their truth or falsity—so far they have been free floating—but even while they are adrift, we can see that some pairs of diagram and sentence will express the same proposition when they are anchored down to express propositions about particular things in suitable ways. For example, Fig. 2.2 gives one such pair.

The term **proposition** causes more confusion in cognitive science than is necessary, or is compatible with a sound theory of representation and reasoning. In logic the term is rather well understood usage and has an important function. Propositions are *invariant* with regard to their representations. The proposition that no A are B is expressed by both diagram and sentence. Propositions are no more sentences than they are diagrams or, for that matter, representations. Propositions are abstract mathematical entities, perhaps best thought of intuitively as like facts, except that facts are all true whereas propositions can be false. Again, issues of mental implementation of processes which compute about propositions are kept separate.

For those of us engaged in developing a theory of the cognitive impact of different modalities of representation, 'proposition', in this interpretation, is an essential concept to pick out what is in common between the sentence and the diagram in Fig. 2.2. These two different representation systems correspond in expressing the same proposition, but in two quite different ways. Similarly, two sentences in two different languages, say

French and English, can express the same proposition in some context. Or, two different sentences of the same language: say, *Some As are Bs* and *Some Bs are As*.

The issue of exactly what propositions are could get us into very deep philosophical waters very quickly. There are different specifications of invariance which classify different aspects of meaning more or less finely. Some philosophers have argued for kinds of content which are not propositional. Some kinds of content might then be more or less suited to expression by some kinds of representation. We take no position on these important matters here. What is important about the meaning of 'proposition' here is that propositions are *not* representations or kinds of representation. For the point made here, a very crude classification of meaning will suffice. Our problem is that 'proposition' has taken on a new meaning in cognitive science which is in direct conflict with the one we need here, and it is important to understand how this has happened.

Theories of representation in cognitive science have developed a virtually opposite meaning for the term 'proposition'. There is much psychological evidence that diagrams and sentences have distinct cognitive properties—the topic of this book. Therefore one might expect cognitive psychologists to talk of diagrammatic or imagistic representations versus sentential representations. But, cognitive scientists are often concerned with *internal* representations in the mind, rather than *external* representations on the paper. The trouble comes because quite a lot is known about the mental representation of sentences, and it all indicates that, however sentences are represented in the mind, it is not simply as sequences of words, like the ones on paper. We demonstrably rapidly lose track of the sequences of words which we have experienced, and instead have a representation of the gist of what they meant. Therefore cognitive psychologists, feeling the need for a term which captures this invariance of meaning with regard to equivalent wordings, have adopted the term 'propositional' for such representations of gist. This usage of 'propositional' is like the traditional one in that it is used to capture an invariance of meaning across different representations—internal ones. But the trouble comes because, whatever these representations of gist are like (and rather little is known), they arguably appear to behave differently from representations derived from diagrams (which are, in turn, demonstrably rather different from external diagrams). In turn, 'propositional' is then used of representations to distinguish ones derived from sentences from ones derived from images. This latter move more or less stands the original term on its head.

Along with this origin of the term 'propositional', the idea sometimes creeps in that after all the processing of external representations, the mind arrives at some representational essence which is the distilled meaning, but itself has no form. It is sometimes supposed that this is the logician's proposition. This idea is pernicious. There is no such thing as a representation which does not have a form. Representations are things arranged in systems which give them forms. Propositions are *not* representations. Another commonly associated error is to assume that there is *one* kind of mental representation for the gist of a sentence. We should, of course, expect as many kinds of mental representations as we find external ones. At some levels of abstraction, these internal representations will no doubt belong to the same categories as the external ones we know and love. Their physical implementations are no doubt rather different.

There is of course nothing wrong with coining new definitions for old terms. But we had better be clear about when we are using old coin and when new. Being clear about commonalities and differences between diagrammatic and sentential representations, and keeping carefully in mind what is known about internal representations, can give us a new perspective on what we know about human representational capacities. Throughout this book, propositions are defined to be what is *independent* of mode of representation. Having limited our scope to systematic representations, it will also be a conceptual truth that all systematic representations are propositional (express propositions i.e. are bearers of truth values). By this we do not mean to denigrate the kinds of content that have been argued to be non-propositional—merely to indicate that our granularity of invariance is here rather coarse. We shall use the term 'sentential' to describe representations of sentences whether internal or external.

A further related misunderstanding arises from the fact that representations, as we have already seen, can be specified at many different levels—the acoustic event, the graphemic pattern, the magnetic pattern on the computer's disc, the phoneme, the word; or the diagram's ink, its pattern of embossing, its abstract description in terms of circles, its electronic pattern of pixels sent to the fax machine, etc. Talk of sentential representations in the mind is perfectly consistent with the idea that the representation of sentences in the mind is not just like it is on paper. Sentences are not just marks on paper or sounds in the air but are abstract categorizations of these marks and sounds. Of course, mental sentences will also have their own particularities, right down to the level of their neural and physical properties. The abstract structure of a sentence is shared between all these physical representations of the sentence—for example, its syntactic tree. 'The cat sat on the mat' has this structure ('The cat' = noun phrase; 'sat on the mat' = verb phrase etc.) whatever physical form it assumes—acoustic, electrical, or whatever.

Beware thinking that this abstract use of sentence is vacuous. Sentences can be represented in many different ways (strings, trees, labelled bracketings, etc.) in many different media, but not just any representation of the fact the cat sat on the mat is a sentential representation of the proposition. For example, we may represent the fact diagrammatically (perhaps we interpret Fig.2.1(a) as a circle A representing the cat's body, circle B representing the cat's head, and the square as representing the mat). Under this interpretation the figure is a diagram which expresses the same proposition as the sentence. But note that it does *not* have the sentence's abstract structure. Nothing corresponds to the noun phrase and the verb phrase. Nothing straightforwardly corresponds to the way that the sentence decomposes the meaning into words. Diagrams can also be described at many levels of abstraction, but their abstract structure is of a quite different nature to that of sentences. It is exactly this contrast in abstract structures, its implications for modes of taking significance, and its consequences for cognition that concern us here.

Propositions are just whatever the mental, the diagrammatic, the sentential, and whatever other sorts of representation we may discover or dream up, have in common when they have the same significance. Therefore propositions are not representations and talk of propositional representations does not make sense in our terminology.[1] We

---

[1] Note that the 'propositional' calculus is, in some logical terminologies, named the *sentential* calculus because it analyses relations between whole sentences (or at least clauses). We shall see below that there are graphical representations of the sentential calculus (Peirce's alpha-diagrams), and it then becomes convenient to talk of propositional calculus as the underlying abstract logic invariant between the two modalities of representation. I have not used the term 'sentential calculus' here for the specifically propositional calculus, wishing to reserve the term for logical languages in sentential modality more generally.

shall gloss talk of propositional representations as sentential representations, always remembering that sentences can themselves be represented in many different ways.

None of this should be allowed to sweep under the carpet the hard empirical psychological questions about what our mental representations that are derived from external sentences and diagrams are like. It *could* be that the sentence *All A are B* is mentally represented by some implementation of a diagram (among other things), and that the Euler diagram is mentally represented by a mental implementation of the sentence *All A are B*, among other things. We know very little about the mental implementation of the 'gist' of either diagrams or sentences. Neither is there any reason to believe a priori that there should be *one* system of internal representations. But without a terminology for talking about what is common between what is represented in different ways we cannot found a psychology of representation.

While on the topic of terminological confusions, there is another which merits attention before we can turn to the differences between diagrams and sentences. This is the use of the terms *medium* and *modality*. There is a tension between usage in computer science on the one hand, and psychology on the other, stemming from the same divergence of preoccupation with either internal or external representations which complicated the use of 'proposition'.

In computer science, *medium* refers to the physical substrate of representations. It started as a term for computer-internal memory substrates such as tape, disk and core memory. But, with the expansion of input and output devices and the problematization of the human-machine interface, it has come to focus implicit ideas about human information processing. Multimedia (pronounced 'multameejah') promises a royal route to the user's mind. Media start to be thought of as ways of presenting information to people.

In psychology, **modality** means sensory modality—vision, audition, olfaction, tactation, . . . This is closer to the original meaning of 'media' in computer science, and it is all too easy to blend the interest in the expanded displays of computers with the psychologists' sophisticated understanding of the contrasts between sensory modalities, into a sort of proto-theory of human information processing which says vision is the thing. But consuming the information on this page is a visual process. If making representations visual were the cure for all interface problems, the ASCII terminal should have been a fine visual solution. It was not.

We need a term which distinguishes between ways of presenting (and expressing) information which abstracts over the physical/sensory properties of representations. We have the intuition that diagrams and sentences have distinct cognitive properties. But both diagrams and sentences can be presented through different sensory modalities. Sentences can be written or spoken. Diagrams can be seen or, if suitably printed by embossing, felt. Certainly there are cognitive differences between spoken and written language, but there are huge commonalities. Braille embossed diagrams which are felt, and conventionally printed diagrams, which are seen, have different cognitive properties, but they also have far more important cognitive commonalities which set them off from sentences consumed in either sensory modality. The evidence is that embossed diagrams are generally useful to the blind just as visual diagrams are to the sighted, even though there are large differences in the acuity and the persistence of the two sensory modalities, and no doubt there are many differences in the detail.

Psychologists already have a terminology which is aimed at this distinction. They use 'visual' to indicate the sensory modality, and 'spatial' to indicate what we are here proposing as a semantic modality. For example, the psychological term 'spatial' picks out what is common between visually apprehended space and acoustically apprehended space. Baddeley's 'pit-and-pendulum' experiment in which subjects track a swinging target in a dark room by pointing with an infrared device, receiving auditory feedback, is perhaps one of the most memorable demonstrations that some phenomena (in this case interference with a certain type of working memory) are spatial and not visual. In this terminology, most of what computer scientists call 'visualization' would be more accurately termed 'spatialization' (and possibly better understood thereby). We will return to the different ways that diagrams and sentences use the visual and spatial properties of representations shortly.

In this book we attempt to understand ways of presenting information which are abstract with regard to the medium of representation. We shall use the term semantic **modalities** for what is common about sentences' ways of expressing meaning and for what is common about images' ways of expressing meaning. Each of these major families of modalities can be more finely categorized into kinds of images and kinds of languages. Some representation systems may even be hybrids of the two, having both diagrammatic and linguistic elements. It is an interesting question whether there are other abstract modalities than language and image, but these are certainly the two founding examples.[2] The possibility of confusing this use of 'modality' with sensory modalities is unfortunate. In default of a better term, we shall try to spell out the intended meaning whenever ambiguity is a real threat.

Our argument will be that distinguishing modalities of information expression is at least as important to cognitive theories of reasoning and communication as distinguishing sensory modalities is to psychological theories of perception.

2.2   Significance and how it is assigned

So what are modalities if they are not physical properties or sensory channels? Our answer will be that they are ways of taking on systematic significance. They are to be analysed through the details of the different ways that representations gain their interpretations. So far this chapter, in specifying what it is to be a representation **system**, has recited a list of ways that diagrams and sentences are the same. But now we must turn to the ways that they are different, and these differences constitute modalities of meaning.

The simplest approach is by comparison with the best understood representation systems—artificial languages. The modern study of semantics began with studies of how artificial languages are assigned interpretations. This study of semantics arose in pursuit of secure foundations for mathematics and has continued on to play a central role in the development and understanding of computational technology, and indeed in the computational modelling of cognition. This provenance can be misleading in that it can suggest that these artificial languages are only suited to communication and reasoning

---

[2]Music appears to be a candidate, but its semantics are sufficiently obscure that it is hard to make out in detail the analogy with language or image.

about the exact. In Chapter 5 we shall argue at some length that the truth is rather the reverse. The history of these systems is the modelling of contentious debate, and few human phenomena are less exact.

Therefore we begin with a thumbnail sketch of what is involved in logical semantics. Our focus, as usual, is on the basic concepts rather than the technical details. The important points hold just as well for natural languages, but they hold amid a welter of what is initially distracting detail.

An artificial language, such as a logical or computer language consists of a vocabulary of symbols, a set of rules for generating sentences from strings of symbols (the syntax), and a set of rules for assigning meanings to these strings as a function of their syntactic structure (the semantics). Thus, for one of the simplest logical languages, propositional calculus, the vocabulary consists of symbols such as $\neg, \wedge, \rightarrow, \vee,), (, P, Q, R, S$ . . . Vocabularies are sorted into syntactic categories. The first four symbols in this list are called connectives. The upper case letters are called propositional variables. They differ from the connectives in that they are an open-ended list. When the calculus is interpreted in a context these variables will be given specific content.

The syntactic rules of propositional calculus are extremely simple, and are given recursively:

(1) any propositional variable alone forms a sentence
(2) any sentence preceded by a $\neg$ is a sentence
(3) any two sentences joined with a $\wedge, \rightarrow$, or $\vee$ and enclosed in parentheses is a sentence
(4) nothing else is a sentence.

Thus, P, Q, R, and S are each sentences (by rule 1); $\neg R$ is a sentence (by rule 2); $(R \wedge S)$ is a sentence (by rule 3). Remembering that these strings are themselves sentences, and applying the recursive rules many times, we can see that they define more complex compounds such as $((R \wedge S) \rightarrow ((\neg S) \vee (R \wedge (\neg P))))$. Note that the parentheses are necessary to make it possible to choose between several different parsings, just as $6 \times 8 - 5$ is an ambiguous expression of arithmetic which needs to be disambiguated by parentheses. Notice that the ambiguities that arise when we leave out parentheses correspond to different histories of rule application.

Linguists generally prefer to specify their grammars in iterative mode—as rewriting systems:

1. $S \longrightarrow \neg S$
2. $S \longrightarrow (S \wedge S), (S \rightarrow S), (S \vee S)$, ldots
3. $S \longrightarrow P, Q, R, S, \ldots$

Here $\longrightarrow$ is read as 'is rewritten as' so that the expression to its left is rewritten as the one to its right. All occurrences of the *non-terminal* symbol S (for sentence) have to be eliminated to achieve a finished sentence. These rules generate all the infinitely many sentences of the language. The right-hand side of rule 2 is a list of alternatives separated by commas and is just shorthand for the three rules that each have one of the alternatives as its right-hand side.

Propositional calculus thus defined consists of an infinite set of sentences (strings of symbols with syntactic structure given by their histories of derivation leaving the trace of the parentheses). It is easy to see that the language is an infinite set because we can apply the rules an indefinite number of times. It is equally easy to see that the definitions rule out an infinite number of strings of symbols as non-sentences. Two examples are $\wedge P$ and $P \neg R$.

So far no significance has been assigned to any of these strings of symbols—they are just marks on the page. Significance is assigned by semantic rules which operate on the structures generated by the syntactic rules. The language of arithmetic provides a familiar analogy: $6 \times 8 - 5$ has two meanings, each corresponding to one of the two ways of parsing its syntactic structure. If multiplication is taken as the main connective (i.e. $6 \times (8 - 5)$), then the value is 18. If subtraction is taken as the main connective (i.e. $(6 \times 8) - 5$), then the value is 43. The syntactic structure defines the 'order of operations' in evaluating the expression. We have conventions for 'operator precedence' which save a lot of parentheses and mean that the first reading of the expression without parentheses is less likely than the second.

Propositional calculus works like the language of arithmetic in the way that significance depends on syntax. For a given **interpretation** of the language, the atomic propositional variables are assigned propositions with truth values (either T for true or F for false), and then the truth value of each syntactic compounding of two sentences is defined in terms of the values of its components. An example assignment of an interpretation is:

1. P is true; Q is true; R is false
2. if a sentence A is true, the sentence $\neg A$ is false, and if a sentence A is false, then the sentence $\neg A$ is true
3. if a sentence A is true and a sentence B is true, then the sentence $(A \wedge B)$ is true; otherwise it is false
4. if a sentence A is false and a sentence B is false, then the sentence $(A \vee B)$ is false; otherwise it is true
5. if a sentence A is true and a sentence B is false, then the sentence $(A \rightarrow B)$ is false; otherwise it is true.

Several things are noteworthy about this definition. First, a technical point. The symbols A and B that occur throughout are *not* propositional variables that actually occur in the language of propositional calculus. They are variables that range over all the sentences in the actual language. They are part of the **meta-language** in which the objectlanguage is described, a concept to which we shall return repeatedly in many guises throughout this book. Conceptualizing part of human reasoning as reasoning *about* representations requires a meta-representational stance. In the current case, propositional calculus is the object language described, and English is the metalanguage in which it is described.

Second, this language differs from arithmetic (and this is the reason why it is worth introducing this exotic example) in that some of the assignments tend to be the same in any interpretation of propositional calculus (e.g. the assignment of $\wedge$ to conjunction is fixed like the assignment of $+$ to addition), whereas others vary from one interpretation to another (e.g., P may be assigned to the proposition 'Bankers are hyenas' on one occasion and 'Hyenas are dogs' on another). Rule 1 perhaps ought to include these propositional assignments to the variables as well as the truth values. But it is conventional to use just

Table 2.1 Truth-tables for connectives

P	¬P		P	Q	$P \wedge Q$	$P \vee Q$	$P \rightarrow Q$
T	F		T	T	T	T	T
F	T		T	F	F	T	F
			F	T	F	T	T
			F	F	F	F	T

the truth values since these are the only factors which determine the truth of compounds. Nevertheless, we should remember that the particular propositions must be there for the language to have meaning.

The other rules assign a fixed meaning to the logical connectives (sometimes called **logical constants** for this reason), and these remain fixed (at least for the classical logic which will concern us here). This feature that some vocabulary is relatively fixed from interpretation to interpretation whilst other vocabulary is highly variable is a property shared with natural languages, although the exact details are complex. Examining the nature of this variability can provide important insights into the human use of representations. Third, whereas it was possible to give one syntactic rule to define the grammar of all three two-place connectives, we need one semantic rule for each because their meanings are distinct. The rules are stated here in their most succinct but not perhaps most comprehensible form. It is perhaps more perspicuous to represent them as truth-tables which tabulate each combination of values of the atomic propositions, and the value of their syntactic compound. The tables for these four connectives shown in Table 2.1. In each case, one column displays the values for each constituent atomic proposition, and another the value for their compound (headed by the connective which compounds).

These are the rudiments of the way in which significance is assigned to artificial languages. They can be seen in outline operating in natural languages, but there they are obscured by many complexities. For example, we can see that the ambiguous English sentence *Old men and women board the boats first* is ambiguous because its constituents can be parenthesized differently, just like the arithmetic example:
((Old men) and (women)) (board the boats first)
(Old (men and women)) (board the boats first). In speech, it is possible to hint at which parsing is intended by suitable pauses and emphases. The operations of computing the meaning are ordered by the syntactic structure of the sentence, just as they are for propositional calculus.

In natural languages, one complication is the stratification we noted earlier: vocabulary items (words) are further analyzable into letters. This also happens when artificial languages are used in earnest—the programmer gets fed up with, or runs out of, Xs and Ys and starts assigning memorable names to variables. The important point is that the atomic letters only serve to identify the molecular words. The syntactic structure (and the semantic structure) is defined in terms of those words, without recourse to their internal structure. But such nice clean generalizations in fact break down in natural languages, some far more so than English. Their words are made up of components that do have systematic structure and meaning—they have what linguists call morphology. Even in English we have plurals and some vestigial tense markings. None of this challenges the idea that the meaning of natural language sentences is dependent on their structure. It merely makes it far more difficult to state how. Since we will be concerned with

Fig. 2.3 Diagram or sentence? And if sentence, then how scanned?

very general principles rather than these linguistic details, we will often prefer artificial language examples.

How does this help us with our comparison between sentential languages and diagrams? In conventional logic courses, because the focus is exclusively on sentential languages, the way languages achieve significance is usually presented at just the level used here. But when we have to compare these languages with other modalities we see that the fundamentals have been glossed over. Consider the representation in Fig. 2.3. We see a square field which defines the extent of the representation, and some symbols placed in the field. We are inclined to see three symbols on a ground, and we shall assume that analysis of the significance of the scene. Of course we cannot be sure how much variation from the particular realizations of the symbols would make a significant difference to what was represented. For that, many examples would be required. This is just the point this chapter set out from. But the important issue now is how are we to interpret the relations *between* symbols?

Suppose we are told that the symbols are drawn from the vocabulary of a sentential language, and that they in fact make up a well-formed sentence. Are we any the wiser as to what sentence that is? Well, as we have just seen, lacking grammatical knowledge we can not say what parsing of the sentence is intended. But even more basically than that, what we lack is a mode of **scanning** for the text. If the scheme is the conventional left-to-right, top-to-bottom one of European writing systems we will have one sentence. If it is the top-to-bottom, left-to-right scheme of Chinese, we have a different sentence. If it is the right-to-left, top-to-bottom semitic system we could have had a third sentence. Just for our amazement, there was an early Greek scanning scheme called Bustrophedon which scanned alternate lines from right-to-left and left-to-right, starting at the top and working down. This appears not to have caught on. A scanning scheme turns a two-dimensional array into a one-dimensional string of vocabulary items. It is this string which is then turned into a tree structure by the imposition of a syntactic scheme.

But suppose that we are instead told that this representation is a diagram? A diagram that contains in its vocabulary the same three types of symbol, but a diagram nonetheless. What now are we to make of the relations between the symbols? Well, of course, the situation is highly indeterminate just as it was for the sentential representation. But for diagrams, the answer will be distinctively different. There is no scanning scheme and no syntactic rules interposed between the spatial relations in the diagram and their interpretation.

Just to take a concrete example, this diagram might be a map. Interpreted as a map, the distances and directions between the symbols on the paper correspond in some way to distances and directions in the part of the world that it maps. There is quite a range of possible schemes of correspondence (different projections, topological correspondences, etc.) but these correspondences are *direct*. No scanning scheme and abstract syntax interpose themselves between the spatial relations on the paper and the spatial relations in the world represented.

This particular example should not mislead us into assuming that diagrams always represent spatial relations with their spatial relations. Euler's circle diagrams are a clear counter-example—the relation between the A and B circles in Fig. 2.2 is spatial, but the relation represented (the non-intersection of sets A and B) is not spatial. Similarly, Fig. 2.3 might be an incomplete line graph with a non-spatial interpretation like that of Fig. 2.4. In both these examples there is a correspondence between spatial relations between symbols in the representation and the relations between the objects they stand for in the world. Neither example has a scanning scheme.

The technical description of the difference between sentential languages and diagrams is as follows. In the sentential case, the correspondence between the spatial relations of the symbols on the page and what they stand for is mediated through the spatial relation of **concatenation**, literally the chaining together of vocabulary items. Concatenation is what is defined by a scanning scheme. Concatenation is the *only* spatial relation between vocabulary items which has significance in a sentential language.[3] But though concatenation is the only significant spatial relation between symbols in a sentential language, it has no *direct* semantic interpretation. Finding that two vocabulary items are concatenated tells us nothing about how to interpret their relation semantically until we also know what abstract syntactic relation they bear to each other. Take for example, the 'old' and the 'women' of our earlier example. Until we know which parsing of the sentence is the right one, we do not know what semantic relation holds between the items.

Sentential languages achieve their significance *indirectly*: abstract syntax mediates between the spatial relation of concatenation and the world described. Diagrams achieve their significance through *direct* semantic interpretation of the spatial relations between their symbols.

A system of representation Σ is *direct*, if, and only if: for any relation R between symbols of Σ, where R is significant in Σ, there is a relation **R** such that it is always the case in Σ that in any complete well-formed representation in the system, a's standing in R to b signifies that the denotation of a (in Σ) bears **R** to the denotation of b (in Σ).

This is our proposal in a nutshell. There is nothing particularly original about it. The fact that concatenation relations and the abstract syntax defined on them are the foundations of linguistic meaning is taught in every first course in semantics. Directness is a consequence of the lack of this apparatus in diagrams. Nevertheless, we will show that these well known facts have consequences, and in particular consequences for cognition. But first it is important to see that they provide a certain precision in semantic affairs which is necessary to make progress on cognitive matters.

---

[3] Footnotes and other interesting exceptions which prove this rule will not interrupt our flow.

One possible response from the reader is that this was hard work for an obvious point—a point which could be more succinctly put by saying that diagrams are like what they represent, whereas sentences are not. Another possible response is that the proposal is clearly false. Diagrams do have a grammar, and in this respect, at least, are just like sentential languages.

The first response, that diagrams are like what they represent, is perhaps the more widespread response, and it at least records an intuition which deserves to be taken seriously if only because it is so widespread. As it stands this idea of correspondence is not sufficiently analytic to serve as the foundation for an understanding of the cognitive impact of different representations, though it is not unrelated to our reformulation in terms of concatenation, syntax, and directness. But in general we reject the intuition as highly misleading. The directly interpreted network in Fig. 2.6 does not look like four people in love. If the 'resemblance theorist' replies that they do resemble each other, then it is incumbent on them to say how, and our claim is that in the end their account will have to come down to something like ours.

Sometimes this point is obscured by confusing mnemonic and semantic issues. Often the shape of an icon may help us to remember what it stands for, just as the morphology of a word helps us to remember what it means. But this mnemonic help must not be mistaken for what systematically determines meaning, which in both the icon and the word cases is highly conventionalized. The meanings of most icons' cannot be guessed without substantial contextual support, and the meanings of many words can be guessed with such contextual support. In neither case are the mnemonic cues what determines meaning.

Nor does this similarity between sentential and diagrammatic representations stop at the level of the isolated symbols they contain. Barwise and Etchemendy (1995) base their distinction between diagrammatic and sentential systems on the existence of ho-momorphisms between representation and represented in diagrammatic systems. But the problem with this approach is that there are well-known homomorphisms between sentences and what they mean. These homomorphisms are the result of the matching between the syntactic and semantic rules which was so evident in the specifications of propositional calculus just given. One might rescue homomorphism as a basis for the distinction between the sentential and the diagrammatic by saying that the homo-morphisms in diagrams are *spatial*, were it not for the fact that the homomorphisms in written sentential languages are also spatial. They are guaranteed to be spatial because concatenation is a spatial relation in written languages. The difference between 'The cat sat on the mat' and 'The mat sat on the cat' is determined by the spatial relations between the words.

In a related vein, Shimojima (1999) has argued that the fundamental difference between diagrammatic and sentential systems is that the former depend on at least some **nomic** constraints whilst the latter exploit only **stipulative** constraints. Nomic constraints are defined as ones arising from natural laws (topological, geometrical, or physical) whereas stipulative rules are conventional in origin. This distinction is related to the distinction between direct and indirect systems, and to the idea of diagrams being similar to what they represent. The semantic rules of propositional calculus are stipulated (as in our grammars above), but they also contain a component of natural relations determined by the compositionality of languages—the correspondence of semantic to

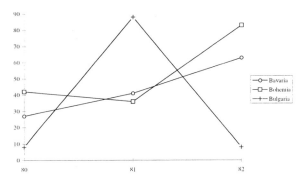

Fig. 2.4 Hierarchical structure in a line graph. The spatial relation between an icon in the body and one in the legend is not interpretable in the same way as that between two icons in the body.

syntactic rules observed in the definitions of propositional calculus. Similarly, when we examine the details of Euler's system, the interpretation of apparently nomic constraints relies on conventional stipulation in a way similar to these sentential language definitions, as we shall see in Chapter 4. It seems that the semantic properties of all systems derive from complex interactions of nomic properties of objects and stipulations about how they are interpreted. When we examine Peirce's system below, we shall see that the very same apparently nomic topological relations that the Euler system uses are employed to do exactly what the concatenation relations plus abstract syntax are used to do in propositional calculus.

What small grain of truth there is to the idea that diagrams are like what they represent lies in how the spatial relations *between* symbols are interpreted—whether with or without abstract syntax, and its concomitant concatenation relation. We shall see this shortly when we look at some critical cases for our theory of the classification of representations as diagrammatic or sentential.

Just before turning to these examples, what about the objection that diagrams do have syntactic structure just as sentential languages do? It is true that diagrams have higher order structure that cuts across the direct interpretation of the spatial relations between their symbols. For example, the line graph in Fig. 2.4 has a legend (the inset explaining which symbols stand for which country). Legends contain tokens of the same symbols that appear in the body of graphs. But we do not interpret the spatial relations between the occurrences of symbols in the legends and symbols in the body directly. The values corresponding to the triangles in the legend are not later than those of the triangles in the body, even though they are to the right on the horizontal axis. The ones in the legend do not have values. The legend is a different spatial field than the body. It has its own semantics. Thus diagrams may have a hierarchical structure between legend and body, and this relation is somewhat like the hierarchical relation which relates the clauses of a complex sentence, but this should not obscure the fundamental dissimilarity between the direct semantic schemes that reign within their bodies, and the schemes of sentential languages.

The real test of the value of our definition in terms of directness of semantics over and above the vague intuition of similarity between diagram and referent, is whether the

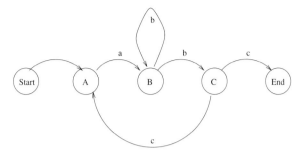

abc, abbc, abbbc, abbcabcabbbc, ...

Fig. 2.5 A finite-state machine with examples of generated strings of its regular language.

approach can throw light on some hard cases. Two kinds of cases present themselves. Are there systems of representation which we conventionally take to be sentential languages which would be differently classified by our proposal, and if so do their properties warrant reclassification? And are there systems of representation which we conventionally take to be diagrams which our proposal might indicate were better thought of as sentential languages? In both cases the answer is positive, and examining the cases is a good way of deepening our understanding of modalities.

The first example is what is known as **regular languages** generated by **finite-state** machines. These simple languages were made famous by Chomsky's application of automata theory to the analysis of natural languages. Chomsky showed convincingly that natural languages have abstract syntactic structure by comparing them with regular languages. Regular languages are probably most easily understood through the finite-state machines that generate them. Finite-state machines are simple devices which are always in one of a finite number of states at any given time. They compute by transitioning from one of these states to another, and emit some characteristic behaviour whenever a given transition takes place. One of the states is designated as the starting state and one as the end state. Therefore their behaviour comes in strings of discrete events. Figure 2.5 shows a simple example and some of the strings it generates. Upper-case letters name states; lower-case letters designate events emitted in the transition between states. Events labelled by the same letter are of the same type.

If the events are interpreted as words, then the strings can be interpreted as 'sentences', and the set of strings which a particular machine can produce is a language—a *regular* one. The machine here is analogous to the syntactic rules for propositional calculus. Regular languages can be represented by rules instead of being visualized in a diagram as here. We are here concerned with the representation of regular language 'sentences' by strings of symbols. The distinction between strings and language is important. The strings of letters are one representation of sequences of events. The diagram in Fig. 2.5 is a representation of a *language*, which is an infinite set of representations of such sequences of events. When it is claimed that the strings are diagrammatic representations, it is the relation between the strings and the sequences of events which is at stake. The fact that the language itself can be portrayed diagrammatically is a separate issue. Just as with the grammar for propositional calculus, a finite-state machine will rule out infinitely many strings as ill-formed. For example, the regular language of Fig. 2.5 will not generate any sequence with a followed immediately by c.

Many finite-state machines (as our example) generate infinite languages—infinite sets of strings. Any machine which has one or more loops of transitions will have this property, since ever longer strings can be produced by traversing the loop(s) ever more times. These are genuinely abstract languages. But the finiteness of the machine's states is what is important in governing the kinds of regularities the sets of sentences can exhibit and in ruling out any abstract syntax. For example, a finite-state machine cannot generate the language of propositional calculus described earlier.

It is instructive, and not difficult to see why. Finite-state machines have no memory for the past history of their current computation. The only information they have about where they have been is where they are now. If there is more than one transition that leads into the current state, there is no record of which one was the path of arrival. An immediate consequence is the impossibility of generating propositional calculus sentences (while avoiding generating non-sentences). Consider a machine that is in the state of having just produced the string $((P \wedge Q)$. To produce all and only the right sentences the machine will need to remember how many left and right parentheses it has produced. At this point, for all it knows, it might have produced $((\neg P) \wedge Q)$ and have no danglers, but in fact it has an unpaired left parenthesis still to discharge. Parentheses require memory. They require memory because they mark abstract structure. Abstract structure is what makes syntactically ambiguous sentences ambiguous—the same string of words is to be parsed in two different ways. Abstract structure is also what makes languages expressive—we shall return to this latter point.

So far we have said nothing about how our regular language's strings are to be interpreted. We can do this by providing semantic rules which correspond to the transitions. A common scheme is simply one in which the words associated with transitions refer to discrete types of event, and their succession is interpreted as their ordering in time. Sentences of such a finite-state language tell us what types of event occurred in what order. The language embodies regularities of sequencing between the types of events.

These may seem rather peculiar 'languages' but they are important in computer science, and at one time were held to be models for human language. They still are used to model many aspects of natural language. Whether exotic or not, they illustrate nicely some consequences of our proposal for distinguishing modalities. If the interposition of abstract syntax between representations and their semantic interpretation is what distinguishes sentential languages from diagrammatic systems, then these regular language strings are an interesting case. They have no abstract syntactic structure. In these languages, concatenation—the chaining together of their words—*does* have a direct semantic interpretation. That word X is left-concatenated to word Y means that an event of the kind denoted by X occurred before an event of the kind denoted by Y. Concatenation is no longer a special spatial relation interpreted only through its coupling with syntactic structure. Now concatenation is a directly interpreted spatial/temporal relation typical of directly interpreted diagrams. The regular 'language' strings of symbols are, in our terms, diagrams of sequences of events.

But, the reader might well protest, these strings are pretty obviously not diagrammatic. Surely this is a knock down argument against our proposal for distinguishing sentences from diagrams? This objection is implicitly that these strings of symbols could be auditory events rather than printed representations and so is an objection about *medium*. We normally think of diagrams as visual objects, on two-dimensional surfaces. Auditory diagrams are not generally possible. For example, we are not good at making sense of the auditory signals corresponding to faxed diagrams. But perhaps we need to loosen up our usage? Perhaps the semantics of lists of temporally ordered event-type names just is a direct diagrammatic semantics, however much that clashes with the vernacular use of 'diagram'. Science often asks us to revise our concepts, and our current proposal asks that, as a modality, we think of diagrams as rather more independent of medium than we are accustomed to do.

The second example tests our everyday intuitions just as thoroughly. Some representations which we are accustomed to think of as diagrams are ruled out by our proposal for distinguishing sentences from diagrams. These are diagrams which *do* have abstract syntax. A well-understood example is semantic networks, a formalism with an interesting recent history in psychology, computer science, and applied information technology.

Semantic networks, such as that in Fig. 2.6, look like diagrams. They are the basis of many so-called 'visual' computer languages which are touted on the basis of their appeal to the human eyeball. What are we to make of these representations? They are evidently systematic. If we shift the links around and alter the symbols, we generate new representations and their significances bear some systematic relation to the twiddlings we have performed. Some rearrangements may turn out to be anomalous (just as with Euler diagrams) but certainly some will represent distinct states of the world. Are these representations sentential or diagrammatic?

To answer this question we need to be a little more analytic. Just what range of representations are we to consider? With what kinds of interpretations? And to answer these questions we shall need to ask, rather more carefully than hitherto, where representation leaves off and interpretation begins?

Let us start by focusing down near the physical. The representations we are concerned with can usefully be called **node-and-link diagrams**. Their vocabularies include nodes (possibly sorted by shapes, sizes, colours, textures, labels, etc.) and links (also possibly sorted by these features and possibly with directionality determined by arrowheads). Some systems of node-and-link diagrams may have some constraints on their form, such as an insistence on every node being connected to a node by at least one link, and every link connecting into at least one node. But this may not be the case. Clearly, this low-level description is already rather abstract as a physical description. It assumes that we perceptually parse the diagrams in this way. But that is the right level to begin at in the study of modality.

If these are node-and-link diagrams, there is clearly a huge range of diagrams which fall in this class: some maps, circuit diagrams, flow charts, ecological system diagrams, semantic networks . . . These kinds of representation system are impositions of quite different *interpretations* on the physical node-and-link representations. Some are 'concrete' interpretations which have all the characteristics which we have ascribed to paradigmatic diagrams. They are directly interpreted so that graphical relations in the diagram have direct correspondences to the real-world relations that they stand for. For these interpretations, there is no abstract syntax to the diagrams. Examples are

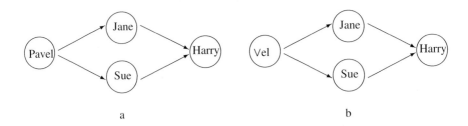

a   b

Fig. 2.6 Direct and indirect interpretations of node-and-link representations.

interpretations of node-and-link diagrams as circuit diagrams and transport network maps. In circuit diagrams, links stand for conductors, nodes stand for various types of component, and the spatial (topological) relations in the diagrams are interpreted as indicating something about the spatial (topological) relations in the circuit. Just as with Euler, the spatial relations in the diagram may be only topologically interpreted rather than geometrically interpreted, but still the interpretation is direct. A similar argument holds for transport network diagrams such as the famous London Underground map.

With these concrete interpretations, our proposal classifies them as directly interpreted diagrams, and our intuition agrees. But node-and-link representations are often interpreted much more abstractly. Figure 2.6 gives us two example representations drawn from a simple semantic network system. Figure 2.6(a) depicts the romantic relations between some people—a love triangle of a sort. Nodes are interpreted as standing for the people whose names label them, and arrows are interpreted as indicating that the person denoted by the tail node loves the person denoted by the head node. So far there is no obvious departure from standard diagrammatic interpretation. The fact that the relation *loves* is *not* a spatial relation is certainly not a departure. In Euler diagrams, containment in a circle stands for properties which are generally not spatial. There is nothing non-diagrammatic about such interpretation.

However, Fig. 2.6(b) introduces a device of a kind which is common in semantic network systems and which radically changes matters. Here another kind of node is introduced which stands for a logical connective ('vel' is the Latin name for the disjunction connective in propositional calculus). What is new is not having several types of node—the most concretely interpreted transport diagrams often have several types, say for towns, cities, etc. What is novel is the way that this new type of node interacts with the other nodes in determining its interpretation.

Figure 2.6(b) is interpreted as meaning that *either Sue loves Harry, or Jane does.* Now look carefully at what has happened here. If Vel is the name of a person, the link from Vel to Sue has one kind of interpretation; if vel is a connective, then the same link has a quite different kind of interpretation. Ambiguity dramatizes the situation, but it is not necessary to make the point. What has happened is that we are now dealing with a diagram with an abstract syntax, in which the arrows are like a concatenation relation— a two-dimensional concatenation relation. This spatial relation (being connected by an arrow) has no uniform meaning without a specification of its abstract syntactic relations to the structure it is part of. The system is not *directly* interpreted. We shall say it is *indirectly* interpreted: pairs of nodes bear the relation R to each other (where aRb means *a is the root of an arrow pointing to b*) for which the denotata of a and b do not bear **R** (where a**R**b means a loves b) to each other. We know a lot about indirectly interpreted node-and-link systems because of work in logic and AI which designed expressive languages based on these formalisms (Schubert 1976).

There are several giveaway symptoms of this shift in kind of interpretation. One is that interpretation is no longer localized. If we see just the right-hand part of either Fig. 2.6(a) or Fig. 2.6(b), we cannot tell whether the representation asserts that Sue loves Harry. However much we can see of what is connected to this visible part of the diagram, we will not know the answer to this question until we can see *everything* that is connected to it. With an Euler diagram, not every local part is interpretable, but neither does the diagram have this drastic non-locality property. If we can see circle A inside circle B, nothing else we uncover will change the fact that the diagram indicates that A is included in B.

One useful question to ask oneself about one's interpretation of a representation is 'what does the *absence* of an element' mean. For example, consider Fig. 2.6(a). What does the absence of a link between Sue and Jane mean? The answer is less than obvious. It is extremely natural for *descriptions* to be arbitrarily incomplete in the sense that they leave lots of things undetermined. But it is more variable whether diagrams can be interpreted to be arbitrarily incomplete. If a circuit diagram has no link between two components, there is a strong inference that they are not connected. This issue is complicated empirically by the possibility of incomplete diagrams—stages of diagram construction.

In this respect, it is interesting to compare Fig. 2.6(a) with Fig. 2.1(a)—both directly interpreted by our definition. In the latter, the relevant spatial relation xRy is 'point x is inside circle y' and the relevant interpreting relation x**R**y is 'individual x has property y'. This interpretation has the property that $\forall x, y(\neg xRy \rightarrow \neg x\mathbf{R}y)$. The question about how to interpret lack of arrows in the former figure is whether we take it to have this property too. To answer is often a subtle matter of the pragmatics of diagram use. The Euler system is one in which all points are always determinately related to all circles— that is a simple theorem of plane geometry. Network systems are such that they allow indeterminacy and a richer range of interpretations.

One last observation about direct diagrams such as Fig. 2.6(a) is about their representation of identity relations by symbol identities. Suppose we ask whether Sue and Jane are one person or two? Most readers have probably adopted the latter interpretation, as they would also adopt the same interpretation for a corresponding description: 'Once upon a time Sue loved Harry. Jane loved Harry . . . '. This is just another case like that of the arrow connections just discussed. If the relation xRy is read as 'node x is identical to node y' and x**R**y is read as 'the denotation of node x is identical to the denotation of node y', then distinct nodes may or may not represent distinct entities, unless it is also true that $\forall x, y(\neg xRy \rightarrow \neg x\mathbf{R}y)$.

For directly interpreted diagrams, this constraint is very natural. When some part of the underground map becomes crowded, it is not open to the cartographer simply to draw another node somewhere less crowded which also stands for a station already represented, even if he or she is kind enough to use the same name. Two distinct copies of the same symbol-type stand for two distinct stations. Resorting to an inset map of larger scale would work, but the identity relations between nodes in a map and its insets are not determined as they are between nodes *within* a map (analogously to the graph and legend of Fig. 2.4). The inset is a different field just as the line graph's legend was. We return to this property later in discussing 'token' referentiality.

The extra constraint on directness that the relation between R and **R** be biconditional rather than just conditional is important in understanding many properties of diagram systems. Perhaps its most natural name would be 'completeness' were that term not fully occupied nearby. We shall use the term **saturated** to describe a representation system which is direct and for which it also holds that, with the same notation as in the previous definition, $\forall x, y(\neg xRy \rightarrow \neg x\mathbf{R}y)$. Diagrammatic systems have a strong, though not inevitable, tendency towards saturated interpretation.

As noted above, apparent failures of saturation sometimes arise from considering diagrams in the course of their construction—a possibility which leads to complexities in interpreting the empirical phenomena of diagram interpretation. We shall often use the term 'direct' and imply that a system is a saturated direct system, though we will be explicit where confusion is likely to arise.

Therefore our general conclusion is that under the more abstract interpretations typical of semantic networks, node-and-link representations cease to be diagrams and become 'sentential' languages. This move expands our concepts of sentential to include languages with a two-dimensional concatenation relation, but languages nonetheless. Concatenation into one-dimensional chains becomes concatenation into two-dimensional chainmail, but concatenation still has its essential property that it is not directly semantically interpretable.

The reader may have the feeling that our language is beginning to creak. First finite-state machine generated strings are seen as diagrams, and now node-and-link diagrams are seen as linguistic representations. In developing a systematic concept of modalities, our terminology is having to cut across our old practices. This intuition is perfectly correct. It seems that our naive intuitions are dominated, or at least heavily influenced by, our grasp of the *medium* of representation. If it is essentially two-dimensional and can be put on paper, its a diagram. If its one dimensional and can be done in time, then it is linguistic. Intuition gets a rough ride under analysis. But I hope to persuade the reader that the ride is worth it; that without a systematic concept of modality, we can not get far with a psychology of representational behaviour; and that our pre-theoretical intuitions, dominated as they are by media considerations, lead us rapidly astray. In the end a developed theory of diagrammatic and linguistic semantics enables us to see that many systems are complex compounds of these modalities, and this plays its part in confusing our intuitions.

In what follows we shall reserve the term 'diagram' for directly interpreted diagrams, using the term 'graphic' for representations such as indirectly interpreted node-and-link graphics that have an abstract syntax and two-dimensional concatenation are not readily called sentential.

If new terminology is to mangle old usage, it had better offer some real excuse. We have to show that basing our distinction between modalities on directness of semantic interpretation offers some real gains in understanding how people operate with different representations. We shall not argue that the difference between indirectly interpreted graphics and their sentential equivalents makes *no* difference to human users. But we shall argue that the differences should be looked for in quite different factors than for the differences between directly interpreted diagrams and sentential systems. Semantics is a necessary prelude to psychology. The kernel of our case will be based on the consequences of directness of interpretation for the complexity of reasoning.

2.3 Modality and the complexity of reasoning

The first section, in the guise of introducing the notion of systematicity, presented a list of ways that diagrammatic and sentential systems are the same. The second section proposed that their central difference is the directness of interpretation of diagrammatic, as opposed to the indirectness of sentential systems with their abstract syntax interposed between representation and interpretation. This section teases out some consequences of directness/indirectness of interpretation for the complexity of reasoning.

A common observation about the semantics of diagrams, at least since Bishop Berkeley's classical eighteenth-century discussion, is that diagrams are highly specific, and that they achieve generality only through complex conventions of interpretation. Berkeley was concerned both with Locke's theory that mental images were what secured meaning for words, and with related observations about how diagrams were used in geometry proofs. Locke's argument was that the meaning of, say, 'dog' is fixed for us by the word's sound conjuring up a mental image of a dog. Berkeley objected that the word abstracts over dogs whereas an image must be of some particular dog. If we know how to interpret the image abstractly, then it is by a process at least as much in need of explanation as the relation between word and meaning.

Certainly we have ways of interpreting images as expressing abstractions, just as we have ways of interpreting words as expressing abstractions, but appealing to images, mental or otherwise, does not help to explain word meaning. Instead, it raises interesting questions about how we abstract from images. An image might serve as a mnemonic of some sort. If we have trouble remembering that 'dog' means dog and 'god' means God, then an image of a dog attached to 'dog' might help, but it does not explain how we understand how abstractly or concretely to interpret the image. Abstraction is one of the chief properties of word meaning which stands in need of explanation, and images will not supply the answer.

Berkeley noted that the dilemma about abstract interpretation of images was given particular poignancy by the use of diagrams in proofs. We draw a diagram of a triangle in, say, proving that the sum of a triangle's angles is 180°. But our proof is quite general—it applies to all triangles. In learning geometry we have to learn how the proof and the diagram are related in such a way to allow this generality. Specifically we have to learn what features of the diagram we can appeal to in our proof without destroying the generality of the proof. Evidently we can appeal to the number of its sides. Evidently, we must not appeal to the fact that angle A is, say, 67°, or even the more general property that it is an acute triangle. The puzzle of just what role the diagram actually plays in the proof is one that is still not completely resolved to this day. Some mathematicians believe that diagrams cannot be more than heuristic crutches to help us grasp the real algebraic proof which must consist of words alone. Others argue that this sentence-centered prejudice is incoherent—that the puzzles of abstraction may not be *solved* by merely providing diagrams, but that at least they are not made any worse than when we use words alone. See, for example, discussions in Lakatos (1976), Chandrasekaran, Narayanan and Glasgow (1995), and Jamnik (2001).

These issues take us rapidly to some deep questions about proof and insight which are closely related to the main themes of this book. Although these questions have arisen in the realm of mathematical knowledge, they are actually just as germane to everyday reasoning. Geometrical intuition and its relation to insight is right at the heart of visual and spatial reasoning.

Extending Berkeley's observations, for all our ability to understand a specific triangle to stand for triangles in general, there are some kinds of abstraction from diagrams which are not so readily performed. Two classes of abstraction which are difficult are abstraction over topological relations and over identity. If we are told that three bodies (say the moon, the earth and the sun) are in line, we cannot draw a diagram that identifies the three, yet leaves undetermined which one is between the other two. Or, if we are told something about the evening star and something about the morning star, we cannot draw a diagram of what we have been told which leaves unresolved their identity (or their distinctness). An immediate objection that we might draw a diagram of the successive stages of the transit of Venus is not a counter-example. In such a diagram, the graphical symbols stand for distinct time-slices of Venus, rather than for Venus. The evening star and the morning star are time-slices of Venus, and as such they are distinct time-slices, and are shown to be distinct in the transit diagram.

Here is a property of diagrams which is distinctive—they are limited in the abstractions they can express, and this property follows from the directness of their interpretation. In a directly interpreted representation, if a spatial relation in the diagram is interpreted for one pair of symbols, then it must be interpreted for all the other pairs because there is no concatenation relation and abstract syntax to 'insulate' some pairs of symbols from others. We return to this insulation below when we discuss the discursiveness of indirectly interpreted representations.

Expressiveness deserves further attention. Expressiveness is the power to remain silent on some aspect of the situation represented. We can describe situations in English and leave out information about betweenness and identity relations. But we cannot draw diagrams that naturally make the same abstractions. The diagrams are specific. They *enforce* the representation of certain classes of information. We use the term **specificity** for this general property of diagrams. Note that specificity is a property not of token representations, but of *systems* of representation. English *can* represent the specifics: 'The moon is between the sun and the earth'. But other sentences from the same language can leave this information out: 'The sun, the moon, and the earth are in line' for example. However, there are no diagrams drawn from a system of diagrams of earth–moon–sun which do not determine this information one way or the other. This ability of language to leave information unspecified is its power of abstraction technically called **expressiveness**. The greater the power of abstraction the greater is the system's expressiveness. The flexible expression of abstraction is one of language's great sources of power as a tool of reasoning.

Diagram use does achieve the expression of *some* abstractions. How can that be? The importance of conventions of interpretation has already been mentioned. We have to learn conventions about what properties of diagrams can be appealed to in proofs. That there is a strong conventional element in what we learn is underlined by the fact

Fig. 2.7 A convention for interpreting blank cells.

Fig. 2.8 Not just any abstraction can easily be expressed by a convention of interpretation. How can the left-hand table be filled out with Xs, Os and ?s to indicate that either of the two right-hand tables are true, but no others? Inventing a suitable annotation trick is difficult.

that different mathematical cultures have used different conventions. For example, in classical Greek geometry, the default triangle used in diagrams in proofs was isosceles—not irregular as we would now choose (Netz 1999). But these external conventions are not the whole story of diagrammatic abstraction. Diagrams are often annotated explicitly with what we will call **abstraction tricks**—devices for introducing limited amounts of abstraction into the interpretation of diagrams through explicit notations.

A common example of an abstraction trick for tables is what might be called the ?-means-unknown-values convention. Suppose that the tabular representations in the system shown in Fig. 2.7 indicate the contents of pigeon-holes, each with four compartments. Xs indicate nests with eggs; 0s indicate empty nests. Suppose also that cells always have either empty nests or nests with eggs in them. There are no empty pigeon holes. A table such as the left-hand one in Table 2.7 is interpreting as asserting that *either* the middle table *or* the right-hand one is true. In other words, the ? stands for an unknown value from the range: with eggs, without eggs. The question mark and its convention for interpretation is then an abstraction trick which allows this system of tabular representations to express limited abstractions. Such devices are common.

This is a (very) limited kind of abstraction, and only some such abstractions appear to be available through conventions of interpretation. For example, it is not easy to fill in the single left-hand table of Fig. 2.8 to be true of *both* the middle *and* the right-hand table, but no others.

An 'indifference to rotation' convention (another common source of abstraction in the interpretation of diagrams) does not partition the space of possibilities in quite this way. In contrast, expressive sentential languages have no trouble specifying any of these abstractions. We shall see that abstraction tricks turn up in many diagrammatic systems and play an important part in determining their usefulness.

This little microsystem provides an encapsulation of the concepts of abstraction and expressiveness. The system has an exactly defined space of possible representations: (there are 3^4 of them) and of worlds to represent (there are 2^4 of them). The number of concepts available for expression is the number of partitionings of this set of worlds into the set of which the concept is true, and the rest of which it is false—i.e. 2^{2^4} or 65536. Concepts are rather numerous precisely because they are partitionings of sets. Nevertheless, a fairly trivial language could be shown to be sufficient for expressing any of these concepts in single sentences (e.g. any language which can list all the positive instances, perhaps using 16 conjoined clauses for each). Of course it is not the numbers that are of interest but the way that worlds, concepts and representations are related. See

Stenning (1999*b*) for further discussion of this example and its application to educational research.

How far can abstraction tricks go in removing the limitations of abstraction from diagrams? Perhaps by judicious introduction of tricks we can extend diagrams to have all the expressive power of sentential languages? The pigeon holes example makes this unlikely. My intuition is that this approach has distinct limits and that the inevitable requirement to ignore spatial aspects of the diagram rapidly destroys the diagrammaticity of the system that remains. The diagram becomes a vestigial organ in what has become a sentential language composed of the conventions of interpretation.

The next question is obvious. Are diagrams that have at least limited power of expressing abstractions through such tricks, directly or indirectly interpreted? Once there is abstraction, is there thereby *in*directness? The answer appears to be no. The diagrams with tricks do not have concatenation or an abstract syntax. Their symbols are simply interpreted on some new categories of thing. Instead of just eggful or eggless nests, the ? symbol stands for sets of kinds of nest.

Abstraction is one vital requirement in a representation system. But, as we have been arguing, abstraction works differently in diagrams and sentences. The latter have an abstract syntax which breaks up their representations into a sequence, each member insulated from the others. The former have no such syntax, and so an interpreted spatial relation between their symbols is interpreted between *all* their symbols. The limited abstractions that they can express are expressed through abstraction tricks which are extra categories of symbol.

Freedom to express abstractions is a boon, but abstraction also has its discontents. Abstraction in general leads to less tractable reasoning. Supposing we describe the arrangement of the sun, moon and earth as follows: 'One body has a larger body to its left. One body has a smaller body to its right. No body is adjacent in size to one that it is adjacent in position to, unless the smaller of the two is on the left.' To deduce the arrangement of the moon, earth, and sun from this representation is considerably harder work, even though only one arrangement is consistent with the information given. This would indeed be an obtuse way to present the information in most circumstances. The obtuseness results from use of the structures in the language which allow us to talk about objects without identifying them—the quantifiers *one, no, all* .... Quantifiers are one crucial source of abstraction in languages. It is precisely such structures which give languages the power of abstraction which is so useful when gainfully employed. Effective communication and reasoning are all about careful matching of our use of abstraction and specificity to the task at hand. The task at hand is defined by many factors, prominent among them are our knowledge (and ignorance), that of our partners in communication/reasoning, and our current goals.

The business of developing a cognitive theory of modalities will bring us back again and again to this issue of appropriate abstraction. In fact the whole enterprise may be seen as an extended meditation on the ability of human beings to employ representation systems which abstract appropriately for the task at hand. And how we can learn to be better at this task—a task which never goes away.

Fortunately, there is a body of work which examines this relation between abstraction of representation and tractability of reasoning which can serve as a foundation for a more cognitively oriented theory. Complexity theory is that branch of logic and computer science which makes an abstract analysis of the relation. Complexity theory's analysis is above the level of *implementation* (the mechanisms that embody a representation system), and will therefore apply as well to minds as to machines.[4] Of course the business of applying a mathematical-conceptual framework like complexity theory to the mind will undoubtedly be more difficult than applying it to a human designed artifact—we cannot look at the design specifications or the wiring diagram. But the harder the project, the more important it is that we have some secure foundation. We shall be less concerned with the technical details of complexity theory than with its fundamental concept—that the more abstractions a representation can express, the more intractable general reasoning within the system becomes. Much of what we have to say follows the work of Levesque (1988).

Even without entering into technicalities, we can see connections between modalities as distinguished here by directness of

interpretation, and the complexity of reasoning with them. If spatial relations between a representation's symbols are directly interpreted, the representation automatically expresses relations between the denotations of all its symbols. A relatively small number of spatial relations can be interpreted, but they simultaneously express relations between all combinations of represented things. Entering a new symbol into the field determines its spatial relations to all other symbols in the field. In contrast, in indirect systems where spatial relations between symbols are merely interpreted as concatenating them (in one or two dimensions), there is scope for indefinitely many abstract syntactic relations to be defined on the basis of the concatenation of categories. And it is perfectly possible to represent a relation between some pairs of represented entities without expressing it with regard to other pairs. An arbitrarily large vocabulary of relations can be asserted of arbitrarily few of the objects that figure in the representation.

Contrast Euler diagrams like those in Fig. 4.1 (p. 96). They represent the relations between sets (e.g. set A is properly included in B) by the topological relation of containment (e.g. curve A is inside curve B). The represented relation in the world has the same logical properties as the graphical relation in the diagram—they are both transitive (if A contains B and B contains C, A contains C), both reflexive (everything contains itself), and both non-symmetrical (if A properly contains B, then B does not contain A). The absence of a mediating syntax means that every circle in a diagram is automatically related to all others by one of the five possible topological relations. It also means that the same graphical relation cannot be made to stand for any other world-relation.

This inheritance of logical properties of represented relations from representing relations gives rise to a particularly interesting semantic property which separates direct and indirect systems of representation. This property is type-referentiality versus token-referentiality (John Etchemendy pointed this property out to me).

All representation systems have symbols which occur as tokens, classified into types. Ʀ, *R*, **R**, r, R, and R are six such tokens, all of the same type (namely Rs), although classifiable into five finer sub-types. For a diagrammatic example, the two circles A and B in Fig. 2.2 (p. 15) are two tokens of the same type. In type-referential systems (e.g. sentential languages) identity of reference is expressed by identity of the *type* of distinct token occurrences. Therefore in the two sentences *All B are A* and *All B are C*, it is the

---

[4]It is true that complexity theory assumes a Turing framework for computation, but this is not a limitation that rules out any extent attempts at computational modelling of cognitive systems.

recurrence of B that indicates that the two sentences are about a shared property B.[5] Such systems are *type*-referential. Diagrams, at least directly interpreted diagrams, in contrast, are *token*-referential. Their tokens of symbols are still categorized into types, and these categorizations are significant, but when two tokens of the same type occur in the same ground, then they refer to *distinct* things. What expresses identity of reference in these systems is identity of *tokens* of a symbol. For example, a map may have a type of symbol for towns, perhaps subcategorized into sizes of towns indicated by shapes or sizes of symbol. Any two distinct token symbols stand for two distinct towns. An immediate consequence is that only one symbol of a given type in a diagram can refer to the same thing. Even two city symbols with the same label on a map (say the two blobs labelled 'Cambridge', one appearing in New England and one in Old England) denote two distinct cities.

Type and token-referentiality are properties of representation systems which are obviously related to media differences. An ephemeral medium like speech can only support type-referential systems, at least if a system is to be able to predicate properties repeatedly of the same object. But the distinction is by no means merely a matter of medium, nor are these media constraints simple. For example, in an ephemeral medium such as video animation, it is not so clear how the distinction plays out. When we see a character in a 'motion picture', we see a succession of ephemeral visual 'icons' which decay rapidly both on the phosphor and in our visual system. We interpret these 'icons' token referentially—if we see simultaneously two icons of Homer, we infer that there are two Homers (or he or we have a hangover and there are two images of him). But once time enters the equation, it is not so clear how to conceptualize the semantics. As we watch Homer move around the screen (perhaps disappearing and reappearing), then the situation appears analogous to speech—repeated ephemeral occurrences of the same type of icon establish that they refer to the same thing by being of the same type. But there is an alternative analysis which sees the type of icon as extended in time, and the system as token referential. Stenning (1997) expands on this discussion of animation. The availability of different ontologies which give different classifications of systems is an issue we return to in discussing Peirce diagrams below. Whatever the details, the directness of the semantics of animations remains—time is interpreted directly, with the resultant inability to express partial orderings except to a limited degree by abstraction tricks.

Whatever is the right analysis of animation, type and token-referentiality are not mere media properties. It may be that speech, because of its ephemeral quality, could only be type-referential. It could even be that evolution was triggered to discover type-referential representation *because* speech was ephemeral. But the semantic consequences are consequences for modality—not medium. The numerosity of relations expressible in a single type-referential paragraph, and the lack of information enforcement by indirect systems with a mediating syntax, are properties maintained when ephemeral speech becomes persistent writing.

Many of the examples given earlier in the chapter illustrate this classification into

---

[5]This property of systems breaks down, at least superficially, once we have ambiguity (existence of two Johns means that occurrence of two tokens of the same type 'John' no longer guarantees the same referent), but it is nevertheless an ideal that we have to reimpose in our interpretation of the messiness of language in context.

type and token-referentiality. Remember the icons of Venus each referring to a distinct time-slice of Venus. Remember also the recurrences of the same letter in the strings of a finite-state generated language each referring to a *different* event of the same type. This is another illustration of why finite-state languages ought to be understood as directly interpreted and thereby 'diagrammatic' in our extended sense. Remember also the nodes of expressively interpreted node-and-link diagrams which could be duplicated without generation of spurious distinctness implications, and the nodes of concretely interpreted node-and-link nodes of the cartographer which could not. Token referentiality is a particular case of sharing of logical properties between represented and representing relations which results from directness of interpretation.

The consequences of token-referentiality for complexity of reasoning are rather immediate. If a referent can only be picked out by one symbol on a diagram, then it cannot be picked out in two logically unrelatable ways. The complexity of reasoning of type-referential systems stems from their ability to pick out the same referent in alternative ways which the consumer cannot tell to be equivalent—remember the obscurantist description of the arrangement of the three planets.

More generally, directness/indirectness of interpretation has consequences for choice of expression for information. We have already seen that direct representation systems enforce the representation of information—one piece of information cannot be expressed without others also being expressed. Therefore direct systems determine the way that a given set of propositions can be expressed, generally restricting expression to in-significant variants on a single expression. In Goodman's (1968) terminology, they are **notations**. Once we have decided to draw a map, and decided what relations will be represented with what representing relations and what set of, say, cities are to be rep-resented, then there is only a set of insignificant variants on one map that we can draw. Exceptions to this sweeping generalization can be contrived using abstraction tricks, but they are rather marginal exceptions in practice.

Indirect systems, in contrast, allow freedom of choice of what is expressed. Each sentence can be syntactically insulated from every other sentence. When clauses are combined they can be combined with selected logical relations. The result is indefinitely many expressions of the same information. Perhaps most basically, we see this in subject-predicate organization of sentences in natural languages, and more generally in what linguists call 'information packaging'. Within a fixed interpretation of properties A and B, *some A are B* expresses the same proposition as *some B are A* but presents the information tailored for an audience with different knowledge or beliefs. We return in Chapter 5 to discuss the significance of this feature of direct and indirectness of interpretation for learning to reason. But the matter deserves some general comment here.

There is something necessary about indirectness representations of knowledge, belief and attitudes. Knowledge is by its nature partial, and attitudes toward the same world essentially may differ from individual to individual. We cannot generally represent what is distinctive about someone's knowledge, attitude or perspective without resort to indirectly interpreted representations. Our very choice of structuring of propositions into subject and predicate indicates something about our mental state and what we take to be the mental state of our audience. The truth of what we say may be independent of those states, but our presentation of it in indirect systems cannot be wholly independent.

With direct systems, what is obligatory is representation of certain facts with other facts. With indirect systems, what is obligatory is *some* choice of information packaging.

This semantic distinction clearly has broad implications throughout psychology. For example, discussions of the 'theory of mind' and the opposing claims of 'mind as simulation' call for some analysis in these terms. If we see someone move something from one concealed place to another while a third party is out of the room, we can calculate that the third party will, other things being equal, believe that the thing is still where it was. It is argued on the evidence of various experimental observations that three-year-olds are not capable of this inference whereas four-year-olds are. 'Theory of mind' protagonists (e.g. Gopnik and Wellman 1994) argue that social interaction requires that we develop a *theory* of others' minds which allows us to predict their behaviour as a function of their knowledge and belief. Simulation theorists (Goldman 1989) assert that the the ability to simulate in our own minds what will happen in someone else's mind by 'resetting some parameters' may suffice for social life and a wide range of the observed inferences.

An interesting speculation is that some of the claims of these opposing camps might be clarified by formulation in terms of direct and indirect representations. Simulations of worlds generally have the property of directness of representation—at least their inputs and outputs have that property whatever their underlying computational architecture. As we remarked above, animations are directly interpreted, and it is no accident that simulations are often 'output' in the form of animations such as moving weather-map sequences. A simulation of a weather system takes as its inputs parameters representing an initial direct mapping of a state of the world, and returns another directly represented end state. The simulation predicts all the simulated parameters mapped onto a complete map of the area simulated. The simulation also yields fully ordered sequences of these maps—time has a direct interpretation in the output of simulations, even if not necessarily a continuous one.

Predictions made by virtue of a true 'theory', in contrast, can make abstract predictions; for example, 'either it will be warmer than X or colder than Y but not in between, depending on whether the low tracks north or south of Z'. Such disjunctive predictions might be based on statistical generalizations over a set of simulations, but then there is a theory operating on top of the simulation.[6] One issue between the theory theorists and the simulationists is about how far we may be able to understand each other's minds using representations of different expressive power. We return to this issue in Chapter 7 when we explore the idea that representation systems come to be implemented in our affective responses.

These distinct properties of diagrammatic and sentential systems of representation also give rise to differences in the ways that representations are used in extended reasoning. Sentential systems such as the usual kinds of logical calculi are used in what I will call **discursive** mode. A proof is a discourse representing an extended episode of reasoning. The target theorem with its premises is written at the beginning, and the rules of inference are applied to these premises to give intermediate conclusions which are written on successive lines, usually along with the rule that was used and references

---

[6]This is not to deny that there may be theories founding the simulation—with the weather there obviously are—but the simulation itself is nevertheless a direct representation allowing the kinds of inferential transformations that direct representation systems allow.

Target theorem: $P \to Q, P \vdash P \land Q$	
1. $P \to Q$	Premiss 1
2. P	Premiss 2
3. Q	$\to$-elimination 1, 2
4 $P \land Q$	$\land$-introduction 2,3

Fig. 2.9 An example proof of $P \land Q$ from the premisses $P \to Q$, P. The rule $\to$-elimination is modern terminology for the medieval *modus ponens*.

to the line numbers of the premisses used. Figure 2.9 gives a trivial example.

In contrast, the directly interpreted diagrams of Euler's system are used in **agglomerative** mode, illustrated in Fig. 4.4(p. 99). The two premiss diagrams appear at the top. The inference rule literally agglomerates them into a single diagram. In fact, the figure taken as a whole apes discursive mode in redrawing the compounded diagram. In more typical agglomerative use, the second premiss would be represented by merely modifying the diagram of the first premiss. If a third premiss were added, then that would also be represented by further modifications to the same diagram. Agglomerative mode results in a single representation, and a loss of the history of accretions. Abstractive conclusions can be 'read off' this single diagram, often expressed sententially, but no inference is possible without going through the agglomeration. Successive stages of agglomeration expand the range of properties or relations expressed. Successive stages of proof may well stay within the same set of properties and relations. Stenning (1992) relates agglomerative mode to working memory structure in human reasoning.

There is an intimate relation between discursive/agglomerative use and the expressiveness of systems. In general, in order to be agglomerated, representations must be directly interpreted. When two representations are merged into one spatial field, all their symbols become spatially related to each other, and in directly interpreted representations, these new relations will be interpretable as expressing new relations. Hence agglomeration is the inferential transformation of choice. Agglomerating indirectly interpreted representations either runs the risk of introducing spurious relations between embedded elements, or fails to make inferences explicit, or both.

An example of the latter would be agglomeration of the premisses of a theorem by conjunction. Conjunction yields one large sentence, but it does not make explicit any of the inferential relations between the premisses, or the premisses and the conclusion. This is because of the syntactic 'insulation' of component propositions under indirect interpretation. If agglomeration was sufficient to make all inferences explicit, mathematics would be an exercise so trivial it would be unknown.

Thus all these dimensions which distinguish diagrammatic from indirectly interpreted graphical and sentential systems stem from the presence or absence of an abstract syntax and the consequent indirectness or directness of semantic interpretation. Stenning (2000) reviews some of these relations between distinctions. Having plumped for directness/indirectness as the essential dimension for understanding differences between diagrammatic and linguistic systems, what can we say from first principles about what direct and indirectly interpreted representations should be good for? When should we draw a diagram, and when write a description or resort to an expressive graphic?

Directly interpreted representations can represent rather few relations between the things that their symbols stand for because there are a limited number of graphical relations on the plane which can be used. And they must represent these few relations between *all* the symbols in a token representation. Thus, for examples, we can draw many thousands of kinds of maps, but each kind must specialize on representing rather few relations and must specify those relations for all the things they choose to represent. If we lack knowledge of the relations between a subset of the entities we wish to map, then we cannot proceed. But if we have sufficiently complete information, drawing inferences from our completed map is extremely straight forward—a matter of reading them off. This style of representation is particularly useful when we do not know what inferences we shall need to draw. We buy a map of the city we live in because we know we shall want to make many journeys, but we do not know which ones.

Direct representations have to express relations between all their chosen objects. When it is necessary to express abstraction, they must resort to 'abstraction tricks', and even then these are of limited expressive power (think of the question marks and empty-cells conventions in our pigeon-holes example). These enable abstraction without introducing an abstract syntax. They do so by introducing an ontology of disjunctive categories—question marks stand for 'either full or empty nests'. These tricks cannot easily be extended to expressing abstractions over relations expressed by spatial relations.

Indirect representations are good for expressing abstractions. They can express indefinitely many relations because their abstract syntactic structure allows them to generate indefinitely many, and they can express arbitrarily few of these relations between any given *n*-tuple of objects. The butcher can be the daughter of the baker who is the neighbour of the candlestick-maker, without us knowing (or caring) about the butcher's neighbours or the candlestick-maker's kin. If we have incomplete information, then we cannot draw a diagram of any relation, but we may be able to make a succinct statement of our relevant knowledge, and we may be able to draw inferences from that statement which will serve many purposes without going via an exhaustive direct representation of *any* relation. We do not need to resort to huge disjunctions of full specified maps or diagrams to express abstractions. However, the price we pay for this tremendous flexibility in choice of information expressed lies in the resulting complexity of inference, which can be arbitrarily great.

Indirect systems typically contain within them inexpressive fragments. One example is the indirect system of which Fig. 2.6(b) is a token member. This system may contain a directly interpretable fragment of which Fig. 2.6(a) is a member. Another would be natural languages which contain inexpressive fragments. Conventions of use will often determine that such inexpressive fragments are used when they can be—witness the inferences we make about the non-identities of the butcher the baker and the candlestick-maker. In the development of representation systems there is also a tendency for graphical systems to start with an inexpressive core to which various abstractive features are added. Thus, for example, semantic networks began with unique-names conventions that allowed simple inferences by spreading activation algorithms (Collins and Quillian 1969), but became ever more expressive in their use as programming languages. These tendencies considerably complicate the interpretation of the use of indirectly interpreted systems.

As users of representations, we operate along this dimension of expressiveness as we have to carry different informational tasks in different contexts of knowledge and ignorance. Most often our circumstances are best suited by something in between the extremes. But when we do need to express abstractions without losing the benefits of directness, then we do so by developing 'abstraction tricks'. In the next chapter we shall see that these 'abstraction tricks' turn out to be the key to understanding some important cognitive phenomena in the use of diagrams. In Chapter 4, we shall see another example of 'abstraction tricks' when we consider a fully developed system of reasoning based on Euler's circles, and its consequences for learning.

With both direct and indirect representation systems, choice of a particular system can make an enormous difference to the complexity of reasoning for solving a given problem, or whether it is soluble at all. But choosing between the two kinds of system is a prior choice.

Before turning from generalities about expressiveness and complexity, to example systems, one more dimension of complexity must detain us. This is the contrast between the complexity of reasoning *in general* and the complexity of a particular problem. When complexity theory tells us that some system is, say, decidable, or that reasoning within it is linear, polynomial or exponential with the size of problem, these are statements about worst-case reasoning. If a problem is of the worst kind drawn from some population of possible problems, then it may take as much as thus-and-so resources (of either time or memory). So, for example, the most efficient known methods for deciding *in general* whether any formula of propositional calculus is a theorem (is true for all assignments of truth-values to variables) are exponential in the number of propositional variables (Ps and Qs). One can obtain an intuitive grasp of this by realizing that the method of truth-tables illustrated above (Table 2.1) will have 2^N rows where N is the number of propositional variables. One method of deciding theoremhood of a formula is to make a truth-table for it and check that its main connective heads a column of Ts in the table. The resources that this procedure will take will be exponential in N. Of course, it is a different matter to prove that there is no method more efficient than truth-tabling, but none is currently known that is not also exponential in its requirements for resource.

The point here is that this is a general statement about a method capable of solving even the worst-case problem. *Particular* problems drawn from this population may be easy to solve with minimal resources, even when they are large by the measures of problem size. It is quite right that a theory of problem complexity should focus on the properties of general reasoning. But it is equally true that in fitting theory to empirical data, it may be hard to know what the characteristics of the actual population of problems are. It may be that the environment only throws up a subset of problems which are in fact much simpler to solve. Or that the vast majority of problems are simpler, even if there are a few insoluble ones. We may be both able and content to give up on a proportion of problems, especially if we can tell which ones are hard. This is one reason why reasoning about how to represent a problem may have such large effects on its tractability.

What this means for the relation of expressiveness to complexity, is that there is no generalization available that relates expressiveness to ease of solution *for particular problems*. For example, think back to our descriptions of the relations between sun, moon, and earth. The impenetrable paragraph in an expressive natural language was a problem representation which was clearly going to make hard work of solving a large class of obvious inference problems, but it might be an ideal representation if the particular inference we were after was closely related to one of the statements it happened to contain. Complexity is a systemic property—rather as we saw specificity was.

2.4 Expressiveness and complexity through examples

The central idea of complexity theory is rather simple—there is a trade-off between a system's ability to express abstractions, and the tractability of reasoning within the system. We illustrate this central idea with examples which reveal the relations between diagrammatic and sentential systems.

2.4.1 From texts to maps

The example concerns a set of representations systems ranged along a dimension of expressiveness. These systems all represent the spatial relations between a set of cities. At one end is a language which can express any abstraction about these relations. At the other, is a directly interpreted diagrammatic system of representation—a system of mapping. Some stages along this dimension of 'regimentation' are:

- a quantified abstraction
- a disorderly text
- an orderly text
- a sequence of successively more graphical tables:
    * an alphabetized table of intercity distances;
    * the same table with cities ordered by longitude in the column labels and latitude in the row labels; and finally
    * a map.

At one end, text is composed of randomly ordered statements of inter-city distances. The next step is to order this text (Fig. 2.10). But such regimented text immediately suggests laying out the information in a table. One dimension of the table corresponds to one of the cities in the relation; the other corresponds to the other city. Tables enforce regimentation in that their cell contents give values for the *same* relation between their row and column headings. But tables still may lack any principled organization of their rows and columns, though they can impose different ordering principles. Ordering alphabetically yields the left-hand table in Table 2.2. Ordering by latitude and longitude of the cities yields the middle table.

But now we can see that under the longitude/latitude orderings, the cells containing the zeros (corresponding to the distances between a city and itself) actually correspond to positions of the cities in a coarse-grained map.

The text of expressive languages can 'bury' information in a manner which requires much inference to unearth. It is too quick to dismiss this as obscurantist—'but no one in their right mind would present this information as the abstract text example above'. On the contrary, the world frequently presents us with information successively and partially in a form exactly corresponding to such texts—a form which is ill-suited to making the decisions that we need to make for the task at hand. Correspondingly, we may have information in the highly regimented form of a map, and yet the task at hand

Quantified abstraction:

Something is to the north of something that is to the south of something that is the northernmost city ...

Disorderly text:

A is 4 miles from C. B is 2 miles from A. C is 4 miles from A. C is 5 miles from B. A is 2 miles from B. B is 5 miles from C.

Orderly text:

A is 2 miles from B. A is 4 miles from C.
B is 2 miles from A. B is 5 miles from C.
C is 4 miles from A. C is 5 miles from B.

Fig. 2.10 Examples of increasingly constrained texts.

Table 2.2 Tables with aphabetical or Longitude/Latitude row/column orders and the corresponding map in which the second table's 0s correspond to cities

	A	B	C			B	A	C				
A	0	2	4		C	5	4	0				C
B	2	0	5		B	0	2	5		B		
C	4	5	0		A	2	0	4			A	

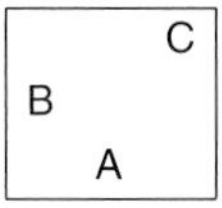

may require us to reorganise it into a set of obscure abstractions if the question we need to decide is posed in those abstractions.

From the example we see that tables are organised texts. Conversely, it is easy to specify how to generate a text from a table by combining the row and column headings with the cell contents to generate a sentence expressing the relation expressed by each cell.

The regimentation of information by tables is analogous to the enforcement of information by diagrams. It is impossible to represent anything about a city in our example table without representing everything (both longitude and latitude) about a city.

Does this mean that tables are just like diagrams in their information enforcement? No. One obvious difference is that tables are not constrained to be internally consistent. It is perfectly possible for there to be no map which corresponds to a table of intercity distances, simply because there is no 'Euclidean' solution for the values the table contains. In contrast, any map represents a self-consistent set of intercity distances. They may not be true, but they tell a consistent story. Therefore regimentation and information enforcement proceed by degrees along our dimension of expressiveness of systems. Tables are an important example because they show how highly expressive languages and directly interpreted diagrams are related by a dimension of increasing constraint.

This example also highlights an important complication in fitting our framework to the real phenomena of human reasoning. Expressive languages, such as English, have inexpressive sublanguages, and are generally used in ways which make them less abstract than might at first appear. Similarly, expressive indirectly interpreted graphical systems such as semantic nets have inexpressive subsystems, as we saw. Inexpressive systems are used with the convention that the least abstraction possible for the task at hand is generally used.

For example, in expository text, there is a convention that we do not use two different names or descriptions to refer to the same thing unless this is retrievable by the hearer. When we start a story 'There was a butcher, a baker, and a candlestick-maker ... ' our hearers expect three people, though this sentence would be true if one person did both the bread and the candlesticks. When a sports commentator refers to the same player as 'Fred' and 'the player of the year' in adjacent sentences, he does so because he can expect his audience to know that these pick out the same individual. Expository prose is produced under the convention that unnecessary abstractions will not be used (see Stenning (1978) for more detail). Later we shall see that inferences made from these conventions are important in understanding reasoning processes. Here we must just remember that inexpressive systems are generally nested inside expressive ones, and this makes interpretation of the systems in use complicated.

2.4.2   Peirce diagrams: direct or indirect?

Charles Sanders Peirce is credited by some with inventing the predicate calculus contemporaneously with and independently of Gottlob Frege. Whether this is a reasonable claim we leave to the historians of logic. Our interest lies in the fact that Peirce presented his discoveries in graphical notations as well as sentential ones. Specifically, Peirce's systems make a particularly interesting case for the study of directness/indirectness of interpretation. Peirce diagrams are logically equivalent to well-understood sentential logics.[7] Peirce diagrams, unlike their semantic network equivalents, exploit the logic of their graphical relations—they use the transitivity spatial containment to significant effect. But equally, Peirce diagrams are *type*-referential rather than *token*-referential in the terminology of section 2.3. How are these statements reconcilable?

Peirce diagrams are known as existential graphs and come in alpha, beta and gamma systems, equivalent to propositional, predicate and higher-order logics. Here, we shall be concerned with the alpha system. Figure 2.11 gives existential graph equivalents for some sentences of propositional calculus. Peirce called the ground on which his diagrams are drawn the sheet of assertion, and by inscribing P on the ground, we assert that P. However, if P is enclosed in a closed curve, then P is denied. Enclosure operates a little like negation—or, to be precise, exactly like sentential negation. If several propositions on the sheet of assertion are surrounded with the same closed curve, then we do not deny each, but rather we deny their conjunction (as might be expected, since their joint inscription on the ground asserts their conjunction). Inscription on the sheet of assertion is like conjunction (if several propositions are inscribed, their conjunction is asserted), but it is formally different in that conjunction is necessarily a two-place operation whereas any number of propositions can be inscribed.

From these two formal operations (inscription and enclosure), Peirce builds up all the expressive apparatus of propositional calculus. Those familiar with propositional calculus will know that a complete sentential treatment can be given with only con-

---

[7]They are also equivalent to 'conceptual graphs', a species of semantic network whose relatives are much used in computer programming (Sowa 1984).

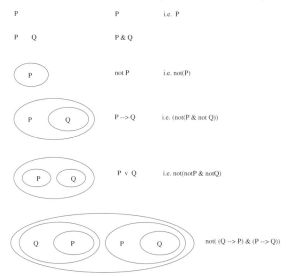

Fig. 2.11 Peirce diagrams for propositional calculus. Each connective is given its graphical equivalent, along with a suggestive reorganization according to the conventional sentential equivalences. The bottom complex formula illustrates that Peirce diagrams are type-referential under the normal interpretation.

junction and negation as connectives, or even in terms of a single connective 'not both ...'.

Figure 2.11 shows how each of the sentential connectives introduced earlier (Section 2.2) can be represented. It also shows a more complex sentential formula represented in Peirce's notation. In that example, we see immediately, that Peirce's system is type-referential. The two tokens of P that occur stand for the same proposition. They behave exactly like recurrences of the same word in a sentential language.

Reconciling the use of graphical enclosure with the type-referentiality of the system is not so hard, but it is illuminating. What Peirce invented was a graphical notation for the *syntax* of what is fundamentally an indirectly interpreted language. Existential graphs of the alpha system are diagrams of complex propositions. But they are not diagrams of what those propositions mean in the way that Euler diagrams are. The same strong logical properties of the graphical relation which we saw directly semantically interpreted in Euler are now interpreted only as determining the abstract syntax of the language. That abstract syntax is interposed between the diagrams and their semantic interpretation.

One way of clarifying what is going on is to think of Peirce diagrams as simply representing *sentences* of propositional calculus—i.e. syntactic objects.[8] Under this interpretation, the diagrams are *directly* interpreted, but they are then *token*-referential—each symbol P in the diagram stands for a *different* syntactic occurrence of P. Under this interpretation, the diagrams do employ graphical constraints—the transitivity of enclosure expresses the transitivity of constituent phrase inclusion. But under this inter-

---

[8]More precisely, invariance classes of sets of sentences, because of the syntactic divergences of Peirce's system from the standard sentential one.

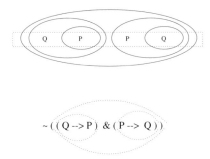

Fig. 2.12 In a one-dimensional regimentation of Peirce diagrams, the closed curves correspond to the parentheses of a sentential system, as indicated here by the dotted lines. The lower propositional calculus formula is equivalent to the upper existential graph.

pretation, the Ps and Qs have no semantic interpretation as propositional constants. That interpretation is only assigned when the pictured sentences are interpreted indirectly in the conventional way.

One way to illustrate this point is through the correspondence between a one-dimensional version of Peirce diagrams and the parentheses of propositional calculus. Figure 2.12 illustrates this correspondence. The closed curves of Peirce express what parentheses express in the sentential system, and, at this level, constitute a diagram of the syntactic object which is the sentence. This does not mean that the difference is trivial. Much of the complexity of parsing one-dimensional strings of existential graphs comes from having to restore the pairings of left and right parentheses which are directly represented in the two-dimensional existential graph.

It is a moot point what cognitive properties we might expect Peirce's notation to have. We might expect the differences to result from differences in parsing complexity, but we should not expect them to be the result of directness of semantics at the level of propositional interpretation. Semantically, existential graphs should be compared with corresponding indirectly interpreted systems such as the abstract interpretations of semantic networks discussed earlier, or with conventional sentential calculi, rather than with the more superficially similar circle diagrams. Predictions of relative difficulty of use of the two formalisms would require a knowledge of the costs to the human perceptual mechanism of parsing strings relative to the cost of interpreting the enclosures. There are also intriguing differences in that the mapping from graph to sentence is one-to-many. This approach does not diminish the differences between existential graphs and sentential calculus but it greatly refines them. Such sharpening of empirical questions is exactly the kind of benefit one might expect from this kind of semantic analysis.

Shin (2002) has made a revealing study of existential graphs showing that their significance has been obscured by the particular reading algorithms which Peirce suggested for translating them into the more familiar sentential calculi. Shin shows that it is more natural to read existential graphs by an algorithm which yields multiple semantically equivalent sentential readings. This insight has important implications for our interpretation of what is cognitively distinct about existential graphs and the contrast between sentential and graphical systems more generally. Shin's analysis suggests the intriguing possibility of performing inferences by parsing. Under the controlled conditions she describes, any two 'parsings' of an existential graph are logically equivalent. Therefore, if we can read a graph in two ways, we know that the two resulting sentences are logically equivalent. Whereas designers of artificial sentential languages go to great lengths to ensure that there is only one parsing, Peirce's diagrammatic system of portraying sentences typically generates multiple parses, all semantically equivalent.

Our approach suggests that *if* there are differences in usability between sentential and graphical presentations of expressive languages, then we should expect a cognitive theory to explain them in terms of the kinds of difference in the role of parsing that this example suggests. It may well be that we have powerful spatial processing mechanisms that can perform inference-by-parsing in the style suggested by this example. Our main point is that this is a different kind of explanation than is going to be required for any cognitive efficacy of directly interpreted diagrams. Existing reviews of what is known about the usability of the two kinds of system bear this out in that they find very different patterns of advantage (Whitley 1997).

Finally, the example of existential graphs shows that actual representation systems can be compounded of direct and indirect levels of interpretation, a lesson that will stand us in good stead when we take our new theoretical tools and set to work on analyzing representations in the wild.

2.5 Cognitive consequences of semantics

Having arrived at a theory about what modalities are, and how diagrams and languages are differentiated by their semantics, what are the general implications for the study of cognition? A redrawing of some intuitive distinctions between diagrams, graphics and languages is a taxonomic exercise, and a conceptual exercise, but not yet a cognitive theory of anything. Conceptualizations have strong effects on what empirical observations we make and how we interpret them, but it is important to preserve the distinction between conceptual and empirical findings. How do our reconceptualizations change our perspective on cognitive questions about reasoning and communication?

As long as we think of sentential language as the modality of thought, and natural languages as the prototypical examples, it is easy to slip into a way of thinking in which there is just *one* language of thought. Mental processes are then modelled by reasoning *within* this representation system. This conception of mental process has been by far the dominant one in cognitive science. Theorem proving in logic, the psycholinguistic processes of parsing and generation within a grammar, the operation of expert systems, and the simulation of cognitive architectures all model mental processes *within* representation systems.

But diagrams and sentences are obviously disparately interpreted representation systems. Once we are forced to give a semantic account of the differences (and the different differences), then we see that sentential languages themselves have to be understood as whole families of interpretations. The chief thing that is wrong with the influential title of Fodor's admirable *The language of thought* is its definite article. Once we see how finely specified representation systems need to be to work in the contexts of reasoning, we see that a more adequate, if less catchy, title would have been *The 10^N languages of thought (where N is large)*, and diagrammatic systems are just as numerous because just as finely specified in context. The argument that natural languages have to be seen as families of fully interpreted languages is made in Chapters 6 and 7. Reflecting on diagrams reflects back on language.

The picture of human reasoning and communication that emerges is of the reasoner navigating or constructing a landscape of representation systems—a highly structured landscape where the systems are intimately related to each other on a large number of dimensions. In cognitive terms, this shifts our focus onto *learning* to reason—learning how to set up an adequate interpretation within which to reason. It also demands a theory of communication which can do justice to the role communication plays in learning, and again this must be communication of interpretations, not just communication *within* interpretations.

Of course, from a computational point of view, this is a possibly paradoxical state of affairs. The picture requires us to think of computations that work over representation systems as objects. This is known to be a hard problem. In its full generality it gives rise to obvious regresses. But that does not mean that it cannot be made to work as a specifically constrained model of mental processes. It accords well with observations that expertise in reasoning is slowly acquired by painstaking learning processes. It makes sense of much of what goes on in formal education. Mathematics, for example, can be seen as teaching some general techniques for representing and re-representing problems in tractable forms. First-language teaching can be viewed analogously. This picture does not mean that we have one all-embracing homogeneous system for reasoning about what system we should use to solve the next problem. Empirical work on how people learn the expertise of representation selection promises to provide some starting points for theoretical analysis of the necessary meta-computations.

There have long been representatives of this way of thinking in cognitive science and some of them go back to its earliest days. The work of Newell & Simon (1972) on representations in problem solving and Amarel's (1968, 1969) work on representation selection are early examples. Chapter 6 reappraises some areas of cognitive psychology (conditional reasoning, analogical reasoning, cognitive semantics) from the perspective of a psychology of representational activity.

The next three chapters describe a series of studies designed to base an empirical psychology on these semantic ideas. Putting the semantics first is a distinctive methodological choice. There is an irony that although psychologists have assembled powerful evidence in every field in which they work that human mental processing is driven by phenomena at the level of semantic interpretation, this poses a severe problem for the experimental approach. Subjects' semantic interpretations are often not immediately accessible for control, and so it is easy to conclude that psychology is forced back to studying the details of the processing of the available 'surfaces' of representations.

But history suggests that this is not a good general strategy. Little insight into the semantics of natural languages was gained until researchers separated off the business of giving a specification of highly idealized structure, from issues about how the real messy physical surface of representations were processed. Only after some methods of describing abstract structure were developed, did whole interdisciplinary fields grow up around the study of the processing of these structures. We conjecture that it will be the same with diagrams as it was with sentences, though hopefully an eye to history may accelerate learning.

When psychology has made claims about systems of reasoning it has tended to ignore semantics at the expense of reinventing it. For example, we shall see in Chapter 4 that the claims that mental models theory's representations are fundamentally different in status from the representations underlying linguistic reasoning is certainly not logically sustainable by the kind of evidence provided. It is not even clear what it could mean for this claim to be sustained by any evidence. Models as abstract objects are very different from sentences as abstract objects, and their differences are formally well understood. Undoubtedly, implementations of both are involved in mental processing. The key to understanding the differences is the concept of expressiveness. Inexpressive directly interpreted diagrams are closer to representations of models. The formal understanding is already there for a reinterpretation of the empirical literature.

Some readers will find this semantic theory an odd place to set out from in search of a theory of representational behaviour. If one wants to get *there*, why start from here? The examples drawn from crisp logical problems, and the paradoxes that lurk only barely beneath the surface, are direly irritating to some temperaments. 'Human reasoning, communication and problem solving are surely much richer and messier than this infertile ground allows' (I hear a voice protest) 'human beings don't reason by logic—that much is obvious.' We return in Chapter 6 to look at some of the widely accepted arguments about the relation, or lack of it, between logic and human reasoning. Throughout the following chapters we shall argue for a different and more productive relationship between formal and empirical research methods.

Meanwhile, the goal of Chapters 3, 4, and 5 is to show how basing an empirical programme of experimental analysis of behaviour on this semantic framework leads to psychological insights. Chapters 6 and 7 reappraise the relation between the cognition of reasoning and our emotional lives, suggesting that the relation is far more intimate than the conventional subdivisions of psychology accept. It is precisely because human cognition is so rich that we need to start with such simplified problems.

2.6 In summary

We began the chapter by distinguishing systems of representation from unsystematic representations, and rehearsed a list of ways in which diagrams and sentences are alike as systematic representations. They are alike in that they both have vocabularies of symbols, some of the features of their symbols are significant, and some not; their overall significance is determined by the way that their symbols are combined; the relation between symbol and what is symbolized may be quite arbitrary; their interpretations may well be inaccessible to the naive reader; the processing of their surfaces must be distinguished from the system of underlying abstract objects that are processed; and they both express propositions.

We distinguished media and modalities: whereas the term media focuses on physical and sensory differences between representations, the modalities are ways of achieving significance. The differences between diagrams and sentences are first and foremost differences in modality, although our intuitive classifications are not independent of the medium of representation.

Then to differences. Sentential languages achieve significance through imposing an abstract syntactic structure on concatenations of their strings of symbols. Concatenation is the only spatial/temporal relation which has significance in relating symbols in sentence strings, but it has no direct semantic interpretation. This stratification of the interpretation of spatial relations in written language is typical of sentences but atypical of diagrams. Diagrams generally interpret the spatial relations between their symbols directly and uniformly. Examination of two limiting cases, regular languages and semantic networks, revealed that this distinguishing feature of the two modalities is obscured in our everyday intuitions by the cross-cutting effects of media. We adopted the terminology of calling indirectly interpreted representations that use two-dimensional spatial concatenation 'graphics' and only directly interpreted representations 'diagrams'.

We related modalities to complexity of reasoning. The power to express abstractions determines a representation system's tractability for reasoning. Being able to express arbitrary abstractions leads to highly intractable reasoning in the general case. Both sentences and diagrams are interpreted to yield abstractions, but they differ in the extent and manner in which this happens. Diagrammatic systems enforce the representation of some categories of information, the opposite of abstraction. The most fundamental kind of information enforcement is in representation of identity relations by diagrams.

Directly interpreted diagrams generally use the spatial relation of 'identity of token symbol' to represent identity of symbol's referent—they are token-referential. Indirectly interpreted systems use 'identity of type of symbol' to represent identity of symbol's referent—they are type-referential. These properties arise from directness and indirectness of interpretation. The nature of media (e.g. whether they are ephemeral) place certain constraints on the characteristics of the modalities they support, but they do not determine those characteristics.

Directness and indirectness of interpretation lead to agglomerative and discursive use of representations respectively in reasoning. In direct systems, inferences are made by making a joint construction of all the individual premises and reading off conclusions from these constructions. History of construction tends to be lost in this process, which depends on certain localness properties of direct semantics. In indirect systems, syntactic units have to be 'insulated' from each other because in general they lack localness properties, and history has to be maintained because it is typically required for later inference. This insulation of syntactic units one from another is also what gives expressive power—a relation may be asserted to hold between some sets of objects without being asserted or denied of all sets.

The major modalities of representation—diagram and language—are chiefly differentiated as tools of reasoning by the ways that they express abstraction. Indirectly interpreted systems have no limits imposed on their expressiveness by the way in which they achieve significance—their abstract syntax ensures that freedom. Directly interpreted systems do have constraints on the expression abstraction which are a result of their lack of abstract syntax. Though their symbols (icons) express abstraction in much the same way that words do, there are distinct limits on their expression of abstractions about relations between the things their symbols stand for, which result from the lack of syntactic insulation between the symbols. Direct systems can only break out of this information enforcement through limited abstraction tricks. These tricks do not express abstractions by introducing abstract syntax. Rather they express abstraction by denoting abstract types of thing, often disjunctions of concrete categories. These two modes of expressing abstraction are what we would expect to have cognitive consequences for mental processes that employ the two kinds of representation. The theory also predicts that the boundaries between what is directly and indirectly interpreted will not correspond exactly to our intuitive classifications of the diagrammatic and the linguistic, and that actual representation systems may have elements of both kinds of system intimately compounded.

Model versus sentence, directness versus indirectness of interpretation, presence or absence of concatenation and abstract syntax, type and token-referential, agglomerative versus discursive use, specificity and information enforcement vs. expressiveness, abstraction tricks and conventions of interpretation, nomic and stipulative constraints: these ideas form the tightly interrelated web of concepts of semantics and pragmatics. They combine to determine the differences between diagrammatic and sentential modalities. These are the computational concepts which are needed to guide the empirical study of representational behaviour, and in the following chapters we shall see some examples of how conceptual apparatus and experimental investigation work together. There is every reason to believe that the differences between image and language are implicated in many psychological phenomena from individual differences and neurological substrates to social and cultural differences. But what the difference between language and image is, is not self-evident. These are the computational concepts that are required to found cognitive analysis. They are computational analyses of external representations, but at an appropriate level of abstraction they are every bit as applicable to understanding mental imagery.

3 Hyperproof: industrial strength logic teaching

3.1 The world of blocks

Figure 3.1 looks down on the Valley of the Ideal Solids, and the ancient parchment reproduced in its caption tells us about the visible blocks. The task is to work out which of the blocks *might* be in the group farthest away? Do try it! It is an example of the kind of reasoning that this chapter studies.

Here is what the great detective Hercule Poirot's mind's ear hears as he solves the problem: '*Alors* . . . since b is between two other blocks, there are just three possibilities for b. Since b is larger than f, b must be the middle pyramid in the group of three. Since f is closer to the front than a, f cannot be in the far group. Block a cannot be in the farthest group since there are no pyramids there. If either e or f is to be in the far group, then they are both cubes, and either e is the big far one and f the small near one, or e is the big near one, and f is the small far one. But f is in the front because a is a pyramid, so e alone could be in the far group . . . *n'est ce pas?*'

Of course, this is not all that goes on in Poirot's mind, but it might be all that his mind's ear can hear, and we shall return for some of the rest later on. This problem is an analogue of a Hyperproof problem. Hyperproof is a computer environment designed by Barwise and Etchemendy (1994) for teaching first-order logic in a novel way that uses

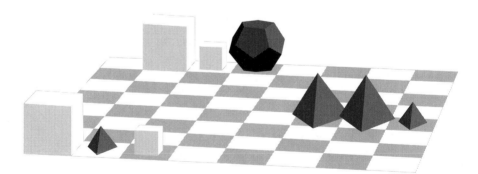

Fig. 3.1 Blocks a and b are pyramids. Blocks e and f are the same shape but e is larger than f. Block f is closer to us than block a. Block b is larger than block f. Block b is between two other blocks.

both graphical and linguistic representations—heterogeneous reasoning. In the program, the diagram of the blocks appears in one window and the sentences appear in another window. The user of the system is set goals (like our goal of deciding what blocks might be at the back), and solves the problem by combining diagrammatic and sentential information as Poirot has just done.

We originally came across Hyperproof in its design stages when working on what became the theory of modalities outlined in the last chapter. Here was an environment in which two systems of representation, one diagrammatic and one sentential, were used together in problem solving. The diagrammatic system was directly interpreted: the sentential system was interpreted through an abstract syntax, and because Hyperproof, unlike Poirot's problem, was couched in an artificial language—the language of first-order logic—this syntax is clear for all to see. Hyperproof's representations and problem goals were sufficiently well-defined that formal rules of inference for combining and abstracting information were built into the computer. Since the user has to tell the machine what to do, the machine could keep a detailed and impartial record of what the user instructed it to do. Here was a 'natural' laboratory for the empirical study of multimodal reasoning.

Most psychological studies of reasoning have been laboratory studies of students doing tasks which are unrelated to their other learning, and which last typically less than an hour. Such studies have given rise to theories that learning logic has little impact on students' reasoning outside logic class. There have been a few studies which have actually looked at the impact of logic classes on reasoning, some positive some negative. We shall review some of this evidence in Chapter 6. Suffice it to say that all our colleagues predicted that we would find no improved reasoning as a result of students taking a logic course.

Even more striking than Hyperproof's mere use of diagrams was its use of what we had been studying as abstraction tricks—notations and conventions comparable to those discussed in Chapter 2, which allow diagrammatic systems to express limited abstractions. Hyperproof's diagrammatic system has several such conventions. Figure 3.2 shows a diagram window in which cylinder and bag icons appear. There are no cylinders or bags in Hyperproof's world. Cylinders show where there is a block of unknown shape (tetrahedron, cube, or dodecahedron) and size (small, medium or large). Sometimes the cylinder bears a badge indicating the block's shape but still not its size. Conversely, a bag icon indicates position and size but not shape. Two blocks appear off to the side of the board. These indicate not that there are blocks off the board, but rather that there are blocks on the board *in addition* to the ones which are shown there. Off-board icons may or may not indicate size and shape but they abstract over position. Finally, blocks may have one or more names (a, b, c, . . .), but these names may or may not appear on the blocks—another source of abstraction.

We proposed in the previous chapter that what distinguishes diagrammatic and sentential modalities is the directness or indirectness of their interpretation, and that these modes of significance result in different ways of expressing abstraction. Here was a diagrammatic system with complex abstraction tricks which would give us some chance of exploring their cognitive consequences. The semantic theory coupled with the cognitive assumption that the complexity of computation is a function of expressiveness suggested that users' performance with the diagrammatic part of the system ought to

Fig. 3.2 Graphical abstraction in Hyperproof. This diagram contains symbols of varying degrees and types of abstraction. The large tetrahedron labelled a is completely concrete. The cylinder with the dodecahedron badge labeled b lacks only a size attribute, and the large paper bag labeled c lacks only a shape attribute. The unlabelled cylinder with the question mark badge on the board lacks size, shape, and label attributes, but still has a position; its twin off the chequerboard lacks even a position. The neighbouring medium sized dodecahedron labelled d lacks only a position.

hinge on their facility at using these abstraction tricks in solving problems.

The designers of Hyperproof did not put these abstraction tricks in for our theoretical amusement. The tricks are essential to the posing of the kinds of problems required to teach reasoning. If the diagrams were completely concrete it would not be possible to give the problem solver partial information about the situation, and so would not be possible to set problems in which graphical and sentential information has to be brought together. Abstraction is essentially involved in posing reasoning problems. Our focusing on the ways representations express abstraction is not just some arbitrary choice.

If abstraction tricks are necessary for posing reasoning problems, the reader might justifiably ask how the Valley of the Solids problem manages without any such tricks? The source of abstraction in that problem is the names of the blocks, and the problem is entirely about the assignment of names. This was necessary for an introductory problem for an audience that has not learned the abstraction tricks of Hyperproof, but it limits the kind of problem that can be set.

Barwise and Etchemendy (1994) describe Hyperproof as a *heterogeneous* reasoning system. Two systems in two modalities are welded together into a single system by the specification of rules for representing information from one modality in the other. For example, a rule called *observe* allows sentences to be concluded on the basis of diagrammatic 'premisses'. Such a rule allows us to write down what we can see to be the case in the diagram. Conversely, a rule called *apply* allows modifications of diagrams on the basis of sentential information: being told something allows us to represent it in the diagram. Reasoning with information gained in different modalities is something we do all the time. Hyperproof's achievement is to demonstrate that a set of rules can be developed which formalize this example system.

Our focus has been on the similarities and differences between diagrammatic and sentential systems of representation and so the discussion has proceeded as if systems were isolated from each other. This implication is an unintended consequence of introductory simplification. Reasoning generally goes on in systems that result from combinations of modalities—heterogeneous systems. The diagrammatic and sentential parts of these systems nevertheless have different kinds of semantics. The idea of heterogeneity is important because it focuses our attention on the modes of inference which glue these parts together. It allows us to think in terms of moving information from one representation to another in the process of problem solving. Chapter 4 examines diagrammatic and sentential systems for solving syllogisms, but the reader will see that the diagrammatic systems are also heterogeneous systems—necessarily so since reasoning starts out from the verbal formulation of syllogisms, and has to return a verbally formulated conclusion.

It is particularly uncommon for diagrammatic systems to be purely diagrammatic without any involvement of language, if only because the symbolic content (the icons) of diagrammatic systems are generally assigned in language—the labeling of Euler circles with verbally represented properties is an example. Sometimes the explicit involvement of language in the use of a diagrammatic system is relegated to problem formulation, and conclusion drawing, but sometimes, as in Hyperproof, the two sub-systems are much more intimately entwined.

Systems which are both diagrammatic and linguistic provide clear examples of heterogeneity, but the concept of heterogeneity, once established, raises intriguing issues for systems of reasoning which are entirely linguistic in modality. Later, in Chapter 6 and 7, we will see evidence that when we insist on considering interpretations in the full detail necessary to explain the computations of reasoning, natural languages have to be construed as highly articulated families of interpretations. Whether to retain the term heterogeneous for systems using more than one modality, or to extend it to systems composed of multiple sub-language interpretations then becomes an active question. We might talk of *representational* and *interpretative* heterogeneity. Stenning *et al.* (2002) analyse episodes of collaborative group conceptual learning in these terms.

Figure 3.3 presents an example Hyperproof problem. It is not necessary to learn the full rule-set to grasp the idea of recasting information from one modality to another in solving a problem. This proof illustrates the use of the rule *apply* as well as the operation of splitting into cases, which is so important in Hyperproof's approach to reasoning. Going through an informal proof of the goals may help to understand the problem.

The board situation shows a small paper bag on the left and a large one at the centre, with a cylinder with a tetrahedron badge on the right. The given sentences can be translated:

- If a thing is large, then its a cube or a dodecahedron
- If a is small and b is a cube, then c is medium
- If a is small or a is medium, then c is left of a
- a is not b and b is not c and a is not c.

'Being left of' is interpreted from the viewer's perspective.

In Fig. 3.4, the rule *apply* is invoked as the first step after the givens. The application is justified by the two highlighted sentences, and it adds the information that the cylinder icon is labelled *a*.

Figures 3.5 and 3.6 show the two situations that appear when the user clicks on the lower diamonds in Fig. 3.4. The user has constructed these two situations by making assumptions about the shape and size of blocks in order to break the problem into two cases. The application of the rule CTA, or 'check-truth-of-assumptions', in each case merely confirms that the constructed scenarios are consistent with the givens.

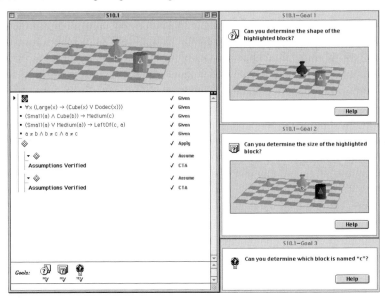

Fig. 3.3 An example Hyperproof problem. The givens of the problem are the diagram in the upper window and the sentences in the lower window. The goals are set at the right.

Finally, the user will invoke the *cases exhausted* rule (not illustrated) and the machine will confirm that these two cases cover all possibilities. Since the size and shape of the blocks highlighted in goals 1 and 2 vary in the two cases, the proof shows that neither can be deduced from the given information—they are logically independent of the information. Goal 3 has been answered affirmatively in passing, and is in fact an essential step in reaching the other two goals. Notice that there are many other possible splittings into cases, and the important insight is that this split is a good one to solve these goals. This is easier to see if the last goal is done first—but then this is an examination! This instant introduction to Hyperproof will be sufficient for our purposes.

The reader will by now be aware of a double involvement of logic in this enterprise. In the last chapter we used the techniques and findings of logical semantics to propose that modalities should be defined by the ways that representations achieved significance. But now, in choosing Hyperproof as a domain for the empirical validation of the the theory, we have not merely chosen logic as method but also the learning of logic as our example domain of diagram use. We make no apology. If logic is a rather abstract study of systems of representation and communication, then learning logic is a domain in which one can expect to develop an empirical understanding of some aspects of reasoning and communication, although not, of course, the only one. But this is a theoretical battlefield and the reader were best warned. The flag is up. We will return to this issue when we have some results.

Before launching in to our study of Hyperproof's impact on John Etchemendy's students, some background to the practices of logic teaching is necessary. Logic is taught in many ways for many different purposes. One major division is between formal and informal approaches. An informal approach focuses on the problems of abstracting

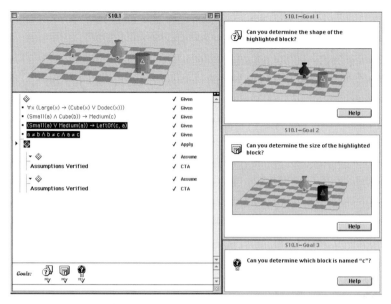

Fig. 3.4 The rule *apply* is invoked using information in the highlighted sentences to draw the inference that the cylinder icon is labelled a.

patterns of reasoning from the variety of ways we encounter arguments in everyday life. A formal approach introduces an artificial language and teaches methods of reasoning within the system. But this is a continuum. Some informal courses introduce at least minimal formality (perhaps at the level of using propositional variables, and classifying patterns of valid and invalid argument). Most formal courses teach something about the correspondence of an artificial language to students' natural language. What varies is the emphasis that is given to recognizing form, relative to calculating within formal notation. This choice of emphasis is something which faces, for example, all mathematics teaching which deals in formalisms. It is a pity that this choice of emphasis is so often seen as an all-or-nothing choice, and a polemical one at that. Proponents generally place themselves in the formal or the informal camp. But there is no reason why this should be. The choice should be related to our teaching goals. It can even be the subject of empirical study. The approach taken in the courses studied here is fairly far up the formal end of the continuum. We return to the issue of relating form to content in Chapter 6.

Logic is taught for many purposes. Here we are mainly concerned with the goal of improving students 'general reasoning' abilities—the traditional role of logic in the college curriculum. Of course, it is theoretically contentious what general reasoning abilities are, and even whether they exist. This issue will be a concern throughout. But it is clear that this goal is the rationale often given for logic teaching. There are many others. Philosophers often explain that they want students to be able to read the logical formalisms common throughout analytical philosophy papers. Computer scientists teach logic because of its relation to the theory of computation or to programming languages. Linguists teach logic as a representation system for natural language phenomena. Electronic engineers teach logic because of the part that it plays in circuit design. Mathematicians teach logic because of its role in the study of the foundations of

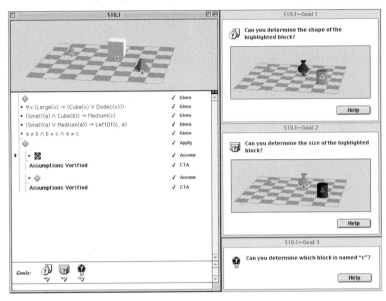

Fig. 3.5 The first case of the proof in which b is a large cube and a is a medium tetrahedron.

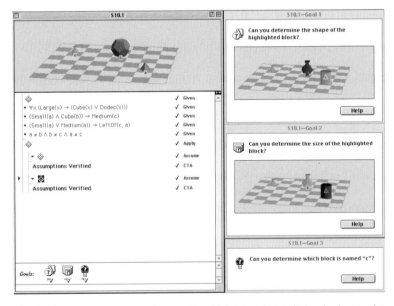

Fig. 3.6 The second case of the proof in which b is a large dodecahedron and a is a small tetrahedron.

mathematics. Despite this proliferation of 'special' reasons for teaching logic, it remains a fact that logic at one time formed a substantial part of the secondary/tertiary curriculum and that it was justified in terms of improving students abilities at reasoning, because that skill was needed throughout the remainder of their studies. It was justified in terms of learning to learn. This goal remains a goal today, and it is this goal with which we are chiefly concerned here.

Chapter 2 introduced propositional calculus, one of the simplest logics, through its syntax, and gave a formal definition of its significance in terms of the truth conditions of its sentences (both as semantic rules and as tables). But this is a minimal treatment of how to apply the formalism to phenomena in the world. Teachers of logic are faced by several choices as to how to go further. They can teach semantics through correspondences to their students' natural language, they can teach the mathematical theory of artificial language semantics, or they can take Hyperproof's line of using graphical representations to aid in grounding their symbols. These are not exclusive choices. In practice, the first option, correspondence to natural language, is by far the commonest choice. The second, mathematical approach is rarely taken in introductory courses, except with mathematics students studying foundations. The third diagrammatic option was pioneered by Barwise and Etchemendy in the design of Hyperproof's predecessor, Tarski's World, although we shall see in the next chapter that they were extending a distinguished tradition of diagrammatic logic teaching that goes back at least to the seventeenth century and beyond.

Barwise and Etchemendy designed Tarski's World and Hyperproof to exploit properties of diagrammatic representations in helping students to grasp the semantics of the language of first-order logic. Their proposal was that diagrams would give students access to the semantics of artificial calculi and that this would their enhance learning. Tarski's World focused entirely on the task of matching the sentences of logic to diagrams of worlds. Hyperproof incorporated a *proof theory*—an inferential apparatus of rules for reasoning with combinations of diagrams and sentences.

Directly interpreted diagrams like those used in Hyperproof certainly give a *different* kind of access to the semantics of the calculus that accompanies them, but we should note that these diagrams are themselves but representations, which themselves have to be interpreted, as we have seen. Even if Hyperproof used real blocks distributed on a real board, the cylinder and bag 'blocks' would still be representations abstractly interpreted as denoting ranges of possibilities. This warning is perhaps a little fastidious, but the distinction is as well to bear in mind when we approach the understanding of what is learned. The distinction allows us to open up the question of whether it is some consequence of the directness of the interpretation which is important. There is a possibility that some highly inexpressive system (perhaps some sort of list representation), which is directly interpreted but not pictorial, might have the same cognitive effects.

Why go to all this diagrammatic and computational trouble? Well, there are notorious problems with the correspondences between natural languages and the language of first-order logic. Even introductory courses are forced to deal, for example, with the paradoxes of implication. We return to these paradoxes in Chapter 6 when we visit the experimental study of conditional reasoning. Many teachers suspect that their students never really grasp the implications of these paradoxes. The divergence of natural language conditionals from material implication arises from the differences in the variation of interpretation that can occur within natural and artificial languages. Natural language 'if' statements require possible worlds for their interpretation: the conditional statements in the calculi taught here are assessed for truth in a fixed-world interpretation. The calculus itself can receive just the range of interpretations formally defined, analogous to the range defined for propositional calculus in the truth-tables of Table 2.1, but in any give argument it has just one of these interpretations. One possible motivation for using diagrams is that anchoring the significance of a logical language may help to give the student access to an interpretation in which these paradoxes do not intrude destructively. This would be one example of many ways in which diagrams might allow access to semantics in a different way than calculi.

Of course, there is a frequently encountered argument amongst logic teachers *against* the introduction of the kind of semantics Hyperproof provides. Hyperproof is, in technical parlance, a *partially interpreted* language. Its predicates (e.g. *tetrahedron*, *between*, *left of*) have pre-assigned meanings. Many formalists would argue that teaching such a formalism prevents students from understanding the full generality of logical formalisms. The retort is that partially interpreted formalisms are perhaps the didactic ladder which can be thrown away when the student has ascended it, but without any aid to the climb, the vast majority never grasp anything, let alone the full generality of uninterpreted languages. In any case, as an absolutist argument it is strange, since even the conventional calculi are partially interpreted in the sense that their logical connectives and quantifiers are interpreted. Yet it is generally accepted that learning these classical 'partial' interpretations is a good waystation on the road to understanding non-standard ones. Absolutism is a dangerous drug for teachers.

There is, of course, ample evidence to back Barwise and Etchemendy's intuition that grasping the semantics of a system is critical for learning it. The classical demonstration of this fact is Miller's (1967) work on the application of information theory to memory, which gave rise to the earliest cognitivist theory of the importance of representation in memory. Miller showed that learning artificial languages without *any* access to their meaning was close to impossible.

Another motivation for incorporating diagrams into logical theory is naturalism. People frequently reason in the real world with a wide variety of representations, not all of which are linguistic. Extending logic to give an account of diagrammatic reasoning, and heterogeneous reasoning with combinations of diagrams and sentences, is an important research goal which may also help students to see that logic is an abstract account of representations—not about a particular mechanism for twiddling sentences. Hyperproof shows that formal rules can be defined for concluding sentences from diagrams, and adding information to diagrams on the basis of sentences.[9] Together these rules can be shown to meet the system-external standards of logical systems—soundness and completeness.

Finally, introducing diagrams enables the solution of much more complex problems than can be tackled in elementary courses using sentential reasoning. For example, think of what would be entailed in translating all the information in the diagram of Fig. 3.3 into sentences. These problems are strategic relative to the tactical focus of sentential courses. Perhaps these strategies are an important part of what students need to improve their general reasoning practices.

---

[9]This notion is challenged in an interesting way in Scotto Di Luzio (2000). His arguments are extremely revealing of what kind of computation is permitted in the application of formal rules.

3.2 What impact does introducing diagrams have on learning?

How is it possible to find out what happens when students learn in the classroom? The basic questions are deceptively simple: what can students do before the teaching 'treatments', and what can they do afterwards? Pre- and post-tests can be set to assess this. An important principle of psychological measurement is that it is much easier to understand comparative measures than absolute ones. Measuring how much has been learned in one course is much harder than measuring how much *more* has been learned in one course than another. In our case, the difference in impact of different modalities is the focus, and so the comparative method is the obvious one.

The hard question is what to assess in pre- and post-tests. Experiments like this always test *transfer* of learning. Transfer of learning from one example problem in the course to a similar one in the test is *near* transfer. Transfer to problems of a different superficial form and content is *far* transfer. How far should the transfer tested be? This is a particularly crucial question when the degree of formality to be adopted is an issue. As mathematics teachers know, teaching students to operate within a formalism is generally much easier than teaching them how to apply the formalism flexibly to new kinds of problems in new contexts. For us, this is *the* issue in assessment. There are views of the formal approach to logic teaching which claim that teaching formal logic teaches students to pass formal logic examinations and *nothing* more. This is a claim that there is no transfer at all beyond examples of the form taught in class. Therefore it is particularly critical for us to assess transfer to some reasoning tasks which are at least superficially different from the content of the course.

The 'far transfer' test chosen is called the Graduate Record Exam's (GRE) Analytical Reasoning Scale. This extra test was added to the GRE's existing battery of tests in response to a complaint from American college professors that the existing battery of testing did not adequately test analytical skills across domains of reasoning. The test has a certain street credibility in the USA since it is used as a component of the decision making for graduate school entrance, and does predict success in subsequent graduate school, to at least some degree. Since the other scales of the GRE do not concern us here, we can refer to the Analytical Reasoning Scale simply as the GRE. Chapter 6 returns to analyse what is involved in some of the GRE problems in the light of our developing theory of what has to be learned in learning elementary logic. It is not necessary to believe that the GRE is a perfect test of some platonic entity called 'general reasoning' in order for this test to be useful for current purposes. The test is a rough and ready research instrument. What is crucial is that GRE problems do not look like the content of a logic test to the students.

The GRE Analytical Reasoning Scale is itself divided into two subscales, a fact which takes on some importance in what follows. These two subscales are called, somewhat confusingly, the analytical and the logical, so the analytical *scale* has to be distinguished from the analytical *subscale*. In what follows we use 'analytical' to distinguish this half of our tests from the other 'logical' half. The choice of the term 'logical' is also rather strange in our context, and we shall use the term 'verbal' in its place. This term will serve to identify its reference without any theoretical commitment to the nature of the test. Two problems, one of each type, appear in Fig. 3.7.

Analytical problem An office manager must assign offices to six staff members. The available offices are numbered 1–6 and are arranged in a row, separated by six foot high dividers. Therefore sounds and smoke readily pass from one to others on either side. Ms Braun's work requires her to speak on the phone throughout the day. Mr White and Mr Black often talk to one another in their work and prefer to be adjacent. Ms Green, the senior employee, is entitled to Office 5, which has the largest window. Mr Parker needs silence in the adjacent offices. Mr Allen, Mr White, and Mr Parker all smoke. Ms Green is allergic to tobacco smoke and must have non-smokers adjacent. All employees maintain silence in their offices unless stated otherwise.

- The best office for Mr White is in 1, 2, 3, 4, or 6?

- The best employee to occupy the furthest office from Mr Black would be Allen, Braun, Green, Parker or White?

- The three smokers should be placed in offices 1, 2, & 3, or 1, 2 & 4, or 1, 2 & 6, or 2, 3, & 4, or 2, 3 & 6?

Verbal problem Excessive amounts of mercury in drinking water, associated with certain types of industrial pollution, have been shown to cause Hobson's disease. Island R has an economy based entirely on subsistence level agriculture with no industry or pollution. The inhabitants of R have an unusually high incidence of Hobson's disease.
Which of the following can be validly inferred from the above statements?

   i. Mercury in the drinking water is actually perfectly safe.

  ii. Mercury in the drinking water must have sources other than industrial pollution.

 iii. Hobson's disease must have causes other than mercury in the drinking water.

- (ii) only?

- (iii) only?

- (i) or (iii) but not both?

- (ii) or (iii) but not both?

Fig. 3.7 Examples of two types of reasoning problem. The top problem is 'analytical' and the bottom problem is 'verbal'.

Figure 3.7's analytical problem is a constraint satisfaction problem. A set of constraints narrow the possible situations which can satisfy them, in this case to a single situation. Deriving this situation (an allocation of offices to employees) allows us to answer each of the questions. Sometimes more than one possibility remains, but usually still a small number. Sometimes the questions are about what could be inferred if the constraints changed.

The verbal problem in Fig. 3.7 is what is sometimes called an 'argument analysis' problem in informal logic courses. It has to do with reasoning about a contingency (between mercury poisoning, environments and symptoms) and about the evidence for and against causal relationships.

Trying these problems for oneself is a useful prelude to understanding the following discussion—there is no substitute for first-hand experience of being a subject in subsequently interpreting experimental results. Yes, these problems are quite hard. They are designed to stretch highly intelligent senior undergraduates, and to be done against the clock.

Several points are worth noting about these problems. First, they are verbally set and verbally answered. Students are told that they can use paper and pencil while solving them, and we shall see below that students' 'work-scratchings' are revealing of their thought processes. Some students draw diagrams for some problems, and these are almost always analytical problems. The problems are designed to test general reasoning. We should think of the reasoning as using content which is available to everyone, rather than content-free reasoning, but what else could general reasoning be? The same is true of Hyperproof. It requires special knowledge about blocks in space, but this knowledge is widespread amongst logic students because it is widespread in the population.

As well as the GRE test of far transfer, we also wanted to know more about what Etchemendy's students could do in reasoning in Hyperproof's domain of blocks before and after the teaching. We could not set Hyperproof problems as a pre-test since they are couched in the language of first-order logic, and even the diagrams demand knowledge of the conventions for interpreting the abstraction tricks. Etchemendy constructed what we call the Blocks World test, which consists of Hyperproof-like problems set in English, using the absence of name-labels as the only abstractions in the diagrams. The problem about the Valley of the Solids which opened this chapter is in fact one of the problems in the Blocks World test. It gives a preliminary idea of what Hyperproof's problems are like. This Blocks World test is, relative to the GRE, a test of *near* transfer from a course taught using Hyperproof. In both cases the machine is a support, especially a support for practice homework examples. In addition to the computer, there is a text book (the conventional 'syntactic' course used Bergman *et al.* (1990); the Hyperproof course used Barwise and Etchemendy (1994), a full set of lectures, and the usual sections supported by teaching assistants, office consultations, etc. Neither course is taught by robots.

Consider the importance of the machine in each course. It is probably best thought of as providing rapid feedback on exercises in a way that tutors could never possibly do. In the diagrammatic case, the graphical system would be completely unwieldy without the computer to effortlessly store, retrieve and modify diagrams. This is almost certainly why this system of teaching did not predate computers. But it is of some importance to us that both courses use the same computerized sentential reasoning system. This at least provides an important control for the motivating effects of computers. Last, but not least, without the machine, there is no way of collecting the kind of detailed data which we are about to describe.

Thus our experiment consisted of two classes taught to mainly freshman Stanford students. This population is rather general in its academic interests (every Stanford student is required to take a course on reasoning skills, and this is a qualifying course), but highly selected for academic ability. Although it was not possible to assign students randomly to the two classes (they could not be run concurrently), the course descriptions were identical and so students could not select the course on the basis of its using or not using diagrams. Students took a pre-test before the course, the 10 week course, the course examination which was set on the computer, and a post-test immediately afterwards. We collected data on all the use of the Hyperproof software through a special version which

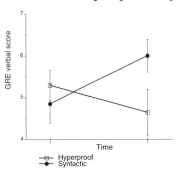 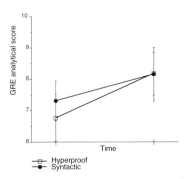

Fig. 3.8 GRE verbal and analytical scores at pre- and post-test by class (Hyperproof versus syntactic.)

logged the user's activity. It would have been useful to be able to test students at some further elapsed interval, but unfortunately this was not pragmatically possible.

Although this description reflects the state of our design before the study, it leaves out one essential element. The real goal of this kind of work is not to measure the relative gain in scores from pre- to post-test. The real aim is to develop a cognitive theory about how characteristics of students interact with teaching methods to result in learning. The really important data for this enterprise are what the students do during the course, as recorded in this instance by the Hyperproof program. Pre- and post-tests are an essential tool, but no more than a tool.

3.3   So, what happened?

All the students in these courses passed well, the vast majority with flying colours. That itself is not unusual in such a highly selected group, but it is important to keep in mind in interpreting some of the problems which we unearth in detailed analysis of the thinking processes involved. Psychology is the second dismal science: it focuses on human error because error is so much more informative than success, but it can be highly misleading if this focus leads us to forget the background of success.

Starting with gross measures of performance first, the good news is that the students substantially improved their scores on the GRE post-test relative to their scores on the pre-test in both the Hyperproof and the conventional syntactic courses. Logic teaching does improve performance on this test of general reasoning. It would have been desirable to have a control group who did neither course—perhaps a term at Stanford is sufficient to make these gains without any logic teaching. Selecting a sample for such a control group has its problems, but we did not have access to such a group anyway. The detail of the effects in different groups which we are about to examine make it extremely unlikely that this is the explanation of the results observed. These results are plotted in Fig. 3.8 by course taken and by subscale of the GRE.

Figure 3.8 shows that both courses are quite beneficial, but the syntactic course does slightly better at improving the 'verbal' subscale scores. This is not so surprising. As we shall see, this scale is probably more closely related to the tactical reasoning on which the syntactic course focuses, than the strategic reasoning of Hyperproof. What is rather more noteworthy when we come to consider the patterns of near and far transfer

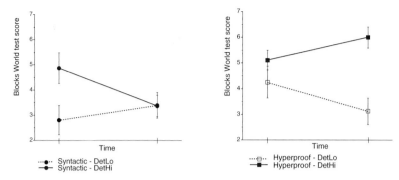

Fig. 3.9 Changes in Blocks World scores from pre- to post-test by course ((a) syntactic; (b) Hyperproof) and by GRE analytical score (DetHi, above median; DetLo, below median).

in all the tests, is that the syntactic course is rather good at improving performance on the analytical subscale. Learning to 'twiddle Ps and Qs' helps people with constraint-satisfaction problems such as office allocation. This is another striking result which poses questions about what is being transferred. We return to this issue in Chapter 6 in discussing what is learned about the process of formalizing content.

In assessing these results, it is important to remember that this was Hyperproof's first time out. That the very first course taught actually measures up to conventional teaching methods honed over about half a century is extremely impressive. At the time of writing, the software has undergone several enhancements, the text book been rewritten, the problems improved, and the teachers practiced. In highly innovative teaching, the first results are often disastrous, and the main consolation for the guinea-pig students is the enthusiasm of the innovators. Not here.

The Blocks World results are rather more complex. When the gross results were plotted in the same way, they showed rather minimal improvement. This is quite surprising. Tests of near transfer reliably show more improvement than tests of far-transfer. A first hypothesis was that the post-test might be inherently harder than the pre-test. We had to design the tests from scratch and we do not have the large population norms which would allow us to equate absolute difficulty. As we shall see, this is not as much a problem as it might appear because absolute effects are rarely what is most interesting—experiment internal phenomena are usually far more indicative of learning processes. It may be that the post-tests are harder and that may account for some of the apparent lack of improvement. However, it does not explain what we observed next.

In looking through the data, it seemed that there was rather great variability on the test items. A great deal of snooping around further suggested that performance on the analytical subscale of the GRE seemed to predict rather different outcomes on the Blocks World test for the two courses. Those who did well on the constraint-satisfaction problems like office allocation improved their Blocks World scores when taught by Hyperproof. But those who did poorly on the constraint satisfaction subscale actually *declined* in their Blocks World score after taking the same course. What is more, the interaction reversed in the students who took the syntactic course. Figure 3.9 shows this interaction.

This pattern of results makes it rather unlikely that the general lack of change in

Blocks World reasoning observed above is simply because the post-test is harder. Some students are showing large improvements; others are showing equally large decrements. This interaction is an example of what is called in the educational literature an *aptitude by treatment interaction* (ATI). Two groups of students categorized by their aptitudes prior to teaching (on the GRE analytical subsubscale pre-test) react differently (as measured by Blocks World post-tests) to two different teaching treatments (Hyperproof versus syntactic teaching).

Aptitude treatment interactions are notoriously slippery phenomena. Snow (1980), who pioneered the study of ATIs himself, published an influential review which showed just how difficult it is to get ATIs to stay still and be measured—they have a history of failing to replicate. Some of this failure is due to well-understood statistical phenomena. In most of the literature, the aptitude that is of central concern is overall scholastic achievement, or some other generalized measure separating sheep from goats. This choice of aptitude has much to do with the social-technological aims of psychometrics and little to do with any theory about the mind. Small shifts in the overall ability level of different classes from one experiment to another, or between conditions in an experiment, either generate or disguise ATIs. If the chosen aptitude is not itself a coherent component of mental process, then there is every reason to suppose that any ATI that it enters into will be labile.

Science overcomes problems of irreplicability by unearthing *mechanisms* which give a uniform account of why nature is so variable from context to context. Unfortunately, psychometrics, wedded as it is to making reliable absolute value judgements across populations, eschews the usual scientific remedy. Psychometrics does not deal in mental mechanisms—only in unanalysed test items.

However, our present predicament is a valuable opportunity. We have an ATI which occurs during the observed courses and reflects mental changes which are brought about in students by the courses. We also have several megabytes of data about how these students went about solving their homework problems and the problems in their final examinations. Surely somewhere in this haystack, a needle (mechanism) can be found, if only we know where to look?

3.4 But why are these the results?

Individual differences between people are a redoubtable weapon in the armoury of the behavioural analyst. If we do not know how people do some task, it may be extremely hard to come up with a general account of how everyone performs it. But if we have two groups of people whom we observe do it differently, then we have a powerful way into the data. Taking the set of example problems and asking which problems are the ones that most discriminate between the groups gives us a subset of problems which we can analyse to produce hypotheses about mental process.

The other royal road into such a set of data is through theory. We have a theory that says that the way that directly interpreted diagrams express abstraction is a highly distinctive property of diagrammatic systems of representation. We can look to see which problems hinge on reasoning with the graphical abstraction tricks of Hyperproof, and chase down the differences that result.

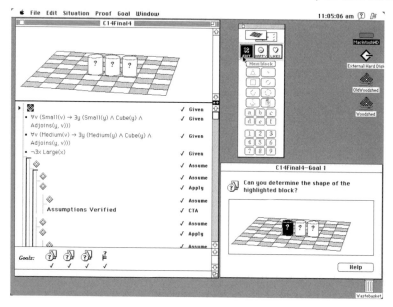

Fig. 3.10 The 'three-cylinders' problem.

A combination of these methods—along with a lot of highly laborious exploration in the data—has actually taught us a great deal about what happened in Etchemendy's two logic classes. The first decision was to concentrate on the examination proof data. The homework exercises turned out to show rather little variation. Perhaps unsurprisingly, students did the exercises the way they had been taught to do them, and were under no formal time pressure. But examinations are designed to stretch students by presenting them with harder problems than they would typically do for homework.

Looking to see which of the four Hyperproof problems in the final examination the two groups of students (sorted by GRE analytical subscale score) did most differently, revealed that it was the problem with the most extreme graphical abstraction which best discriminated them (Fig. 3.10). Figure 3.11 shows two student's solutions of this problem. These two proofs were selected as intuitively at extremes, but they also turned out to be by students with extreme scores on GRE constraint satisfaction. The left-hand proof is by a low scorer and the right-hand proof by a high scorer. When trying to get a foothold, studying extreme cases can be instructive.

Just as in the simpler problem in Fig. 3.3, each of the diamond icons in the sentence window proofs stands for a Hyperproof diagram used in the section of proof directly following. If this figure were the screen, the user could click on the diamond icon and the relevant diagram would appear in the diagram window. Each diagram represents a 'case', and this problem demands that the goal conclusion be proved in several cases. The sentences of first-order logic in the sentence window of Fig. 3.10 translate:

If a block is small, then there is a small cube next to it.
If a block is medium, then there is a medium cube next to it.
Nothing is large.

As usual, the experience of solving the problem for oneself is invaluable for assessing

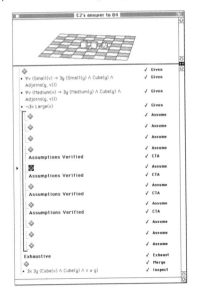
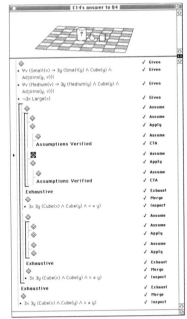

Fig. 3.11 Two contrasting proofs of the 'three-cylinders' problem.

what follows. And yes, the problem is quite hard. Remember that it was set to stretch clever test savvy undergraduates after a 10 week course on this kind of problem solving.

Even the novice eye can see that the left-hand proof in Fig. 3.11 has a flat structure relative to the right-hand proof which has hierarchical indentation (look at the 'proof bars' on the left of the proof). The flat and the hierarchical structures reflect the way that these students use graphical abstraction. The left-hand proof starts from the graphically abstract line of three cylinders, and concretizes it by assuming information until it is as concrete as it will become in the proof. Unfortunately, the reader cannot click on the page and see this diagram but will have to take what I say on trust. Having proved the goal for that concrete case, the next case is concretized from the abstract graphic by making a different set of assumptions, and so on for each of the 10 cases. When the cases have all been completed, the proof includes an application of the cases exhausted rule, which checks to see whether the student has missed a possibility, and when that is successful, the goal is solved.

In contrast, the right-hand proof uses graphical abstraction tricks to stage the concretization of cases. First, one piece of information is added, say being small, by using a small paper-bag icon, and then this subproof is further divided into three subsubproofs, one for each shape. When this is completed, the proof backs up not all the way to the top, but only to the point at which the paper bag assumed a size value. Then a different size value is assumed, and the subsubproofs for the three different shapes are done again. In this style of proof, the use of the abstraction tricks to stage the concretization of cases leads to the proof defining a principled structure for the space of cases. In the flat proof, the process of generating the space of cases is not reflected anywhere in the proof, and places a considerable memory load on the reasoner (possibly held in paper note form).

Note that both these students succeed in giving a valid proof, and in fact the flat proof is slightly shorter, and completed slightly quicker. Nevertheless, a trained eye regards the right-hand proof as more elegant—it 'shows its working' in a way that the flat proof does not. This might be only an unwarranted prejudice for a style, but it turns out to correlate with objective reasoning performance elsewhere, as we shall see.

An analysis of two proofs in terms of differences in the use of graphical abstraction is all very well, but what does this have to do with our aptitude treatment interaction? Have we not just found what we set out to find—an involvement of graphical abstraction. Might not another theorist have found their favourite hobby horse just as well?

It is hard to tell how many hobby horses there may be in this haystack, but can we at least show that this observed phenomenon does explain something of why these two groups of students respond so differently to teaching? This is not quite as simple as it might appear. Proofs are highly structured abstract objects, and it is not immediately clear what measures to take to show that one kind of students' proofs are more this or that than another's. It turned out that just counting the number of levels in the nesting of the proof (and several other trial measures) always yielded suggestive differences which hovered short of truly persuasive statistical significance. In an attempt to resolve this impasse, we produced some graphical representations of our own.

If abstract proofs are highly structured, people should be able to make reliable judgements of their similarity of structure even without knowing much about what they are judging. The proof-o-gram is a representation built on this principle. A proof-o-gram is a plot of the number of units of graphical abstraction at a point in a proof against the step number of that point. They look, to my inexpert eye, rather like patterns from Caucasian rugs (Fig. 3.12).

Giving the set of proof-o-grams for the problems like the three-cylinder problem with much graphical abstraction (one proof-o-gram for each students' proof of each of four problems) to a set of judges, and asking them to sort them into two piles on the basis of similarity, showed that there was indeed something to our intuition that these groups of subjects' proofs were different. Despite the fact that the student judges were told nothing about the semantics of proof-o-grams (they might as well have been rug patterns), judges unknowingly sorted our logic student subjects' proofs of this problem reliably into those done by students good at constraint satisfaction problems of the GRE, and those done by lower-scoring students. So there is something systematically different in these structures for the two student groups. But this demonstration does not go far in saying what it is.

Knowing that something humanly detectable about the abstraction structures of the proofs is different between the groups of students is reassuring. But what is the difference? At each point in a proof, there are many rules that could be applied, and even more ways in which they could be applied. How are we to abstract over all this detail to understand the similarities and differences in what students are doing? We needed to think at a strategic level about all this tactical detail. What is being learned? What is going on in Poirot's mind as he conducts his proof?

The Valley of the Solids problem at the outset of this chapter is useful for giving an intuition about the Hyperproof domain, but it could give the impression that what is being taught is merely to be better at Blocks World problems. This kind of misapprehension lies behind many of the dismissals of logic teaching as being useful for general reasoning.

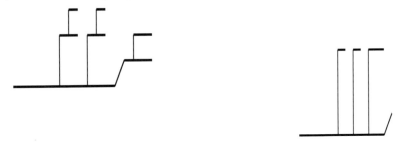

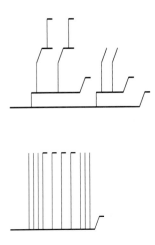

Fig. 3.12 Example proof-o-grams displaying amount of graphical abstraction by proof step. The upper two are nested and flat proofs of the one problem: the lower two of a different problem.

Reasoning about blocks on a board might have a little more street credibility than twiddling strings of Ps and Qs, if only because arguing about where things are is a common experience. But even if we could turn every student into a calculating genius for Blocks World problems, it is not clear why this would help them do anything else. Transfer at this level would be mysterious, even if true.

But this is not what Hyperproof is teaching. The chief thing that Hyperproof is designed to teach is the concept of proof, and the skills of finding proofs for target problems. Poirot gives no justification for his monologue—his mind's ear just has to take it on trust that the master is not having an off-day. If he were feeling more cryptic, he might merely announce the answer as obvious—to him. The steps in Poirot's monologue are sufficiently large that they may not be self-evident to us apprentices. Mathematics students know the old story about the professor who one day says, in the middle of a difficult theorem, 'from this it obviously follows that ... ', but suddenly breaks off in a state of high anxiety, and abruptly leaves the room. When he returns a hour later he continues 'from this it *is* obvious that ... ' and continues writing the thing which now is obvious to him. The business of proof is to reduce the span of these leaps to the obvious.

Logic makes a radical distinction between *discovery* of a logical or mathematical truth and *justification*. Logic provides a mechanical criterion of justification. A conclusion is logically justified if it appears in a sequence of steps of derivation all of which follow from the problem statement or earlier derivations from it by one or other of the rules of inference. Each rule application is 'small' enough that it can be checked mechanically. But how we are to find such a chain of rule applications is a matter of *discovery*. Discovery can be (and historically has been) by dream, hallucination, or revelation. Logic does have something to say about discovery, but by far its most intense focus is on the apparatus of justification, and on the very concept of justification itself.

This distinction in slightly different guise also lies at the foundations of our ideas of computation (historically no accident, since logic was the origin of our theoretical understanding of computation). Checking whether a rule application is a valid step in a proof is a mechanical operation: deciding what rule to apply and how in order to reach the goal is not, in general, a mechanical matter. Logicians distinguish between **logic** and **theorem-prover**. A logic (in this narrow technical sense) is the system (vocabulary, syntactic and semantic rules) and rules of inference (axioms, whatever...). Most abstractly a logic is simply an infinite set of theorems—pairs of sets of premises and valid conclusions from them. This is what is known as a consequence relation. It says nothing about how to find the chain of steps that will get from the premises to the conclusion. This latter is the task of the theorem-prover—to discover the path from premises to conclusion (if there is one). Theorem-provers may be algorithmic (follow a mechanical recipe for guaranteed success), or heuristic (offer rules of thumb which may increase the likelihood of finding proof, but offer no guarantees). All these technicalities are directly germane to understanding student learning.

The mechanical nature of each rule application is critical to logic's approach to justification, but unfortunately casual acquaintances come away with the impression that logical reasoning is mechanical. This is deeply paradoxical, since the main advances in logic in the twentieth century stemmed from the demonstration that even deductive reasoning cannot, in general, be mechanized. For example, there is no algorithm for deciding the truth of an arbitrary candidate theorem in the first-order predicate calculus. Discovery is not, in general, a mechanical but a heuristic process. Even if Poirot's steps in reasoning were as small as single rule applications, what his mind's ear does not hear is the processes which lead him to discover his path to the conclusion. A very important part of what is being learned are heuristic methods for finding proofs.

For example, why does Poirot start at the end of the list of premises, by noting that: 'since b is between two other blocks, there are just three possibilities for b'? A flippant answer is that the awkward people who construct these problems always put the best place to start at the end. But Poirot knows a thing or two about where to start, and he would not be fooled even if a super awkward test author had put it at the beginning to catch the half-savvy student.

What Poirot has done is called 'splitting into cases'. 'Since b is between two other blocks, there are just three possibilities for b.' These three possibilities are cases. In general, it is a good idea to choose to split on a premiss which leads to a small number of cases.[10] There is more than one splitting in Poirot's monologue, and there are other sequences of splitting that he could have used. Perhaps Poirot is a self-taught genius. Perhaps he does not know that this heuristic for splitting is something that he knows. If asked why he started there, he might give a Gallic shrug and say that it is because it is obvious. If so, he would be a typical expert.

Poirot would also, in this respect, be like a typical student of logic. Students in first-year college are experts at solving a great many kinds of reasoning problems. They use the structure of their natural languages, and diagrams, in highly sophisticated ways. But in general, they know little about how they do this. Logic, like many university subjects (linguistics, psychology, physics, . . .), is substantially aimed at making explicit what students already at least partly know implicitly. All these disciplines turn implicit knowledge embedded in complex contextualized skills into explicit theoretical knowledge.

Perhaps the effect is comparable to asking the centipede which leg it should move next? Indeed, the immediate price of explicitness may well be regression to a lower level of skilled performance. Researchers may justify this simply by saying it is a price we pay for theory, and theory is the only goal. But a teacher's justification must be that making skills explicit can lead not just to theory, but also to subsequent improvement in performance. This is one of our proposals in this book, though it is hardly a novel one.

Logic teaching to improve general reasoning abilities gambles that making explicit the distinction between justification and discovery, and providing a language for thinking about these matters, as well as developing the skills of applying the concepts, *can* eventually lead to better performance at both tasks. Poirot's implicit heuristic is about knowing where to attack a set of premisses in the course of splitting into cases. How can we approach the analysis of the heuristics that our Hyperproof students are using to produce their different kinds of proof? This is where the statistics become vital.

Each proof starts with a diagram (a graphical situation in Hyperproof terms) and a set of sentences which are *given* (they define the problem). A sequence of rule applications, and citations of the earlier lines which justify them, then yield new lines in the sentence window, or changes to the diagram. The conventional sentential rules of logic which take sentence premisses and yield sentence conclusions are included.

For example, P and $P \rightarrow Q$ as premisses justify the addition of Q as a new line of the proof. This particular inference rule is known medievally as *modus ponens*, or $\rightarrow$ *elimination*, the former from Latin and the latter for obvious reasons. Hyperproof adds rules for moving information between diagram and sentence windows. So if we can *observe* that there is a cube in the current graphical situation, then we can add the sentence $\exists x, x\, a\, cube$ with the justification *observe*, to the proof. Conversely, if a sentence such as *cube a* appears in the proof already, either as an assumption or derived by an earlier rule application, and an icon in the diagram is already labelled a (perhaps it is a cylinder icon without a shape badge), then we can add a cube badge to a's cylinder, citing the rule *apply*. We have *applied* the sentential information to the diagram. Alternatively, if a is currently represented by a small paper-bag icon (remember paper bags hide shape

---

[10] Think of the alternative splittings into cases involved in the proofs of the theorem in Fig. 3.3.

but indicate size), then we can change the bag to a cube citing the same rule *apply*. There are altogether about a dozen rules of inference like → *elimination*, *observe*, and *apply*.

If we take rule of inference applications as the unit of analysis, we can look for patterns of sequences of rule use. In fact, the simplest methods amount to analysing the proofs as if they were produced by a finite-state machine (as described in Chapter 2); we analyse the probability that one rule will follow another, regardless of what went before.

This is a common technique used in the statistical analysis of natural language discourses, usually applied at the level of words rather than rules. But there is nothing to prevent its application to unnatural languages. Just as with natural languages, it is possible that there are longer distance dependencies than between adjacent pairs of words (certainly there are, because proofs are hierarchically structured). Our choice of this simple technique is not because we want to claim such structure is unimportant, or because we think our students are finite-state machines, but is made in the spirit of using the simplest tool first.

Feeding the students' examination proofs into the analysis program as strings of rule applications returns a square matrix of rules, with cells which correspond to the frequency with which the row-rule was applied immediately after the column-rule. This frequency can be compared to the chance frequency that the two rules would occur as often as this if they simply occurred at their observed frequencies but independently of each other. Two kinds of departures from independence are possible: an ordered pair of rules can occur in the data either *more* frequently or *less* frequently than independence would indicate. The probability of an observation as extreme as that actually observed is calculated, and a list prepared of the 'bigrams' (sequenced rule pairs) which occur more or less than expected on the assumption of independence. In fact, two lists are prepared, one for students who were good at GRE analytical subscale reasoning, and one for students who were less good. Examining the lists then indicates which bigram profiles discriminate the groups of students.

The resulting ungainly lists and tables are condensed in Fig. 3.13. Each box represents a rule; its size represents the overall frequency of the rule's use and the thickness of the arrows joining boxes represents the proportion of the transitions from the arrow's tail-rule which go to the arrow's head-rule (percentages also appear on the arrows). The data has been thresholded, so that rule transitions which occur less than 10 per cent of the time are excluded to avoid clutter.

The data have also been tailored somewhat to our quest. Examination of the data indicates that there might be something special about different uses of the same rule *assume*, which is related to the flat and hierarchical proof examples in Fig. 3.10. We distinguish uses of *assume* from a special subset of its uses which we call *fullassume*. These are applications of *assume* adding information to diagrams, which take the diagram to full concreteness (i.e. eliminating all graphical abstraction tricks). Absence of name labels is not treated as graphical abstraction for this purpose. These fullassume applications correspond to the spikes in the proof-o-gram of the flat proof in Fig. 3.12. Finally, proofs start with givens, so the *given* box is like the 'start' box of our example in Fig. 2.5. There is no single Hyperproof rule which ends all proofs, and so there is no 'end' box in this representation.

Even without knowing much about the rules, this rather crude representation reveals some differences between groups of students in their patterns of rule use: the balance of

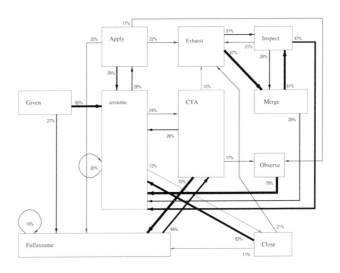

(a)

(b)

Fig. 3.13 Finite-state machine representations of rule-transition frequencies for the two groups of student defined by GRE analytical score: (a) below-median students; (b) above median students. Hyperproof rules correspond to boxes. Area of box represents frequency of rule use. Thickness of arrow represents the proportion of transitions taking that path. Data are thresholded to remove transitions accounting for less than 10 per cent of transitions out of a box.

assume and fullassume applications is different. GRE high students show more *assume* than *fullassume*, whereas GRE low students show the reverse); the GRE A low students have an arrow from *given* to *apply*, whereas the other students do not; GRE A low students use *close* much less, and none of the transitions from *close* are above threshold, whereas GRE A high students have several transitions out of *close*. Each of these differences can be related to graphical abstraction behaviour.

Distinguishing *assume* from *fullassume* picks up on the habit of low GRE students of fully concretizing situations. Using *apply* after assume is another aspect of this habit—*assume* begins a subproof, and *apply* is the rule that concretizes diagrams using sentential information. The relation of *close* to graphical abstraction is somewhat more indirect. *Close* plays a part in a particular kind of *reductio ad absurdum* proof—a proof that assumes the negation of its target conclusion, and then shows that that the assumptions are now jointly contradictory. Teachers of logic will not be surprised that there is a subset of students who do not use *reductio* proofs.

Statistical tests on whether the frequencies of these bigrams (and some others) are significantly distinct in these two groups of students show that indeed they are. It was not just our theorists' blinkers which hallucinated the trends for flat and hierarchical proof styles in the two groups.

So much for detective work. Let us step back from the level of the evidence—the fingerprints—and summarize at a more synoptic level what we have found—the culprits' characters. What are the differences between the two groups of students who we are now satisfied really do prove things in different ways?

Synoptically, this is a remarkable result. The Hyperproof students were given 10 weeks intensive teaching in how to reason in what appears to many a rather arcane computer system using formal rules of reasoning which are, on the face of things, new even to logicians. Indeed, analysing the students' homework exercises shows that considerable uniformity of proof method reigned. When they were put in an examination and set problems rather harder than they had experienced before, these two distinctive styles of proof emerge from the data, and can be predicted from pre-course scores on a 20-minute reasoning test which uses quite different problems. The first point must be that if Hyperproof teaching just taught a new rigamarole quite unrelated to anything else students had ever done, then one might expect them to all do it the same way. Remember, this is not a question of good and not so good performance. The students are producing valid proofs and passing examinations. But they do it in quite different ways. They have learned something different, and there is also some indication that they 'knew' different things before they started.

When it comes to summarizing what this difference is, the results are rather paradoxical. Psychologists presented with these results are initially inclined to categorize the students who learn well from Hyperproof (GRE A high) as 'visual' and the ones who learn well from the syntactic course as 'verbal'. This is a well-known psychometric distinction, and is often backed up by appeal to speculations about differences between the balance of processing in the two brain hemispheres.

But look carefully at what is actually observed here. The students who do not improve and even decline in Blocks World scores are exactly the group of students whose first impulse in finding a proof is to concretize the situation by translating sentential information into diagrams. Conversely, the students who do improve their Blocks World scores are exactly the group of students who refrain from translating sentences into the diagram, and actually instead express things they observe in the diagrams through graphical abstractions, or in sentences. This hardly sounds like 'verbal' and 'visual' vignettes. Remember, the diagnostic test for the distinction, the GRE analytical, is *not* a visual test. It is set verbally and answered verbally. It is true that many students draw diagrams while solving these problems, but it is not like classical visual/spatial tests, nor does it behave like they do, as we shall see.

The best summary of these differences between student groups is in terms of *strategies* of reasoning—strategic aspects of their theorem provers. The group whose Blocks World scores increase after Hyperproof teaching have learned something of Poirot's genius for splitting into cases. In particular, the 'visual' students are the ones who learn well when to avoid overly specific 'visual' representations, especially when solving graphically abstract problems! A nice paradox.

Another paradoxical aspect of these results is that there is rather good *far* transfer to the GRE test, but mixed transfer to the near Blocks World test. This is the reverse of the usual case. Far transfer is the Holy Grail, not often achieved. Near transfer is more often achieved. This paradox raises the question which is likely to have been troubling the teachers in this readership—how are we to interpret these significant decrements in performance in the groups that 'get into the wrong class'? This result sends chills down the spine of any responsible teacher.

First we should remember that, overall, all the students show gains in the test which was chosen to reflect (if imperfectly) general reasoning ability. The decrements in performance show up when we test (in the Blocks World test and in the examination) the special techniques which have been taught in the class. The most likely interpretation is that students are adopting methods of reasoning which they have been taught to adopt, but which are not well suited to some pre-existing reasoning style onto which the course has grafted them. We doubt that the teaching is causing brain damage. It is quite likely that if the students were tested in some context where they felt less bound to apply the methods they have learned in this course, they might well have gone back to whatever they would have done before the teaching (a case of non-transfer bringing the teacher relief?). But these results are an eloquent reminder that students learn different things in different ways, and teachers can but do their best to cater to variety.

Another striking aspect of these results, and another that casts some doubt on the idea that the effects are due to preferences for visual or verbal media, is the finding that conventional sentential logic courses lead to good improvements in blocks world reasoning amongst GRE low scoring students; but brings about decrements in blocks world scores in GRE high scoring students. 'Verbal' students taking a 'syntactic' course improve their 'visual' blocks world reasoning. This result is even more remarkable when we remember that these students did not see a single Hyperproof diagram between taking the pre- and post-tests.

Unfortunately, analysis of the sentential proofs collected from the syntactic course has not so far proved nearly as revealing as the Hyperproof analyses. This is because with the much shorter sentential proofs of examination problems (remember our earlier remarks about the tactical nature of the sentential course reasoning relative to the strategic nature of Hyperproof problems), students either get a proof (and usually it is basically the same proof), or they fail to find any proof at all. They do not come up with a variety of different methods of proof. This is a pity because it would be valuable to have a detailed analysis of what is transferring from the syntactic course to the Blocks World problems for some students and not others. But even without such a detailed analysis, their transfer to Blocks World reasoning from the syntactic course is completely comprehensible if we think in terms of the transfer of reasoning strategies. Splitting into cases is as much a skill in sentential reasoning as in Hyperproof's diagrammatic reasoning.

We conclude that both high and low GRE scoring students, when they learn successfully, transfer similar skills (notably strategic skills like splitting into cases) from the respective courses to the post-tests. High scoring GRE students find this easier to do from the Hyperproof course; low scoring GRE students find this easier to do from the syntactic course. Only at this abstract level can transfer from logic teaching be understood theoretically, or achieved practically. In Chapter 5, we return to the problem of characterizing what is learned in elementary logic class.

Details of the evaluation study of Hyperproof can be found in Stenning *et al.* (1995*a*) and Oberlander *et al.* (1999*a*).

3.5   But how general are these differences?

Probably the question uppermost in the reader's mind at this point is: 'but what can we tell from 60 kids?' Surely psychometrics is done on populations of thousands carefully balanced for gender, socio-economic background, race, birth month, etc., etc.? The question is a good one. How can we generalize from these data? And how not?

First there is a paradox of sample size—if an effect is large enough to reach statistical significance in a small sample (and all the effects reported here are significant), that is stronger evidence for their existence than if they are only found in large samples. A small experiment is a low-power microscope, and what it can see is correspondingly large. The catch, of course, lies in the relationship between the small sample and the general population. What statistical significance tells us is that if we find another small sample from the same population, we stand a good chance of getting the same result. But we do not really know what properties define the population other than that they were Stanford students enrolling in a particular class in a particular year.

We do know that these are a highly selected group for their academic ability, and they are from relatively affluent backgrounds; they are highly motivated to learn; they are rather easier to teach than some other groups, or at least the problems encountered by teacher and learner are different. This relationship to the general population is what tells us what kinds of generalization it is sensible to consider. If we are interested in how difficult a set of test items is for the cohort of 18-year-old members of the human race, then our experiment tells us almost nothing. But if instead our goal is to try to characterize the mental processes of one population of students and the learning that happens under different teaching regimes, then our sample is quite useful. It provides strong evidence that if we ran a few thousand such students, we would observe the same effects. If it can reveal some mental mechanisms, then we have a basis for seeking generalization to other kinds of students. Even if their mechanisms of learning turn out to be somewhat different, we will have made a start.

It remains an open question whether such results will transfer to other populations. But there are many reasons for wanting to start studying the learning of reasoning amongst populations who are rather successful at it. There are large numbers of students who are prevented from learning by factors which we have little to say about—lack of opportunity or intrinsic motivation being the most important—but these are not the populations to choose initially for basic research into learning reasoning. If we can say something about the mental processes of this group of students, then we have some hope of transferring insights into other groups, even if their processes are substantially different. Without a characterization of mechanism, as psychometrics keeps exemplifying, there is no prospect even of replication, let alone extension.

A more serious question for our research programme is what relation the differences in reasoning style we have found bear to other tasks and other cognitive differences. Are there other things that these groups of students do differently? Are there other groupings of the students along other dimensions that would show other differences in reasoning processes? We shall address both these questions by looking for broader evidence.

With a complicated evaluation of students learning in real-world courses, there are many factors beyond the experimenters' control and even knowledge. We felt it important to seek both convergent evidence and replication. We looked for the former in an analysis of students' own spontaneous use of representations, and the latter in a second evaluation study.

3.5.1 Spontaneous representations in reasoning

Most students use the pencil and paper provided with the GRE test, and most draw some diagrams for at least some of the problems. These 'work-scratchings' offer an opportunity to see whether the same kind of differences in reasoning style that appeared in the examination-proofs also show up in pre-course spontaneous graphical behaviour. The GRE is normally taken just before applying for graduate school, and so few freshman undergraduates have done much cramming for GRE analytical problems.

Students do a variety of things with paper and pencil while solving GRE analytical tests. Unsurprisingly, the office allocation problem produces a variety of directly interpreted diagrams, though some of these are hard to distinguish from word lists.[11] In contrast, the mercury problem produces little in the way of diagrams but a variety of verbal and symbolic efforts. On the other hand, some problems produce a wide range of different kinds of representations ranging from direct diagrams through node-and-link graphics to formal language notations.

Analysis of the students' work-scratchings from both pre- and post-test GRE Analytical problems showed that getting the right kind of representation was an important determinant of success at solving the problem. Representation selection accuracy was defined by applying our distinction between direct and indirectly interpreted representations. Tables, ordered lists, spatial layouts, set-diagrams etc. were scored as directly interpreted: textual descriptions, expressively interpreted network graphics, and logical calculi were defined as indirectly interpreted. It is obviously an imperfect art applying our semantic distinctions to students' private work-scratchings, but inter-rater reliability was high. We derived representation selection accuracy scores for each subject and problem by comparing our ratings of the students' work-scratchings with the type of representation recommended for each problem by a selection of GRE crammers, in turn scored as directly or indirectly interpreted by ourselves.

Using this measure, the Hyperproof students' mean representation selection accuracy scores improved from pre- to post-test, indicating that the Hyperproof course significantly improved representation selection skills applied to the GRE constraint problems,

---

[11] Remember that word-lists are directly interpreted too, as our discussion of regular languages in Chapter 2 argued.

and that these might well be part of the mechanism of improvement of GRE reasoning in this group. The syntactic logic course also slightly improved students' skill at choosing representations but this did not reach significance. As Fig. 3.8 showed, the students in the syntactic logic course improved their GRE analytical subsubscale scores *as much* as the Hyperproof students, but this improvement is not much reflected in improved representation selection accuracy. It looks as if the syntactic course is leading to improvements in some other subskill. Further analysis shows that the two courses lead to improvement on different GRE problems at post-test. In other words, the different courses lead to the same amount of improvement in scores on this sub-test, but they do so in different ways. We return to this issue in Chapter 6 when we discuss content effects in reasoning.

The differences between the two kinds of student, which played such a large part in our analysis of what was learned in the logic courses, is also reflected in their spontaneous representation construction. Selecting an appropriate representation had a different impact on the problem solutions of the two groups of students. To show this we had to resort again to our semantic theories. The obvious way to analyse these data for our purposes is to divide the representations according to their modality of interpretation—direct or indirect. It is possible to do this with reasonable agreement, as checked by inter-rater reliability.

It is also possible to categorize the GRE problems as to whether they lend themselves to direct representation, or whether they require representing with the expressive power of indirect systems. Problems whose constraints specify a single model (or possibly a few models) lend themselves to direct representations: problems whose constraints can be satisfied by many models require the greater expressive power of indirect diagrams. We shall call the former *determinate* problems and the latter *indeterminate* ones. This dimension is something of a continuum since problem constraints may only narrow possibilities rather than specify a unique one, and the issue is then whether there is some direct diagram which can achieve the limited abstraction necessary by using suitable 'tricks'. Nevertheless, raters achieve high agreement on classifying problems, as well as on classifying students' work-scratchings. An interesting side finding is that the experts' recommendations found in GRE crammers did not always accord with our analysis in terms of expressiveness. The experts several times recommended approaches which were demonstrably inapplicable in detail.

The question then is whether the two different groups of subjects defined by the GRE analytical scale behave differently in constructing representations classified this way, for classes of problem classified this way? And what impact does their choice of construction have on their accuracy of solution? Remember, the groups are being classified on the basis of their pre-test scores on this selfsame test, and so one group is guaranteed to be better than the other on GRE analytical reasoning accuracy at pre-test. The issue is whether their success can be related to their representation selection behaviour, and how the relationship changes with logic teaching, as measured at post-test.

Figure 3.14 shows that there is the expected determination of reasoning accuracy by the expressiveness of the representation chosen, interacting with the determinateness of the problem tackled.

Figure 3.15 shows how differently representation selection affects reasoning accuracy for the two groups of students. Although determinate problems are in general best solved by weak (directly interpreted) representations (maps, tables, set-diagrams,

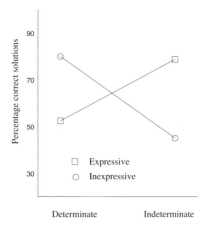

Fig. 3.14 Frequency of correct solution by expressiveness of representation selected and by problem type.

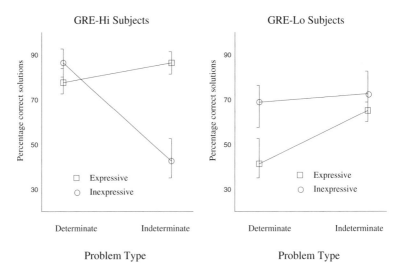

Fig. 3.15 Frequency of GRE analytical problem solution for high and low scoring subjects, by determinateness of problem and expressiveness of representation constructed.

etc.), and indeterminate problems by strongly expressive (indirectly interpreted) representations (networks, logical notations, reordered texts, etc.), the relationship between problem type and representation used in determining problem-solving success is quite different in the two student groups.

Students who are good at GRE analytical problems at pre-test show a significant positive determination of their reasoning scores on indeterminate problems by their selection of strongly expressive representations. These students are in general good at selecting the correct 'strength' of representation, but when they make the mistake of trying to draw, say, a table or a map of a problem which requires something more expressive, then their solution accuracy really suffers. In contrast, the group weaker on solving GRE analytical problems show a rather weak and statistically insignificant relationship between choice of representation and reasoning success. They are poorer at selecting the right representation, but getting it wrong has a less adverse effect on their reasoning. Probably, they place less reliance on their representations, and indeed there are many cases of the work-scratching being clearly in error, whilst the student gets the right answer. The reasoner may well be aware of errors in their representations but not correct them.

Further analysis to see whether the two kinds of course affect the representational behaviour of the two kinds of students differently does not reveal any clear effects, possibly because of sparseness of data when this much subdivided. There are much fewer data because many problems are solved without any work-scratching. The trends are in the suggested direction but it is not possible to reproduce the full aptitude by treatment interaction between kind of student and kind of course in this analysis of spontaneous work-scratchings. However, this analysis does support the generality of the individual differences, and the idea that representational behaviour underlies some of the differences observed earlier in styles of proof. The analysis also provides an important kind of generalization. The processes which go on in GRE problem solving appear to be susceptible to the same analysis in terms of direct and indirect representations, and related individual differences. The details of this analysis of work-scratchings can be found in Cox *et al.* (1995).

3.5.2 Replicating the study

Aptitude by treatment interactions have proved notoriously difficult to replicate. We claim that this is because of the lack of attention paid to the mechanisms which underlie learning. Getting an insightful description of what are the crucial differences between these groups of students is central to understanding our results, and also central to getting them to replicate. So we set out to study the next Hyperproof course that we could find—in Sweden.

We were able to find a willing colleague, Cecilia Sönstrod, who was preparing to teach a Hyperproof course in Göteborg University. Unfortunately, there was no available conventional 'syntactic' control course, but nevertheless this offered an opportunity to examine the robustness of the individual difference findings of the initial study and to extend them in some new directions.

A few changes were made to the teaching, to the testing, and to the examination problems used. On the teaching side, Cecilia Sönstrod had decided to increase emphasis on the sentential component within her Hyperproof course. She did not make this change as a result of our findings, but it was a change entirely consonant with those findings. For some students, (perhaps the lower GRE scoring ones?), more emphasis on the sentential component of Hyperproof might be expected to be beneficial. These changes to the sentential teaching show up in the data as we shall see.

On the testing side, we wanted to explore the relations between the individual differences which we had discovered to be so dominant in the results of the first study, and other psychometric tests of spatial abilities. We added several tests to the pre- and

Fig. 3.16 Example item from the Paper Folding Test. Two folds and a punching are portrayed in the left-hand three diagrams. The task is to select from the right-hand five diagrams the pattern of holes that results.

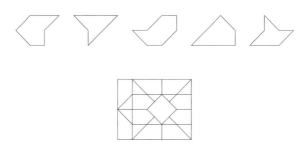

Fig. 3.17 Example Hidden Figures Test item. The task is to select which of the outline figures in the row above is contained in the complex pattern below.

post-test battery: the Paper Folding Test (Ekstrom *et al.* (1976)), the Hidden Figures Test (Witkin *et al.* (1971)), and the Serialist/Holist Learning Styles Test (Pask (1975), Ford (1984), Clarke (1993)). The Paper Folding Test (PFT) was designed as a test of spatial ability, but is one that has been shown to be subject to strategic variation, including the use of verbal strategies. Both the Hidden Figures Test (HFT) and the Serialist/Holist Test are intended to be tests of how flexibly the problem solver can bring a 'frame' to bear top-down on a problem. The HFT is perhaps one of the tests least dependent on the first language of the subjects tested—an important criterion in a study of Swedish students for whom we did not have translations of these tests.

On the examination problem side, we increased the number of problems which involved rather high levels of graphical abstraction, since we now had some justification for the belief that this tested a rather critical aspect of learning from the course.

A brief description of the new tests is helpful for understanding the results. Each item of the PFT consists of a diagram of a sequence of folds made in a sheet of paper. After folding, the paper is punched as marked, and then opened out. A set of diagrams of alternative pieces of paper is presented, from which we must choose the one with the correct pattern of holes which would result from the punching. Figure 3.16 shows a typical item with two folds. The correct answer is the option on the far right.

Figure 3.17 shows an item from the HFT. It presents a row of candidate subpatterns, only one of which can be found embedded in the complex pattern without reorienting, flipping, or resizing. In this case the rightmost pattern can be found in the top left quadrant of the larger pattern. The test requires suppressing alternative interfering visual 'parsings' of the large figure to find the small one.

The serialist/holist test, the short 'self-rating' version of which is used here, simply asks the subject the question which appears in Fig. 3.18. A wholist reading strategy makes active use of the high-level structure of the text being read, while a serialist approach passively accepts the linearization which the author has imposed. Note that this dimension is not evaluative. Some texts are undoubtedly better read one way and

When I'm reading a book (or other information source) for my studies, I prefer to spend quite a long time skimming over and dipping into it to get a clear picture of what it's about and how it will be relevant.

When I'm reading a book (or other information source) for my studies, I prefer to get quite soon into a fairly detailed reading of it once I know that it's going to be useful, in the knowledge that its precise relevance and contribution will become clear from a detailed reading.

Fig. 3.18 The serialist/holist self-rating scale.

some the other, and the effects of approach will interact with the reading task at hand.

The same GRE and Blocks World tests were set as in the previous study. Having no Swedish translations to hand, and granted the excellent English of most of these students, we set the tests in English. More of this later.

Otherwise the design of the study was like the first one. Students took the pre-tests before instruction began. Instruction took 10 weeks, and was followed by the course examination, and the post-tests. About 80 students took the course, although there was an unfortunately high drop-out rate at the final post-tests. The students were first-year students, rather narrower in their range of subject specializations in that they were all students of philosophy, but rather broader in their ability range, because Goteborg is a less highly selective university than Stanford. These ability range differences, combined with sitting the tests in a foreign language, combined to depress GRE performance somewhat relative to the Stanford students, more so on the verbal than on the analytical subscales, as one might expect.

The results of the study are reported in Monaghan *et al.* (1999). The effects on Blocks World scores broadly replicated the Hyperproof half of the previous study. Students who did well on the GRE analytical subscale increased their Blocks World scores more than did those who did less well on the GRE. In fact, the latter group barely improved at all, though they did not decline in Blocks World scores as the corresponding Stanford students had done. This is the half of the original aptitude treatment interaction which this study can compare, and it replicates fairly well.

So far, so good. But detailed study of the examination problem proofs of these students indicates a mixed pattern of replication and non-replication. The absolute measures of amount of graphical abstraction used in the examination proofs for indeterminate problems is not different between the two groups of students. Ironically, the HFT *does* predict the difference which the GRE predicted in Stanford. Students who score highly on the HFT do use more graphical abstraction in their proofs of indeterminate problems. The HFT is less dependent on the language it is set in than the GRE, and may be a more reliable test of the difference we are studying than the GRE in this population with Swedish as a first language. HFT and GRE analytical scores are significantly correlated.

This is rather unsatisfactory, but rather typical of the problems of replicating aptitude treatment interactions. In fact the replication is rather good in comparison with the field. These results prompted us to try to extend our analysis of what underlies the learning. The advantage of our approach is that we can collect detailed records of rather complex structures and processes—the construction of complex proofs. We can relate these

Table 3.1 Mean number of situations used in proving single and multiple-goal problems, by PFT score (high and low) and GRE analytical score (high and low).

	PFT Lo	PFT Hi
Multiple-goal problems		
GREA Lo	13.40	9.86
GREA Hi	12.33	10.89
Single-goal problems		
GREA Lo	1.15	2.00
GREA Hi	1.71	1.21

structures and processes to the semantics of the representations that enter into them, and to the problems of finding proofs in this domain. These data can characterize the 'theorem-prover' that constitutes these students' skills at the end of their course.

What is needed is a classification of problem types and proof methods which will allow a more abstract analysis of what students with different ability profiles do in constructing their proofs. Kinds of problems can naturally be classified in terms of: whether the problem can be expressed graphically, or has to be expressed sententially (modality); whether the proof is of consequence or non-consequence (that something follows or that it is logically independent); and also by the number of cases required to be considered in the least-case proof. A useful and easily applied measure of a student's method for a proof is the number of cases used.

Using this classification it is possible to show that the reason that the Stanford results for the three-cylinders problem did not entirely replicate is related to Cecilia Sönstrod's teaching innovations. A substantial number of her students devised purely sentential proofs of this problem (something that never happened in the original study). This change almost certainly resulted from her new emphasis on sentential methods. A purely sentential proof of the problem is yet further along the dimension of abstraction than the hierarchically nested proof of Fig. 3.11. The data bear this out. The mean scores on the two spatial tests (HFT and PFT) and the Blocks World test for students doing the three kinds of proof (sentential, abstract graphical, concrete graphical) are ordered from high to low respectively. The more abstract your proof, the higher you scored on the spatial pre-test measures. The sentential proofs behave as if they are the abstract end of the dimension we found in the first study.

However, the results with the GRE analytical test are still not exactly as they were in Stanford. To find full analogues of the original interaction in these data it is necessary to look across all the problems in the new study, and to analyse by proof method, as well as problem type. When this is done there are a number of significant aptitude by treatment interactions involving GRE analytical scores even in this population, where native language probably obscures results. An illustrative example is presented in Table 3.1 which shows mean number of cases used for multiple and single-goal problems by PFT and GRE analytical pre-test scores.

With multiple-goal problems, high PFT scorers use less cases regardless of their GRE scores. But the *low* GRE analytical scorers who are also high PFT scorers are the most efficient solvers of these problems of all four groups. With the single goal problems (where complete efficiency would be represented by a group mean of 1.00), these same low GRE but high PFT students are actually the *least* efficient. Strategies honed for one kind of problem lead to poorer performance on another kind. The PFT, designed as a 'spatial' test is picking up on some mental ability or strategy substantially independent of HFT/GREA score. Whether this is some component of three-dimensional spatial operations, or yet another strategic factor, we cannot at this stage say. As we develop a more principled taxonomy of problems and methods, so the prospects of generalizing from one study to another are improved.

The analysis of the Swedish Hyperproof study was part of the work reported by Padraic Monaghan (2000) in his thesis. He also took this approach a step further, turning the methodology back onto analysis of the GRE and Blocks World tests themselves. The problem with psychometric tests is that they merely summarize performance on a set of items which are unstructured and unrelated (as far as the tests measure). Monaghan asked whether our analysis of Hyperproof's case-oriented reasoning could be applied to the GRE test items themselves. Could it be used to analyse the students' strategies and to predict the aptitude treatment interactions we observe? After all, if what is going on in Hyperproof proof construction is a process of any generality, perhaps we can find it going on in GRE test reasoning and explain the pre and post-test scores in terms of the logical relations between course and test? Put another way, are the changes in the students' theorem provers wrought by Hyperproof teaching evident in their performance on post-test Blocks World and GRE reasoning?

To illustrate with the nearest transfer first, the Blocks World test items demand splitting into cases (as we noted in Poirot's soliloquy) just as the Hyperproof problems do. Can we analyse which Blocks World problems which students get right in the same terms that we can analyse their Hyperproof proofs? This is a small jump, one might observe, since the Blocks World test was designed to emulate Hyperproof reasoning. But GRE analytical problems can also be analysed in this way. The office allocation problem involves case-oriented reasoning. Can we extend our methods to the GRE analytical test itself? Could we take this line of reasoning all the way to its conclusion and base a psychometrics of reasoning on logical theories of reasoning?

Monaghan's studies show that indeed the Blocks World and GRE tests can be analysed along the dimension of how many models satisfy their constraints. Logical and analytical problems in fact form a continuum with the office allocation problem at one end and the mercury problem at the other, and this continuum reflects students' problem solving behaviour. The students who show strong preferences for solving Hyperproof problems using single cases are better at the GRE problems which are at the determinate office allocation problem end of the dimension. The students who show strong preferences for multiple model solutions to Hyperproof problems are better at the GRE problems at the indeterminate mercury problem end. Teaching often improves their ability at the problem types they are initially poor at, but often at the expense of making them weaker on the ones they were good at. Only a relatively few students show a real increase in flexibility and accuracy of strategy choice across the full range of problem methods.

Monaghan shows, in an extensive review of the psychological literature about in-dividual differences in reasoning, that this strategic interpretation of the differences between reasoners, accounts better for the evidence than an account in terms of capacity for reasoning with visual of verbal representations. His interpretation of the evidence argues that these individual differences are not only strategic, but also that they are stylistic preferences rather than ability differences, a distinction that has become prominent in differential psychology in recent years. Briefly, the contrast is between styles as alternative approaches to reasoning which are equally good but differ in their efficacy on different problem types, as opposed to a unidimensional capacity which measures reasoners' success on a unidimensional range of problems.

One way of clarifying this far-reaching distinction is to think evaluatively. The members of a contrasting pair of reasoning styles are neither good nor bad. One will be more effective on some problems but less on others, and vice versa for the opposing style. In contrast, more of a capacity is by definition, in the words of *1066 and all that*, a 'good thing'. Monaghan's evidence is that whatever strategy difference it is that underlies the aptitude treatment interaction between the GRE, modality of logic teaching, and learning outcome, the GRE's two subscales are measuring stylistic preferences more than simple reasoning capacities. This conclusion has far-reaching implications for interpretation of the individual differences observed here, which we return to in Chapters 6 and 7. Note that the test has two subscales and that this is often a sign of a style difference in the population. The designers have to resort to different subscales in order to reflect the fact that equally good reasoners (as judged by some informal socially based criterion) are good at different kinds of problems. The balancing of 'verbal' and 'performance' subscales in intelligence tests is the classic example.

Monaghan's review places our paradoxical finding that students who learn well from diagrams are ones who know when to avoid them in a wider psychological setting. He argues convincingly that those who score highly on spatial tests are those who flexibly apply non-spatial strategies to the test items when that is more efficient.

3.6 The diversity of intelligence and the status of *g*

Looking back on all this empirical work, the main surprise was that the findings are dominated by differences between students rather than overall differences between courses—a complexity we should perhaps have foreseen, but did not. However, the really striking finding was that the differences between students were hidden beneath surface homogeneity. Global performance was uniformly good, as we should expect from this highly selected group. But this uniform excellence obscured quite dramatic equal and opposite differences in subgroups of students. The detailed analyses show that even when we look at a group of highly able students, all of whom are succeeding at the course—passing the examinations, and increasing their scores on a test of general reasoning—what we find is that they are starting at quite different places, learning quite different things and succeeding in quite different ways, and also that their successes often mask declines in performance on some microskills. Rather than progression toward some homogeneous ideal from various starting points on some linear dimension, we see changes in the balance and tuning of strategies to optimize reasoning by students who start with qualitatively different approaches.

This is, of course, reminiscent of a familiar question in psychometrics. Is there *g*, some general intelligence which underwrites our ability in all intelligent tasks? Or are there lots of specialized abilities which make us good at one thing but rather poor at another equally eligible task? Our methodology has been almost the opposite to that of psychometrics. Instead of taking a huge sample across an entire population we have focussed on a tiny sample from right up one extreme end of the range of academic abilities. Instead of being content with randomly gathered theoretically unrelated test items, we have tried to relate logical tasks to mental processes. But our results raise fundamental questions for the psychometric approach.

The psychometric approach is coherent as social engineering. On normative grounds, societies value some attributes, and some societies believe that a meritocracy should be defined on those attributes. A society might use inherited wealth, political connections, skin colour, gender, speed at running a 100 metres, prowess in battle, score at *Trivial Pursuits*, or lottery number (or any function of the above) to define its concept of merit. Or it can construct problem-solving tests of various kinds—perhaps to get away from inherited wealth, race and gender, and the rest. Merit is then defined as some number—the test score—and so merit is guaranteed to be a unidimensional phenomenon. Unidimensional meritocracy is a general political position that has its pros and cons, and within meritocracy, specific functions for defining merit also have their pros and cons. As they stand, none of these normative issues even touch on any scientific issue about how minds work.

In order to establish any connection, a theory is required that shows that certain mental abilities are causally involved in individuals' success at the life tasks they face in their culture, and that promoting individuals with these abilities leads to benefits for the society. This requires some understanding of what the population of abilities is and what the population of tasks facing individuals is, and how the abilities contribute to the completion of the tasks. A moment's thought about this prospect should be enough to cast some scepticism on unidimensionalism as a *scientific* account of mind.

The kinds of results which we have reported here are fuel for that scepticism. If a group of exceedingly able people (as defined by the culture) are shown to be succeeding at a difficult intellectual task but employing quite distinct computational mechanisms, we should have some doubt that their ordering on the next task which the environment throws at them should be the same. Even within our tasks, we see students honing themselves for one subtask only to decline on performance on another set of subtasks. Our modern computational understanding of the complexity of the landscape of reasoning tasks should be enough to cast further doubt on any connection between unidimensional meritocracy and science. Information-processing tasks are not strung out along a single dimension of difficulty. A monstrously complex function sensitive to the way problems are represented produces a high-dimensional space. Complexity theory shows us that there is no one 'golden algorithm' to be had, even for single systems of reasoning, let alone across all systems of representation. To set up any single dimension of difficulty for problems, we need to know with some precision what the population of tasks will be, and what range of representations will be employed for each.

However, there is an entirely other kind of justification for unidimensional meritocracy and the homogeneity of *g* which one might entertain. There are many attributes of people that we expect to influence their performance across a wide range of tasks. Many of these attributes may not be cognitive at all (general health, level of energy, social dominance, confidence, motivation, ...). We should expect these attributes to have effects on success on a wide range of tasks precisely because they are insensitive to the computational character of tasks. Some function of these attributes might well then define a unidimensional value which would turn out to be related to success at a culture's chosen basket of valued tasks. Here could reside a justification of psychometric testing as social engineering. On this account, measuring peoples' scores on this function is a good way of predicting their success on mental (and non-mental) tasks irrespective of the nature of the tasks. On this view the informational relations between test tasks and life tasks are quite irrelevant except as they are mediated by non-mental attributes which have generalized effects across mental tasks. Whether or not one accepts this as social engineering, notice that it has almost nothing to do with how the mind performs any of the tasks, because the attributes measured are not mental attributes: they are at best enabling conditions for mental attributes. Notice also that these non-mental contributors to g are not only non-mental but also quite unhomogeneous.

Granted that for these reasons one would expect an attribute that behaved like g to emerge from psychometric methods, the onus is on the psychometrician to show that what is being measured by g is even a mental kind at all, let alone a mental natural kind. The only way to do that would be to show some commonality between the mechanisms by which people perform the tasks in the tests, and the tasks in life which they predict. This is what psychometricians signally refuse to do, and this refusal is what indicates that they are engaged in social engineering—not social science. As social engineering their procedures may or may not be justified, but the only conceivable kind of justification must be cultural and political.

If we did have scientific theories that could connect the mechanisms by which people perform the test tasks and the life tasks, then those theories might feed into justifications of certain meritocratic programmes. But it seems that the methodology of classical psychometrics precludes progress toward such a goal. Of course, there have been many contributions toward a cognitively founded psychology of individual differences; Sternberg (1984) and Lohman and Kyllonen (1983) are examples that spring to mind.

Things are, as has often been pointed out, somewhat worse than this scientifically for psychometrics, because our argument has entirely ignored the feedback loops that exist between social judgements of performance and subsequent success at life's tasks. If, for example, social standing, health, and confidence are predictors of test scores, and social promotion is a result of test success, it would not be too surprising if increase in social standing and confidence were to be correlated with test scores. If social standing and confidence are predictive of life-task success for the same reasons they predict test success, then that too will also be correlated with test score. To the confident shall confidence be given.

This critique of psychometric method as science does not mean that we need be sceptical about there being any causal relation between the mental mechanisms of test performance and life-task performance. For example, Monaghan's analysis of the GRE test items in terms of the logical theory of models, and the demonstration that the analysis can predict behaviour, gives some encouragement that a coherent theory of mental processes of reasoning can cover both test-task and, with some imagination, life-task mental processes. We are not sceptical that test mental processes and school mental processes are related to real-life tasks and real-life mental processes. We do, after all, earn our living teaching in the belief that some of what students learn is useful to them after school.

But then we are not committed to g being a mental natural kind, nor to the relation being a unidimensional one, and we are committed to the analysis of mental processes that are causally related to task performance. The whole idea that mental processes are computational processes and that logical analysis is the fundamental basis for understanding computation, encourages us to be anything but sceptical about the causal relation between mental processes and social functioning. But our findings are of diversity, and the unidimensionalism of g is scientifically irrelevant to them.

Separating these two kinds of influence on test scores—non-specific, possibly non-cognitive enabling attributes on the one hand, as opposed to attributes of information-processing mechanisms actually performing the tasks—is conceptually critical but, of course, a massive simplification. One of the reasons to set such store by the acknowledgement that different people do the same mental task in radically different ways is that their choices of methods appear to interact strongly with general social and emotional factors in their temperamental makeup. Students have to be strongly motivated to perform the apparently strange tasks we ask of them, but they are also strongly motivated to approach these tasks in one representational manner rather than another. Diagrams are a highly affectively laden topic in learning—students either light up or glaze over when diagrams appear. I firmly believe that the kinds of reasoning process we are investigating here are intimately connected to students' affective responses. Chapters 6 and 7 look at some reasons why this might be so. The current argument for distinguishing non-cognitive effects on test performance from the cognitive processes of reasoning is a conceptual argument, rather than an argument that the two kinds of process are in fact separable in the mind. Confidence and social standing are intimately related to how we justify our knowledge. In Chapter 5 we shall make some proposals about how cognitive and social processes are intimately linked in learning to reason.

I hope that this digression may help to explain our methodology. If the goal is to study the mental process by which people reason and learn to reason, and a significant problem is to disentangle the computational processes that underlie performance from such factors as motivation, confidence, and social standing, then choosing to study populations judged by their culture as able, decreases the variation in these extraneous variables. If the mental processes which are revealed are shown to be highly and systematically variable even *within* this group, then this suggests that variability in these cognitive processes is what we should expect in more varied groups. It also suggests that the apparent homogeneity of g is due to non-cognitive factors. There is no conflict at all between there being a general measure combining such factors as social standing and confidence, and there being huge variability between people of the same score in how they perform the same task.

Most cognitive psychologists probably regard this critique of psychometrics as old hat. Of course we need accounts of mental structures and processes. That is what the cognitive revolution established several decades ago. But the implications for cognitive theory are just as radical. The paradigm of cognitive explanation has been to analyse cognitive phenomena as computations *within* systems: logics, grammars, expert systems, etc. The thinking subject is conceived as running a 'theorem prover' over its system to achieve some goal. The issues of the day have been about *what* system they operate within. In reasoning research, this has meant that there has been much focus on the nature of the mental representations which define the system, but rather little attention to representational behaviour—how people choose systems and what they actually do with observable external representations. The goal has been to define the 'fundamental human deduction mechanism' for the language of thought, or the system of mental models, or whatever the theorists' chosen approach suggests.

The present approach from the semantics of publicly observable representations, and observations of what subjects *do* with those representations, vindicates the meta-systemic perspective suggested by our semantic investigations. How do people decide which representation system to use and when? It turns out that different learners employ rather different strategic answers to this problem, and those strategies change in different ways in response to different teaching methods employing different representations. In the next chapter we shall analyse in some detail some theories of the mental representations involved in reasoning, using the same semantic techniques as we used for external representations in Chapter 2.

These theoretical questions have their practical counterparts. If different students respond so differently to presentations in different modalities, should we teach to their strengths or their weaknesses? Should we choose the presentation they find easiest? After all, the GRE pre-test only takes 20 minutes to find out which method is likely to be preferred. Or should we deliberately try to remedy their modality deficiencies by teaching, say, a remedial graphics curriculum to the students scoring low on the GRE analytical test before their Hyperproof course, and perhaps a remedial language curriculum to the high scorers? These are special cases of venerable questions. These questions plainly require much more empirical research about the malleability of profiles of aptitudes or styles, and also contain moral elements which may not be scientifically decidable however much evidence we can marshal. But the general approach certainly suggests an intriguing idea—that we should have a representational curriculum.

Some might argue that that is, in a good part, what we have. Large parts of the mathematics and language curriculum could be seen as teaching little other than representational skills. This may be true, but this is not generally how these curricula are seen. Even in mathematics and science, the common pattern is to teach representation in the context of solving a certain kind of problem. Students develop skills of going from problem type to representation type, but these skills are rarely made explicit. What are rarely taught are the properties of representation systems that suit them to the kinds of problems for which they are useful, or conversely, the properties that make kinds of representation useless for kinds of problems. This representational curriculum would have to take a much more *meta* stance, and to develop a terminology for talking about representations. It might be reminiscent of a modernized version of what the logic curriculum once was. With modern understandings, that curriculum could be extended beyond sentential representations, and incorporate explicitly some of what we know about strategies of reasoning.

4 Back to the Age of Reason

Leonhart Euler, the famous eighteenth-century German mathematician, invented Euler's circles when faced with the task of teaching a German princess her syllogisms (Euler 1772). Those were the days when royalty had intellectual aspirations! Fortunately, the princess was a distance student on a correspondence course, and so some of the conversation, and particularly the diagrams, survived. There are claims that Euler's circles are really Leibniz' circles, but be that as it may, syllogisms, and graphical and other methods for solving and teaching them, figure large in this chapter. We have presented a theory of what is distinctive about diagram semantics, and some evidence that its primary distinction between direct and indirectly interpreted systems can play a useful role in understanding students' reasoning and learning. The example system which originally inspired this theory was Euler's circles, and our interest in them arose from their various employment by psychologists in their theories of human reasoning. We now seek to deepen the role for our semantic theory of diagrams in the heartland of the psychology of deductive reasoning.

This field has overwhelmingly concentrated its attention on the mental representations involved when undergraduate subjects solve deductive reasoning problems without recourse to pencil and paper, i.e. the *internal* representations involved in mental reasoning, where 'mental' has the same meaning as it does in 'mental arithmetic'. This is a foundational area of psychological theory. It seeks to give an account of central mental processes which are not, like perceptual or motor processes, direct interactions with the environment, i.e. an account of thinking processes. Such process accounts were prominent in early cognitive psychology, notably in the work of Newelland Simon (1972), who, for example, constructed simulations of the working memory and rules involved in artificial task like cryptarithmetic.[12] How much more exciting and important to give an account of natural thinking processes which are mentally omnipresent!

Of course, this viewpoint it highly controversial. There are those who believe that the mind does not have processes which compute on internal representations—that all processes are direct interactions with the environment in the way that perceptual motor interactions are held to be. Even if we accept that there are internal representations and processes, there is the question about what relationship laboratory deductive problems such as syllogism solving have to natural mental processes. One view is that they are not much less artificial than cryptarithmetic, even if they are a little older. For those concerned with representation, reasoning, and the learning of reasoning, these are important questions. However, we shall postpone the question of what relation syllogisms bear to people's reasoning before they encounter syllogisms in the laboratory until the next chapter, where we develop a theory of this relationship. Here we will

---

[12]Cryptarithmetic is arithmetic with a letter code for digits, where the subject's task is to discover the code from such equations as DONALD + GERALD = ROBERT.

assume, for the sake of argument, that the mental processes of solving syllogisms in the laboratory bear some correspondence to natural reasoning processes, in order to challenge the kinds of psychological theory that have been proposed to account for these mental processes. This challenge is pertinent whether you believe that syllogisms are as artificial as cryptarithmetic or are the foundations of our daily thought processes.

After a brief introduction to what syllogisms are, we shall present Euler's diagrammatic system for solving them and relate this system to our account of diagrammatic semantics. We then briefly sketch a number of other diagrammatic systems, which provide illuminating comparisons, before introducing the main psychological theories of mental syllogism solution. Although the subjects in the experiments that underpin these theories are allowed no external representations beyond their unrepressed mutterings, the theories themselves have to be given external expression. This allows a semantic analysis of their claims, and especially of their claims about how one theory differs from another. We then show how the theoretical frameworks—mental models and mental logics—are equivalent to each other for the kinds of evidence sought in their experimental programmes.

These equivalences are fatal for the empirical claims made, but they are not merely 'philosophical' objections to a psychological programme. The equivalences can be exploited to reinterpret old results and to reshape experimental programs. An example study is presented which uses a new task suggested by the metalogical properties of syllogisms to throw new light on how subjects make conclusions that no valid conclusions can be made.

The new semantic insights also allow us to return to our previous focus on and teaching, with a study using two teaching systems which are much more closely equivalent than was possible in the Hyperproof case. This study replicates the findings of the last chapter of aptitude treatment interactions, but it also suggests that we need to reappraise the connections between the semantic framework and its cognitive application. The findings highlight the need to pay attention to the issue about what fragments of reasoning systems are 'in play' during an episode of reasoning. We end the chapter by illustrating some of the problems involved through an extension of the Euler system.

4.1 Syllogisms and ways of solving them

The syllogism is a fragment of logic which deals with reasoning about properties of things abstracted from their identities i.e. with *types* of entity. Modern logic sees the syllogism as part of monadic predicate logic. It adds names and quantifiers to the basic apparatus of propositional calculus, but it lacks many-placed relations. This last restriction makes reasoning within it particularly tractable. For our concerns with reasoning as the search for systems that make problems tractable, this is an important fragment.

Syllogisms are no longer a prominent fragment of any modern logic, and disappeared from most logic courses as modern symbolic logic arrived. However, the syllogism should not be dismissed as a historical relic too quickly. As Peirce said:

It is easy to over-rate the importance of syllogism. Most of the older logics do that in teaching that the substance of all reasoning lies in this. It is also easy to underate it, as many have done.

The truth is, it is an essential part of almost all reasoning, perhaps of all. (quoted in Bird(1964))

4.1.1   What are syllogisms?

The syllogism is the logic of *all, some, no* and *some_ not* as applied to one-place predicates. One-place predicates (such as *-is red, -is running*, or *-outgrabes*) are contrasted with many-placed relations (such as *-is equal to-, -is the mother of-*, or *-was born before the youngest uncle of-*.

Syllogisms are arguments having three predicates *A, B, and C* appearing in two sentences—the first and second premisses. The *B* term appears in both sentences and is therefore called the 'middle' term, whereas *A* and *C* are 'end-terms'. The *A* term appears in the first premiss and the *C* term in the second. Terms appear as subjects or predicates of sentences. A quantifier (one of *all, some, no, some_not*) precedes the subject and predicate terms. These constraints allow four **figures** or patterns of terms in syllogisms. Illustrating with the quantifier *all*:

> Figure 1 *All A are B. All B are C*
> Figure 2 *All B are A. All C are B*
> Figure 3 *All A are B. All C are B*
> Figure 4 *All B are A. All B are C.*

Since there are four quantifiers to substitute into the first premiss, four to substitute into the second, and four figures, there are 64 such premiss pairs.

The conclusions of syllogisms relate the terms *A* and *C* by one of the same four quantifiers, thus eliminating the middle term *B*. Therefore there are eight possible conclusions from each of 64 premiss pairs—the four quantifiers each with the terms in the order *AC*, or in the order *CA*. Only 27 of these conclusions are valid conclusions in the conventional interpretation of the syllogism—more on this presently.

Medieval logicians produced some fiendishly ingenious mnemonics for remembering which 27 were so favoured. Some of them really did seem to believe that a look-up table for syllogism forms was what was worth learning. But Aristotle had already proposed a systematic theory about *why* these 27 and only these 27 were valid arguments—arguably the earliest logical metatheory (Lear 1980). Aristotle's assumptions about the interpretations of these arguments are not quite as general as the modern logically accepted ones. He assumed that the arguments were interpreted with the properties A, B and C always exemplified—the 'no-empty-sets' axiom. This does not accord with modern logical practice, but it does accord with psychologists' assumptions (and probably those of the majority of their subjects). We shall see later that these differences of interpretation have some interesting historical reasons and offer some interesting psychological insights.

If the reader has never consciously tried solving any syllogisms its worth going through a few to convince oneself that the answer is not completely self-evident in all cases. There is no substitute for trying a few for yourself when it comes to generating intuitions about the psychological theories which we discuss later.

In the spirit of our guiding question about the impact of modalities of information presentation, we shall approach syllogistic reasoning through various graphical methods and return to sentential approaches afterwards. We start with Euler, and move on through Venn to Carroll's diagrammatic method, mental models (a method proposed as a theory

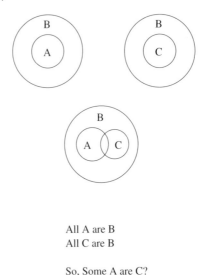

All A are B
All C are B

So, Some A are C?

Fig. 4.1 A syllogism and potential conclusion represented by Euler's circles.

of mental reasoning), and a sentential logical method, ending with the metalogical method known as the Sieve. Our interest in explaining more than one system is in what comparisons can tell us about respects in which apparently similar systems are in fact diverse, and also in which apparently diverse systems in fact have hidden equivalences. The equivalences are particularly important when we come to try to discriminate systems of internal representations on the basis of the highly indirect kind of evidence we currently have.

4.1.2 Euler's circles

Most diagrammatic methods for solving syllogisms are based on the same spatial analogy—the analogy between an item's membership in a set and the geometrical inclusion of a point within a closed curve in a plane. Euler took this analogy, represented the first premiss as a pair of circles, represented the second premiss by adding a third circle; and finally read off the conclusion from this construction. So, for example, Fig. 4.1 shows how one might solve the syllogism *All A are B. All C are B.*

This is an interesting example for working through what we said in Chapter 2 about the inexpressiveness of diagrams. While we may feel that Fig. 4.1 is helpful in clarifying the reasoning, as a method of reasoning it is obviously fallible. Even setting aside the several different diagrams we could have chosen to exemplify the premisses, there are several ways of combining the two premiss diagrams that we did choose. The conclusion drawn here is true in the combination we chose, but if we had only tried a different combination, we might have found that the conclusion did not hold. Diagrams exhibit specificity. How are generalizations to be extracted from them? A familiar question.

Figure 4.2 shows the mapping of the sentence forms onto primitive Euler diagrams. The problem of the explosion of combinations of diagrammatic elements is particularly

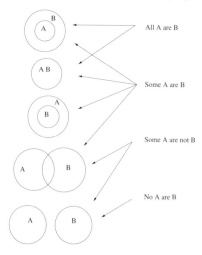

Fig. 4.2 The five topological relations between two circles mapped onto the quantified sentences they model—the Gergonne relations.

acute in the case of *some* where four of the five topological relations between two circles exemplify the sentence. Imagine having to solve the syllogism *Some A are B. Some B are C* by this method. There are four diagrams of the first premiss, four of the second, and several ways of making each combination to derive a composite diagram. There are about 50 diagrams we should consider. In many of these diagrams, it is true that some A are C (or, diagrammatically, that circle A intersects circle C), but not in all. If we chanced to construct a diagram where some A were C, we might make this conclusion without realizing that it did not follow because there were other situations which made the premisses both true, but in which this conclusion was nevertheless false.

This problem for diagrammatic methods of reasoning stems exactly from the lack of abstraction inherent in diagrams discussed in Chapter 2. This problem has been used to argue the hopelessness of diagrammatic methods (Johnson-Laird 1983). How could a brilliant mathematician like Euler make such a fundamental mistake? How did the poor princess gain anything from this flawed system?

The answers, of course, are to be found in what Euler taught about the *strategy* for choosing which diagrams to use when. Euler taught that one should select what we might think of as the 'weakest' case. If we want to represent *Some A are B* we do not choose a diagram where all A are B. If we want to add a third circle to a diagram, we do so in the way that represents the most possibilities—graphically we include the most circle intersections that are consistent with the premisses. Although Euler did not burden his princess with adding these strategies explicitly to his notation, it is rather simple to do so. Figure 4.3 shows four diagrams for representing the four premisses.

The crosses mark what are technically known as minimal models. If there is a cross in a minimal subregion of the diagram, then there *must* be something in the world represented with the properties corresponding to that subregion. One thing corresponding to a cross is the absolute minimal 'furniture' there must be in a world for the sentence to be true in that world. There may be more, but this much there must be. If there is more than one cross, there is more than one minimal model. It is a property of the syllogism,

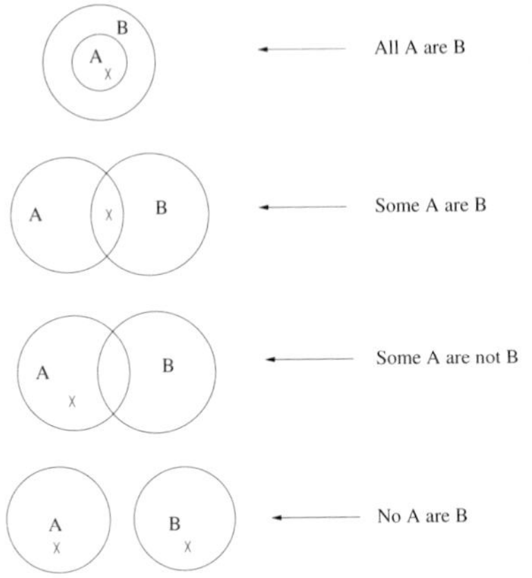

Fig. 4.3 The four quantifiers mapped onto their characteristic diagrams using the cross notation for their minimal models.

that minimal models are always single-element models.

The crosses help capture the right strategy for combining diagrams. Figure 4.4 shows the process of solving the syllogism *All A are B. Some C are not B* exploiting the cross notation. The two premiss representations are combined by registering the B circles (which are, after all, the same circle). There is then a choice about the relation between the A and C circles. They could be placed in one of three arrangements consistent with the premisses. The rule is that the arrangement which creates most subregions is chosen. A simple rule determines whether the crosses persist or are eliminated during this combination process. If a subregion containing a cross is bisected in combining the diagrams, then its cross is eliminated. If not, then the cross persists. Finally, we need to determine what if any conclusion follows from the represented syllogism.

It turns out that every valid conclusion is based on the three-property description of a subregion containing a cross (in the case of Fig. 4.4, the subregion with a cross in the final three-circle diagram corresponds to *C*s that are not *A* and not *B*). No cross, no valid conclusion. Conversely, if there is a cross remaining in the final diagram, then, with a couple of interesting exceptions which we shall come to directly, there is a valid conclusion. To generate a conclusion, first describe the type of individual corresponding to the cross's region and eliminate the *B* term (in the case of Fig. 4.4 this yields 'things that are *C* and not *A*'). Now, if the subregion containing the cross is circular, its label becomes the subject of a universal conclusion. Otherwise the conclusion is existential (with *some* or *some not*). If the cross is outside one of the two A and C circles, then the conclusion will be negative; otherwise it will be positive. This algorithm will generate all the valid conclusions of the 64 syllogisms. Try some!

The attentive reader will be asking why this graphical rigamarole leads to the right answer? How is it any more insightful than the medieval logician's mnemonics about Barbara and her exploits? We shall look at the differences between readers who find it satisfying, and those who do not later. But a few hints might be helpful. Combining the circles to give the maximum number of subregions consistent with the premisses guarantees the exhaustiveness of the search for kinds of things there may be in a world in which the premisses are true. A cross's subregion is guaranteed to have something in

All A are B   Some C are not B

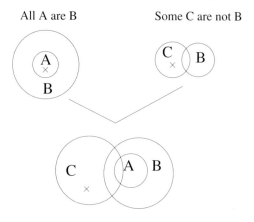

Therefore, some C are not A

Fig. 4.4 An example syllogism solved by Euler's method augmented by the cross notation.

it. If the region is bisected during the addition of the third circle, then it is no longer clear which subsubregion the cross should go in, and so neither of the new subsubregions is guaranteed to have anything in it. And so on for the rules about drawing conclusions. If there is no cross left in the diagram there is no type of individual defined for all three properties which must exist. It turns out that the syllogism has the rather special metalogical property that all its valid conclusions follow in respect of such maximally defined individuals. If there is such a cross, then its subsubregion defines the type of thing that must exist. At least an existential conclusion is therefore justified. The rules about when universal and negative conclusions are warranted are left as homework.

Our cross notation abruptly turns Euler's method from one mired in up to 50 diagrams for a syllogism, to one which provides a one-pass algorithm for solving any problem. The cross notation is an abstraction trick. It allows exactly the abstractions required, but little more. The result is a kind of mechanical calculating device. Imagine the circles as wire hoops of variable size, and the crosses as drawing pins (thumb tacks in American). This mechanical device models the logical constraints of the premises. If a drawing pin prevents the A and C wire hoops from being pulled horizontally apart, then a positive conclusion follows about the fact they must intersect. If the drawing pin prevents the A and C hoops from being pushed into complete correspondence, then a negative conclusion is justified by their non-correspondence. No drawing pin—no conclusion. Euler's genius was to appreciate this correspondence between logical and mechanical constraints.

Euler's method exposes metalogical properties of the syllogism which are important to their implementation in representation systems. As we just noted, conclusions require there to be a cross in the final diagram, and the cross corresponds to a completely described type of individual. The diagrammatic representations make this especially easy to see. The geometrical properties of closed curves (such as circles) mean that every point in a plane is either inside or outside any closed curve. Therefore any cross defines its corresponding type of individual with regard to all three properties. Every valid argument can be made in virtue of a cross in a final diagram. We shall call this property of the syllogism revealed by the diagrammatic system *case identifiability*, there being always a single 'case' that founds a valid argument. Most logical systems do not have this property. A further obvious question is whether the converse of this no-cross—no-conclusion generalization is also true? Does every cross give us a valid conclusion?

For Aristotle's system the answer is no. There are syllogisms which give rise to final diagrams containing crosses which do not allow any Aristotelian conclusion. Figure 4.5 shows two such syllogisms and their diagrams. If we think for a moment about whether there *should* be a conclusion to these problems, we can see that in all cases it is true that *Some not-A is not C*. This somewhat inelegant expression is not included in Aristotle's system, but if we add it, then we can catalogue more valid conclusions. Since the conventional abbreviations for *all, some, none, some_not* are respectively *a, e, i, o* (from the Latin mnemonics), we shall abbreviate this new quantifier *u*.

It is quite unlikely that Aristotle's omission is to be put down to the inelegance of phrasing of this proposition (in English or in Greek), nor to mere oversight. He had much more systematic reasons for excluding these conclusions which turned out to be at the heart of one of the critical developments of twentieth century logic. Aristotle did not make a distinction between the domain of interpretation of a logic, and the universal domain (everything in the universe–the whole lot). He thought of all sentences being interpreted on the universal domain. This is why the no-empty-properties assumption was more natural for him than for a modern logician. If all sentences are thought of as interpreted on the universal domain, then the proposition that there is something somewhere that does not have properties A and B is fairly vacuous (I say 'fairly'). It amounts only to the claim that not everything does have one or the other property. The development of twentieth-century semantics grew out of the realization that logics *must* be interpreted on local domains, and that the idea of the universal domain is incoherent. Russell's paradoxes, which brought down Frege's anti-semantic approach to predicate logic, were what finally exposed this incoherence at the turn of the twentieth century. This twentieth-century insight into the distinction between local and universal domain is the logical foundation for our cognitive focus on the importance of reasoning externally about systems. The logical discoveries have not yet permeated psychological theories of reasoning.

Quite apart from his metatheoretical reasons, Aristotle would have had some discomfort about admitting these u-conclusion syllogisms as valid because they violated one of his two major generalizations about validity, namely:

1. at least one of the premises must have a universal quantifier for a syllogism to have a valid conclusion
2. at least one of the premises must have a positive quantifier for a syllogism to have a valid conclusion.

Syllogisms with only valid u-conclusions violate this second dictum. These logical observations are not merely historical curiosities. They raise interesting psychological questions about whether logically untrained students have any metalogical, if implicit, grasp of these principles. And does their grasp agree with Aristotle, or with these more

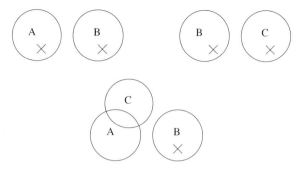

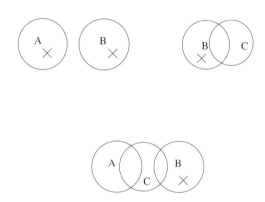

No A are B. No B are C. So Some not-A are not C.

No A are B. Some B are not C. So Some not-A are not C.

Fig. 4.5 Syllogisms with valid conclusions *Some not-A are not-C*—the 'u-conclusions'.

recent insights? We return to these questions when some data on how students reason allow logical insights to be put to good psychological effect.

A final metalogical property of the syllogism that is emphasized by Euler's system is what we might call its self-consistency. Euler's system is self-consistent in that no single diagram can represent an inconsistent set of propositions—the diagrams are models.[13] Strictly speaking, we need to make some assumptions explicit before this statement is true. We have been assuming that Euler's system represents properties by *continuous* closed curves (ones which are not composed of separated regions); and that distinct closed curves in the same diagram represent different properties. For an example of a discontinuous closed curve, imagine the two circles in Fig. 4.4 interpreted as a single closed curve called A. The possibility of discontinuous curves would be incompatible

---

[13]Logically, a model of a set of sentences is an interpretation (assignment of content) which makes the sentences all true.

with the reasoning algorithms. Similarly, in the same figure, if the two circles A and B denoted the same property, then the diagram would express a contradiction. Self-consistency is a consequence of saturated direct interpretation.

Just before passing on to compare Euler with some related systems, we should pause to ask what our semantic framework has to say about the system. The system just described is clearly a directly interpreted system. The relation of spatial containment of a point in a curve in the diagram corresponds to the relation of an individual having a property in the represented world. Furthermore the system is saturated because the converse holds. The crosses are a prominent example of an abstraction trick as can be seen by comparing Figs. 4.2 and 4.3. The crosses allow what would be disjunctions of diagrams to be expressed by a single diagram. Without these tricks, the system would specify exactly one model per diagram and suffer from the combinatorial explosion of diagrams for very simple arguments. These tricks are possible because syllogistic minimal-models have single elements. If minimal-model specifications had to specify relations between elements, no abstraction trick would be available. Euler's circles can and are used to reason agglomeratively.

Diagrammers coming after Euler were much taken up with the question of how Euler's system could be extended beyond the logic of the syllogism and their quest provides interesting examples for our theory of diagrams. The next in the sequence was Venn.

4.1.3 Venn

Venn is now best known as the inventor of his diagrams, but he was the author of one of the main nineteenth century logic textbooks, and an important figure in the logic of his time. His diagrammatic method is the one that has survived, probably because it is used for teaching elementary set-theory, and elementary set-theory showed more stamina than the syllogism. In Venn's system the variety of diagrams is impoverished (there is only one diagram, in the sense of topological arrangement of three circles and so the mechanical analogy disappears) but the notations are enriched. The single diagram is the one with all possible subregions represented—the seven region plus background diagram.

The notations we shall use, in order to be consistent with our Euler notations, are not quite the conventional ones: a zero will represent emptiness of its minimal subregion; a cross represents non-emptiness of its region. It is common to use shading to indicate emptiness, and sometimes question marks are used to represent explicitly the undetermined status of a region. The notations can be placed on the boundaries between regions as well as within subregions. In this case, a zero means that both adjacent subregions are empty; a cross means that at least one of the adjacent subregions is non-empty.

Figure 4.6 shows the same example syllogism of Fig. 4.4 solved by Venn's method. The sequence of operations might run something like this: The first premiss is represented by placing zeros in the two subregions of circle B which are also in A—these must be empty for the premiss to be true. Now we can place a cross in the subregion of C which is outside the other two circles because the second premiss tells us that there is something outside B, within C, and the zero inside A and B means the cross cannot go there. The conclusion can then be read off that some thing (represented by the cross) is C but not

All A are B   Some C are not B

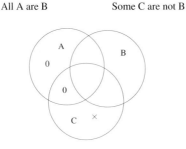

Therefore, some C are not A

Fig. 4.6 An example of a syllogism solved using Venn diagrams.

All A are B   Some C are not B

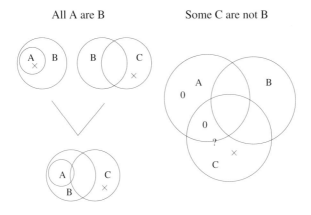

Therefore, some C are not A

Fig. 4.7 Euler and Venn systems compared.

A.

If the premises were reversed in order, we should have to start by placing the cross on the boundary between the C, A and not B subregion and the C, not A and not B region, and only subsequently moving it to the C and not A not B region when the second premiss put a zero in the A and C and not B subregion.

We are initially more concerned with what these methods can tell us about the semantics of diagrammatic systems, than with which is better for solving syllogisms. Figure 4.7 compares the two systems. Although they are based on exactly the same fundamental analogy between graphical containment and set membership, the details of their semantics are starkly contrasting. We can see immediately that Venn's system loses all mechanical analogy. It has become a cunning device for laying out what is essentially a table. Figure 4.8 illustrates this point.

The tabular nature of Venn's system is reminiscent of the discussion in Chapter 2 about abstraction tricks. Empty subregions indeed are interpreted according to the empty-cell-means-undetermined-value convention mentioned there. Although the changes from Euler initially seem very slight, the system is deceptively different in a number of its properties. For example, the interpretation of empty subregions in Venn is quite different

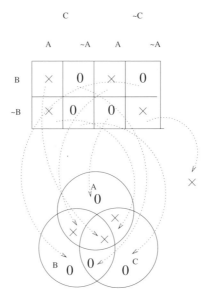

Fig. 4.8 Correspondence of a Venn diagram to a tabular representation.

from what it was in Euler. In Euler the existence of an unannotated subregion indicated that it was possibly non-empty. But in Venn such an unannotated region might be *necessarily* empty. In Euler necessarily absent kinds of thing correspond to no subregion. A further difference resulting from Venn's expansion of the annotation, and reduction of diagrammatic richness, is that, whereas Euler's circles are naturally self-consistent, Venn diagrams can only be made so by stating graphically arbitrary notational conventions. In Euler, no pattern of crosses in subregions of any diagram expresses inconsistent propositions: in Venn a cross and a zero in the same subregion express inconsistent propositions, unless they are arbitrarily ruled out as ill-formed. Does this mean that Venn is indirectly interpreted? I think the answer should be yes. The zero notation has to be interpreted as of a different syntactic category than the cross notation. Zeros are not icons standing for things, although crosses are.

The notational devices of Venn can be extended further beyond what is required for syllogistic reasoning. For example, Shin (1994) shows that by including the use of links to express disjunction, the system can model the monadic predicate calculus. Figure 4.9 illustrates Shin's linking device. The linked crosses are read as meaning that at least one of the crosses indicates the non-emptiness of its subregion. Chains of linked crosses may contain any number of crosses. Needless to say, introducing such extra expressive power means that reasoning becomes less tractable. For example, the testing for self-consistency just pointed out in the simple Venn system (a cross and a zero together) can no longer be done purely locally once links are introduced. We shall return to the self-consistency property of Euler diagrams at the end of this chapter when we raise the question how expressiveness can explain modality differences.

On the cognitive front, Shin's augmentation of notation by links appears to scupper the cognitive transparency of the system, at least according to my intuition and Shin's teaching experience (personal communication). The only experimental comparison of

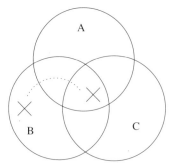

Fig. 4.9 Venn's system augmented by links to express the disjunction *Either there is a B not A and not C or there is an A B C.*

the two systems available stops short of Shin's augmentation, and poses some interpretative problems because the student subjects do not appear to reach a firm grasp of the systems (Dobson 1999, discussed in Stenning 1999*b*).

Perhaps the most important moral of this comparison of Euler and Venn is just how much can change in the semantics even when the fundamental graphical relations employed remain constant. This comment also holds for the next system too.

4.1.4 Lewis Carroll

Charles Dodgson the logician (geometer, logician, photographer, puzzle wizard, and author of Alice's adventures, better known to us as Lewis Carroll), invented a *Game of Logic*, a board game for two players which amounts to a diagrammatic method for solving syllogisms. He had much fun arguing with Venn about the merits of their respective systems. His complaint about Venn's diagrams was that they were all very well for three-property syllogisms, but for many-property syllogisms (classically known as **sorites**) the two-dimensional nature of paper sorely restricted their generality. There is a fascinating diagram from the Venn-Carroll correspondence preserved in Carroll's *Symbolic logic* (Dodgson 1896), which was Venn's convoluted attempt at a diagram for a five-term sorites.

Carroll's system is mainly interesting for the relation between its method of circumventing this problem, and the local-universal domain distinction which had not yet been clarified in the logic of the time. Carroll's system is an eight-region-plus-ground system which makes clear the distinction between local and universal domains. It is interesting that Carroll's choice of examples and their introduction, throughout his writings on logic, is often designed to emphasize that some local 'world' is the intended interpretation. Figure 4.10 shows a Carroll diagram solution for a favourite example 'syllogism', alongside Venn and Euler solutions. This is, of course, what we have been calling a u-type syllogism.

No philosophers are conceited. Some conceited persons are not gamblers. Therefore, some persons who are not gamblers are not philosophers. Or symbolically,
No y are m. Some m are not x. Therefore, some not-x are not y.

Carroll's game was a board game and the circles in the diagram can be interpreted as black and white counters. *No y are m* is represented by placing the two white counters in

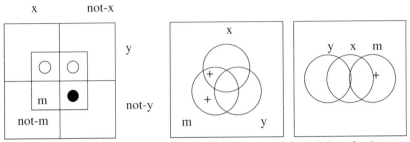

Fig. 4.10 A Carroll diagram alongside Venn and Euler solutions for the same syllogism.

the two top inner squares, signifying their emptiness. *Some m are not x* is then integrated with this diagram (board position) by adding a black counter in the inner bottom right square. If it were a matter of representing *Some m are x* on a blank board, the black counter would go on the border between the inner top and bottom right squares instead, but the inner top right is already marked as empty, and so the black counter goes below (analogously to Venn's placement of notations on borders). Up to this point, Carroll's system is close to Venn's save for the modification of shapes. In fact, if we allow any convex curves in Venn's system, Carroll's board *is* an example of Venn's diagram, save for the addition of the outer frame which sets off the part of the world which is outside of the domain of interpretation.

Having distinguished the region that corresponds to things with none of the three properties of a syllogism which are nonetheless within the domain of reasoning (things in the lower right quadrant), from the region that represents the things outside the domain of reasoning (things outwith the outer square frame), Carroll can represent sorites of any number of property terms. But he does so at the expense of having properties represented by discontinuous curves. The diagram for a four-property problem simply replicates the diagram for the three-property case, and labels one subdiagram *z* and the other subdiagram *not-z*. The property *z* is now the only one represented by a single continuous curve. The other three properties x, y, and m are now represented by discontinuous curves distributed between the two halves of the diagram. By this innovation Carroll can represent reasoning with any number of properties. Figure 4.11 depicts the evolution from Venn to Carroll.

Using discontinuous regions is what purchases extensibility to any number of properties, and it relies on distinguishing local domain from the larger universe. After what we just said about the importance of continuity of curves for Euler's system, the obvious question to ask is what Carroll's system looses by its introduction. In fact Carroll's system only allows highly constrained discontinuity of curves. Although looking at the Carroll diagram in Fig. 4.11, we cannot tell whether there are things which are x represented elsewhere (in another part of the diagram not shown representing the property z, for example), we can tell that there are no x things in the not-x subpart of the diagram. The discontinuity which is allowed is highly circumscribed, and since, like Venn, the system uses annotation rather than Euler's topological relations to specify its reasoning operations, the discontinuity does not destroy the system. Nevertheless, it would be

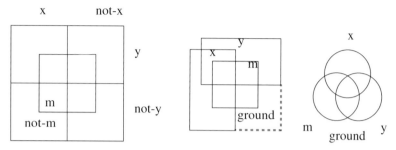

Fig. 4.11 The evolution of Carroll's diagrams from Venn's. The three circles are replaced by rectangles, and the ground of Venn's figure, which represents the local domain, is enclosed to distinguish it from the outer universal domain, which is the ground of Carroll's diagram.

interesting to know more about its cognitive properties.

Apart from some antique curiosity, our reason for looking at these three systems of syllogism solution is that they illustrate how the same spatial analogy can be the basis of such different systems. It is all too easy to think that Euler, Venn and Carroll are simply additive accretions of more complex notations which leave the interpretation unaffected. It is not so.

The only aspect of their semantics that the Euler, Venn and Carroll diagrams share is the designation of types of thing by regions in the diagrams. What the regions and their annotations assert about these types of thing are quite distinct. A subregion in a Venn or Carroll diagram which is empty of annotation asserts nothing. A subregion of an Euler diagram without annotation asserts that the corresponding type of thing *may* exist. In Venn and Carroll all subregions are always represented. The absence of a subregion in Euler asserts that its type of thing does not exist. Real errors of interpretation have been made in the literature because of this contrast. When it is claimed that diagrammatic semantics is transparent, here is a useful counter-example (if Carroll will forgive the pun).

4.1.5 Mental models

Mental models are the basis of one of the current theories about how reasoners solve syllogisms 'mentally' without recourse to pencil and paper. However, like all the others reviewed here, they are a formal system in that they make no connection with the content of the individuals and properties represented. Euler's and Venn's systems were invented as formal analyses and only later pressed into the service of psychological theory. Mental models reversed this development. The original system of Johnson-Laird and Steedman (1978) is presented in Fig. 4.12. The columns of letters represent individual types with the properties designated by the letters. Parenthesized letters indicate that the individual type corresponding to their columns of letters may or may not exist. The vertical links indicate positive predication. Dotted arrow links indicate negative predication (not illustrated).

The system is used agglomeratively, and the bottom half of Fig. 4.12 shows the representation of *All A are B* being agglomerated with the existing representation of the

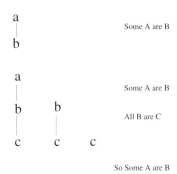

Fig. 4.12 A mental models representation of the syllogism *Some A are B. All B are C.*

first premiss. Only columns completely made up of unparenthesized letters figure in the read-off of conclusions. Here a single column represents an individual which has all three properties A, B, and C, and so justifies the conclusion *Some A are C.*

Reasoning with mental models is done cyclically. A model is constructed, and a candidate conclusion drawn. Processes than check whether this conclusion can be defeated by an alternative construction, or whether alternative constructions throw up any alternative conclusions, which in turn can be tested for defeasibility. If a conclusion holds in all the models constructed to represent the premises, then the conclusion is valid. If no such conclusion can be found after exhausting these processes, then there is no valid conclusion. We return to mental models when we discuss psychological theories in the next section.

4.1.6 Natural deduction applied to syllogisms

At one level, it is obvious that the syllogism can be represented and solved in logical systems such as the natural deduction window we saw in Hyperproof. The syllogism is just a small fragment of such logics. But our purpose here is to reveal representational homologies between systems, and so what we present is a particular fragment of propositional calculus which emulates syllogistic reasoning in Euler and mental models systems.

The best way to abstract away from the specifics and understand abstractly what is in common between the methods for doing syllogisms is to think in terms of *critical individuals*—the types of individual marked by the crosses in completed Euler diagrams. A critical individual is one fully specified in terms of all three properties or their complement properties—in fact by a conjunction of literals. As we have seen, the syllogism is a fragment in which pairs of premises only have a valid conclusion *if* they entail that there is such a critical individual.

To take the simplest case first, suppose that we have an existential premiss. Then it specifies a conjunction of two properties of at least one individual. *Some A are B* specifies that there is something that is $A\&B$. Now, to reach any conclusion we must also have a universal proposition that allows us to conclude something about this individual's property on the third dimension. A universal proposition is a conditional such as: $B \rightarrow C$ (or $B \rightarrow \neg C$ in the case of *none*). We can apply $\rightarrow$-*elimination* to conclude that our thing that is A and B is also C (or $\neg C$ if the conditional is negative), and we can then conjoin the result C to our previous two-term conjunction $A\&B$ getting $A\&B\&C$—a specification of a critical individual. This linguistic rigamarole corresponds to establishing a cross in a three-circle Euler diagram, and to a column of unparenthesized letters in mental models.

The most glaring hole in this simple recipe for solution is that the conditional may not be in the applicable form to yield the literals wanted for the construction of a description. The conditional may have to be reorganized. The transformation for doing this is called, in Latin, *modus tollens* (to contrast with *modus ponens*). It is not a fundamental rule of most natural deduction systems, but rather a derived one (i.e. it can be proved from the fundamentals). Its pattern is that from $\neg B$, and $A \rightarrow B$ we can conclude $\neg A$. If the reader seeks an intuition to go with the formalism, the following might help. If the consequent of a true conditional is false, then its antecedent must also be false because, if the antecedent were true, the truth of the consequent would follow (by $\rightarrow$ *-elimination*). Syntactically, note that whereas simply reversing the order of the antecedent and consequent of a conditional $A \rightarrow B$ to $B \rightarrow A$ is *not* valid, combining this reversal with negating both clauses *is* valid.

The addition of this rule will allow us to apply the method of building individual descriptions to syllogisms which otherwise would prove intransigent; for example, *All A are B. Some C are not B.* The latter premiss provides the literal $\neg B$. This literal cannot combine with the first premiss by $\rightarrow -elimination$, but it can by *modus tollens*.[14] Therefore we could now detach $\neg A$ and conjoin it with the first premiss to yield $C\&\neg B\&\neg A$ as a description of a critical individual, just as we found a cross in the corresponding region in Fig. 4.4 when we solved the same syllogism using Euler. Table 4.13 presents a set of rules for solving any syllogism by this method.

The attentive reader will have noticed something rather odd going on here. We have been using natural deduction rules operating on propositional calculus sentences to model syllogistic reasoning, but the syllogism is about quantifiers, and quantifiers are not modelled in the propositional calculus. How come? The answer is that we have been modelling the different quantifiers through our use of connectives. Existential quantifiers yield conjunctions ($\&$) whereas universal quantifiers yield implications ($\rightarrow$). But we can only do this without introducing the quantifiers of first-order logic because of a special property of the syllogistic fragment. That property is what all the direct-graphics methods we have described depend on which we called case-identifiability. Namely, there is a critical individual on which any valid syllogistic inference depends—just one single one, corresponding to each cross in final Euler diagrams. Therefore we can think always of a world in which there is just one thing and our reasoning will not go awry as long as we choose carefully what kind of thing we consider. Stripping away quantifiers reveals the structural homologies between natural deduction and the graphical methods. The method was originally published in Stenning and Yule (1997).

Figure 4.14 is designed to bring out some of the graphical/sentential correspondences. The left-hand column shows the six alternative Euler representations of possible source premisses. With positive universal premisses, *modus ponens* applies to each of the top five, yielding the top right-hand five conclusion diagrams. Graphically, when

---

[14] It is the negation of the consequent of the second premiss—strictly speaking we also need a rule of 'double negation' which rests on the equivalence $\neg\neg P \equiv P$.

1. Seek a unique existential premiss.
   - (a) If there are two, then respond NVC and quit.
   - (b) If there are none, then go to 2.
   - (c) If there is a unique one, make it the source premiss and go to 4.

2. Seek a unique positive universal-premiss end-term subject.
   - (a) If there are none, then go to 3.
   - (b) If there is one choose its premiss as the source premiss and go to 4.
   - (c) If there are two, conclude NVC.

3. Seek a unique positive universal-premiss middle-term subject.
   - (a) If there are none, then conclude NVC.
   - (b) If there is one choose its premiss as the source premiss and go to 4.
   - (c) If there are two, choose an arbitrary source premiss.

4. If the source premiss is existential, then take its two terms as the first two clauses of the individual description. If the source premiss is universal, assume its antecedent. Apply *modus ponens* and conjoin the consequent to the antecedent to make the first two clauses of the individual description.

5. Compare middle terms.
   - (a) If a source middle term matches (with regard to negation) the antecedent middle term of the conditional premiss, apply *modus ponens*, and conjoin consequent term to individual description. Go to 6.
   - (b) If the source middle term mismatches (with regard to negation) with the conditional consequent middle term, apply *modus tollens* to the conditional premiss and conjoin the consequent term to the individual description. Go to 6.
   - (c) ELSE conclude NVC and quit.

6. individual description is now complete.

7. Draw abstract conclusion from individual description:
   - (a) Delete B conjunct from individual description. Quantify existentially for an existential conclusion (reordering any negative conjunct into predicate position).
   - (b) If clause 2(b) was satisfied, then there is a universal conclusion with the source premiss end-term as subject.

Fig. 4.13 A sentential algorithm based on the process of constructing an **individual description** by conjoining terms for each predicate or its negation. (NVC–no valid conclusion)

the diagrams are unified, the × *within* the source premiss diagram falls within the b-circle of the universal premiss to license a conclusion to the containing property of the conditional.

With a universal premisses, *modus ponens* or *modus tollens* applies to each of the top five source premisses, yielding the middle right-hand five conclusion diagrams. The rule choice will depend on which term is subject in the conditional premiss. Graphically, when the diagrams are unified, the × within the source premiss diagram falls *outside* the end-term circle of the universal premiss.

Finally, in the bottom row, with an existential negative premiss in which the end-term is subject, and a positive universal conditional premiss with end-term subject, only *modus tollens* can be applied and unification of the diagram places the source × *outside* the other end-term circle.

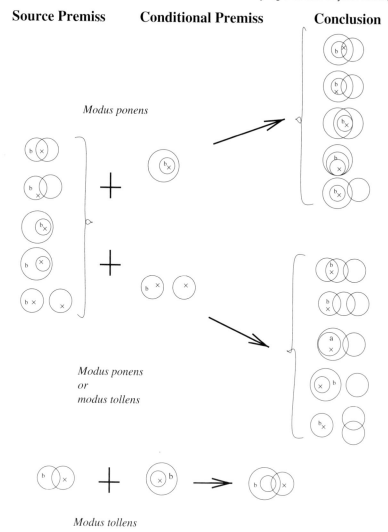

Fig. 4.14 Correspondences between Euler diagrams and natural deduction system.

4.1.7 To sea in a sieve

All the methods we have examined so far share the feature that they focus on the process of drawing valid inferences, and they make decisions about pairs of premisses which do not have valid conclusions as a side-effect of these inferential processes. But this is not a necessary feature. **The Sieve** is medieval method which consists of a set of constraints for filtering out problems that do not have any valid conclusions. This change of perspective provides a useful counterpoint to the other methods so far described, particularly when we come to ask psychological questions about how people make judgements of the *absence* of valid conclusions. These are important questions if we are to develop a psychology of reasoning as representation selection. For this discussion we shall assume the conventional definition of syllogistic validity which excludes u-conclusions.

Several of the Sieve's constraints depend on the concept of a term being *distributed* in a proposition. In each premiss type, subject and predicate terms are either distributed or not, according to whether the proposition asserts something of all of the term's extension set. So in *all A are B*, the subject term is distributed but the predicate term is not. The proposition asserts something about all *A*s but not about all *B*s. In *some A are B*, neither term is distributed. In *no A are B*, both terms are distributed (something is asserted of all *A*s (i.e. that they are not *B*s) and of all *B*s (i.e. that they are not *A*s)). And in *some A are not B*, the subject term is not distributed but the predicate term is (something is asserted of all *B*s (i.e. that none of them are the *A*s that the proposition is about).

Armed with the concept of the distribution of terms, Copi (1978) gives the following rules which exclude all invalid conclusions. The rules are adapted for our adoption of the no-empty-sets axiom.

1. The middle term must be distributed in at least one premiss.
2. For a term to be distributed in the conclusion, it must be distributed in its premiss.
3. If there is a negative premiss then any valid conclusion is negative.
4. Two negative premisses have no valid conclusion.

The fourth rule is violated if we include u-conclusions. Defining the concept of distribution allows the rules to be stated particularly succinctly, but the method is of more importance here because of its general structure than its particular rules. Without introducing distribution one might, for example, use Aristotle's metalogical principles that there must be at least one universal and one positive premiss for there to be any valid conclusion in a similar method. To use the Sieve as a complete method of drawing valid conclusions requires iterating through all the candidate conclusions. The Sieve is the complement of the other methods we have seen. It is good at detecting rapidly a wide range of problems with no valid conclusion which the other methods can only discover by running their conclusion drawing mechanisms to exhaustion. Conversely, using the Sieve to draw valid conclusions requires potentially exhaustive search. The Sieve focuses our attention on what metalogical principles subjects know, implicitly or explicitly.

For example, most naive reasoners have little trouble rapidly deciding that a double existential syllogism has no valid conclusion, thus leading to a confident and rapid rejection of such examples as *Some B are not A. Some B are not C*. Extant psychological theories generally fail to give a good account of such easy rejections, because they assume that such conclusions can only be reached by running object-level systems to completion and finding no conclusions. In Section 4.2 we present some evidence which suggests that some meta-judgements are reliably available and tells us something about their flexibility.

If, as we have argued throughout, human reasoning is as much a matter of deciding on a representation as reasoning within it, then access to metaknowledge of systems is to be expected, and its empirical exploration is a neglected major goal of reasoning research. There is of course no reason why reasoners should not use such meta-level knowledge alongside reasoning within object-level systems. If a decision that there is no valid conclusion can be arrived at quickly, even in a proportion of cases, it can forestall exhaustive reasoning in the object-level system.

4.1.8 The representational supermarket

This review of alternative representations for syllogisms is intended to highlight the surface variety that is possible in systems specified for solving the same small set of problems. We find both systems which are rather similar on the surface but which have very distinct semantics beneath that surface, and systems which appear to share no representational resources but which nevertheless emulate each others' operations. Any syllogistic system has to specify the same consequence relation, and so tracing the corresponding structures across systems is revealing of underlying homologies where the surface disguises them.

This exploration naturally raises the question of whether there is some way of specifying the space of all possible representations, together with an insightful classification. This is an important open question for an approach to reasoning which sees representation selection or construction as a major component. While we cannot yet give a general exposition, we have explored several other representational possibilities elsewhere (Stenning and Tobin 1997).

Before moving on to the psychology, one logical result is of direct significance to psychological claims about what sense can be given to processes being syntactic or semantic. Logic conventionally distinguishes between model theory and proof theory. Model theory is the study of logical consequence relations (mappings from premises to valid conclusions) *without* recourse to ways of computing these mappings. Proof theory is the study of the computations of these mappings. The distinction is given meaning by completeness and incompleteness results which show that some important systems (e.g. first-order predicate calculus) have *no* model-theoretic consequences which *cannot* be computed by proof theory, whereas others (e.g. formalizations of number theory) do have model-theoretic consequences which cannot be encompassed in any consistent proof theory. For the latter, semantics always extends beyond what can be captured in a formal system.

Mental modellers have been tempted to claim that their mental models are semantic in the sense that logical model theory is semantic relative to syntactic proof theories. However, this cannot be what gives meaning to their distinction between semantic and syntactic processes. For all decidable systems, any model-theoretic result can be mirrored in some proof-theory. Mental models (as a formal system) are finite, let alone decidable. For these tiny systems, any account can be construed as either model theory or proof theory. There is nothing particularly deep or mysterious about this collapse of the distinction in simple systems. Stenning (1992) spelt out the significance of this result for mental models theory using the example of a 'syntactic' emulation of truth-tables (a method usually thought of as 'semantic').

None of this denies the importance of the abstract objects known to logicians as 'models'. The differences between models and other abstract objects such as sentences is of critical importance to cognitive theory. But these abstract objects are not representations of anything, and the psychological task is to explain the probably many ways in which computations about them are implemented in minds.

In the next section we review some of the psychological literature which claims to explore alternative *internal* (mental) representations involved in syllogism solution.

4.2 Psychological theories of syllogism solution

Psychologists studying syllogisms have more or less agreed from the outset that their aim was to investigate a single fundamental mental mechanism that underlies the reasoning that occurs when subjects (usually undergraduate students) are given syllogisms to solve. From early on, there has been an interest in the effects of different content on reasoning with problems of the same form (an issue we shall come back to in Chapter 6), but the majority of effort has focused on representations of form and how they are mentally manipulated.

There has been little investigation of how people use externally observable representations in solving these problems, and little attention to individual differences between subjects. But there is already some evidence that different subjects go about the task very differently (Ford 1995). The range of apparently disparate representations for solving syllogisms just reviewed should make us ask just why there should be *one* fundamental internal representation system or reasoning mechanism, any more than there is one external one; and how we can distinguish (if we can at all) between these (and other) representation systems for syllogistic reasoning, on the basis of subjects' reasoning behaviour (the conclusions that they draw from the premises we present). But first we give a brief history of psychological work on syllogisms.

One of the earliest studies of syllogistic reasoning (Sells 1936) observed the *atmosphere effect*: problems with at least one existential premise tend to produce existential conclusions; problems with at least one negative premise tend to produce negative conclusions. These observations were offered as explanations of *error*, on the analogy of grammatical errors of agreement between subject and verb. Of course, as our review above of Aristotle's principles indicated, these simple heuristics embody valid principles of reasoning and do actually predict valid inference in a substantial proportion of problems.

A little later, Chapman and Chapman (1959) brought the logical literature on fallacies into the psychological laboratory, focusing on well-known fallacies such as 'illicit conversion'—the invalid inference from *All A are B* to *All B are A*, which was well known to be prevalent amongst learners of logic. We return to this fallacy in Chapter 5.

Erickson (1974) introduced Euler's circles into the field as a model of students' mental representations during syllogism solution. He used the concreteness of the primitive diagrams without abstraction tricks to explain how students made illicit inferences through overspecification of the premisses (illustrated in Fig. 4.1). The model overcame the problem about multiple diagrams for premisses simply by stochastic choice from the possibilities displayed in Fig. 4.2.

Johnson-Laird and Steedman (1978) made a decisive break with their predecessors by shifting the focus from simply the making of errors, towards a **competence model** of correct reasoning, combined with a psychological theory of how errors arise. This was an important innovation. People do not have mental processes whose function is to produce errors (whatever the logic instructor may sometimes feel as the end of term nears). People have mental representations and processes whose function is to produce correct performance (they may, of course be mechanisms developed for other purposes), but these mechanisms are subject to errors. This pattern of scientific development is common in psychology. The psychologist starts with a focus on error. There would have been no research on syllogisms if people solved them flawlessly. But error is

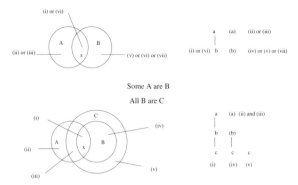

Fig. 4.15 The correspondence of mental models (MMs) to Euler's circles (ECs). Lower-case numerals represent the types of entity which correspond to minimal subregions of ECs, and to columns or parts of columns of MMs as follows: $(i)abc(ii)a\neg b\neg c(iii)a\neg bc(iv)\neg abc(v)\neg a\neg bc(vi)ab\neg c(vii)\neg ab\neg c$. Note that $\neg ab\neg c$ and $ab\neg c$ are not represented in either completed MM or EC. These are the only two types inconsistent with the premises. Letters in MMs without parentheses correspond to Euler subregions with crosses: Letters in MMs with parentheses correspond to Euler subregions without crosses.

only comprehensible against a background of the system 'working correctly'. This is a crucial innovation for integrating the insights of logic with psychology. Logic is the source of competence models in this domain, along with the abstract understanding of the computation on which cognitive models are based.

However, our case will be that Johnson-Laird and his coworkers, although they were the first to make this distinction clearly in this field, have pursued the idea without sufficiently careful consideration of the logical basis of competence models. This has been to the detriment of both the empirical understanding of what people do when they solve syllogisms, and our theoretical understanding of models of reasoning processes.

Johnson-Laird (1983) proposed that people solve syllogisms by constructing mental models. He motivated the introduction of mental models by attacking Erickson's Euler-based theory. The argument was exactly the argument from combinatorial explosion which we mentioned earlier in this chapter. But despite this motivation, mental models are a re-creation of Euler's circles in a more opaque form. The combinatorial explosion can be emulated in mental models (by unwise or random choice of model sequences), and it can be avoided in Euler's system by the cross notation shown in Fig. 4.4 (Stenning and Oberlander 1995).

Section 4.1.6 revealed a correspondence between a sentential logic fragment and Euler's circles with the cross notation. But mental models are also equivalent to the same Euler system. Figure 4.15 displays the correspondence between mental models and Euler's circles.

Let us look more closely at how Johnson-Laird sees the issue. Mental models theory is proposed as fundamentally different from formal logical theories (Johnson-Laird 1983, Chapter 11). Mental models are claimed to provide for 'semantic' computation as opposed to formal syntactic computation, and this is claimed to explain how human reasoning is affected by content (we further examine this claim in Chapter 6). He says, for example, that the tokens in mental models (the *a*s, *b*s, and *c*s in Fig. 4.15) stand for individuals through a relation of similarity. Despite the fact that the theory is presented as a system of formal representations and manipulations on them, the mechanisms in the mind are supposed to be non-formal and contentful. This is fine as long as we remember that the presentation of the formal system has done nothing to explain how the mental representations are contentful. However contentfulness is to be explained for mental models (we have some proposals below), it *could* apply to equivalent sentential systems like the fragment described above.

Mental models theory is presented as an approach to the psychology of syllogisms contrasting with 'mental logic' theories (Rips 1994) which posit that the mental representations of syllogisms are similar to the usual sentential formulations of natural deduction systems (a subsystem of the system that appeared in Hyperproof's sentential window, augmented by a particular heuristic theorem-prover).

We do not need to look far to see why it has proved so difficult to see this correspondence. In all the arguments about fitting the data of student reasoning to mental models and to mental logics, it has been assumed that the right measure of complexity of a problem is, for mental models, the number of models that have to be explored, and for mental logics, the number of rule applications. But Fig. 4.15 should make us immediately suspicious of this metric. What corresponds to a mental model in natural deduction is not a sentence-step in natural deduction, but a *case* (as in Hyperproof). We can mimic the consideration of models in mental model theory by structuring our natural deduction proofs as case-based proofs. It is true that the proofs we construct are often not the shortest proofs which can be found. But whether they are the cheapest will be a matter of how the theorem-prover is implemented. The underlying correspondence is of cases to models.

Since we know virtually nothing about the mental implementation of any of these systems, we simply do not know how mental cost will attach to rule applications versus case representation. Rule applications may be virtually 'free' while shifts from representing one model to the next might be expensive, and prone to interference. Stenning and Oberlander (1994) propose some kinds of working memory representation which would explain exactly why consideration of proofs might occur one case at a time—because the binding of properties to individuals in working memory is done by constraint satisfaction on contentful representations of properties. This is a substantive account of how content is implicated in processing of these representations. But notice that it is as applicable to other case-based methods as it is to mental models or Euler's circles.

Because mental models theorists believe that they have made an empirical claim about the nature of the mental representations, they have failed to ask the important psychological question. How are abstract models (complete mappings of properties to sets of individuals) implemented in working memory?

Using cases as an alternative measure of mental cost for sentential proofs (as we did repeatedly in Chapter 3) makes sense of the arguments that have reverberated back and forth between the mental modellers and the mental logicians. The latter often point to places where the data show students taking 'short cuts' relative to full case-based proofs, and the mental modellers' responses have been to build notation into mental models which enables one model (with notation) to do service for several (i.e. abstraction tricks). As long as one misses the overall formal correspondence between the systems, it is easy to think that one is engaged in substantive disagreement.

One interpretation that would make sense of Johnson-Laird's claims about mental models representing through similarity is that it is implicitly a proposal that mental models are *direct* in our sense of interpreted without an abstract syntax. Mental models tokens $(a, b, c, \ldots)$ can be construed as icons whose type is determined by their letter, but whose identity is given by their spatial relations in their diagram (columns). In the version shown in Fig. 4.12, the spatial relations are essentially those of tabular representations, being determined by (unlabelled) columns and rows. Note that the letters are token-referential—a different token of a represents a different individual in the domain. More accurately, we should say that the *columns* of letters are token-referential—one column, one referent. Two token letters, say an a and a b in the same column, have the same referent. The columns are then interpreted as conjunctions of the properties denoted by the letters in the column. The parenthesized elements that appear in some mental models (see Fig. 4.12) are abstraction tricks in the sense of Chapter 2. Interpreting mental models as a claim for the directness of the mental interpretations underlying syllogistic reasoning helps with interpreting some of the literature on mental models and mental logics and removes mysterious claims about reference by similarity.

Some care is required in interpreting these equivalences between mental models, Euler's circles and natural deduction fragments. What the equivalences show is that reasoning processes modelled within one system can be emulated within each of the other systems. What the equivalences do *not* show is that the algorithms (Euler, the natural deduction fragment, mental models, etc.) are equivalently easy to implement on any 'device'—human or silicon. If a device cannot perform the elementary topological operations on circles that Euler demands, or the elementary syntactic operations that natural deduction demands, then that algorithm will be unimplementable. Or, if the device can perform the operation, but only very slowly or only using large amounts of memory, then that will also have an impact. The force of the equivalences for psychological theory comes from the epistemic situation of the psychologist with regard to internal mental representations. If we only have access to inputs and outputs (premises and conclusions), and perhaps reaction times or whatever, then the equivalences are a serious problem. Conceivably, in the future we may learn how to interpret such alternative sources of evidence as functional MRI scans or evoked reaction potential traces, or whatever other technological wizardry the physicists conjure up, so that they give us evidence of the nature of the representations in the brain, comparable to the evidence that we have of the semantics of the representations on paper that we can now watch. I see no sign yet, but I keep an open mind.

There are two further important caveats about these equivalence of representation systems—one about extensions, and one about external reasoning about systems.

The fact that these small systems coincide does not mean that their extensions will coincide, or that there are equivalent extensions. Most obviously, there is no extension of Euler's circles or mental models which is equivalent to the full propositional calculus.[15] Direct diagrammatic systems are usually small fragments of expressive languages. Put the other way, expressive languages contain small inexpressive fragments.

---

[15] Peirce's alpha graphs are equivalent, but although they use the same transitivity of containment, they only use it directly to represent syntactic objects.

None of the Princeton letters is in the same place as any of the Cambridge letters
All of the Cambridge letters are in the same place as some of the Dublin letters

So, none of the Princeton letters is in the same place as some of the Dublin letters

None of the Princeton letters is in the same place as any of the Cambridge letters
All of the Cambridge letters are in the same place as all of the Dublin letters

So, none of the Princeton letters is in the same place as any of the Dublin letters

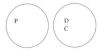

Fig. 4.16 Two supposedly undiagrammable multiple-quantifier arguments from Johnson-Laird *et al.* (1989) with their Euler diagrams.

The different extension possibilities offer one possible way of getting evidence about which system reasoners are using. If we could show that human reasoners' ability to shift problems was more in keeping with one set of boundaries than another, this could be a kind of indirect evidence for one system over another. For example, the mental models theorists have claimed that mental models representations can express multiple quantification and Euler's circles cannot. In addition, they claim that people shift easily from single- to multiple-quantifier reasoning and that this is evidence against their using Euler's circles (Johnson-Laird *et al.* 1989).

Such arguments about fragment boundaries are important from the perspective of a psychology which takes representation selection seriously. However, these particular claims are just wrong. Euler's circles can express a subset of multiply quantified arguments ones that can be recast monadically) and these appear to be just the ones which people do handle, with roughly the range of difficulty they exhibit with the corresponding syllogisms. Certainly they are the range of examples used in the experiments by Johnson-Laird *et al.* (1989). I know of no experiments which study multiply quantified reasoning outside this fragment, nor have I seen any explanation of how mental models would express such reasoning. Far from supporting the independence of mental models, this work reinforces the equivalence. Two examples of a multiple quantifier arguments from Johnson-Laird *et al.* (1989) are given in Fig. 4.16 along with the obvious Euler diagrams. It is an interesting homework exercise to formalize the method of translation into the two systems. Given human reasoners' flexibility at shifting ontologies evidenced in such reasoning, understanding what fragment of what representation system is *in play* as a subject reasons is perhaps the most pervasive empirical issue for modelling the data of reasoning.

The second caveat is about the inequivalence of external reasoning about internally equivalent fragments. If reasoners have meta-knowledge of the representations used in two internally equivalent systems, that may enable them to reason differently. Euler's graphical system makes some of its metalogical properties available to reasoners who have an intuitive grasp of some simple geometrical truths about the plane. These same reasoners could not so easily deduce these properties from mental models theory because it does not exploit the topology of the plane in a transparent way. Neither does the natural deduction equivalent. Being able to see these meta-properties might well allow reasoners to exploit the tractability of a system, and so play an important part in reasoning and learning to reason.

These equivalences between Euler, mental models, and fragments of natural deduction systems offer many possibilities for reconstruing the existing empirical findings, and for shaping future empirical work. For an example of the former, many of the truly empirical claims of mental models theorists are about the sequence in which people consider cases in reasoning, in whatever representation systems they use. We return to this important theme in considering information packaging in the next chapter. An example of the latter is the design of new tasks which we illustrate now.

Tidying up Euler by incorporating the cross notation into his system, raised some intriguing questions about Aristotle's formulation of syllogistic validity. Noting that every Aristotelian conclusion corresponded to a surviving cross in the diagram integrating the two premises, suggested the question of whether every surviving cross corresponded to an Aristotelian conclusion. The answer was 'no'. There are syllogisms such as *No A are B. No B are C* which have a cross in their final diagram, but there is conventionally no way of drawing the conclusion which it marks: *Some not-A is not C* (Fig. 4.5). The syllogism solved in Fig. 4.10 provides another example. This inadequacy of Aristotle's theory was the ground of Carroll's complaints. Do logically naive reasoners have access to such logical facts prior to being taught logic? How could we find out?

The discovery of the case-identifiability property of syllogisms suggests a new task for investigating peoples' reasoning. Every cross in an Euler diagram corresponds to a type of individual fully determined with regard to all three properties. The obvious psychological question is whether people can describe the individuals corresponding to crosses. This is not done as a basis for some spurious decision as to whether people really have Euler diagrams in their heads. We have seen that cross-marked individuals can be defined within the other systems. In mental models, they are columns of three letter-tokens, none of which is parenthesized; in natural deduction they will show up as conjunctions of three *literals*.[16] Rather, the object is to provide a new task which can throw some light on a new question. Do people have a grasp of these conclusions which Aristotle 'disallowed'? The new task, which we shall call the **individual description task**, is simple. Instead of subjects being instructed to 'draw a conclusion relating A and C by one of the four quantifiers', they are asked 'Is there any type of individual fully specified in terms of having or not having each of the three properties A, B and C, which *must* exist?'. An example from Fig. 4.5 would be, 'Something is not-C and not-A but B', corresponding to the cross in either subdiagram.

A beneficial side-effect of this new task is that it gives us information about the sequence of all three predicates in subjects' conclusions, an issue which is important in understanding the mental processes of syllogistic reasoning, as we shall see in Chapter 5. One detailed prediction of mental models theory is that the mental representations of the properties A, B, and C always have to be brought into an arrangement in which B appears in the middle and can be removed by a kind of cancellation operation in drawing conclusions. No evidence is presented for this view apart from an appeal to 'first-in–first-

---

[16]Literals are atomic predicates or their negations.

out' (FIFO) working memory organization. Such implementation details are not logical consequences of the representation system chosen (a FIFO memory could be used to hold literals in a sentence-based theorem-prover) but they are sometimes suggested by the details of systems. Mental logic theorists generally have not concerned themselves with memory implementation, though this detail could be built into their accounts. By the same token, mental models theory could be reformulated to avoid this rearrangement and cancellation mechanism. On any theory of representation, finding out more about ordering or terms in working memory is an interesting psychological issue. But these details should not be claimed as consequences or support for particular representational theories.

Figures 4.17 and 4.18 compare the reasoning accuracy in the two tasks on problems with and without valid conclusions (Stenning and Yule 1997). The annotations of the problem types used in these figures are defined in Figs. 4.19 and 4.20. Each row of each table gives, in order, the name of the problem type, the corresponding registration diagram, and the full set of instance problems using the standard mnemonics (A = all, I = some, E = no, O = some... not), broken down by figure. The problem names have some mnemonic significance: the first letter specifies whether the problems have valid conclusions (v) or not (n); the second letter indicates whether both premisses are positive (p), at least one is negative (n), or the problem type has u-conclusions (u); the final digit just reflects the listing order.

Problem types are sets of logically equivalent problems, abstracting over premiss order (and hence end-term assignment) and over the valid conversion of *no* and *some* premisses. Graphically, each problem type corresponds to a different Euler final diagram. Each subject only did one or the other task to avoid interference between them. Needless to say, u-conclusion problems belong on one side according to Aristotle's criterion, and on the other as defined by our new individuals task. We arbitrarily include them here with the valid conclusion problems but the reader should remember that in the conventional task, subjects are responding 'no valid conclusion' to these problems.

These graphs show several important things about people's reasoning. First, on the whole, performance on the two tasks correlates rather highly (the problems are scattered around the positive correlation diagonal). This is reassuring—if the tasks showed wholly different profiles we would be hard put to interpret them. Second, there is a group of problems without valid conclusions in the top right of the first scatterplot which are rather easy in both tasks: better than 90 per cent of subjects correctly judge that *Some B are not A. Some B are not C*, for example, has no valid conclusion. These problems are as easy as the easiest ones with valid conclusions. This grouping is rather revealing about how NVC decisions are made. Aristotle's generalizations appear to go some way to explaining the patterns observed. The easy NVC problems are the ones that can be decided by Aristotles' generalisations that two negative or two existential premisses do not have valid conclusions. The harder problems are those that cannot be decided this way. The easiest problems that Aristotle's generalisations cannot weed out are the 'np2' *All/Some* problems at the lower left of the ellipse of easy problems. All other problems in this ellipse are rejected easily on the basis of the generalisations.

The u-conclusion problems (Fig. 4.18) are by no means trivial, but by no means impossible. Substantial numbers of students (on average about a half) get each u-conclusion problem right when set the individuals task, and even more set the standard

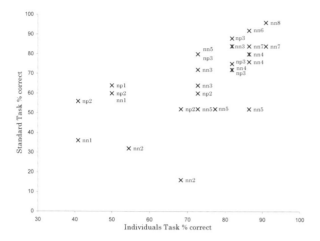

Fig. 4.17 Scatterplot of percentage of subjects getting no-valid-conclusion problems correct in the two syllogistic tasks. The problems are indexed by their Euler diagrams as in Fig. 4.19.

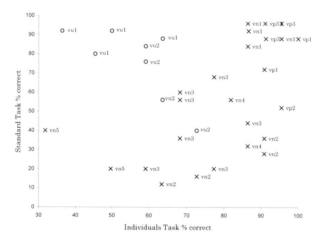

Fig. 4.18 Scatterplot of percentage of subjects getting valid-conclusion problems correct in the two syllogistic tasks. The problems are indexed by their Euler diagrams as in Fig. 4.19.

task (on average two thirds) get u-conclusion problems right (by making the NVC response). Therefore an appreciable number of totally logically naive students implicitly judge validity in the two different ways demanded by these tasks. This is a rather impressive sensitivity to logical context, given the problems that they show elsewhere. Although no subject in this experiment did both tasks, the numbers are such that we can be confident that some students who correctly drew u-conclusions in the individuals task must also have correctly rejected them in the conventional task.

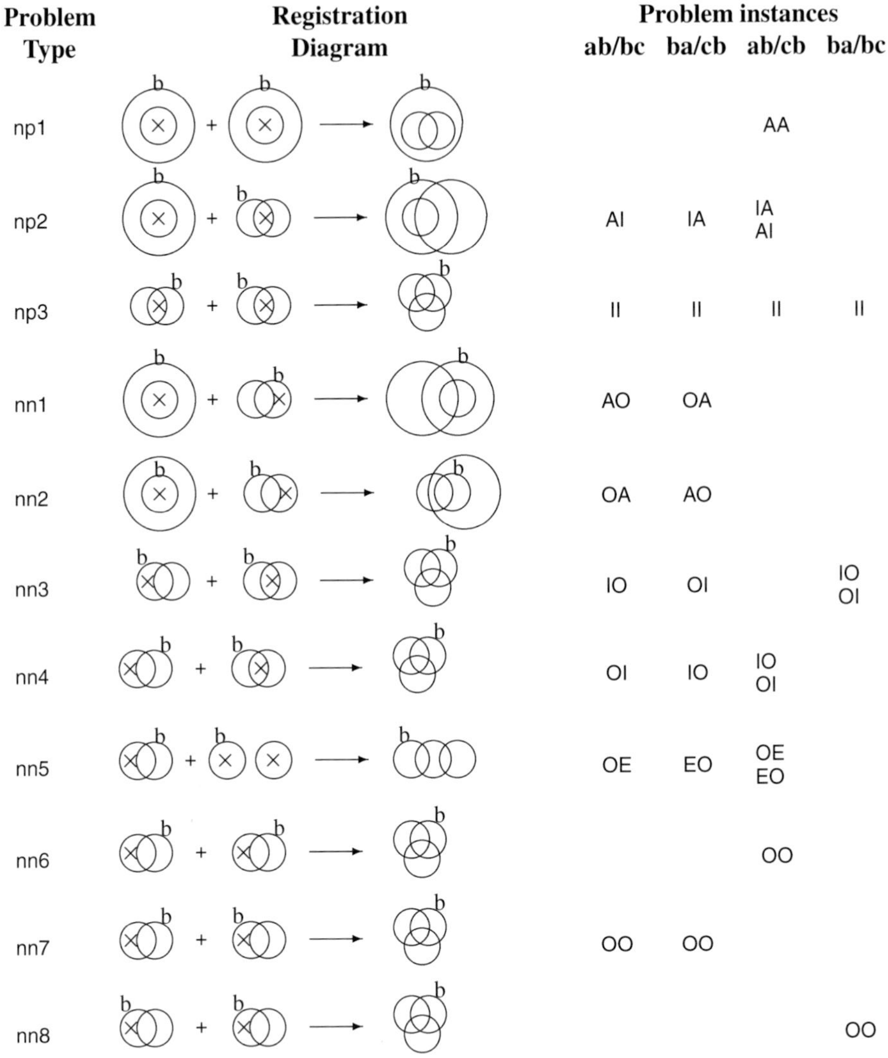

Problem Type	Registration Diagram	Problem instances			
		ab/bc	ba/cb	ab/cb	ba/bc
np1				AA	
np2		AI	IA	IA AI	
np3		II	II	II	II
nn1		AO	OA		
nn2		OA	AO		
nn3		IO	OI		IO OI
nn4		OI	IO	IO OI	
nn5		OE	EO	OE EO	
nn6				OO	
nn7		OO	OO		
nn8					OO

Fig. 4.19 Euler diagram key to Figs. 4.18 for problems *without* valid conclusions.

What about term-ordering in the individuals task, and FIFO memory? Examining the sequences of description of all three properties reveals rather strong evidence against this proposal by Johnson-Laird. Table 4.1 shows the percentages of individual descriptions with each term order as a function of syllogism figure (Stenning and Yule 1997). It is especially noticeable that less than half of all conclusions place the middle term in the middle. Stenning and Yule's explanation is that conclusions are founded on the term order of the 'source premiss'. Be that as it may, the idea that the middle term must be got into the middle to be 'cancelled' receives no support at all.

Therefore the new individuals task suggested by semantic analysis also provides useful information about students' metalogical knowledge. There is still much to explain,

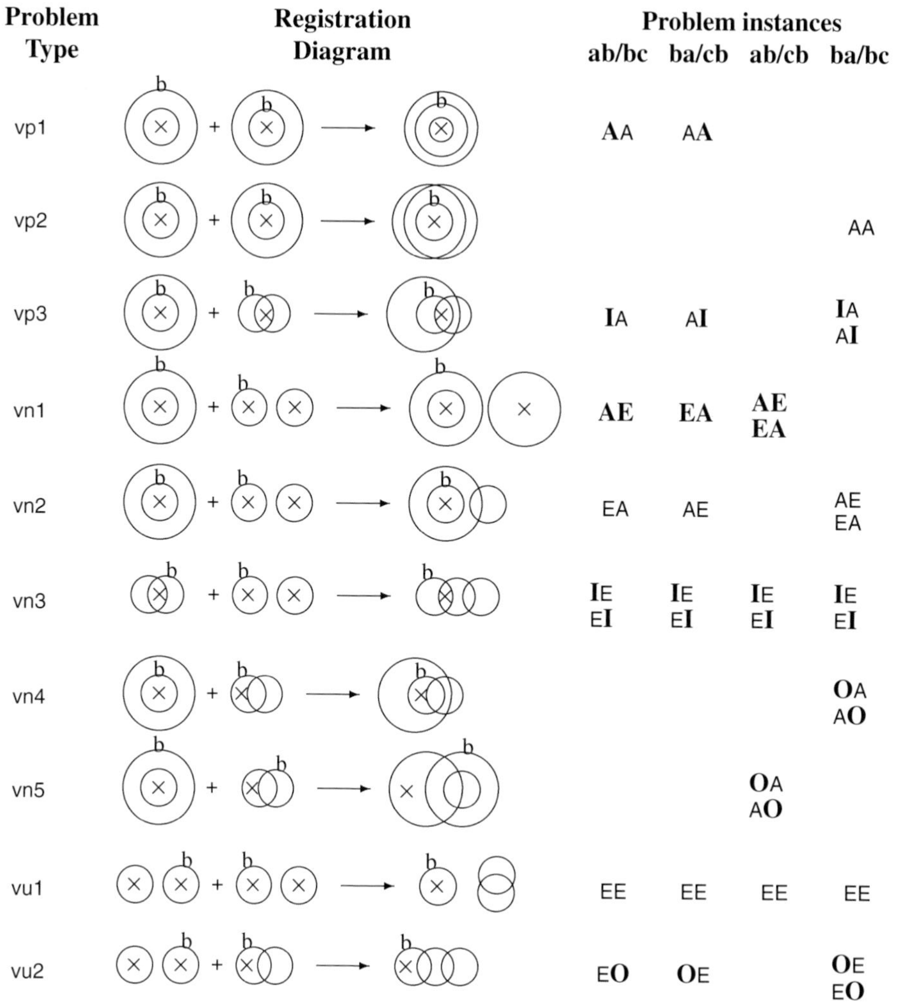

Problem Type	Registration Diagram	Problem instances			
		ab/bc	ba/cb	ab/cb	ba/bc
vp1		AA	AA		
vp2					AA
vp3		IA	AI		IA AI
vn1		AE	EA	AE EA	
vn2		EA	AE		AE EA
vn3		IE EI	IE EI	IE EI	IE EI
vn4					OA AO
vn5				OA AO	
vu1		EE	EE	EE	EE
vu2		EO	OE		OE EO

Fig. 4.20 Euler diagram key to Figs. 4.17 for problems *with* valid conclusions.

but the study highlights the general lack of attention that has been paid to how NVC decisions are made. It seems that an appreciable proportion of students have some quite flexible, if possibly implicit, grasp, not only of Aristotle's generalizations, but also of the fact that they do not hold in our new task. The Sieve does seem to be a suggestive starting point for a model of this neglected aspect of students' knowledge. It is, of course, perfectly possible that reasoners might use *both* a method focused on drawing valid inferences, and one (like the Sieve) focused on making NVC judgements in parallel. They might use the Sieve as a shallow analysis of the problem, only reasoning within some object-level system for the problems that the Sieve retains?

This is of some theoretical importance. The Sieve is couched in distinctively meta-logical terms. These are generalisations about valid inference in the syllogistic system. They are not statable, let alone inferable, as object-level propositions within the domain. Theories which assume that no-valid-conclusion judgements are made simply on the

Table 4.1 Percentages of individuals task conclusions with each possible term order in each figure[17]

			Order				
Figure	bac	bca	abc	cba	acb	cab	*N concs*
ab/bc	7.5	**23.9**	59.2	3.5	1.5	4.5	201
ba/cb	**37.3**	6.5	4.3	**44.3**	4.3	3.2	185
ab/cb	13.1	4.1	**36.6**	**35.2**	3.4	7.6	145
ba/bc	**52.6**	**35.6**	5.5	3.2	1.2	2.0	253
Overall %	**30.1**	**19.9**	24.7	18.9	2.4	4.0	784

[17] Orders predicted by premiss-founding are in **bold**, and orders predicted by mental models theory are boxed.

grounds of failure of an object-level inference mechanism to come up with a conclusion are not plausible faced with data that indicate that problems without valid conclusions show the same range of difficulty as valid conclusion problems. This is another piece of evidence that theories of human reasoning must incorporate accounts of metalogical knowledge.

Our formal equivalences between representational systems can enrich empirical study of human reasoning using classical experiment methods. But in the context of this book, perhaps the most obvious use of these studies of syllogistic representations is to see if the individual differences we observed in the Hyperproof study replicate in the teaching/learning of syllogistic inference. Learning should be our empirical focus if understanding reasoning in terms of representation selection and construction is our theoretical goal.

The equivalences between Euler's circles, mental models, and sentential systems provide methods of teaching which are strictly equated. This is a much stronger starting point than the Hyperproof domain where we had to acknowledge that there were differences in *what* was taught as well as in *how* it was taught. We can also teach this far simpler domain of reasoning in about an hour instead of 10 weeks, which means that we can look at dialogues between teacher and student using on-line measures of the process of learning, rather than measures of the finished product (exam proof structure).

Relative to the way that the field of the psychology of reasoning has defined itself, we are studying behaviour with external representations—diagrams, language, speech, . . . We would be the last to make any quick inferences about the existence of corresponding internal representations from observations of behaviour with external representations. At the very least one would expect external representations to obviate the need for some internal memory representations, replacing them by perceptual-motor processes with their own more ephemeral representations. Nevertheless, watching the use of representations which we can observe, is one of the few roads to gaining evidence about what goes on when representations disappear inside the mind.

4.3 Teaching the syllogism graphically or sententially

When we first constructed the sentential method described earlier, the equivalent of Euler's method, we were extremely dubious that it would be a serviceable teaching method. It looked like an arbitrary set of rules with no why nor wherefore to its design. All the explanation was left outside the rules. In the nature of these things, as a researcher, it is hard to be sure that one has not loaded the dice for one's favourite method (it will be no secret by now that the author and several of his graduate students find diagrammatic methods rather fun). We tried hard to come up with more perspicuous sentential methods which were still equivalent to the Euler method. We achieved some simplification over the original, but the method was essentially unchanged.

Dubious as we were, we took this specification of a teaching method and carried out a study to compare its effects with the effects of Euler's method on our long-suffering students. At this stage the only teaching study of syllogisms we had done was to run a few pilot subjects through an Euler-based tutoring regime. Interestingly for the subsequent controlled study results, the very first two students we ran, had very different 'feels' to the tutor's intuition. Although both actually grasped the mechanics of the Euler system adequately and made rather few mistakes, debriefing them produced starkly different reactions. Whereas the first student was already explaining the basis of the diagrammatic method to the tutor during the teaching session, and at debriefing gave an eloquent account of the diagram's logical transparency, the second student sounded quite different. Though this student remained very polite, and attested to the the usefulness of the diagrams when asked (students always try to humor what they assume to be professor's hobby horse), it emerged when he was asked a few meta-questions about why the system was as it was, that, for him, the whole diagrammatic system was just a graphical rigamarole. This two-subject pilot was a taste of things to come.

In the study proper (Monaghan and Stenning 1998), 20 first-year Edinburgh students from a range of academic backgrounds were tutored, randomly assigned, half using Euler's method and half the sentential equivalent. All did some pre-test practice problems to give a baseline and to get them into thinking about the domain, and all did several subsequent post-test problems after the teaching session to assess their performance in the domain after teaching. We also ran some of the psychometric tests used in the Hyperproof studies. The tutor (and the students, for that matter) was 'blind' with regard to the psychometric pre-test results. All the tutoring sessions were videotaped, and were subsequently analysed to assess teaching/learning effectiveness. The two measures we chose to focus on were number of errors made by the student, and number of interventions made by the tutor.

The first, and to us amazing, result was that the two methods of teaching worked exactly as well as each other overall. One woman's logically transparent diagram is another's graphical rigamarole. One man's fundamental rules of thought are another's syntactic spaghetti. We ceased worrying whether we might, under the spell of some subconscious urge, have cooked the books in favour of diagrammatic methods.

The question at hand is, of course, whether this overall similarity masked the same aptitude by treatment interactions as the Hyperproof studies. We analysed using several psychometric tests of pre-tutoring aptitudes. As well as using the GRE analytical constraint satisfaction problems from the Hyperproof pre-test, we also used Pask's Serialist/Holist self-rating test, and the Paper Folding Test. The analysis separated the

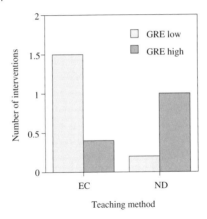

Fig. 4.21 Number of tutor interventions at translation-in phase by GRE score and by teaching method.

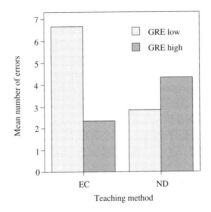

Fig. 4.22 Number of reasoning errors at manipulation phase by GRE score and by teaching method.

reasoning process into three phases. Because of the theoretical equivalence of the methods, it was possible to make the same division into stages of reasoning for both. The three phases were translating into the formalism (graphical or sentential) from English, manipulating the formalism, and translating back into English. The tutoring made these phases relatively easy to distinguish.

The results for the aptitude treatment interactions involving the GRE are shown in Figs. 4.21, 4.22, and 4.23, and are rather clear. There were several other significant aptitude by treatment interactions with serial/holist and PFT scores which we shall not present here for lack of space. Students scoring high on one of the three psychometric tests reacted differently to the two teaching methods—graphical and sentential—than did the students scoring low on the same test. All these interactions were in the expected directions—students scoring high on the tests (or toward the holist end of the dimension) made fewer errors and required fewer interventions by the tutor when taught using Euler diagrams than their peers who scored lower on these tests. But when taught the natural deduction method, the effects were reversed—students scoring low on the tests

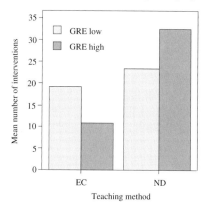

Fig. 4.23 Number of tutor interventions at manipulation phase by GRE score and by teaching method.

made *fewer* errors and required *fewer* teaching interventions than their higher scoring peers.

The symmetry of these aptitude treatment interactions is particularly striking. *Higher* test scorers show *poorer* performance with a teaching method, and *lower* test scorers show *better* performance. This means that there is more here than merely the tendency of any psychometric test to test 'general aptitude' or, worse still, 'general test savvy'.

Analysing the three stages of reasoning separately also showed that the different kinds of student classified by the tests generate these aptitude treatment interactions at different stages of the reasoning. The GRE analytical differences predict different responses to the different teaching methods at the translation-in and the manipulation stages, the serialist/holist differences predict differences in response at the manipulation and the translation-out stage, and the paper folding test predicts differences at the translation-out stage. In all cases except the translation-in stage, where there are rather few errors and the interaction does not reach significance, all these interactions hold for both errors and for tutor-interventions. They constitute a rather remarkable replication of the Hyperproof studies in a different though comparable student population, in a totally different teaching problem domain, with rather different diagrams, and completely different measures of performance.

Notice how different the Euler diagrams are from Hyperproof diagrams. The Hyperproof diagrams are rather 'realistic', in the particular sense that the spatial relations in the diagrams represent the same spatial relations in the Hyperproof world. It would be possible, if unwieldy, to teach Hyperproof using real solids on a board. In contrast, the spatial relations in the Euler diagrams represent non-spatial logical relations in their domains, and the domains are never specified beyond the abstract properties A, B, and C. The Euler diagrams are highly non-realistic in this sense. However, both kinds of diagrams share two features of their interpretations: they are both directly interpreted, and they employ abstraction tricks to express limited abstractions—the cylinder and bag icons, and off-board area of Hyperproof; the crosses of the Euler system.

Having designed two methods of reasoning in two different modalities, carefully equated so that each structure in one is mirrored by a structure in the other, each process in one by a process in the other, we still find that students react to the teaching methods in systematically contrasting ways. What conclusions can we draw?

First, acknowledging problems of inferring internal representations from behaviour with external ones, this result still suggests that there is more than one mental representational approach to syllogisms. The general agreement that the search should be for one fundamental mental mechanism stands in need of justification. No justification has been provided other than a theoretical desire for homogeneous foundations which has no logical justification now that logic acknowledges a plethora of representations. Second, it is fruitful to look at *learning* to reason syllogistically rather than assuming that we are tapping into a pre-existing mechanism. An approach through representation construction and meta-knowledge is supported. Third, we should not dispute that there *may be* representational and strategic differences between direct and indirectly interpreted representations for solving syllogisms. What we dispute is three claims of the mental modellers: that any evidence has been provided by their experiments as to which system is used, that only *one* system is used prior to logic teaching and what is the important distinction between the two kinds of representation—whether the important distinction is between semantic and formal processing or between the formal processing of direct as opposed to indirect representations.

4.3.1 Languages within languages—revisiting expressiveness

If these results raise further problems for mental models and mental logics as exclusive systems of representation, they also challenge our own theory developed in Chapters 2 and 3 that expressiveness of systems can explain cognitive characteristics through its effects on tractability of reasoning. If the two teaching methods implement the same logic, how can the complexity of reasoning in the two be different? And if two different groups of student find different representations and algorithms preferable, is not this an elegant refutation of the idea that complexity theory has anything to offer at all to a theory of human reasoning? We need to revisit our original theoretical proposals.

We started out by pursuing the idea that the framework of computational complexity theory should be as applicable to human reasoning as to machine reasoning—it is, in the jargon of the field, an architecture-free theory of computation. The idea was that an important class of diagrams (directly interpreted ones) were inexpressive and therefore led to tractable reasoning, for all the reasons that complexity theory explains. But what we have found (twice now) is that when we resort to carefully controlled study of human performance with diagrammatic and non-diagrammatic systems, what we see are benefits of one for some groups of user, and benefits of the other for other groups. We do not see an overall modality superiority of the sort that might simply be explained by diagrams providing more tractable reasoning.

None of this shows that there are not tasks and representations which would show such overall modality effects for all users. There is, after all, in the everyday world, quite a bit of evidence of strong preferences widespread in the population for one type of representation for some tasks. For example, there are some tasks which make the vast majority of people reach for a map. But the problem with studying these tasks is that the range of explanations for the preferences are rather wide. The individual differences we find certainly pose some hard questions for theory, but they offer a unique route deeper into those questions.

There is, after all, something deeply paradoxical about using computational complexity theory to explain modality differences. It was some time before the paradox struck us, though it has probably been staring the attentive reader in the face for several chapters. Complexity theory is entirely based on the analysis of representations and processes of reasoning over them in terms of logics, and computations over them. If complexity theory has anything to say about an inexpressive diagram system, it says it by specifying an equivalent weak sentential logic. So how could expressiveness possibly explain modality differences? For any analysed weak diagrammatic system there is a corresponding weak sentential system. This weak sentential system will offer *ex hypothesi* exactly as tractable reasoning as its diagrammatic counterpart—no more, no less.

Perhaps we should throw out the idea that complexity theory is any basis for understanding human reasoning, and find some other starting point? Psychometrics or the study of brain imaging? Alternatively, we could deepen the theory. We believe the resolution of this paradox lies in thinking about *interpretation*. Interpretation cannot only be thought of as distinguishing its products (different representation systems), but also as a process (how people come to grasp an interpretation). If this is right, then it is a signal piece of luck that we chose for empirical study situations in which people are *learning* new interpretations for diagrammatic (and sentential) systems.

Complexity theory always assumes the kind of situation in which a processor (person or machine) embodies an (optimal) theorem-prover for reasoning over a representation system in accordance with a *known* interpretation. It could similarly concern itself with a diagrammatic theorem-prover working over a diagrammatic system, according to a prearranged interpretation for the system. What such a theorem prover does *not* have to do is to figure out how to interpret a novel system of representations—the situation that most readers of this book will have been in for at least some of the diagrammatic systems presented here. It is of course the same situation in which all of the various students in our experimental studies find themselves.

This process of acquiring an interpretation for a diagrammatic system was indirectly exemplified by the observation in Chapter 2 that the very same node-and-link notations were capable of interpretations of extremes of expressiveness—circuits, maps, abstract languages. Another example that made the point was consideration of the similarities and differences between, Venn, and Carroll diagrams. These interpretations were similar enough to be easily confusable, but different enough for confusion to be fatal. Someone new to the systems could easily import parts of one interpretation into diagrams of another system—interpretations could interfere. The same applies to languages, as we shall see later in Chapter 6.

Perhaps differences between modalities can be explained in terms of the ease or difficulty of *assigning* interpretations for new systems. We shall call this property the **availability** of interpretations. We do not need to give up on the involvement of expressiveness, because expressiveness will have its effects once we have found an interpretation of some particular power. The theory might be rephrased as saying that when diagrams are efficacious it is because they make available (to some class of user) their inexpressiveness, and this allows the exploitation of the resulting tractability of reasoning. For another kind of reasoner who brings different knowledge and skills, it appears that sentential systems make selection of a system with appropriate expressiveness easier.

This idea has at least some superficial plausibility. Diagrams are often used in teaching, and often subsequently disappear from practice, being superseded by more general or less laborious linguistic methods. But if this is true, at least in the domains of our studies, there have to be traceable differences between students in how they learn from the different kinds of system. Otherwise, simply changing from a theory that tractability explains usability, to a theory that availability of a new interpretation explains usability, would leave us in the same position of being unable to explain individual differences.

So why are we any better off with this revised theory? One answer is that we are theoretically better off because if the differences are due to the availability of interpretations for new users of representation systems, then we would expect performance to be highly sensitive to differences in background knowledge, and this is somewhere where learners really do differ, either through constitution or experience. An opponent might feel that this is simply helping the theory to a whole bundle of new degrees of freedom. That undoubtedly is so. But if the phenomenon is complex in this way, then the degrees of freedom will be needed, and will have to be reduced by empirical observation. Such abstract theories can do no more than point empirical study at the right place. If this is the right place, then our modified theory will have been a good theory.

Why should modalities make differences in availability of information about their interpretations? We are only beginning to understand how to investigate this question. So what follows is preliminary and speculative. Our hypothesis is that directly interpreted graphics offer some hooks into their interpretation for some naive users which sentential languages do not. If there is some correspondence between the logical properties of the significant spatial relations in the diagram and the represented logical relations of the domain (because the diagrams are directly interpreted), then this correspondence should be available to a user with suitable knowledge of graphical relations. It *could* be available in a way that similar correspondences will be obscured by abstract syntactic relations in a sentential language which is indirectly interpreted.

Take as an example, the metalogical property of syllogisms which is the foundation of most of the methods of solution presented here. Case-identifiability is the correspondence of maximally specified critical individuals and valid arguments in the syllogism. This is what enables us to add the cross notation to Euler's circles. We do not know of any discussion of this property in the large sententially oriented logical literature of the syllogism, yet it is at the heart of all the extant methods of solution. The property is discussed (though not in this terminology) by earlier graphical investigators of the syllogism—notably Carroll. The cross notation makes this metalogical property of the syllogism immediately available to anyone who looks at Euler diagrams and has a basic grasp of geometry. Every point is inside or outside all closed curves in a plane, and therefore fully specifies a type of individual.

The fact that naive students are quite good at finding critical individuals corresponding to pairs of premises (as demonstrated by the study above) perhaps indicates that at some level they have access to this property of the reasoning domain. We can see how Euler's circles *might* make this implicit fact more available to them. What is the situation with deriving this property and others like it from sentential systems of representation? What might some users know about sentential systems which would make this property available to them? Our results suggest that some students actually find accessing interpretations and exploiting their inexpressiveness *easier* with sentential languages. How could that be explained in terms of availability?

Even having asked the question opens up a new perspective on the problem of understanding the linguistic case. Students come to this task with an immensely sophisticated grasp of their native language. We deliberately taught an artificial language in our syllogism study so that we could track its correspondences to the diagrams. But we taught the formal language by appealing to translations from the pre-existing natural language. What did the students know beforehand, and what did they learn?

The syllogism is a tiny fragment of English. When students solve syllogisms using a linguistic representation, how much of their whole English 'theorem prover' is operating? If only the syllogistic part, how is this cutting down, or how is specialization achieved? Whereas the border of the graphical systems like that of Euler are fairly distinct—it is clear what range of reasoning they can deal with—it is far from clear what range of reasoning fragments of English can encompass if only because it is quite unclear how English is to be dissected into fragments. And this is because words, and strings of words, all look the same. More accurately, being indirectly interpreted, there is nothing available in the spatial relations between words which will help us in this dissection, without access to their abstract syntax. This is not to say that reasoners experienced with some language will not be able to isolate and optimize a new module for solving a newly presented range of problems such as syllogisms. It is just that we know little about how they do this.

This reformulation of our problem offers a new perspective. There are a pair of subtle analogies which pervade this perspective. For the diagrammatic systems we think of them as scattered around in a landscape and adopted by some metalogical examination of their properties, guided by our geometrical knowledge of their diagrams. For the sentential systems, we think of them as part of an omnipresent universal language which is narrowed down by specializing theorem-provers to the constraints of a new domain. Neither analogy is yet a theory of how either kind of system works, but analogies are where theories come from. If these different ways of thinking about representation selection can be given substance, then they might be the theoretical basis for explaining differences in reasoning and learning styles.

The suggestion the reformulated theory makes is that characterizing the *initial* interpretations of systems of reasoning might be expected to be particularly informative—where a 'naive' reasoner starts from. This is the topic of the next chapter.

To exemplify this rather abstract set of ideas, we shall finish this chapter by exploring the relation between Euler and our natural deduction system equivalent. This will provide an example of a study of the nesting behaviour of graphical fragments of logics. We shall show how Euler, as currently defined, is limited by showing how to expand the system a small step toward a larger part of natural deduction by adding a graphical operation. We shall add the operation of turning circles inside out.

4.3.2   Circles turned inside out

In sentential languages we can negate a predicate and so have a tool for asserting the complement-property to that picked out by the predicate itself. There is a property *red*, and a complement property *non-red*. True, we have to be careful to keep track of what domain of things we apply these terms in, or there will be things which are neither red nor non-red, but this point serves merely to reinforce the fact that we are always concerned with a local domain of interpretation—perhaps coloured shapes or some such. The obvious topological Euler-equivalent of this operation of property complementation by negation is the distinction between the inside and the outside of the closed curves.

In sentential languages we can additionally vary which of a pair of contradictory properties is expressed positively, and which negatively. Therefore we could define 'blah' to mean non-red, and then 'non-blah' would mean red. I am not suggesting that blah is likely to catch on, merely that we have the apparatus for defining such reversals of negative-positive character. The Euler equivalent of this operation is to turn a circle inside out—or to think linguistically, to allow negation into labels. So far we have followed the convention that the sets represented by containment within a circle are positively characterized, and we have implicitly interpreted the outside of the circle as representing things with the complement property. But if we overthrow this convention we produce the alternative encoding of each syllogistic premiss shown in Fig. 4.24.

When we augment the system in this way interesting things happen. For example, if we try solving the syllogism shown in Fig. 4.4 with the augmented system, we find that on some encodings the two premiss diagrams will not unify, as depicted in Fig. 4.25.

This is an exact parallel to what happens in the natural deduction method when the encoding $B \rightarrow \neg A.B \rightarrow C$ will yield a conclusion by forward reasoning, but the encoding $A \rightarrow \neg B.B \rightarrow C$ will not. Adding the cross notation to Euler diagrams already made them much more like the simple sentential reasoning of the syllogism. The crosses mark a 'focus of attention' for the goals of reasoning. The cross expresses some of what is expressed by the logical subject-predicate distinction in sentential systems—the cross marks the subject term. The further addition of the turning-inside-out operation takes the system another step towards the sentential system. The new representations mean that every premiss has both a graphically symmetrical and a graphically non-symmetrical form, which may be a disadvantage for those students helped by the simple Euler system representation of logical symmetry/asymmetry by diagrammatic symmetry/asymmetry.

The augmented graphical system now offers choices for reasoning which are available in the propositional calculus but were previously unavailable in the graphical system. Notice that our sentential algorithm in Fig. 4.13 is arranged around the goal of avoiding these blind alleys of getting the incompatible encodings of the two premisses. The theorem-prover cuts off paths which the language in its generality allows, thus effectively defining a fragment. If we had started with the augmented graphical system, we would have to modify our diagrammatic algorithm for solving syllogisms in a similar way. In both cases, the theorem-prover builds in constraints which restrict the fragment of the representational system which is 'in play'.

Therefore we can devise nested graphical fragments of larger graphical systems by analogy with nested fragments of sentential languages, and we could take the system internal perspective of thinking of these constraints as residing in the skill of reasoning embodied in the theorem-prover. The reader should try using the augmented system for solving a few syllogisms. My intuition is that it creates problems which have a similar feel to the problems of reasoning sententially. Turning inside out seems to be a rather unnatural diagrammatic operation. Or, put another way, there is a natural preference for having positive information represented by the visual focus of the circle figure on the

Euler   Euler-inside-out

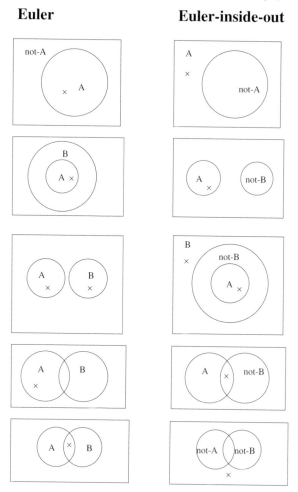

Fig. 4.24 The Euler system augmented by representation of negatively defined sets within circles—Euler inside out. The right-hand column gives equivalent representations in the augmented system for the left-hand column's diagrams.

diagram ground.

But is this just an intuition of one group of reasoners? We have already confessed to being rather poor at predicting others' intuitions on these matters! Turning circles inside-out really may be an operation that all human processors only implement at high cost. Adding it to the Euler system may be disastrous for all users. Perhaps the Euler system is effective for those people it is effective for precisely because it cuts out these blind alleys of non-integrable premiss encodings. But if this is so, then it seems highly likely that the other students who do not benefit from Euler but do benefit from the natural deduction approach, have some other way of avoiding these impasses in the sentential case. Which again reminds us of the need to know more about what the low scoring GRE students gain from the syntactic logic course. We believe that this issue of how to explain how reasoners control the fragment of reasoning systems which are 'in

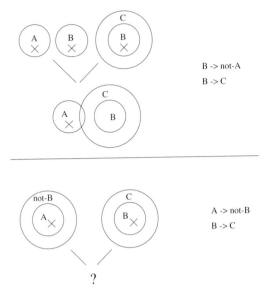

B -> not-A
B -> C

A -> not-B
B -> C

?

No A are B. All B are C.

Fig. 4.25 An example in the augmented Euler system in which premiss representations do not unify, with propositional equivalents.

play' at any given time is one of the central issues for understanding the computations of human reasoners. Although we know a good deal about the processing of negations in language, we have less information about how they are processed when attached to diagrams.

In this chapter we have seen that a modern logical analysis of the many representations for syllogisms and their relations to each other can serve as the basis for richer empirical study of human reasoning. Subjects have choices in how they interpret materials and these choices are critical in determining the course of their reasoning. Accepting multiplicity of systems and interpretations as a fact of logical life throws the pscyhological focus onto meta-reasoning, onto learning to reason, onto individual differences in reasoning and learning styles, and onto the processes of interpretation. So far we have concentrated on alternative ways of representing deduction from syllogisms, but now we must stand further back and look at alternative ways in which subjects interpret the very task which they are set.

5 Students' models of communication

5.1 Professor Grice's logic tutorial

Picture the oak panelled Oxford room, with the white-haired don sunk in his archetypal philosopher's armchair, facing two fresh-faced undergraduates in their first term of university life. Professor Grice is teaching introductory logic, a subject taught to a wide range of students during their first year. Grice opens the afternoon's session with a question—opening the topic of logical validity:

Suppose I tell you that some A are B', snatching a different example than his usual one from the air, 'What follows from this statement?', asks Professor Grice.

'Some A are not B', comes the reply from the less diffident of the two students.

'Ah, is that so? Tell me why you answer thus', says Grice, struggling for control of his eyebrows.

'Well, sir, you said that some A are B. You are a helpful sort of fellow, and if *all* A were B, you would have said so. So it follows that some A are *not* B.'

Professor Grice, despite the lateness in the term and the frequency of similar tutorials in his teaching career, is struck by a blinding flash of insight and runs from his rooms shouting 'Eureka! I have it! A theory of pragmatics!'

Our aim in this chapter is a rational reconstruction of the difficulties that students face in learning the core concepts of elementary logic. We begin by observing that the idea of learning logic has an air of paradox about it—resolving this paradox will force us to be clearer about exactly what has to be learned, and that in turn will help us to understand what other tasks we might expect such learning to transfer to. By far the most influential relevant theory is Grice's theory of communication as a co-operative activity. A brief exposition of Grice's theory illustrated by the material of elementary logic learning sets the stage for the empirical study of students' naive intuitions about logical consequence.

Past studies have provided evidence that students draw the inferences that Grice's co-operative model of communication predicts. But the same studies claim that the theory fails to accord with students' patterns of extended reasoning—their solving of syllogisms. We shall show that semantically informed empirical study of student intuition coupled with a theoretically principled operationalization of the concepts of Grice's theory can resolve this impasse. Students models of communication do determine how they reason. However, there are several qualitatively different patterns of intuitions which play complex parts in determining reasoning, and these patterns can be related to the individual differences that we found in the impact of modalities on learning.

Our empirical studies of naive intuition point up needs for theoretical development of Grice's theory to cover multiple kinds of discourse and the involvement of natural language structures in tailoring information for recipients—information packaging. This excursion into empirical work on logical intuition and its implications for theory also offers some more morals for relations between theory and experiment in psychology and cognitive science.

5.2 The paradox of logic learning

According to an important current of thinking about natural languages (such as Chinese and English), natural languages are in fact logical languages, only thinly disguised. Montague's (1974) work is perhaps the classical focus for this point of view. The logical languages which are argued to be equivalent to natural ones are much more expressive languages than first-order predicate calculus (the logical language which Hyperproof is designed to teach). They contain first-order logic as a fragment. Undergraduates, it is observed, are fluent speakers of natural languages well before coming anywhere near a logic course. Therefore, if English, say, is a formal logical language, and first-order logic is a small fragment of it, why is there anything to learn in logic class? The paradox of logic teaching is that logic learning goes on.

For the philosophical reader, I do not intend to claim that this paradox is necessarily particularly deep—at the very least it would require much more sharpening to make it cut deep. Once we were clearer about the many ways languages can be identified and enumerated it might become less paradoxical. But that is my point. In order to understand what it is that could conceivably be learned in logic class, we need a more finely graded notion of language, interpretation, communication, and learning. My excuse for presenting this as a paradox is that I believe that responses to it reveal how logic teachers see what they are teaching. I believe that we need a resolution that can explain why highly intelligent undergraduates exhibit intuitions and behaviour which logically sophisticated faculty find incredible. And we need a resolution which can do justice to the importance of elementary logic learning and explain the impact on general reasoning which our evidence supported in Chapter 3.

This paradox of logic learning applies with even more force to the syllogism which is an even tinier fragment of first-order logic, and is a fragment of each natural language with no extra symbols. Yet we have seen in the last chapter that solving syllogisms is by no means a trivial task for intelligent undergraduate students. How can this be?

We shall attempt an answer which can be encapsulated in the slogan 'It's the discourse stupid!'. What people have to learn is a new kind of discourse, or at least an explicit grasp of a kind of discourse which we might call the discourse of 'proof', and the balance between exposition and proof in communication more generally. This discourse is highly aberrant relative to other kinds of discourse of which undergraduates have more prior experience, and so much of logic class involves unlearning a set of highly ingrained habits—always hard work.

This is the reason for opening with our fictional, and perhaps fanciful, staging of Grice's tutorial. Grice (1975) did more than anyone else to lay the groundwork for the empirical study of how logic is embedded in communicative phenomena. Whether or not his experiences of teaching logic played an important role in leading him to his theories, he certainly deserves centre stage in a resolution of the paradox of logic learning. Grice's work can serve as the foundation for a rational analysis of learning to reason.

Grice's theories have had a huge impact on philosophy of language and on the branch of linguistics known as pragmatics—the study of the use of language. For those studies, logical semantics is an underlying theoretical framework and set of methods. What philosophers and linguists less often consider is the pragmatics of the kind of discourse that is proof—deduction as an actual human discourse rather than some theoretical analysis or 'ordinary discourse' or 'conversation'. Grice was motivated in his programme by the desire to retain logic as an underlying theory of the meaning of sentences. I think Grice would have been quite happy to apply the same kind of approach to the communications involved in proof. But it never became a major focus. After our investigations we shall be in a good position to raise some questions about Grice's programme as it applies to the discourse of proof.

5.3 A sketch of Grice's theory

Grice's great contribution was to show that if logic is to be used as a basis for studying natural language semantics, then it must be augmented by a theory of pragmatics—what people are doing when they use language to perform communicative acts. Grice's programme was essentially conservative—it sought to preserve the insights of formal logic as an account of semantics, by enriching the theory of meaning with a much elaborated theory of language use. The context in which Grice wrote was the Oxford of Austin and the ordinary language philosophers who were quite allergic to systematic treatments of the meaning of natural languages, let alone treatments couched in formal calculi. Grice's programme may have been technically conservative, but it was philosophically radical.

Grice entitled the central exposition of his work *The logic of conversation*. 'Conversation' functions as a place-holder which gestures at all uses of language which are not themselves analysis of language, though Grice was rather vague about just how widely his theory was intended to run. At the time, what was important was to consider what (at the least) would have to be added if formal logic was to be the kernel of a theory of some prominent everyday uses of natural language. Grice saw conversation as a collaborative activity in which interlocutors had to observe certain maxims of co-operation if they were to succeed in their shared aims. Note the undergraduate's 'You are a helpful sort of fellow' in our fable tutorial. It is from the assumption that the participants are co-operating, among other assumptions, that the undergraduate's inference 'You must mean that some A are *not* B' follows.

This particular inference is, for Grice, an example of an implication generated by one of several maxims, together with contextual information. These maxims make up the core of his theory. A very brief example must suffice for exposition here. Two of Grice's maxims were the Maxim of Quantity: *say as much and not more than is necessary* and the Maxim of Quality: *be truthful*. Illustrating from our fictional student's reasoning, 'If Grice knows that all A are B, then he would have said all A are B, so the fact he said less, namely that some A are B means that it must be that some A are not B'. It is the Maxims of Quantity and Quality which figure most prominently in the kinds of quantifier inferences which concern us here and so we shall omit the others.

Implicature was Grice's technical term for the implications generated by these pragmatic inferences. First note that implicatures are not logical entailments. is perfectly possible for it to be true that some A are B *and* that all A are B. Second, note that even when the conversation is co-operative, these inferences involve quite a few contextual assumptions. Suppose Grice was known by his hearer to be ignorant of whether all A were B. Then the inference that *if* all A are B, then Grice would have said so, fails. With this ignorance the implicature that some A are not B also fails. As Grice's theory spells out, these implicatures depend on a certain kind of assumed contextual omniscience, as well as co-operation and truthfulness, and once ignorance becomes a good reason for not having said something stronger, then the implicatures cease.

Grice's theory seeks to give a schematic account of this balance between knowledge, truthfulness, and informativeness in our everyday communication. In passing, note that assumed omniscience (at least with regard to the technical topic at hand) is an attribution some students make, or at least act as if they make, in some circumstances, of their teachers.

Where does the gap between implicature and entailment arise from? It arises from the co-operative nature of the kind of discourse Grice calls conversation. Logic originated as a model of what we might call **adversarial** communication—at least in a technical sense of adversarial. What *follows* in deduction is anything that is true in *all* interpretations of the premises—that is the definition of logically valid inference. We have to be careful to give a precise meaning to *all interpretations*, but Fig. 2.1 already gave an idea of how that might be done for the propositional calculus.

Think of the contrast between 'co-operative conversation' and deduction. In conversation hearers try to arrive at the speaker's 'intended' model of their utterances. We jump to all sorts of conclusions about this model on the basis of assuming mutual habits of communication and mutual beliefs about the topic at hand. When we hear someone say: 'Max fell. John pushed him', we jump to all sorts of conclusions about what was meant—probably that John pushed Max before Max fell, and that the pushing caused the falling. We generally jump correctly to the intended model, ignoring many models logically compatible with what was actually said. A certain sort of conversational joke can be made out of refusing to make these jumps, though with repetition such jokes wear thin rather quickly. Jumping to conclusions is a staple of co-operative communication, but it is bad logical form.

In logical deduction, matters are different. Our job, as speaker or hearer of a discourse that purports to be a deduction, is to test the drawing of inferences to destruction, to ensure that what is inferred is true in *all* models of the premises, not just the intended one. It is in this technical sense that logic models adversarial discourse. We may actually be socially co-operating in testing a deduction for validity, and certainly we have to co-operate a great deal to be sure that we are assuming the same things about the range of interpretations which are intended, but there is a core of seeking out all possible assignments of things, not simply finding one intended one. This is perhaps not accidentally related to the fact that logic arose as a model of legal and political debate. We return to the issue of how Grice's theory applies to argumentative discourse itself below, and to the social arrangements of authority in arguments in Chapter 7. Meantime we shall use the terms co-operative and adversarial with this somewhat technical meaning to contrast what Grice called conversation with deduction.

Another technical expression of this distinction between co-operative and adversarial communication is found in formulations of logic based on abstract games. Expressions such as quantifiers 'some' and 'all' can be defined in terms of strategies in a game between opponents. One player tries to establish the validity of a conclusion, and the other tries to defeat that demonstration by choosing example objects from the domain. If

I am trying, in the course of proposing the validity of a conclusion, to establish the truth of an existential statement, then I have free choice of exemplar. But if you are trying, in the course of attempting to refute a conclusion, to defeat a universal statement, you have free choice of the exemplar. The meaning of quantifiers and the validity of arguments can be defined in terms of whether or not there are winning strategies in such abstract games. The adversarial nature of the game guarantees that validity of inference is tested in all interpretations. The degree to which such games provide a foundation for logical concepts is debatable. The point here is that they do illustrate how adversarial games can serve to implement a search for counter-examples, and this search contrasts with the co-operative goal of finding an intended model.

This contrast between co-operative and adversarial elements of communication and reasoning is worth emphasizing because audiences schooled in the ways of literate cultures are so skilled at moving between modes that they may find it hard to notice the transitions. Scribner's work (see Scribner 1977; and Scribner and Cole 1981) on reasoning compared the responses of schooled and unschooled populations to syllogisms. She quotes the following dialogue between herself (E) and an unschooled villager (S) presented with the syllogism: *All Kpelle men are rice farmers. Mr Smith is not a rice-farmer. Is he a Kpelle man?*

S: I don't know the man in person. I have not laid eyes on the man himself.
E: Just think about the statement.
S: If I know him in person, I can answer that question, but since I do not know him in person I cannot answer that question.
E: Try and answer from your Kpelle sense.
S: If you know a person, if a question come up about him you are able to answer. But if you do not know a person, if a question comes up about him, its hard for you to answer it.

Another example answer to the syllogism *All people who own houses pay a house-tax. Boima does not pay a house-tax. Does Boima own a house?* is

S: Boima does not have money to pay a house tax.

In both examples the subject construes the problem as one of expanding on the situation of the problems' words, even though the reference is known only to E. In the first case, the subject points out that she cannot join in this discourse on these terms, for lack of first-hand information. In the second case, the subject adds a plausible further assumption, perhaps in the spirit of telling a fictional story communally authored with the experimenter? The story thus embellished starts with a dramatic impasse, and would no doubt continue with a resolution as to how Boima coped. Both of these responses treat the experimenter's invitation as an invitation to co-operative communication which will construct a mutual model of a particular situation (real or fictional respectively). These responses are not the exercise of some special logic that only members of unschooled societies possess. They are exactly the kind of responses we make in different circumstances. It is just that we rarely interpret this as the kind of discourse invited in this context by the experimenter's words.

Scribner's schooled subjects almost never interpret the experimental task in this way or make either of these kinds of response. They understand, as we educated folk do, that the task is to accept the words and draw something from them, based only on knowledge of the words and not mediated through personal experience of the particular referents of the words. The schooled subjects may not have a complete or explicit grasp of the concept of valid derivation, or of the calculative complexities of the more difficult syllogisms, but they understand something more about the intended game. In the experiments we are about to describe our undergraduate subjects rarely make the responses of the unschooled even though analysis will show that a good proportion have at best a weak grasp of what is involved in valid inference—adversarial communication. The difference between Scribner's schooled and unschooled reasoners comes with literacy rather than logic teaching. Examining the extremes of the dimension is instructive if we have forgotten a mind set, and is a useful reminder that there is nothing irrational about the game that the unschooled choose to play in this circumstance, and we often play ourselves in other circumstances.

Grice's theory, considerably modified and extended, has been extensively applied to cognitive phenomena by Sperber and Wilson (1995) as relevance theory. Grice's theory has also been widely used by computational linguists who need a pragmatic component in their models of communication. From this community, there comes some criticism that the theory is not computable. That is, researchers argue that the maxims cannot be made sufficiently explicit or tractable to underpin actual conversation. Some of the artificial intelligence literature on agents has criticized the idea that conversation is inevitably co-operative (Castelfranchi 1992). From the present point of view, Grice might have been quite content to have established that the issue is whether the theory can be computed in actual circumstances, and been happy to have extension made to fit more complex blends of co-operative and adversarial communication. He set out with adversaries who did not think that any generalizations could be made. Our investigations will suggest some directions for extending Grice's theory which might help with fitting some of the recalcitrant data.

5.4   Taking Grice into the laboratory

Grice's writings and those of linguists influenced by him became widely dispersed in the late 1970s. Some psychologists saw that Grice's theories might help to explain some of the apparent divergences of undergraduate reasoning from the normative deductive models provided by logic. Notably, Newstead (1989, 1995) conducted a number of groundbreaking studies which tried to explain undergraduates' reasoning performances on the basis of Grice's theory of interpretation.

Newstead's results uncovered a deeply problematical situation for the psychology of reasoning. Newstead's observations showed that indeed plenty of undergraduate subjects did make Gricean inferences of the kind illustrated above when their interpretations of single sentences were elicited. But when the same subjects reasoned about syllogisms, their reasoning was not congruent with their interpretation. Here was a yawning gap between interpretation and reasoning by the very same students minutes apart. It was this gap between interpretation and reasoning which initially engaged our interest in the empirical phenomena of naive logical intuitions. It turned out that the methods Newstead used are quite informative about psychologists' conceptualization of deductive reasoning. We first describe what Newstead did, and some of what he found, before describing our own empirical study.

The first thing that a psychologist needs in order to study interpretation is an instrument for measuring it. The instrument used here is usually referred to as the 'immediate inference task'. The subject is given a single premiss, and asked whether a candidate conclusion follows from it. A sample immediate inference question is the following:

Assume that *All A are B*. Does it follow that *All B are A*?

This question has subject and predicate reversed relative to the assumption, and we shall call such questions **out-of-place**. If the question had been **All A are B?** then it would have been an *in-place* question. Here we use 'abstract' material with As and Bs. Newstead systematically compared responses to this material with responses to so-called 'thematic' material where logically unrelated common nouns replace the letter variables. Little difference in students' responses in this task emerges from the comparison. In the next chapter we return to the issue of form and content. Our experiments here used formal As and Bs.

In the psychological terminology, immediate inferences contrast with extended inferences such as syllogisms themselves where more than one premiss has to be combined, or a sequence of intermediate inferences is involved. From the point of view of a particular logical system (say, a natural deduction system), there might be intermediate steps in a proof of what psychologists call an immediate inference and, conversely, it could be that a multi-premiss inference is logically immediate (a single application of *modus ponens* is an example).

The immediate inference task is supposed to collect intuitions of logical consequence. However, there is a twist to the way that Newstead collected subjects' logical intuitions. Told to assume that the premiss, for example, *All A are B* was true, and asked, for example, *Are all B A?*, the subjects had to answer the question: 'Is the conclusion sentence definitely true? Or else false?'. Subjects had to respond either 'true' or 'false' Newstead 1995, (p. 652). Unfortunately, this is not the question that needs to be asked to tap subjects' notions of logical validity, though it says something interesting about psychologists' understanding of validity that this paper is published in a prestigious peer reviewed and prestigious journal. The difference between validity and truth is at the very foundation of what logic, and learning it, are about.

Faced with this question, a subject with perfect 'competence theory' logical intuitions would have to answer, 'Neither of the above', but Newstead's subjects were not offered this choice. Crucially, subjects could not register a judgement of **logical independence**, which is the relation between the two example statements in our question, i.e. the truth of the conclusion is independent of the truth of the premiss. As we shall see, it is certain that many of the subjects also lacked this explicit concept of logical independence, but the fact that the experimenter did also is a warning against the all too common dismissive reaction that subjects are simply irrational, unco-operative, stupid, or malevolent. It also serves to remind us that, before logic class, subjects generally lack a vocabulary for distinguishing the many different relations that may hold between assumptions and conclusions, and that when psychologists use the expression 'follows logically' in their instructions (as they often do), they should not expect these words to connect with their technical meaning. Without instructions to the contrary, subjects may quite reasonably construe our questions as questions about whether the truth of what they have been told to assume makes the truth of what they have been told to question *more likely*. This inductive question is a perfectly good construal of the question. Merely putting in the word 'logically' is not going to differentiate it. The immediate inferences of intelligent alert subjects (and experimenters) are a substantive topic.

Newstead also used a graphical task for eliciting logical intuitions. He presented a sentence together with a diagram of the five possible topological relations between two circles A and B (Fig. 4.2) and asked 'Which of these five diagrams makes the statement true?' Subjects were explicitly told that they could choose more than one of the five. This is a well-posed question, at least given the unproblematical semantics intended for the diagrams. In logical terms, it asks which of the diagrams are *models* of the sentence. The 'competence theory' answers are, of course, the ones shown in Fig. 4.2.

Newstead asked both sentential and diagrammatic questions of all of the four syllogistic premisses. Thus there are 32 sentential questions (four premisses by eight possible conclusions), and each should have three possible answers (yes, the conclusion follows; yes, its negation follows; no, it is logically independent). There are four graphical questions (the four possible premisses) each with 2^5 possible answers (all combinations of choosing, or not choosing, five diagrams).

Newstead observes that the sententially and graphically collected intuitions do not correspond. They are logically quite different questions, so this is hardly surprising. It is true that it is possible to derive judgements of validity from the graphical judgements of modelhood—a valid inference is one in which the conclusion is true under all interpretations (assignments) that make the premiss(es) true. Therefore if all the subjects' choices of diagram for the potential conclusion are also choices for the premiss, then the subject is indirectly claiming that the former follows validly from the latter. But transforming graphical judgements of modelhood into judgements of valid inference relations between sentences is a non-trivial recombination of the data which Newstead did not attempt in order to compare graphical with sentential judgements—or the part of them that is comparable. Again, this transformation would not bring perfect 'competence' order to the data because it is quite apparent that the subjects did not have an explicit grasp of these interrelations any more than the experimenter, but this is the logic of the situation.

Finally, Newstead collected syllogism solution data from the same group of subjects and looked at correspondences between their immediate inference judgements and their extended reasoning performance. He looked at subjects who made Gricean interpretations (say, inferring from *Some A are B* that *Some A are not B*) and checked what they then did faced with a syllogism such as *Some A are B. All C are B.* If such a subject were to add the premiss *Some A are not B* to this syllogism on Gricean grounds, then they might well conclude that *Some C are not A*. However, they did not, or did not more often than subjects who did not make the Gricean interpretation. Newstead's conclusion was that subjects' interpretation of quantifiers, as measured by the immediate inference task, does not indicate the interpretation with which they reason when faced with extended inference tasks. His explanation is that the extended inference task leads them to bring into play a quite separate set of procedures—namely mental models.

This conclusion would be alarming, if warranted. It would be alarming because it would mean that there was no connection between subjects' immediate and extended inferences. It is all very well saying that mental models theory cuts in when subjects are asked to reason, but what are they doing if not reasoning when asked to make judgements of immediate inference? Here is a another challenge for those who believe that logical concepts are an essential basis for a psychology of reasoning. It is a challenge that takes us into some old issues in reasoning, such as the origin of fallacies (e.g. the illicit conversion of the conditional), and some new ones (e.g. the status of Grice's theories as treatments of empirical observations of behaviour). Time to put Grice into a white coat. We made a study of the naive logical intuitions of Edinburgh first-year undergraduates' (Stenning *et al.* 1995b), simply re-running the first part of Newstead's experiment with modified questions, for example:

Assume that *All A are B*. Does it follow that *All B are A*? Or does it follow that *It's not the case that all A are B*? Or does neither conclusion follow? (Choose just one option!)

We concentrate here on the sentential answers. The diagrammatic answers are interesting in themselves. Many subjects, just as Newstead had found, showed a strong tendency to choose a single diagram for each assumption, and that was usually the diagram which was used in our extended Euler system (though without the cross annotation). But the diagrammatic responses are a story for which we should not delay here.

How can these data be analysed? Certainly there was no expectation that putting the question right was suddenly going to turn all the subjects into 'competence model' performers in this task. Sure enough, a cursory check indicated that there were lots of divergences. But these are rich data. There are 32 questions each with three possible answers, and so there are 3^{32} possible responses—a fair amount of room for variation. How to search this haystack?

This is a good example of the need for exploratory observation in psychology. The conventional approach is to choose a hypothesis (preferably before running the experiment) and then calculate the probability that we should reject the 'null hypothesis' in favour of our chosen one. Hypothesis: *Syllogisms that allow implicatures will be solved as if those implicatures were added to the premises.*

Nothing could be much further from the way that any other science is conducted. As Newell (1973) pointed out so eloquently, playing twenty questions with nature is a fool's game. Testing hypotheses is fine as long as we have a well-developed body of theory and observation that give us criteria for evaluating which hypotheses are worth testing, how our tests might generalize, and how to operationalize the concepts that we need to express our hypothesis. We beg the reader's patience in recounting some of the narrative of how our explorations went. We believe they have some methodological morals for the place of experimentation in cognitive research.

Our study is typical of where psychological investigations should begin. It is a fishing expedition. 'I wonder what first year undergraduates' naive logical intuitions are like?' This seems like a good scientific question. Of course, like all explorers, we set out with a conceptual system–to have left it at home would have been both unhelpful and impossible, if only because, like all conceptual systems, some of ours was explicit, and some of it implicit. Because we were engaged in a fishing expedition what we caught was partly determined by our tackle. Therefore we did have to be on the lookout for the restrictions in our conceptual system of which we were unaware. Our expedition began with a period of looking at the data for patterns which were striking—striking to our naive conceptualizations.

The focus of the investigation rapidly became the students' grasp of the concept of logical independence—just what was missing from the way the questions were originally posed. The key initial observation was that there was a substantial group of students (about 20 per cent of the 120) who would nearly always make a judgement of logical independence when asked a question which involved inversion of the subject-predicate structure between premiss and conclusion, such as 'Assume Some A are B. Does it follow that Some B are A?' These 20 per cent of subjects would reject this conclusion (and its negation) regarding the two sentences as logically independent. Our initial observation was that for this group of students, it did not matter much which quantifier was in the premiss, or which in the conclusion. For the questions where they should have said that the conclusion was true, or should have said that it was false, they would answer that neither the conclusion nor its negation followed. In all, there are eight questions which invert subject and predicate, for which the right answer is that the conclusion follows, or its negation follows; and eight where neither follows because premiss and conclusion are logically independent (Table 5.1).

Now come the health warnings about fishing expeditions. Several questions must continually be kept in mind. First and most obviously, there are the questions as to whether interesting patterns are merely random distributions of observations, or whether they are 'real' phenomena. Are we just staring at the waves and hallucinating? But less obviously, and probably more importantly, there are other questions. Are the phenomena we find interesting? What other phenomena have we not seen? What other phenomena *should* we have looked for?

We take these latter less-asked questions first. The first thing to bear in mind is that there is always the possibility that there are other patterns we have not found—we have done our best with the conceptual tools at hand. And there are opportunity costs of looking. Of more concern are questions about what else we should have looked for? If there are competing explanations of phenomena which involve searching in other parts of the data, or searching it in other ways, then we had better investigate those alternatives. But more often than not, psychology is not at the stage where there are lots of competing alternative explanations. Indeed, we have seen at least one case where apparent alternatives are in fact indistinguishable. With regard to describing naive logical intuitions, no one has done the preliminary trawling to find the phenomena which are in need of explanation.

For example, readers will already have noted that logical independence was important in our theoretical scheme before we went fishing. We inherited it from our logical background. If it had not been salient, we probably would not have noticed that Newstead's question precluded him finding out about it. And sure enough, a phenomenon focused on logical independence is what we first found in the data. We make no apologies. It is for the reader to judge at the end of the chapter whether we found any more than we first knew.

But what of the question about randomness and reality? This is the question that always gets most of the attention. In practice it is often not nearly so burdensome as it is made out to be. Figure 5.1 shows the number of subjects responding to N questions that reverse the premiss subject and predicate, with the answer 'Neither conclusion follows', when this is incorrect. That is to say, the question should receive the answer 'Yes, the conclusion follows' or the answer 'No, its negation follows', but these subjects wrongly believe that neither conclusion can be drawn. This graph is striking! One does not need any elaborate statistical tests to realize that something non-random is afoot, though such tests are easy enough to provide.

What is so striking about this graphic? There are eight questions (of the 32) which

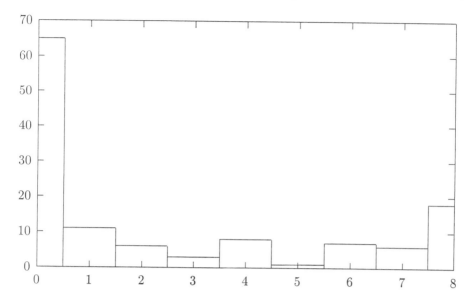

Fig. 5.1 The number of subjects responding to N out of eight questions that reverse subject and predicate with the answer 'Neither conclusion follows', when this is incorrect.

constitute opportunities to make this kind of 'error', i.e. error according to the logical competence model. So the possible scores for a subject range from 0 to 8. Repeated binary judgement errors usually show almost the complement of this distribution. We might expect a roughly normal distribution of errors—rather few people making very few or very many errors, and rather many people make a middling number of errors. Here we see the two most frequent responses being to make no errors or all errors.

However, none of these statistical surprises would make the pattern shown in Fig. 5.1 in the least bit interesting if there were no interpretation of what it meant. We do not need some complete, neat, and all-encompassing interpretation, but we need something that relates the observation to the major conceptual issues of interest. As we shall see, this histogram takes us rapidly into central issues in the investigation of subjects' naive logical intuitions. But first let us look further at what it constitutes, and see where else it leads us in the data.

Table 5.1 shows the 32 questions of the immediate inference questionnaire classified into those in which the subject/predicate structure of the premiss and conclusion are the same and those in which the structure is reversed; and into those in which the candidate conclusion or its negation is entailed by the premiss and those where premiss and conclusion are logically independent. The eight questions in the bottom right quadrant are the ones which have reversed subject-predicate and for which the logically correct answer is 'independent'. These are the questions generating the data plotted in Fig. 5.1. The questions eliciting responses classified as Gricean implicatures by Newstead fall in the top right quadrant, although Newstead initially only used two of them.

One question which follows naturally from the observation of this curious pattern of responding to questions about logically independent propositions is whether responses to

Table 5.1 All candidate 'immediate' inferences classified into those in which the subject-predicate structure of the premiss and conclusion are the same (AB,AB), and those in which the structure is reversed (AB,BA); and into those in which the candidate conclusion or its negation is entailed by the premiss, and those where premiss and conclusion are logically independent[18]

Inference structure	Logically dependent			Logically independent	
	Premiss	**Conclusion**	**Correct**	**Premiss**	**Conclusion**
	All A are B	All A are B	T		
	All A are B	Some A are B	T		
	All A are B	No A are B	F		
	All A are B	Some A are not B	F		
	Some A are B	Some A are B	T	Some A are B	All A are B
AB, AB	Some A are B	No A are B	F	Some A are B	Some A are not B
	No A are B	All A are B	F		
	No A are B	Some A are B	F		
	No A are B	No A are B	T		
	No A are B	Some A are not B	T		
	Some A are not B	All A are B	F	Some A are not B	Some A are B
	Some A are not B	Some A are not B	T	Some A are not B	No A are B
	All A are B	Some B are A	T	All A are B	All B are A
	All A are B	No B are A	F	All A are B	Some B are not A
	Some A are B	Some B are A	T	Some A are B	All B are A
	Some A are B	No B are A	F	Some A are B	Some B are not A
	No A are B	All B are A	F		
AB, BA	No A are B	Some B are A	F		
	No A are B	No B are A	T		
	No A are B	Some B are not A	T		
				Some A are not B	All B are A
				Some A are not B	Some B are A
				Some A are not B	No B are A
				Some A are not B	Some B are not A

[18]T, the conclusion follows; F, the negation of the conclusion follows.

questions about logically related propositions with reversed subject predicate structures (the bottom left quadrant) show equally bimodal distributions? Figure 5.2 shows the frequency of N responses of either T or F to questions which should be answered 'independent'. There is much less tendency for subjects to cluster at the extremes. But certainly the distribution is nothing like a normal distribution.

Both these population density distributions are remarkable as distributions. When we consider their content they become even more remarkable. First, there are some logical intuitions amongst these sets which are highly familiar from the literature on human reasoning. *All A are B so All B are A* is the fallacy of illicit conversion, by far the most observed fallacy in this literature (see reference to Chapman and Chapman (1959) in Chapter 4). Often observed, but little explained. Then there are intuitions which are

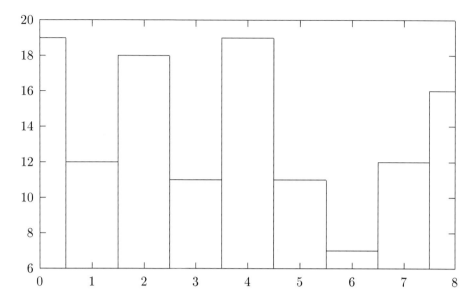

Fig. 5.2 Frequencies of N out of eight responses of either T or F to out-of-place questions which should be answered 'independent'

remarquable because they have never been reported in the literature: the commonness of the judgement that *Some A are B* is logically independent of *Some B are A* is perhaps the simplest one. A logically sophisticated audience quite often responds to this latter intuition with disbelief—'the students must have been filling out the questionnaire at random!'

But whatever is going on, randomness is not it. The clustering of students at the ends of the first histogram shows quite clearly that the tendency to respond one way to one question is highly correlated with tendencies on the other questions. The relevant questions are scattered about the questionnaire and not readily identified by any surface feature. And there are more complex correlations.

An obvious question is: What is the relation between the two histograms? What does a student who gets all the independence cases wrong do on the logical dependence cases, and vice versa? Note that it is *logically* possible to get everything wrong—to judge all the independent cases dependent and all the dependent ones independent. But the answer is that there is some tendency for the two groups to be disjoint. If they illicitly convert, then they do not fail to infer *Some B are A* from *Some A are B*. And if they do fail to make this inference, then they are far less likely to illicitly convert.

This throws some interesting if perhaps rather worrying light on the fallacies. These tendencies are rather independent of particular quantifiers, and that means that, for a good many students, their success at avoiding illicit conversion may not be due to logical insight. Rather, it may be due to a tendency to reject *any* inference which reverses subject and predicate. Symmetrically, answering correctly that *Some A are B* and *Some B are A* are logically related may be due to believing that there is such a relation between *any* two propositions that have undergone predicate reversal.

To reassure ourselves that subject/predicate structure is really so important, we should also consider what happens in the two top quadrants of Table 5.1. Are the tendencies to infer, or to refuse to infer, just as strong when subject and predicate are not reversed? Perhaps we are looking at general temperamental tendencies toward risky or safe inference making.

Again, the patterns are distinctive. There are very few subjects who respond 'independent' to immediate inference questions where subject and predicate structure remains unchanged and they should draw an inference (the top left quadrant). There are some who make these inferences when they should not (the top right quadrant). Some of these last are the 'Gricean' implicatures with which we opened this chapter. The tendency to draw these Gricean inferences is slightly positively correlated with the tendency to draw the illicit inferences when subject and predicate are reversed. But there are plenty of students who respond 'independent' whenever subject and predicate are reversed, but illicitly draw inferences when they remain in place. These tendencies are not temperamentally global caution and riskiness in decision-making—they are specific to the subject-predicate structure of the question.

Note that failures to infer *Some A are B* from *Some B are A* (and other such judgements that logically related propositions are independent) have received barely any attention in the literature. Apart from the lack of attention to validity and logical independence, there is an obvious reason. Fallacies are sins of commission. Teachers hear and see students committing errors. Logic teachers since Aristotle have observed the attractions of illicit conversion for their students. Grice's anecdotal data were observations of fallacies of commission. But the failure to convert the existential statement is a sin of omission, and omissions are silent and invisible. A student may, as a result of failing to draw an inference, fail to find a proof, but there are always so many possible reasons for that failure, that only systematic elicitation of intuitions is likely to unearth these subtle but no less logically important errors. There are good reasons why sins of omission are not detected until we get into the laboratory.

How can we visualize the patterns in this complex dataset? There are two kinds of question (subject-predicate in-place and subject-predicate out-of-place), and two kinds of error (making an inference where there is logical independence; and failing to make an inference where there is logical dependence). For mnemonic convenience we shall call the former kind of error one of **rashness** and the latter one of **hesitancy**, though we should remember that these are *not* personality or general decision traits. Therefore there are four dimensions on which we can score subjects' performance. Scores will range from zero to the maximum number of opportunities for each kind of error (four in one case, eight in two cases, and twelve in the last (see Table 5.1)). As it turns out, extremely few subjects are hesitant on in-place questions, and so we are conveniently left with three dimensions to visualize. Figure 5.3 shows the first set of immediate inference data we collected laid out in this way.

This visualization reveals several features, such as the negative correlation between being rash on out-of-place questions and being hesitant on them, and the positive correlation between being rash on in-place and on out-of-place questions. There are also more complex contingencies: students are rarely rash-in-place without making one or both of the other possible errors as well; and they are somewhat rarely rash-out-of-place and hesitant-out-of-place without also being rash-in-place. Again, the default model in which the three errors are independent of each other would yield an extremely different

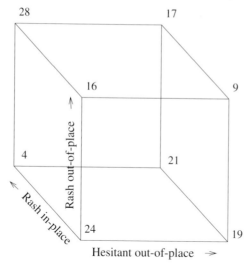

Fig. 5.3 Frequencies of immediate inference errors. Each error dimension has been discretized to force each subject to one of the cube corners.

kind of distribution.

The conclusion that is perhaps so obvious that we might forget to draw it, is that simply classifying students as prone or not prone to Gricean errors or not would be to look at one exposed face of this ice-cube while the rest remained submerged. Grice pointed out a critical axis of divergence between students' naive logical intuitions and the competence model's valid inferences. But he was not engaged in describing students' intuitions. When we explore we find that there are several *kinds* of student defined by different patterns of intuitions.

Why should subject/predicate structure be such a driving force? And is it a driving force in extended reasoning as well as interpretation? Or is it just something invoked by superficial responses to questions about pairs of sentences? We now look at extended reasoning before coming back to the question about the reason for the dominance of subject-predicate structure in these data.

5.5 And how do they reason about syllogisms?

To investigate how these patterns of interpretation influence extended reasoning, we ran further studies (Stenning *et al.* 1996; Stenning and Cox submitted). After filling out a similar questionnaire about quantifier interpretations, students were given the full set of syllogisms and asked to draw valid conclusions, or to respond that there were none. The data from this study reveals that indeed the individual differences in interpretation observed do have reflections in the patterns of subsequent student reasoning. Newstead's findings of disconnection are the result of failing to focus on logical independence, and, it turns out, on having too simple an operationalization of 'Gricean implicature'.

Interestingly, if we just look at overall accuracy, the correlations between each of the three individual difference dimensions and overall reasoning accuracy are weak or nonexistent. Subjects who are rash on in-place questions are slightly less accurate reasoners, but hesitant students are no more or less accurate in their reasoning than non-hesitant subjects. However, the mistakes of rash-in-place subjects are concentrated in their responses to NVC problems. That is, students rash on in-place questions (making Gricean implicatures) make more invalid inferences to problems without valid conclusions.[19] Students hesitant on out-of-place questions make fewer of these errors. The two groups are not so distinct in their responses to problems with valid conclusions.

Once we measure interpretation in an insightful way focused on students' intuitions of logical independence as they interact with subject/predicate organization, and once we measure reasoning accuracy in a way which distinguishes errors of omission and commission, we immediately find correspondences between students' intuitions and their reasoning. Students who respond in a Gricean way to a whole subset of eligible immediate inference questions also over-infer more than their colleagues when solving syllogisms. But rashness is something more than this narrow Gricean tendency defined in terms of a couple of patterns of implicature.

Newstead draws the quite correct conclusion from his data that the specific Gricean implicatures he selects for attention do not predict specific invalid conclusions based on their implicatures. But there are many reasons why this might be. The students who make these 'errors' also make a host of other interpretation errors, relative to the competence model, and may be making these responses for a variety of reasons. In fact this raises the question of exactly which errors should be considered as 'Gricean' implicatures. Suppose we start from the paradigm case of *Some A are B* generating the conversational implicature that *Some A are not B* (one of the cases that Newstead uses to define implicature), then why should we not take *Some A are B* as generating the implicature that *Some B are not A*? Or *All A are B* generating the implicature that *Some B are not A*? Why should implicature respect subject-predicate structure?

The point is that if we take a simple logical interpretation of these statements and apply Grice's theory of informativeness, then we cannot resist these extra implicatures of subject-predicate reversed propositions. Grice's theory is simply mute on these implicatures, and we shall see directly what is missing when we come to ask what subject-predicate organization reflects in natural language. The inference to be drawn here for psychological interpretation of Newstead's data is that it is not reasonable to define 'Gricean' interpreters by fiat as all and only people who respond in a particular way to two particular inferences. The operationalization is inadequate. If students draw a broad pattern of implicatures for roughly reasons related to the ones Grice suggests, we have to assess them across the broad pattern of their responses, and the broad pattern of their subsequent reasoning. That is what our more descriptive approach is designed to do.

What is the basis of these traits of rashness, and of hesitancy on out-of-place questions? Hesitancy is just as much an error as rashness, yet hesitancy is associated with *good* performance, especially on a difficult class of reasoning problems—no valid conclusion problems. This is reminiscent of the contrast between styles and abilities noted in Chapter 3 and again in Chapter 4 when we discussed alternative approaches to individual differences. Can we say any more about the basis of hesitancy? Hesitancy is particularly

---

[19] It is perhaps worth adding the reminder that these are operationalized as 'Gricean' errors. We do not, of course, know whether students make them for the reasons in Grice's theory.

related to subject-predicate reversal. Remember, there are virtually no subjects who are hesitant on in-place questions. Why should that be?

Apart from reasoning accuracy, syllogism data have often been analysed for what are called 'figural effects'—tendencies to impose certain subject-predicate organizations on conclusions as a function of the figure of the premises (as noted in Chapter 4). So, for example, the syllogism *Some A are B. All B are C* much more often elicits the conclusion *Some A are C* than it does the equally valid *Some C are A*. By the same token, *All B are A. Some C are B* much more often elicits the conclusion *Some C are A* than it does the equally valid *Some A are C*. One can summarize these effects by saying that syllogisms in the first two figures, where the middle term is subject in one premise and predicate in the other, tend to elicit conclusions which *preserve the subject-predicate status of the A and C terms*. In the other two figures, both end terms are of the same grammatical status and so we cannot observe this tendency. These effects are not plausibly interpreted as simply effects of grammatical tidying after inference. Invalid conclusions show just as strong if not stronger figural effects. Syllogisms with only counter-figural valid conclusions are harder to solve and are generally responded to as having no valid conclusions. The grammatical organization of problems has real effects on the processes of reasoning.

Figural effects appear to be an obvious area in which to look for patterns of reasoning behaviour related to the tendencies for interpretation that we have seen to be linked to subject-predicate organization. Statistical models of the figural effect data show quite clearly that students' patterns of quantifier interpretation have reflections in their reasoning processes. Students who are hesitant on out-of-place questions are more affected by premiss order (they have a greater tendency to draw *AC* conclusions overall). But the most interesting effects are interactions between rashness-in-place and hesitancy out-of-place with the quantifiers *no* and *some _ not* respectively, and with the grammatical organization of premises.

Hesitant subjects are particularly influenced by the positioning of the quantifier *no* in the premises and by the differences between Figures 1 and 2. They have a generally greater tendency to conclude *CA* when there is a single *no* quantifier and it is in the second premiss, but when the problem is in Figure 1 with *no* in the same position, they have a strong opposite tendency to conclude *AC*. Rash-in-place subjects show a similar pattern but with the quantifier *some _ not*. They have a generally greater tendency to conclude *CA* when there is a single *some _ not* quantifier and it is in the second premiss, but when the problem is in Figure 1 with *some _ not* in the same position, they have a strong opposite tendency to conclude *AC*. Finally, subjects rash on-out-of-place questions show a tendency to conclude *AC* when *no* is in the first premiss.

These tendencies are sufficiently strong that examination of the data of the rash-in-place students who are not hesitant reveals that they show little figural effect if any, i.e. their *AC* conclusion proportion in Figure 1 is barely higher than in Figure 2. Despite the prominence that this effect achieves in the literature, and despite the use of supposedly universal features of the architecture of human working memory to explain the effect (namely FIFO memory as discussed in Chapter 4), there is a substantial subgroup of students who barely show the effect.

Explaining why the differences should revolve around the negative quantifiers and take this form lead us into some further logical insights about the syllogism. It turns out that *no* has the peculiar feature as a quantifier that whenever its logic determines an obligatory grammatical organization for a problem's conclusion, the end-term of the *no* premiss always goes in predicate position. There is no such logical generalization for any other quantifier. In general, hesitant subjects seem to comply with this regularity better than other subjects when *no* is in the second premiss, but this compliance is overridden when grammar goes against it in Figure 1. In this case, their reasoning, like their interpretation, is particularly driven by subject-predicate organization.

Why should rash-in-place subjects show a special reaction to *some _ not*? This has to be interpreted against the background of another logical generalization namely that **source** premisses[20] can always contribute subjects of conclusions, and existential premisses are always the source premisses of any valid conclusions. There is also a tendency to place negative information in predicate position. In general, these two tendencies interact so that the existential quantifier's premiss contributes subject terms, and with rash-in-place subjects, when *some _ not* is in the second premiss, the existential wins over the negative effect more than with other subjects, leading to even more *CA* responses. But when this configuration appears in Figure 1, grammar appears to lead to the effect of negation becoming uppermost, leading to *AC* responses.

Thus the negative quantifiers are each distinctive in their own ways for two different groups of subject. As was highlighted in our extension of Euler at the end of the last chapter, although *no* is logically symmetrical, when it is formulated linguistically, it has to be given one or another linguistic form. Hesitant subjects, who are more susceptible to linguistic form, comply less with the generalization that *no* end terms become predicates of conclusions, except where the strong grammatical organization of Figure 1 aligns with the tendency.

Some _ not has an ambiguous life—it can be thought of either as an existential assertion of a negative property, or as a universal denial of a property of the reference set (cf. the definition of *distribution* in the Sieve). With rash-in-place subjects, the 'referential' interpretation prevails, generally leading to treatment of the *some _ not* premiss as source of the subject term. Although all subjects are somewhat affected by the grammatical difference between Figures 1 and 2, rash-in-place subjects are less affected than hesitant ones. Thus the fact that when *some _ not* occurs in the second premiss of Figure 1, the rash-in-place subjects respond *AC* is perhaps an indication that the strong grammatical organization of Figure 1 induces the universal-denial perspective and the negative-at-the-end effect then produces this island of grammatical sensitivity. Notice that in the rash-in-place students, Figure 1 with *some _ not* in the second premiss produces more *invalid* responses; in hesitant subjects Figure 1 with *no* produces more *valid* responses.

Therefore students' interpretations of quantifiers can be seen to influence their reasoning with syllogisms, and the influences are generally consonant with what we might expect. The details of those influences provide leads as to how to develop fuller explanations of the basis of the interpretation traits. There is much work to do, but at least we have a bridgehead for attacking the threatened gap between interpretation and reasoning. By focusing on logical independence (by asking the subjects the appropriate questions, and analysing the results with regard to the 'third category') and by not jumping too quickly to a narrow operationalization of Grice's theory, a cognitive account is restored.

---

[20] Source premisses contribute the crosses which establish conclusions in the Euler system. They are what entails the existence of necessary types.

But above all, what our kidnapping of Grice into the laboratory shows, is that there are several quite distinct patterns of quantifier interpretation which are not sensibly understood as simply ranged along a dimension of being more or less close to the competence model. Students come in different kinds, and will need to be understood as different kinds if we are to understand what happens when they learn elementary logic.

Like Victorian biologists faced with Petri dishes of obviously distinctively structured sea creatures, we are not yet in a good position to decide whether the kinds we are observing are different animals, or different stages of the same animal. Are these patterns of interpretation stages in learning about logical concepts? Or are they the different starting points of students with different styles of reasoning and learning? Our Victorian biologist forefathers often mistook stages of sea creatures for distinct species of sea creatures. We have the benefit of their experience. But either way, we do have strong evidence that what we are looking at are not merely different *sizes* of fish. Without venturing on fishing expeditions, one rarely learns much about fish.

5.6   A rational reconstruction of kinds of student

It is one thing to exhibit interactions between interpretation traits and reasoning traits experimentally, and another to provide a synoptic theory which can be intuitively grasped and used for exploring what has to be learned in logic class by different subgroups of student. How can we relate these details to an overall view? Can we take the logical competence model of reasoning seriously both as a theoretical specification of valid reasoning and as a useful educational aim, and simultaneously make sense of the data of naive student intuition?

Two underlying dimensions of students' models of communication seem most in need of our understanding. The first is the one with which we began this chapter—the contrast between co-operative and adversarial communication. Some students lack an explicit grasp of which model to apply to the syllogistic task. Rashness both on in-place and out-of place questions is evidence of this problem.

The second underlying dimension is that of grammatical organization. Hesitancy is a rather specific tendency to reject valid deductive inferences when they involve reversal of the subject predicate structure of premiss and conclusion. Why should subject and predicate play such a central role in organizing logical intuitions—even to the extent of almost obliterating the components of intuition attributable to the logical nature of particular quantifiers?

Chapter 2 explored what it meant for a representation to be part of a system of representations, and we noted that both sentences and diagrams expressed **propositions**. In fact we defined a proposition as a bearer of truth values that is *invariant* with regard to its representation. Whether represented by a diagram or by a sentence, the proposition that no *A* are *B* is the same proposition. Proposition is one of the fundamental abstract concepts which has to be acquired by students of elementary logic. What is it that we abstract from when we say that propositions are invariants? When students deny that *Some A are B* implies *Some B are A*, they respond to a difference which the question intends them to ignore. What is this difference?

Linguists' general term for the difference is **information packaging**, continuing the philosopher's metaphor of the kernel proposition wrapped in superficially different representational husks. The difference of husk between the diagram and the sentence is obvious. But why should natural languages provide alternative husks? The two sentences are designed for hearers with different background knowledge. Crudely, *Some A are B* is designed for a hearer who can identify *A*s, but does not know whether they have property *B*, whereas *Some B are A* is designed for a hearer who can identify *B*s but does not know whether they have property *A*. Another way of presenting this intuition is to say that the sentences are designed to answer different questions. 'What things are *B*?' seeks an answer such as 'Some A are B', while 'What things are *A*?' seeks an answer such as 'Some B are A'. The same proposition is packaged for different communicative destinations.

But with our sophisticated hindsight, it may still seem hard to understand why an intelligent undergraduate would have trouble seeing that when the one is true the other will also be true, and vice versa. Perhaps it may help the readers' empathy if we consider figurative interpretations. Consider the Lewis Carroll example *Some bankers are hyenas* and its relation to *Some hyenas are bankers*. Interpreted figuratively, as is most likely without further context, the first of these might be glossed as saying that bankers make their profits from others' adversity, but the second as making a perhaps rather unlikely assertion that hyenas are tidy-minded future-oriented bean-counting sort of animals much taken to delayed gratification.

Or to take a contemporary example, a renowned English libel lawyer defended his comedian client against tax avoidance charges by observing that 'Some accountants are comedians, but no comedians are accountants'. This might be glossed as saying that while some accountants are laughably incompetent, no comedians are financially well organized. Reversing the subject predicate order radically alters the interpretation that we find first for these sentences.

These examples do not show that logic is wrong about the logical relations between *Some A are B* and *Some B are A*, nor that the lawyer was logically challenged. In 'conversational' communication, much of our work is in continually finding new interpretations for speakers' utterances, not in operating on interpretations fixed within the span of an argument as deduction demands. Information packaging has profound effects on this process of finding interpretations. In 'conversation', finding a plausible interpretation of a predicate draws on its concept's typicality structure in a different way than finding a plausible interpretation for a subject term. Inverting subject and predicate with emotively laden terms leads saliently to different interpretations—choosing terms that invoke figurative readings merely exaggerates the effects, though the effects also apply to literal language. But logic is about operations within arguments *under a fixed interpretation*, whether figurative or literal, and students have to learn an explicit grasp of what counts as a fixed interpretation.

The stance toward meaning which elementary logic adopts is called *extensionalism*. This stance treats both terms and predicates as denoting sets of things. According to this stance, in a particular local domain, bankers are just a subset of all the things that there are in the domain, and hyenas are another subset of the domain (logically possibly the same subsets in some local domains). It is a great mistake to think that logic deals only with terms that have a fixed meaning (across arguments rather than within them). On the contrary, logic originated as a theory about shifting meanings and how to hold the still for the duration of an argument. 'Bankers' and 'hyenas' (along with all other natural language words) shift meanings from context to context. Sometimes they overlap or even coincide.

Learning about extensional interpretation in elementary logic class is about learning to recognize that in each of the pairs of contrasting glosses there is a proposition which both sentence and its reversal can share, even if the salient interpretation changes with subject-predicate reversal. The purpose of our examples here is to try to make plausible the predicament of the student who has not developed the ability to shift contextualizations of these various communications flexibly. Subject and predicate make a great deal of difference to the packaging of information even when they do not affect truth values.

But once we have settled on an extension for the words involved, then to assert that some bankers are hyenas is merely to assert that there is a non-empty intersection of these two subsets. From this stance it really is obvious that some hyenas are bankers will be true whenever some bankers are hyenas is true and false just when it is false, just as long as the interpretation of the terms within the argument is held constant. From this extensionalist stance, one might still acknowledge that the two sentences are best packaged for different audiences, but if so, it will not be a matter of logic. We shall have more to say about the problems of detecting prevarication and equivocation—concealed shifts of interpretation during argument—when we consider the skill of argument analysis in Chapter 6. Here the suggestion is that hesitant students have a tendency to refuse to infer conclusions with switched subjects and predicates because they realize that something is changed (the packaging) but fail to distinguish this from the proposition expressed.

Now we have arrived near the heart of this account of what has to be learned in learning elementary logic. The concept of **valid conclusion** is just defined as a proposition that is true *in all interpretations* which make the premisses true. Premiss and conclusion must be interpreted under the same assignments, but *all* such interpretations must be considered.

Along with validity go **premiss, conclusion, proof, consequence, assumption, follows from** and **proposition**. These are the tightly knit field of abstract concepts which define the subject matter of logic. They are all dependent on having an explicit grasp of the idea of *the range of possible interpretations*. Logic is about understanding the relation between this external semantic stance towards representation systems, and the patterns of inference within them. Remember the truth-table we introduced in Chapter 2 to give a concrete grasp of all possible interpretations in terms of all possible assignments to the variables—one in each column.

Subject and predicate play an important role in information packaging in 'conversation'. They cease to play the same role in logical deduction, though subject-predicate structure does not suddenly become logically irrelevant (*All A are B* continues to contrast logically with *All B are A*).[21] If we want to understand our students' problems more deeply, and to find a real explanation for why some students do not jettison the packaging in the quantifier interpretation experiments, then we need to understand the functioning of information packaging at a deeper level. The key to this understanding lies in the *social* relations of communication (Stenning 1996).

---

[21] Modern artificial logical languages actually replace the subject-predicate distinction with a function-argument distinction so that the terms *A* and *B* are both logical predicates, and the remaining logical asymmetry is captured by the conditional connective.

Grice defined conversation as a co-operative activity, and his explanation of how implicatures arise rests on this fundamental co-operative nature. As we stated above, co-operative communication involves the hearer trying to guess the intended model of the speaker's utterances, and using all the information available (shared but unstated assumptions, general probabilities, etc., etc.) to do so. What is this kind of communication to be contrasted with? Let us adopt 'proof' as a convenient name for the discourse which contrasts with 'conversation'.

Communicating a proof contains an essentially adversarial component. Imagine that the role of a hearer of a proof is to ensure that each of the speaker's steps in the proof follows *in all models* of the explicitly stated premises. If a step should turn out not to follow (i.e. a counter-example can be constructed in which the premises are all true and the conclusion false), then some repair is required. Either the 'intended model' of the discourse is narrower than that captured by the explicit assumptions, and the proof can be repaired by making the extra premises explicit and thus producing a valid proof of a more specialized conclusion, or the proof is in error in that there is a gap in the reasoning which must be filled.

It is clear from this specification of the discourse of proof that it actually involves an intricate interaction between co-operative and adversarial relations. Those engaged in the discourse must co-operate to agree a set of explicit assumptions, but must also operate adversarially to test that the conclusions follow under all interpretations of those assumptions. Actual communications of proof may involve a cycling between these phases with impasses in the proof leading to changes in the assumptions.

However complex the intertwinings of co-operative and adversarial elements of discourse may prove in actual communication, the underlying contrast remains a bold one. In co-operative communication, the speaker is telling the hearer something contingent. The participants behave as if the speaker has authority for the information and the hearer accepts that authority. In adversarial communication, the participants do not behave as if they agree such a partitioning of authority for information. They regard each other as of equal authority, and so the drawing of conclusions from premises does not rest on either participants' authority, but on the authority of the rules of inference.

Before proceeding, some caveats are in order. In these definitions, both 'co-operative' and 'adversarial' are being used in their previously used technical senses. Neither is intended to fix overall social attitudes. To help someone assess a proof one adopts a technically adversarial stance, but this does not have to be due to disagreement, still less being a social adversary.

Furthermore, both kinds of transition occur during what we would normally call conversation. We make deductions from what we take to be mutually held assumptions, and when we detect inconsistencies we have to repair them by making explicit where our assumptions implicitly diverge. But despite all these caveats, the underlying opposition between co-operative and adversarial transitions in discourse is absolutely central to understanding the two modes of communication. In the one, we try to find a model for 'new information'; in the other we try to check that the new statement is true in all the possible interpretations of the assumptions already made.

Grice's theory needs to be brought into line with this more articulated concept of communication. Grice's theory is predicated on what we have called the co-operative mode of expository communication—the kind of communication where someone is telling us 'new facts'. The maxim of quantity, for example, tells us to be informative, and this is easily understood in co-operative mode. The speaker will make statements which allow us to guess his or her intended model of the domain, thus narrowing down our range of uncertainty. For these facts to be informative they must, by definition, be logically *in*dependent of our existing assumptions and conclusions. But this definition of informativeness will not work for the discourse of proof. A deductive transition is valid just in case it is *un*informative in this sense of narrowing down object level possibilities. $P \rightarrow Q$ and P entail Q just because Q tells us nothing that the two premises together did not already tell us. Conclusions have to be logically *de*pendent on their premises.

This is not to say that a theory of informativeness of deductions cannot be developed. One place to begin is in terms of the guidance of proof. Not just any valid application of any old rule at any point in any proof is as informative as any other (in the sense of informativeness appropriate to proof). The informativeness of rule applications in proofs is informativeness that the step leads nearer to the proof goal. But this is a quite different notion of informativeness—a meta-level phenomenon relative to the object level informativeness of narrowing possibilities of the way the world is. At this meta-level of proof communication, the discourse of proof becomes just like the discourse of exposition. At each twist of the argument we learn something new about the direction of our journey from premises to conclusion. The proof is a story. At this meta-level, even the concept of information packaging is reintroduced, though not necessarily in terms of subject-predicate, more in terms of sequencing of statements. There are features of the layout of the proof which do not express propositional differences but which have effects on 'processors' of the proof (either human or machine) such that they make make the proof easier or harder to process. These matters are extensively studied in so-called 'logic programming'.

This starting point is not adequate for a full theory of the informativeness of deductions. Informativeness is ultimately about epistemic possibility, not logical possibility. A full theory is well beyond the present scope of this book. But the important point here is that to understand each other we need to know what kind of informativeness speakers believe their utterances have for their audiences. Grice's Maxim of Quantity can only be preserved for the discourse of 'proof' as opposed to the discourse of 'conversation' by realizing that its quantities have to be quantities of different stuff in different kinds of discourse.

Therefore our claim is that there is a fundamental distinction between two kinds of process in discourse—the co-operative and the adversarial. In real communication, these may be intricately entwined. The distinction depends on being able to enforce a further distinction between what is explicit in an argument and what is implicit in shared knowledge or belief. Adversarial communication enforces explicitness. Gaining an explicit grasp of these underlying distinctions and how to operate them is the topic of learning in elementary logic. Logic teaches the ability to make explicit what is implicit in knowledge of new domains, and in communication with parties who may be conceptually misaligned.

There are at least two ways that this theory could be applied to the data of students' logical intuitions. One would assume that students are well acquainted with the co-operative processes of communication. Their understanding of these processes is nevertheless implicit. On this view, learning logic is learning a new set of processes which constitute adversarial communication. What has to be learned is both an implicit grasp of this new mode, and an explicit grasp of both co-operative and adversarial modes. This might explain why students do make inferences consistent with implicatures. However, it does not go very far towards showing why students do have some grasp of when there is no valid conclusion (witness Fig. 4.17).

A contrasting view is that students already have an implicit grasp of adversarial communication just as they have an implicit grasp of co-operative communication, but that what has to be learned is to make both of these modes and their interrelations explicit. On this view, one needs to provide an account of when the adversarial model and when the co-operative model is engaged by a problem. This view can potentially make sense not only of students drawing implicatures in deductive tasks, but also of showing some quite sophisticated knowledge about when there are no conclusions.

We lean toward this second alternative. It seems rather unlikely that students lack implicit models of adversarial communication, but these models are probably only invoked by some kinds of social situation, and do not make explicit the distinction between assumption and derivation which logical argument requires. Kids are good at 'arguing', in the sense of disagreeing, from an early age. However, in doing so, they do not generally preserve a distinction between a set of mutually accepted premises and the derivation of conclusions from them. What they typically do is to bring whatever assumptions suit their cause, whether they are acceptable to the other party or not. They attempt to tell a story which has a different punchline; not to show that their conclusion follows from the adversary's agreed premises (adults of course do not necessarily give up this kind of argument, but do widen their repertoires to engage also in something more like proof). Even when Harris' (Leevers and Harris 2000) four-year-old subjects mentioned before can do syllogisms contextualised in fictional worlds, they probably cannot separate what they implicitly guess those worlds are like from what has been explicitly stated about them. See Stenning and Monaghan (2000) for some proposals about these two different ways of regarding logic learning.

It is instructive to compare this position that logic learning is a matter of differentiating discourses and gaining explicit control of the differences, with the comments made in Chapter 2 on the contrast between theory of mind and simulationist accounts of our reasoning about other minds. The present deductive tasks are much more demanding than the false-belief task's questions about what a character would believe in some context. Out of any particular communicative context students have to answer questions about the truth of some representation (the conclusion) in all situations in which certain other representations are true (the premises). Just as young children have to acquire the ability to answer false-belief task questions, our students have to learn to answer deductive questions in the abstract laboratory situation. Our account says that they do so by making explicit existing implicit grasps of the generalizations about the form of their native language, and that this can make a real difference to what reasoning they can subsequently do. This is a simulationist view. It sees learning as gradual making explicit of the contextual parameters previously encapsulated in a simulating 'black box'. On this view, the analogy to a theory of mind explanation would be to explain learning on the incorporation of logical theory into the mind. Positing such full-blown theories that have to be couched in expressive languages helps the theorist to too much, and fails to acknowledge that much of the learning is about how the theories operate in contexts.

If that's what Harris's four- or five-year-old syllogiser has, why is it not sufficient for elementary logic class? At least attempting to sharpen the difference between theory and simulation through the distinction between the direct and indirect representations involved in simulations and theories offers promise of deeper insight.

It also raises the possibility that there are different kinds of solution to the problems of understanding deduction (or understanding other minds, for that matter), and that these might lie at the bottom of the styles we have seen to differentiate students' learning. Some speculations about the social foundations of styles of reasoning are offered in Chapter 7.

What is distinctive about the adversarial communication of proof is that it drives its participants to make explicit all the relevant assumptions in their search for a set of premises on which they can agree. This in turn focuses on the representations involved whether language or diagram. This model of communication and the role of logic in it is developed in Chapter 7. In Chapter 6 we revisit Wittgenstein's argument about the concept of game, and some attempts to invoke implicit theories to explain what a child acquires when learning a new word. Something very like this theoretical move has also been made to explain word meaning, and we shall evoke a similar scepticism about full-blown theories being involved and argue instead for a foundation on affective structures.

The particular social arrangements of the classroom (and the rather closely related psychology laboratory), in which the teacher (experimenter) is a highly authoritative source of information, may play an important part in inducing the 'set' which we observe in psychological experiments towards treating deductions as expositions. Teaching students to argue with each other may be easier than teaching them to argue with the teacher, for these social reasons. The relations of authority between peers are more nearly symmetrical at the outset.

This train of thought suggests a resolution to the paradox of logic learning. What has to be learned is an explicit model of how two modes of discourse—the co-operative and the adversarial—fit together in communication. 'It's the discourse stupid!'. An example analysis of the GRE mercury problem from Chapter 3 in these terms is given in Chapter 6 by way of illustration.

Note that on this view of logic and what is involved in learning it, logic and its attendant skills should be most involved when the task is finding interpretations for new representations and languages, rather than when the task is doing extended reasoning within an established representation system. The minding of Ps and Qs that has to be learned is not so much minding the twiddling of Ps and Qs within a formalism, as the minding of the slithering of Ps and Qs as we search for a representation. This refocusing onto the skills of finding new interpretations may go some way to explaining why logic learning can play an important role in learning to learn.

5.7 Revisiting modalities

We began this book with a question about the effect of modalities of information presentation and we focused on information presentation in teaching and learning. Our observations of learning revealed robust differences between students in their responses to the modalities, and this revealed a need to characterise the basis of these differences.

The dominant finding in our empirical study of students' interpretation of quantifiers was again that there were robust differences in interpretation. This time there were more than two patterns of response, but again the different patterns appear to be broadly based—styles or models of interpretation to go alongside the styles of reasoning and learning invoked by different modalities of presentation.

An obvious question is whether these students' models of communication as revealed in their patterns of interpretation are related to students' responses to the modalities of teaching presentation. Are they merely different aspects of the same phenomenon? Are they conceptually different but empirically related phenomena? Or are they just more individual differences to go alongside the ever-growing battery of traits tested by different psychometric tests?

Unfortunately, we do not have immediate inference data for the Hyperproof students either before or after their courses. But the work on interpretation had started before the study of syllogism teaching, and we did have time to collect immediate inference data from those students before they received either graphical or sentential tutoring on the syllogism task. As described in Chapter 4, these students also did a GRE pre-test before the tutoring.

From these data it is possible to say that there definitely is some systematic relation between styles of interpretation and styles of learning from the modalities. Students who see *Some A are B* as independent of *Some B are A*, and, even more so, students who see *No A are B* as independent of *No B are A* tend to benefit from graphical tutoring on syllogisms, but less from sentential tutoring. What is more, these students are significantly *higher* scorers on GRE analytical problems. In other words, they would tend to fall into the group that benefit from Hyperproof diagrammatic teaching. It is the interpretation of the quantifier *No* which is most diagnostic of response to modalities of teaching, and we have just seen in Section 5.5 that it is the same quantifier that most characterises differences in figural effects in the syllogistic reasoning of hesitant students.

The fact that students hesitant about converting *some* and *no* are better at GRE analytical items is another example of the phenomenon we saw earlier of students making *more* errors on one task (giving certain logical intuitions) being better at another (no valid conclusion syllogisms). Again, making *more* of these errors of interpretation actually makes for *less* of a specific type of error in problem solving.

There is also some correlation between rashness and GRE performance, and the correlation is stronger on the analytical (constraint satisfaction) problems than on the 'logical' problems of argument analysis. But here, as we would expect, students who are rash on in-place questions are worse on GRE logical problems and very much worse at GRE analytical problems. If rashness indicates a failure of explicit grasp of the adversarial nature of problem solving this is what would be expected. This difference in GRE reasoning of rash students also means that they would tend to be over-represented in the group of students who benefit most from sentential teaching in Hyperproof (and the syllogism).

There is clearly some relation between interpretation, reasoning, and learning styles as affected by the modalities, even if we are at an early stage of understanding it. But why should this relation exist at all? Why should hesitancy at inferring logical relationships between subject-predicate inverted sentences predict better learning from diagrams? And

Logically symmetrical quantifiers---Q AB = Q BA

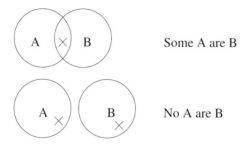

Some A are B

No A are B

Logically asymmetrical quantifiers---Q AB not = Q BA

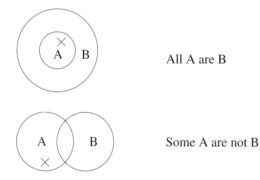

All A are B

Some A are not B

Fig. 5.4 Graphical symmetry mirrors logical symmetry and strips away information packaging.

why should rashness in drawing immediate inferences about quantifiers when subject and predicate structure is the same in premiss and conclusion perhaps be associated with learning better from sentential presentations? Speculating about mechanisms may help us to find stronger relations in the data.

An obvious comment about the benefits of diagrams for the hesitant is that diagrams of logically symmetrical quantifiers are graphically symmetrical. As is illustrated in Fig. 5.4, there is no graphical difference in status between subject and predicate in the diagram representing *Some A are B* and in the one representing *No A are B* (see Fig. 4.3). But there is graphical asymmetry in the diagrams representing the logically asymmetrical quantifiers *All A are B* and *Some A are not B*. In both diagrams, the cross appears in the subregion corresponding to the subject term of the sentence. Euler diagrams represent the critical feature of logical symmetry or lack of it. This is an example of the generalization observed in Chapter 2 that indirect systems offer the possibility of information packaging whereas direct ones do not.

Perhaps this feature of diagrams explains why tutoring with diagrams might aid hesitant students who are perhaps sensitized to the fact that the subject-predicate distinction plays some novel and distinctive role in the new 'game of deduction', but are in need of help in understanding how to differentiate just where subject-predicate remains relevant and just where it is mere packaging.

How are we to understand rashness in both its in-place and out-of-place guises? And why should rash students benefit more from linguistically oriented teaching than from diagrammatic? Rashness is first and foremost a failure to distinguish co-operative and adversarial modes of discourse, and to follow through the implications of this distinction. The confusion is between what we would sensibly infer from the utterances of a speaker whose co-operativeness and authority we accept, allowing whatever general knowledge we ourselves may have about likelihoods, on the one hand, and what we can logically infer without recourse to our knowledge of likelihoods from some speaker whom we do not assume to be either co-operative or authoritative, on the other. Two kinds of discourse have to be differentiated—two criteria of what legitimately 'follows from' what in a sequence of utterances.

The graphical procedures for using Euler diagrams do not map easily onto this new kind of discourse, and even when they are mapped, the mapping tends to diminish the prominence of the difference between the two kinds of discourse. This was the topic of the distinction between agglomerative and discursive uses of representations in Chapter 2. True, we can think of the first premiss (in the form of its diagram) arriving first; the next premiss next; the process of integrating them coming third; and the abstraction of a conclusion coming last. But this diagrammatic sequence does not correspond superficially to the sequence of events in either kind of linguistic discourse—exposition or proof.

In the sentential representation of proof, there is something that is prominently new. Citing the justification for each transition from statement to statement in the discourse is a highly distinctive feature of proof systems. It has no analogue in co-operative discourse. The only 'justification' for each new informative statement is that it is true (suitably informative, relevant to existing knowledge, etc., etc.). These are meta-justifications comparable to proof-guidance in deduction. If the greatest need of rash students is to develop a differentiated concept of the social relations in co-operative and adversarial discourse, then sentential teaching would emphasize this more than diagrammatic teaching by enforcing the giving of justifications.

At least that is a hypothesis that might guide further exploration of the relations between interpretation, reasoning, learning and modalities of presentation. Interestingly, it is a hypothesis which has a distinctively social dimension to it—a dimension that will be expanded in the next chapter on form and content in reasoning.

Before finishing with students' models of communication, it is perhaps worth noting a level of abstraction revealed by the current analysis at which logic shares a great deal with many other subjects taught at the end of secondary and the beginning of tertiary education.

Logic is just like physics and psychology (to take two poles of the university science curriculum) in that it works on pre-existing implicit knowledge which the student brings to the classroom. Without this pre-existing knowledge it is rather unlikely that anything could be taught, and even after theoretical insight is successfully gained, student remain dependent on their pre-course implicit habits for most of their transactions with the world (social or physical). We largely avoid bumping into things (either physical or social) through our implicit grasp of these topics even after theoretical training. The question as to what extent theoretical learning modifies real-world behaviour is an interesting one in all these fields.

In all three subjects, we learn a tight-knit field of abstract concepts and the skills required to operate with them. In fields of abstract concepts like logic, physics, and psychology, learning can only take place through learning what transformations leave which of the concepts invariant. We have discussed the invariance of propositions under transformations of information packaging. In physics, students must grasp *mass, volume, density,* etc. in terms of their variances and invariances under various physical transformations. Psychology also has its field of abstract concepts such as *stimulus, response, memory,* . . . . In all subjects, what makes these concepts abstract is that they cannot be learned by simple ostension. One cannot usefully point to masses to teach *mass* because every mass has a weight, a volume, a density, etc. One cannot learn *proposition* (or *validity, consequence, interpretation,* . . .) by pointing to propositions because every representation of a proposition has its packaging (see Stenning (1999*a*) for an extended discussion of these similarities).

Seen in this light, logic is both a special science, like the other special sciences in that it has a particular subject matter (the structure and functioning of representation systems), and universal, in that all thinking, reasoning, and communication are conducted with representations.

Chapter 2 set out a a semantic theory about the difference between diagrams and sentential languages. Chapter 3 produced some initial evidence that the theory's main distinction between direct and indirect representation played an important part in explaining how students learned to reason in elementary logic class. Students learned different strategies for reasoning according to whether they learned best with or without diagrams. Chapter 4 explored the equivalences and distinguishing features of systems for representing syllogisms, and then showed that again the directness or indirectness of representations used in teaching played the same role in differentiating students' learning styles evidenced in the same aptitude by treatment interaction. This chapter has presented evidence characterizing the variety of students' naive models of communication and relating them to the difficulties encountered by the various kinds of student in learning elementary logic. One part of the problem is differentiating co-operative and adversarial elements in communication and understanding how they interact; another is unwrapping the propositions of their native language from their information packaging. Again, direct and indirect representations support different aspects of these learning problems.

In the next chapter we turn to the problem of how formalisms are related to their contentful interpretations. Hyperproof provided fixed content for its relations and predicates. Our discussion of the syllogism in Chapters 4 and 5 has been satisfied with stopping analysis at abstract *A*s and *B*s. But any account of the role of learning formalisms on thinking and reasoning cannot be content without a treatment of the process of getting formalism to contact content.

The empirical work presented so far on the teaching of reasoning with diagrammatic and linguistic representations provides evidence that the interventions of teaching form *can* lead to improved skills of contentful reasoning. Analysis revealed some of the strategic mechanisms that underlie those improvements. Studying naive logical intuitions unearthed a variety of student starting points on the road to understanding and applying logical form.

But the main direction of research in the psychology of deductive reasoning, since the 1970s has been in the opposite direction. Observations of students' reasoning with statements of different content which apparently share the same form have been used as evidence that reasoning is not based on form but rather on content, and has led to the development of theories like mental models which propose to do away with logical accounts and replace them with supposed alternatives which are directly semantic and not formal. As we saw in Chapter 4, the psychological theories offered as alternatives turn out to be wholly formal themselves—reinventions of logics and their theorem-provers in disguise.

Work on Wason's selection task, which requires both conditional reasoning and reasoning about conditionals, has been the most important locus of this anti-logical argument. The conclusion has been that formal theories have little to contribute to understanding human reasoning. One might take the stance that form can have an impact on reasoning once one has learned logic, but that, prior to that, some other mechanisms were at play. But this would be utterly unsatisfactory. It would pose a problem about how learning forms could impact reasoning, and a problem about what on earth these 'other mechanisms' could be if not computational mechanisms working on forms. Time to see whether formal theory cannot guide better experiment and yield a better theory of how form contacts content.

6 Form and content: three illustrations

Logic is a theory that reasoning operates on *forms*. The two statements A and B have the same form but differ only in content. People are observed to reason quite differently from A than from B. Therefore, human reasoning does not operate on forms.

This syllogism has dominated the study of the psychology of reasoning for the last thirty years. The thesis of this chapter is that it is far too quick.

An account of the relations between form and content is the foundation of any cognitive theory because computation operates in virtue of interpreted form. Theory cannot be generative without resorting to form. But neither of these propositions mean that cognitive theory can be *only* formal. Cognitive theory must account for the relation between form and content in the very concrete sense that it must account for how content is encountered, formalized, operated on, and issues in contentful action. In developing computational models of behaviour there is no alternative to refining a theory of how form is accessed through content. The processes of interpretation are, as we saw in the last chapter, real mental process and they assign form to content. As Peacocke (1994) argues, this is as true for understanding and explaining computations of arithmetical functions by Turing machines as it is true of computational models of human communication and reasoning.

Understanding cognition as being as much about how representation systems are selected or constructed as about how reasoning goes on within them recasts the problem of how to model the imposition of form onto content into more tractable form. If reasoners are always situated somewhere in a space of possible systems, and the data that arrive can be interpreted as cues to whether the current system is appropriate, needs reinterpreting, or more radically replacing, then interactions between form and content are the most natural thing to expect.

Three diverse methods applied to three diverse topics will illustrate these advantages. First, we take Wason's (1968) 'selection task'—the lion's den for logic-based accounts of human reasoning—and meet the psychological objections to any role for formal theory head on. We shall show how semantic and pragmatic analysis of Wason's task using more adequate ideas of form and content can be used to explain why subjects encounter such difficulties in this task, and can make predictions suitable to guide the empirical investigation of 'content effects'.

Wason's selection task is one specific reasoning task which highlights one particular aspect of content, susceptible to a range of formal analyses. The selection task focuses on one particular linguistic form *if . . . then*, the conditional, and therefore makes the formal analyst's task more tractable, if not easy. But content is, by its very nature, omnipresent and unconfined to particular linguistic expressions or particular logical functions. Therefore our second area of investigation will be analogical reasoning. Analogical reasoning is normally taken to be at opposite ends of a dimension of rigour to deductive reasoning. Analogical reasoning is certainly thoroughly contentful, and not susceptible to formal analysis of one particular linguistic structure. Our approach will be to reconceptualize the relation between representation systems and analogies, and to show that our semantic distinction between directly and indirectly interpreted systems throws new light on the empirical evidence about the basis for human analogical capacities.

Our third area is the relation between logical semantics and word-meaning. Here is an obvious general meeting ground for form and content. We approach the topic through two arguments about lexical meaning: Lakoff's arguments for founding semantics on cognition; and a reappraisal of Wittgenstein's classical argument about the meaning of the word 'game'. Our purpose in both cases is to clarify the relation between psychology and semantics. Where some approaches would psychologize semantics, we propose that a multiple level theory of word meaning can treat logical semantics as a highly abstract sociological theory about fully contextualized communication, while assigning psychological theory the role of explaining how systems are implemented in minds.

In all three areas, we propose that logical semantics can be construed as a theory of both the domain dependence and the domain independence of human reasoning, and of the interactions between. Logical semantics is not a cognitive theory, but it is the only coherent conceptual framework that we have for conducting empirical studies of human reasoning, and on which a cognitive theory can be built.

6.1 Losing our shirts at cards

Wason's (1968) selection task, known as the **selection** task, is one of the main sources of evidence that turned psychologists against assigning logic any role in understanding human reasoning. In Wason's task, subjects are told that they will be shown four cards, and that these cards have letters on one side and numbers on the other. They are then given a conditional rule which they are told is about just the four cards, and are asked to turn over all and only the cards that they need to turn over in order to check that the rule is true. Many different rules have been used, and it is variation in the rules which has been the main focus of investigation in the paradigm. Wason's original rule was 'If there is a vowel on one side of a card, then there is an even number on the other'. Faced with this rule, and four cards with A, K, 4, and 7 on their visible faces, the commonest response of first year undergraduates is to choose A and 4. Yet a 7 with an A on the back is as surely a counter-example to the rule as is an A with a 7 on the back. In fact it is the same counter example. And whatever the 4 has on its back, it cannot be a counterexample. Thus students' choices appear to be at variance with the meaning of a simple English sentence. Only about 5 to 10 per cent of this population choose the A and 7 dictated by the competence model. It is this reliable observation of error in an apparently simple task that has rightly fuelled investigation.

Content effects in reasoning have been investigated by using different kinds of rules in this schematic task. The most reliable improvement (in the sense of increased choice of the 'false-consequent' (7 in this version) and decreased choice of the true antecedent (4 in this version)) has been observed with the use of rules which are laws—legal laws rather than scientific ones. For example, the cards might have the name of a drink on one side, and an age of the drink's drinker on the other; the rule would be 'If you drink alcoholic drinks, you must be over 18', and the task is to turn only those cards required to see if the drinkers comply with the law. Now, far more students select the cards with 'whisky' and '17', and far less select the card with '19'. These rules are called **deontic** rules as distinguished from Wason's original 'abstract' abstract rule. None of these three labels is particularly felicitous. Wason's rule is just about as concrete as it is possible to be since the letters and numbers actually appear on the cards rather than just referring to some unknown cases; the legal law is a very particular kind of deontic statement; and 'indicative' is technically a syntactic category of sentences which, when interpreted, can have either descriptive or deontic force. But since these are the terms of the field we shall, for the most part, stick with them. We shall use 'descriptive' to distinguish conditionals (usually indicative ones) which describe states of affairs, rather than stipulate deontically how affairs should be. The oddities of the field's terminology should be kept in mind because it is material at some points.

Therefore, the argument goes, the two rules (descriptive and deontic) have the same *logical form* (namely *if P then Q*) and most people reason wrongly with the first one, and correctly with the second one. Therefore content drives reasoning, not logical form. This is the chapter's epigrammatic syllogism.

Cosmides (1989) in particular has built a whole edifice of evolutionary psychology on this interpretation of findings that reasoning with deontic 'social contract' conditionals is achieved by innate encapsulated 'cheating-detector' modules which evolved in our Pleistocene ancestors under the selection pressures of social life. Cosmides does not specify much about the characteristics of cheating-detectors but we are to understand that they are contrasted with more general reasoning methods working over natural language conditionals. We return to this point. A number of other researchers have argued for reasoning mechanisms more general than cheating-detectors but nevertheless more contentful than logics. A good example is Cheng and Holyoak's (1985) proposal of pragmatic reasoning schemas.

The literature sees the main problem as explaining why the abstract task is so difficult. Stenning and van Lambalgen (2001) review the variety of explanations offered from the perspective of the semantics and pragmatics of rules and tasks. Much of the current discussion is derived from that paper. We shall focus here on the comparison of abstract and deontic tasks. What part do form and content play in determining reasoning in this task? Are the two rules 'If there's a vowel on one side, then there is an even number on the other' and 'If you drink alcoholic drinks, you must be over 18' (the A and the B of our syllogism) really of the same form? What account can we give of what subjects are doing in the selection task?

6.1.1 What form do the rules have?

First the semantics—we shall review some of the main relevant issues about the semantics of conditionals, and only then look at the applicable data. A semanticist's reply to the question as to whether A and B have the same form is always likely to be 'Well, yes and no'. Form is not an absolute concept. Descriptive and deontic conditionals share form with each other. In natural languages there are a host of other superficially different sentences which also express conditional relations both descriptive and deontic. For example, the universal quantifier is often another expression of logical implication; 'all cards have letters on one side and numbers on the other' is another conditional that occurs in the instructions to the task (we shall call this the background rule). At this first level of analysis, descriptive and deontic conditionals are of the same form—both conditionals. But statements are subject to analysis of further form. The fact that they need further analysis to capture the inferences we make from them is not difficult to see. The easiest way to illustrate is by asking the straightforward semantic question: What is the relationship between the rule and the cases (cards) with the two types of conditional?

With the legal law, and other deontic conditionals, the semantic situation is rather simple. People either break the law or comply with the law. Their drinking behaviour does not affect whether a law is in force or not. More especially, one person's drinking behaviour does not affect whether another person's drinking behaviour complies with the law, and from an epistemic point of view, turning a card to discover something about one person's compliance with the law has no impact on whether we need to turn any other cards to find out about others' compliance.

With descriptive conditionals, the situation is far more complex. The cases *do* affect whether the rule's description is true, and they do so in very complicated ways. In particular, if we turn one card which shows us that a universal rule is false of that case, then that act may change for us what other cards can tell us—namely it may mean that cards that would have previously been informative become uninformative because we may now know that the rule is false. We shall refer to this feature of the semantics of descriptive rules as the **contingency** of evidence from one turn, on evidence from other turns.

But indicatives are more complicated still in that their susceptibility to counter-example varies enormously, and one important factor in this variation is the backing for the rule. If the backing is a law of nature, then rules are typically highly resistant to falsifying instances. All ravens are black despite albino ravens, ravens' eggs (which are blue), newly hatched ravens (pink), punk ravens (various), ravens that have tangled with bleach, ravens viewed under polarized light, etc. In contrast, if the backing is highly contingent, as in the case of such happenstantial regularities as that all the coins in my pocket this morning are copper, then the rule is typically brittle to counter example—one gold sovereign and the statement is false (the example is Goodman's 1954). The subject in the abstract task is given no idea what the backing for the rule is, but this does not mean that the subject will not be influenced by implicit assumptions about backings.

It is rather unusual to utter 'if ... then' statements without any general backing. Notice that the example of the copper coins becomes rather unnatural if expressed with 'if' in cases where we imagine that I know this because I have inspected them all. 'If a coin is in my pocket this morning then it is copper' only sounds natural if I am asserting it on the basis of partial knowledge, usually some generalization. Perhaps British academics are so impoverished, or perhaps a hole lets all the smaller non-copper coins out. Although Wason's task explicitly says that the rule is only about the four cards, that does not mean that subjects do not imagine that its backing may be a generalization. The statement about the coins is only about the coins in my pocket this morning, but it may still be backed by a generalization about a population of coins. The nature of the backing and how much one's concern is the truth of the backing or the compliance of the particular cases, tends to be what determines brittleness or robustness to counter-example. This general issue about the domain of interpretation of the rule will return later.

Robustness to counter-example makes Wason's task hard to construe. If we interpret the conditional as robust to counter-examples, what should we do? Turn nothing, on the grounds that nothing could falsify? Turn all but K on the grounds that the number of exceptions might be relevant? There is a very strong presumption in the instructions that the task makes sense, and that some cards should be turned and others not. Wason simply assumed brittleness in fitting his assumed competence model. Yet most conditionals are robust to counter-examples to at least some degree. Rather few students do turn everything but K, but this may nevertheless be a source of confusion which interacts with other problems.

The material conditional (the one defined in propositional calculus in Chapter 2 and assumed by Wason in his interpretation of his evidence) is still different in other respects from scientific and everyday conditionals. The material conditional's peculiarity is that the mere absence of counter-examples is *sufficient* to establish the truth of the conditional. In a world where there are no boojums, the material interpretation of *If a thing is a boojum, then it is a snark* is automatically true. *If a thing is a boojum, then it is not a snark* is also automatically true. This is one of the paradoxes of material implication. A false antecedent is sufficient to establish the truth of any conditional. The other paradox of material implication is that a true consequent is also sufficient to establish a conditional's truth. (Think of any conditional with a consequent true in all circumstances—*if the snark is a boojum, then 2 + 2 = 4* and *if the snark is not a boojum, then 2 + 2 = 4* are equally good examples).

The best way of thinking about these paradoxical assignments of truth is in terms of the fact that the structure of the statements rules out the possibility of deriving false conclusions, and that is enough for validity. The paradoxes highlight the localness of interpretations of formal calculi. What is true in one local domain of interpretation (snarkless environments) becomes false in the neighbouring (snarkful) ones. Our natural rejection of these paradoxes testifies to our tendency to think of language as uniform across local domains as well as within.

The naturalness (unnaturalness) of the material interpretation of conditionals interacts with the issue about the domain of interpretation of the rule and its backing. Interpretation as a material conditional is somewhat more natural if conditionals are explicitly or implicitly universally quantified (as they are intended to be in the selection task) than if they are interpreted propositionally on a domain of a single case. To see this consider a material interpretation of Wason's abstract rule, interpreted propositionally and applied separately to each of the cards. Consider the case of the card with 4 visible—the true consequent card. Under a propositional material interpretation this card is sufficient to make the rule true. It is not merely, as in the case where the rule quantifies over the four cards, that whatever is on the back cannot make it false and that the truth of the rule will therefore depend on other cards. On this interpretation the rule is simply true. Similarly with the false antecedent card showing a K.

Universal quantification over a population of cards at least allows for an implicit backing generalization to motivate the use of 'if', and only gives rise to paradox if the antecedent is *always* false or the consequent *always* true. Since the subject knows that there are both consonants and vowels, even numbers and odd numbers on the four cards because an example of each is visible, and since the rule is quantified, the quantified material interpretation coincides with the subjects' natural interpretation of the rule as having some generalization as backing. However, there is some evidence that the possibility of a material propositional interpretation, interpreted card by card as four separate domains and with an overall deontic interpretation that all domains should comply, may be yet another source of confusion in the task. This evidence comes from performance with conjunctive rules, but should not detain us here (Stenning and van Lambalgen submitted).

Of course matters are still further complicated by pragmatics. First, grammatical form is an unreliable guide to whether a conditional is deontic or whether it is descriptive. 'In the UK, cars drive on the left' may be an approximate description of behaviour or a statement of the law. Conversely, subjunctive statements can be assessed as to whether they state a law that is in force: 'In the UK, cars must drive on the right' is a subjunctive statement which is false as a description of a legal situation. Although laws do not have truth values, statements about laws do. Whether a particular utterance is interpreted as a promulgation of a law, or as a description of the legal situation, is a complex matter of context. The complexity of the relation between rules, descriptions and laws of various kinds, and the evidence for them is the bread and butter of the philosophy of science and of language.

All this puts the selection task subject in a complex situation. Or better, subtle features of the task pragmatics involving the instructions, the rule, and the cards will determine which of these complexities come into play. Our argument is that the deontic conditionals used by Cosmides are designed to put the subject in a very simple reasoning situation in which the law is in force and all that is required is to see whether the cases conform. This view is supported by existing experiments in the literature. Gigerenzer and Hug (1992) showed that inducing a descriptive perspective on deontic rules (placing the subject in a position of seeking evidence about which law is in force) reduces subjects' performance towards the level shown with descriptive rules. Once some of the complexities of indicative semantics come into play, performance declines.

The descriptive 'abstract' task, in contrast, is calculated to maximize the possible problems with interpreting the indicative semantics of conditional rules. The subject has no information about the background warrant for the rule and no guidance about whether to interpret it as brittle or as robust with regard to exceptions, let alone as a material conditional. Contingencies between card choices and feedback come into play.

There are still more semantic complexities, probably many more that we have not even considered. One more will be mentioned here for its relevance to the relation between interpretation and reasoning. The indicative rule contains a linguistic structure usually referred to as **variable anaphora**: 'If *one side* has a vowel, then *the other* has an even number'. The phrase 'one side' is an antecedent and 'the other' is an anaphor. The semantic structure is like saying 'If x has a vowel, then y has an even number' where the variables x and y range over card-faces and the substitution value of the variable y depends on the value of the variable x (being the other face of the same card). In contrast, a *constant* reading of the antecedent/anaphor relation would simply take the antecedent to be a constant like a name for a face, fixed for each card, and then the anaphor would be a name for that card's other face. Gebauer and Laming (1997) proposed that students make a constant anaphor interpretation and then reason correctly from that interpretation. If they did so, they would turn only the true antecedent card (the A). They provided some experimental evidence that this is compatible with some students responses. The issue of whether this is the interpretation adopted and whether students then reason correctly from it is like the issues surrounding Newstead's arguments about implicature and subsequent reasoning. Note that there are no anaphors in the deontic rules.

Apart from the complexities of the available semantic interpretations, there are other social pragmatic factors which might be expected to affect subjects' behaviour. One is what we might call the authority structure of the task. In the indicative task, there is only one authority for the information and that is the experimenter. The subject is being asked to accept that authority for some information but to test it for other information (just like the mixture of co-operative and adversarial stances required in the mercury problem discussed in Chapter 5). For example, the subject has to accept the background rule that cards have numbers on one side and letters on the other, but test the foreground rule. In contrast, the deontic tasks divides up authority between at least three sources—the experimenter, the law, and the drinkers corresponding to the cards. Perhaps this division externalizes the source of authority and makes it more likely that student subjects will challenge the drinkers, along the adversarial lines suggested in Chapter 5, because they do not have to challenge the experimenter in doing so. Here the social psychology of psychology experiments comes to the fore. In these experiments, the experimenter is often also the students' professor.

Before moving to the empirical evidence, we need to ask how these potential explanations of why the abstract task is so difficult sit with Cosmides' claims about cheating-detectors, and the modularity, innateness and evolutionary history of students' reasoning. Psychologists often react to these semantic observations of complexity and multiplicity of interpretations of the conditional with a commonsensical scepticism that matters cannot possibly be that complicated. Cosmides and Tooby (1992), for example, claim:

After all, there is nothing particularly complicated about the situation described in a rule such as 'If a person eats red meat, then that person drinks red wine'. Cosmides and Tooby (1992), footnote 14, page 223.

Well, just which of the many simple situations? Does this person *never* eat red meat without drinking wine? Or is it that if they drink wine with red meat it is red wine? Are there no exceptions? And just what cards should we turn in whichever simple situation it is that Cosmides has in mind?

Of course within a single context with suitable support for constructing an interpretation, reasoning is so simple as to be invisible. But what is complicated is the variety of interpretations for conditional sentences across contexts. Wason's task exactly denies such contextual support.

Linguists and philosophers of science who have studied the semantics of the conditional do not just dream up the complexities. But in using natural language we ordinarily only catch glimpses of complexity when the context does not sufficiently determine the interpretation and misunderstanding arises. If we are to characterize speakers' competence we need to characterize the full range of interpretations and their contextual sensitivities. That is not to claim that speakers consult some list of possible interpretations—just the model we reject. Hearers construct their interpretation according to a host of information of the kinds we have reviewed here, and many others. Subjects do not have an explicit grasp of these complexities, but they most certainly have an implicit grasp that allows them to construct a wide range of appropriate interpretations with suitable contextual support.

Cosmides, in contrast, believes that her evidence tells her that the computations involved in the deontic tasks are done by cheating-detectors which are special purpose devices for reasoning about social contract conditionals, that they are innate, and that they evolved in the Pleistocene era. Implicitly, Cosmides asserts that our ancestors' experiences in the Pleistocene did not equip us with the apparatus for communicating with descriptive conditionals. This is implicitly her explanation of why subjects fail the abstract selection task. She does not have any suggestion about what computational capacities explain the competence we do have for communicating with descriptive conditionals (see comments below on good performance on the construction and tasks with the same descriptive conditionals) or whether these capacities are modular or innate or when they evolved. We shall argue in the next chapter that the evolutionary truth is plausibly very nearly the reverse.

One more obstacle remains before we can move to observation, and that is the ill-specified nature of cheating-detectors themselves. Cosmides tells us little about cheating-detectors. The nearest we get to an explicit characterization of the functionality of cheating-detectors is that they detect violations of social exchange conditionals. Social contract conditionals in this context are ones based on exchange. If we make a contract in which I undertake to provide you with specified benefits for specified rewards, then I break that contract if I fail to provide, and you break it if you fail to reward. We know where to look to detect cheating.

Detecting under-age drinkers is the most widely used example of a deontic task, and it was among the earliest examples of material which was shown to reliably have a large facilitating effect in the selection task. Yet it is not obvious why this should be regarded as a social contract conditional. Cosmides claims that the drinking age law 'expresses a social contract in which one is entitled to a benefit (beer) only if one has satisfied a requirement (being a certain age)' Cosmides and Tooby 1992 (p.183). Of course they mean *entitlement to drink beer* rather than beer, but this strange wording obscures the dissimilarity between laws and exchange contracts. A footnote attempts to blur the distinction further by claiming that roads free of drunken under-age drivers are the relevant benefit, but on this benefit, everyone 'free-rides', even the few(er) drunken youths themselves. Laws, unlike exchange contracts, are not voluntarily entered into by those governed. Of course there are many political theories, not universally accepted, which attempt to explain how laws are based on exchanges. As we have cause to return to in the next chapter, rational choice models (such as the ones' Cosmides and Tooby base their psychology on) have notorious problems getting from exchange contracts to laws. Drinking-age laws (and many of the other examples used) are not based on exchange in any simple sense, but they do obviously have the deontic semantics described earlier with all its simplification of inference in Wason's task.

Another kind of conditional that was shown to be facilitating well before Cosmides' work was 'inspector' scenario conditionals. Wason and Green (1984) gave subjects conditionals specifying constraints that products on an assembly line had to meet in order to pass inspection. The subject was instructed that the cards represented particular product items and asked to turn over cards in order to ensure that the products they represented met the constraints stated in the rules. 'If the wool is longer than a foot, then it must be blue', with cards showing 6 inches, 2 feet, blue, and red would be an example. This rule was found to facilitate performance as much as a drinking-age rule, yet it is not a social contract conditional unless that concept is extended in a highly elastic fashion. However, it does have exactly the deontic semantics which allows such simple reasoning in Wason's task—namely that the relation between the cases and the rule is symmetrical and one-to-one. Whether one case passes has no bearing on any other cases; the conditional can naturally be construed as applying to an open-ended population of cases; all cases could fail and the rule would still be in force etc.

The underspecification of the functionality of cheating-detectors is not just a problem with laws and inspector scenarios which are not exchange contracts. It is also a problem with the abstract conditionals. Why is detecting whether the experimenter's descriptive rule is true or false in the abstract task not a case of cheating-detection? What more fundamental social contract is there than to speak the truth? Are not social contracts about exchange all parasitic on this fundamental contract to communicate faithfully? Liars are, after all, cheats.

Three kinds of attempts to drive a wedge between the kinds of cheating involved in descriptive and deontic cases should be seen to fail. First, it might be objected that telling a falsehood is not sufficient to achieve a lie. To tell a lie one has to utter a known falsehood with intention to deceive, and more . . . Therefore lie-detectors are not going to be activated by mere false saying. But this wedge finds no place of insertion. Exactly the same kinds of extra clauses apply to deciding whether parties are cheating on contracts. If, for example, I fail to deliver you the benefit of our contract because I subsequently realize that my compliance would be to your detriment, I do not break our contract (see Manktelow *et al.* (1999) for discussion of the many subtleties that go in to real cheater detection). There are similar background conditions on social contracts of exchange as there are on social contracts of exchange of information, and for similar reasons.

Second, it might be objected that in the deontic case, the contract is something that the rule is reporting on, and in the descriptive case, the contract is something actually being exemplified by the utterance of the rule. But one might expect this very directness to make things easier. Deciding whether one is actually currently being sold a lie ought to be more vivid than deciding whether some unknown agents described by squiggles on a card are complying with a contract described by some other squiggles in the instructions. The abstract task has presence in that the transactions are actual rather than hypothetical, and the objects described in the rule are concretely present and not merely referred to.

Third, the subjects in the abstract task may not have been given enough scenario to know why someone might be trying to deceive with false conditional statements, and so to trigger their 'liar detectors'. This may very well be true, but if it is then it argues for a theoretical conclusion opposite to that of Cosmides'—it is not that we cannot do descriptive reasoning by 'cheating-detectors' but that subjects need to be given a suitable context in which to apply them. We shall see presently some evidence that at least some subjects' responses are being guided by the social psychology of attributing dishonesty to the experimenter.

If detecting liars is a species of cheating-detection, then cheating-detectors can no longer explain differences between the deontic and abstract tasks. The only plausible account remaining of the difference between the deontic and descriptive tasks is the complexity of the consequences of descriptive semantics in this task setting, as described above: the fact that only *sets* of cards can (at best) make a rule true; contingencies between card turns and feedback hypothetically received; the variable brittleness/robustness to exceptions; challenging the authority of the information source for the rule; understanding the relevant domain of interpretation; the need to assume the background rule but challenge the foreground rule; and so on. We return to this question about the relation between social exchange and communication in human evolution in the next chapter.

If cheating-detectors are underspecified in Cosmides' account, the cheating-detector account is differentiated from logic-based accounts in odd ways. Describing what they purport to be 'The standard social science model', Cosmides and Tooby claim that:

On this view, reasoning is viewed as the operation of content-independent procedures, such as formal logic, applied impartially and uniformly to every problem, regardless of the nature of the content involved. (Cosmides and Tooby 1992, p. 166)

This characterization of logic comes from the same authors who wrote in the introduction to the same book:

Conceptual integration—also known as *vertical integration*—refers to the principle that the various disciplines within the social and behavioural sciences should make themselves mutually consistent, and consistent with what is known in the natural sciences as well. (emphasis in the original) (Cosmides and Tooby 1992, p. 4)

Perhaps logic is neither social nor natural science and so psychology is exempt from integration with logical understanding? But logic is the only sustained attempt to give a theory of how domain-specific and domain-general reasoning interacts through its apparatus of general logical principles operating on domain principles, and of interpretation on local domains.

This is not merely a general problem of misunderstanding logic. It is played out in the details of Cosmides' interpretation of how her cheating-detector account differs from what she supposes to be a logical account. To quote but one example, Cosmides and Tooby (1992, p. 187 *et seq.*) claim that social contract scenarios cannot simply aid performance in the selection task by facilitating logical reasoning. This claim is based on subjects performance in the selection task with 'reversed social contract conditionals'.

- Rule 1: If you give me your watch, I'll give you $20 (standard form).
- Rule 2: If I give you $20, you give me your watch (reversed form).

Cosmides and Tooby observe that given the second rule in selection task, subjects tend to select the $\neg P$ and Q cards, and they claim that logic-based accounts must claim that they should select the same cards as for Rule 1. They reasonably assume that cheating-detectors will be brought to bear on a representation of the problem which imports a great deal of information about the likely situation from subjects' general knowledge of exchanges, while at the same time assuming that logic will operate only on the sentences as printed. But any reasonable logic-based theory would assume exactly similar importations of general knowledge of the likely intentions of the experimenter with regard to interpretation of the material. Cosmides and Tooby (1992, footnote 13, p. 223) finally acknowledge that 'Social contract theory is, in fact, a circumscribed form of deontic logic'—a none too subtle shift of emphasis from the quote above rejecting logic-based understandings. They go on to claim that it cannot be a generalized form of deontic logic and that controversies between deontic logicians about whether rules like Rule 1 above are to be interpreted reversibly. But the logician's technical concern is what can be captured in a 'pure system' whereas for the modelling of psychological data, one can perfectly accept the reversibility as a non-logical assumption about exchanges, imported or not, on the basis of cues about the scenario. The issue of whether an inference is 'purely logical' in the sense so important in the foundations of mathematics is universally irrelevant to the cognitive modelling of inference.

The same problems of understanding persist through all the other attempts to separate cheating-detection and social contract theory from logic-based accounts. When Manktelow and Over (1990) show that deontic 'precaution schemas' produce good selection performance but are not based on social contracts or cheating, Cosmides and Tooby (1992, p. 205) invoke new evolved modules for 'hazard management'. They fail to see that what is common to all these scenarios is that they have the simple deontic semantics governing the compliance of cases that we have emphasized here. The logical generalization cannot be made if we balkanize the basis of subjects' performances into cheating algorithms, precaution algorithms, threat algorithms, permission algorithms, . . . to name but a few proposed.

The issue at stake then is about the generality of subjects' reasoning. Logic-based accounts do not suppose that subjects will cast the rules in these tasks into logical forms irrespective of any other information supplied about their suitable interpretation. Logic-based accounts do suppose that subjects will reasonably import all sorts of general knowledge about the scenarios described in imposing form on the problems. Therefore reasoning will be thoroughly domain specific and sensitive to content. But logic-based accounts also seek a theory of Wason's task which is in accord with what is known about subjects' reasoning and communication abilities more generally—their extraordinary flexibility in interpreting the likely meaning of conditional statements in the rich contexts of their actual use and their flexibility in getting knowledge of one domain to interact with knowledge of another; all tempered by the great difficulties presented to them by the fine balances between co-operative and adversarial stances in many laboratory problems. Also logic-based accounts are the only accounts that have contributed insight about the differences in the semantic relations between cards and rule in descriptive and deontic cases. This distinction is the main predictor of selection task performance right across the literature.

Before seeking new evidence tailored by semantic considerations, in line with these observations that the generality of reasoning capacities is what is really at stake, we should mention some old evidence that is easily forgotten. It is all too easy to assume that the selection task is obviously about failures of deductive reasoning with the conditional. This may be so, but if it is, then there are other reasoning tasks which elicit perfect or near-perfect deductive reasoning with abstract descriptive conditionals from the same subjects.

The **evaluation** task presents subjects with conditionals and asks them to evaluate the truth of the conditional given the truth values of its antecedent and consequent. The **construction** task presents conditionals and asks subjects to construct cases (in terms of the truth values of antecedents and consequents) which make the conditional true, and cases which make the conditional false. There is some tendency for subjects to regard some cases as irrelevant to the truth value of conditionals where the logical competence theory would assign a value. This may be because they lack the differentiated technical vocabulary for describing the possibilities. In general subjects reason with conditionals quite in line with the logical competence model in these tasks. Specifically, they demonstrate that they know that a false consequent and a true antecedent make a conditional false under at least some assumptions (i.e. that a 7 with an A makes the original rule false).

Such observations must throw considerable doubt on any proposal that failure in the selection task can be explained in terms simply of failure to grasp the consequence relations of the conditional. If cheating-detectors are the basis of deontic selection task performance, then what is the basis for the good performance in descriptive evaluation and construction task performance?

Our abstract selection task subject was left, some time ago, pondering cards and rule. We have taken a rather extended look at the various factors that might be expected to affect reasoning in this situation, to remind ourselves that 'content' involves much more than the different rules involved. On the basis of this survey, we can expect certain factors to affect judgements.

6.1.2 Basing empirical explorations on semantic analyses

The observations that follow seek to extend the kind of evidence brought to bear on Wason's task, in fact returning to an earlier exploratory tradition of experiment on the task which Wason himself instigated. This should be viewed as another fishing expedition. Again, circumstances conspired to lead us to study evidence from teaching, of a certain kind.

The most frontal approach is to talk to the subjects. Psychologists have not, in general, been keen on this approach. It is granted to yield information about some consciously accessible processes but not about the fundamental unconscious processes of the 'universal reasoning mechanism'. This scepticism is healthy but in need of examination. There are several kinds of evidence that need to be distinguished. Thinking-aloud protocols are generated when subjects are asked to do a task and to explain what they are doing simultaneously. These methods can yield interesting data but they meet a brick wall when the subjects do not understand their own mental processes, or lack a vocabulary to talk about them, or are simply too busy with the primary task. Post-process self-descriptions are especially dubious. These are only too likely to be based on 'folk theories' which cannot be taken at face value.

However, thinking-aloud protocols are not the obvious way of talking to students. The most obvious way is to engage them in dialogical reasoning, and to see what evidence emerges about the processes involved in their reasoning. These dialogues are then not *reports* of anything. They are arguments. They constitute the students' reasoning itself. As usual, the relation between this public reasoning and whatever private reasoning goes on during the conventional selection task may be complex. For one thing, this evidence suggests that not a whole lot of reasoning does go on in the classical task. We need an account of what this complex relation between external and internal reasoning is, using as many kinds of evidence as we can obtain.

At this stage, our tutorial dialogues provide preliminary evidence. They motivate the hypothesis that the kinds of interpretative problems which are suggested by formal analysis of the task can actually be found causing difficulties in the students' public reasoning. If we could find no such evidence, that would make us think hard about the applicability of the analyses. On the other hand, if public dialogues do reveal evidence congruent with the analyses, then other methods are available to examine the relation between the private reasoning in the conventional task, and what the dialogues reveal. Besides, the public reasoning is of at least as much *prima facie* interest, especially for us teachers.

In fact our observational approach harks back to early experiments on the selection task (e.g. Johnson-Laird and Wason 1970). The exploratory technique is perhaps best thought of as Socratic tutoring. The experimenter-tutor has a schedule of issues to explore, and the students were asked a series of questions to elicit their understanding, with a minimum of intervention from the tutor. What could be on the back of this card? Write it down! If you found an X on the back, what would that mean for the rule? Now that you have turned the card, and found a Y, what does that tell you? . . . The sequence was to ask of each of the cards, all the hypothetical questions about what could be on the back and what it would mean, and then go through turning each card and asking about the significance of what was found. At each stage students would be asked whether they wanted to change their mind about selections, and if so why. What intervention there was consisted of questions designed to be as little leading as possible, and subjects were never given direct feedback that they were 'right' or 'wrong' (whatever that might have meant). Although we have no illusions that the outcome is unaffected by the questioning, the effect is mainly to provoke reflection.

At the beginning of our one-to-one sessions, subjects performed several versions of the task without dialogue to afford us a baseline of their reasoning before tutoring. This was to get a measure of students' interpretations of rules to compare with the previous classroom data, and with the dialogues later in the session. Here we report only a few relevant features of the data (see Stenning and van Lambalgen (2001; submitted)). We focus here on the issues relevant to Cosmides' content effects by concentrating on what makes the abstract task so much harder than the deontic one.

The interactive nature of tutoring might itself be enough to produce richer evidence about the subjects' problems, but we sought to improve our chances by incorporating new tasks and a number of instructional variations. One task was designed to throw some light on the semantic complexities of the relations between cards and rule, and the different relations between rule and cards in the descriptive case. We call this the two-rule task because it presented the two rules:

(1) if there is a U on one side, then there is an 8 on the other side;
(2) if there is an I on one side, then there is an 8 on the other side.

The cards shown were U, I, 8, and 3.[22] The instructions were the same as in the classical abstract task, except that the subjects were instructed that one of these two rules was true, and the other false, and their task was to discover which by turning all and only necessary cards. This task was designed to focus attention on the fact that a card can comply with a rule without thereby making the rule true, and so help subjects differentiate the many card–rule and rule-card semantic relations. It also pushes issues of robustness to exceptions into the background.

---

[22]Using particular letter pairs rather than categories vowel and even number may have a small facilitating effect, but later experimental comparisons were made with the appropriate single-rule task.

Another instructional variation we used was to spell out the constant and variable anaphora readings of the rules in both directions to see whether subjects could adopt these interpretations and reason from them.

- If there is a vowel on the *exposed face*, then there is an even number on the *hidden back*.
- If there is a vowel on the *hidden back*, then there is an even number on the *face you can see*.

Such instructions are not infallible tests for spontaneous interpretations, but if subjects can adopt the required interpretation and reason from it, then that provides some support for this as a possible source of confusion. The reason for the two spellings out is to test a hypothesis about reasoning and interpretation. If variable anaphora is the problem, then both these constant anaphora rules should be equally easy. But they impose different memory loads in reasoning (at least if we assume that subjects tend to reason from antecedent to consequent); the second spelling out demands that two hypothetical possibilities about the backs of cards are entertained. If interpretation is partly determined by the complexity of the reasoning that would ensue from an interpretation, then we might expect these rules to behave differently. Gebauer and Laming (1997) claim that students reason faultlessly from their initial constant anaphora interpretations.

We also paid careful attention to whether students' interpretations were logically reversible (i.e. did they 'convert' the conditional as we saw some of them do to the abstract conditionals in Chapter 5?)

Our first observation was that the baseline tests administered at the beginning of the session yielded data indistinguishable from that in the literature on the abstract task, in this small sample. Once socratic tutoring begins, student interpretations change rapidly. Not surprisingly, engagement in a teaching dialogue changes minds—although not always in the 'normative direction' nor always for very long! But tutoring does precipitate intense engagement.

The second finding comes from the explicit attempt to teach the distinction between the constant and variable anaphora interpretations. In the initial baseline tests, merely spelling out the classical variable rule by adding *(front or back)* in the two relevant places had no effect (see Stenning and van Lambalgen for discussion of the significance of this observation). But once in tutorial mode, students almost all adopted the constant anaphor interpretation of the rule when it was made explicit. Given the 'If there is a vowel on the *front*, then there is an even number on the *back*' rule, they chose just A, even when they had previously made other choices. Being asked what might be on the back and what consequences it would have for the rule was sufficient to induce the correct interpretation of this rule, without any feedback from the tutor. This is at least some evidence that students can adopt this interpretation, and reason normatively from it.

However, given next the rule 'If there is a vowel on the *back*, then there is an even number on the *front*' the students mostly chose just the 4. No one chose correctly just the 7. This choice does at least show some influence of the wording of the rule: no student made this choice in the earlier conditions or the baseline tests. Attending to the rule carefully enough to analyse the possibilities for the backs of the cards was sufficient to invoke a distinctive reading, but a wrong one. The students appreciate that it is the cards with numbers on their fronts that are now relevant, but reasoning about two hypothetical antecedents (i.e. possible backs) defeats them.

So here we immediately have evidence that interpretation and reasoning interact. The 'front-back' rule simplifies reasoning to being about one case, and the antecedent of that case is concretely given on the face of the card. The fact that students reason correctly with this 'front-back' rule indicates that we are succeeding in getting them to adopt the reading intended. In contrast, the 'back-front' rule uses the same 'constant' anaphora but demands reasoning about two hypothetical cases whose antecedents are not visible. If students spontaneously adopt constant readings and reason perfectly from them, and our spelling-out is sufficient to establish a constant reading for the face-back rule, then why not for the back-face rule too? The linguistic interpretation of the latter rule should be as easy as the former. The fact that it is not suggests that the main source of complexity is in the reasoning, not the interpretation. There is a possibility that the complexity of reasoning with the variable interpretation is in fact what triggers a resort to the rather implausible constant interpretation in the classical task with the normal wording. The mental process is not a pipeline beginning with interpretation and ending with conclusion, a point we take up in the next chapter.

However, what happened next was even more interesting. Moving on to the issue of whether it was permissible to reverse the rules, the tutor explicitly asked whether the 'conversion' of the rule held by spelling it out. It was quite clear that several students who had spontaneously stated that the rule was *not* convertible (earlier in their baseline test behaviour and in their prior dialogue) were now, after the anaphora intervention, prepared to convert the rule. Having had 'reversibility' of the variable anaphora emphasized, this seemed to have confused their previous grasp of the fact the conditional is not *logically* symmetrical. The first example shows Subject 12 who explicitly changes the direction of the implication when considering the rule *If there's a vowel on the invisible back, then there's an even number on the visible front*, even though at first well aware that this did *not* follow.

Subject 12:

E. The first rule says that if there is a vowel on the face of the card, so what we mean by face is the bit you can see, then there is an even number on the back of the card, so that's the bit you can't see. So which cards would you turn over to check the rule.

S. Well, I just thought 4, but then it doesn't necessarily say that if there is a 4 that there is a vowel underneath. So the A.

E. For this one it's the reverse, so it says if there is a vowel on the back, so the bit you can't see, there is an even number on the face; so in this sense which ones would you pick?

S. [Subject ticks 4] This one.

E. So why wouldn't you pick any of the other cards?

S. Because it says that *if there is an even number on the face, then there is a vowel*, so it would have to be one of those [referring to the numbers].

⋮

E. [This rule] says that if there is a vowel on one side of the card, either face or back, then there is an even number on the other side, either face or back.

S. I would pick that one [the A] and that one [the 4].

E. So why?

S. Because it would show me that if I turned that [pointing to the 4] over and there was an A then the 4 is true, so I would turn it over. Oh, I don't know. This is confusing me now because I know it goes only one way.

⋮

S. No, I got it wrong didn't I, it is one way, so it's not necessarily that if there is an even number then there is a vowel.

An example of influence in the opposite direction, from a logically asymmetrical reading of the rule to an asymmetrical reading of variable anaphora, is provided by Subject 23:

S. Then for this card [2/G] the statement is not true.
E. Could you give a reason why it is not?
S. Well, I guess this also assumes that the statement is reversible, and if it becomes the reverse, then instead of saying if there is an E on one side, there is a 2 on the other side, it's like saying if there was a 2 on one side, then there is an E on the other.

Later, in doing the 'fit' instructions part of the task (see below), which uses the variable anaphora rule, the subject explicitly states logical symmetry and later justifies it on the basis of the 'exposed or hidden clause'. The tutor then explicitly distinguishes the two senses of reversibility and this is successfully taken up. But later, in the two-rules-one-false task, the subject induces that the anaphora is asymmetrical from the logical asymmetry, whereas it should be symmetrical:

Subject 23 (continued):
E. Now we'll discuss the issue of symmetry. You said you took this to be symmetrical.
S. Well, actually it's effectively symmetrical because you've got this either exposed or hidden clause, for each part of the statement. So it's basically symmetrical.
E. But there are two levels of symmetry involved here. One level is the symmetry between visible face and invisible back, and the other aspect of symmetry is involved with the direction of the statement 'if . . . then'.
S. Right, O.K. so I guess in terms of the 'if . . . then' it is not symmetrical . . . In that case you do not need that one [2], you just need E.
[While attempting the two-rules-one-false task he makes some notes which indicate that he is still aware of the symmetry of the cards]
S. For U, if there is an 8 on the other side, then rule 1 is true, and you'd assume that rule 2 is false. And with I, if you have an 8, then rule 1 is false and rule 2 is true.
[The subject has turned the U and I cards, which both carry 8 on the back, and proceeds to turn the 3 and 8 cards.]
S. Now the 3, it's a U and it's irrelevant because there is no reverse of the rules. And the 8, it's an I and again it's irrelevant because there is no reverse of the rules. . . . Well, my conclusion is that the framework is wrong. I suppose rules 1 and 2 really hold for the cards.
E. We are definitely convinced only one rule is true . . .
S. Well . . . say you again apply the rules, yes you could apply the rules again in a second stab for these cards [3 and 8] here.
E. What do you mean by 'in a second stab'?
S. Well I was kind of assuming before you could only look at the cards once based on what side was currently shown to you. . . . This one here [8] in the previous stab was irrelevant, because it would be equivalent to the reverse side when applied to this rule. I guess now we can actually turn it over and find the 8 leads to I, and you can go to this card again [3]. Now we turn it over and we apply this rule again and the U does not lead to an 8 here. So if you can repeat turns rule 2 is true for all the cards.
E. You first thought this card [3] irrelevant.
S. Well it's irrelevant if you can give only one turn of the card.

The fact that the subject wants to turn the cards twice is evidence for the constant (asymmetric) reading of the anaphora.

We observed influence in both directions in different subjects: interpretation of anaphor affecting interpretation of logical reversibility, and the reverse. This was especially obvious in the 'two-rules' experiment described below. This result suggests some interference in working memory for reversals. It offers a fascinating glimpse of how different factors can interact in interpretation and reasoning.

The tutorials then went on to explore how subjects see the relationship between cards and rule. The technique used was to alter the instruction. Instead of asking subjects to find out whether the rule was true, they were asked to see if the cards *fit* the rule. This instruction was intended to induce the interpretation that the rule might admit of exceptions even though it was still regarded as true. Several kinds of confusion about the relation between rule and cards were elicited by this manipulation.

Some students simply assumed that the rule was true—a phenomenon of obvious relevance to the issue about the social psychology of the task. Others asked whether they were being asked about relations between single cards and the rule, or about *sets* of cards and the rule. They asserted (correctly) that no single card could make the rule true, and that what cards they would want to turn later would depend on what was on the back of cards they turned initially (what we have called contingency). This is a legitimate question even according to the competence model.

Subject 10

> S. OK so if there is a vowel on this side then there is an even number, so I can turn A to find out whether there is an even number on the other side or I can turn the 4 to see if there is a vowel on the other side.
>
> it E. So would you turn over the other cards? Do you need to turn over the other cards?
>
> it S. I think it just depends on what you find on the other side of the card. No I wouldn't turn them.
>
> :
>
> it E. If you found a K on the back of the 4?
>
> it S. Then it would be false.
>
> :
>
> it S. But if that doesn't disclude [*sic*] then I have to turn another one.
>
> it E. So you are inclined to turn this over [the A] because you wanted to check?
>
> it S. Yes, to see if there is an even number.
>
> it E. And you want to turn this over [the 4]?
>
> it S. Yes, to check if there is a vowel, but if I found an odd number [on the back of the A], then I don't need to turn this [the 4].
>
> it E. So you don't want to turn . . .
>
> it S. Well, I'm confused again because I don't know what's on the back, I don't know if this one . . .
>
> it E. We're only working hypothetically now.
>
> it S. Oh well, then only one of course, because if the rule applies to the whole thing then one would test it.
>
> :
>
> it E. What about the 7?

it S. Yes the 7 could have a vowel, then that would prove the whole thing wrong. So that's what I mean, do you turn one at a time or do you ...?

⋮

it E. Well if you needed to know beforehand, without having turned these over, so you think to yourself I need to check whether the rule holds, so what cards do I need to turn over? You said you would turn over the A and the 4.

it S. Yes, but if these are right, say if this [the A] has an even number and this has a vowel [the 4], then I might be wrong in saying 'Oh it's fine', so this could have an odd number [the K] and this a vowel [the 7] so in that case I need to turn them all.

it E. You'd turn all of them over? Just to be sure?

it S. Yes.

This expression of contingencies between cards is evidence that subjects appreciated that single cards could not make a rule true. Even more fundamentally, it provides evidence that even under this 'fit' instruction, subjects still have difficulty keeping clear the distinction between being asked about what the cards say about the rule, as opposed to what the rule says about the cards. It is this confusion which cannot arise in the obvious primary interpretation of deontics in which the law is accepted, and the cases are assessed relative to it. It seems to us a perfectly reasonable confusion, in the light of the complexity of the semantics of descriptive conditionals.

The interviewer now moved on to the novel two-rule task. Subjects' choices in this task before any tutoring were different than in the classical one-rule task, though they were not competence model responses. The modal choice was to turn U and I. Something about the task seemed to enable the subjects to see the irrelevance of the 8 card, but not yet to see the relevance of the 3 card, or the irrelevance of the U and I cards.

The subsequent tutoring consisted of the usual pattern. The dialogues revealed even more frequent confusions about contingency—'whether I turn that depends on what happens when I turn this.' Other confusions were also evident, particularly about what single cards could indicate about rules, and hence the asymmetry of truth and falsity in this regard. Several subjects reasoned that if one card complied with one rule (reported as 'making it true'), then they could conclude that the other rule must be false. They failed to see that since some cards could comply with rules which were nevertheless false (of other cards), it is possible for some cards to comply with both rules.

But the response to tutoring was what was most distinctively different from results of the classical single-rule task. A substantial proportion of subjects moved to competence model responding after non-directive tutoring on this novel task. Very often they had an identifiable episode of insight, usually involving insight into the error of thinking that only one rule could be complied with by each card. They would say something like 'Ah! This card fits this rule, but one further along may not, so I can't conclude anything', followed by an explicit search for a card which would definitely falsify one or other rule; this search was usually successful. Not all subjects had such insights. Some subjects, after they had turned the U and found 8 and the I and found 8 would claim that the instructions must be faulty—this response was commoner amongst the males!

Merely introducing the novel task was not enough to produce a radical alteration in baseline reasoning performance (in this handful of subjects), but it did seem that Socratic tutoring in this task had a greater impact than it did in the classical task. This is some evidence that inducing a choice between alternative rules is a good direction from which to approach teaching students to adopt the competence model. This is probably because having two rules encourages clarification of the fact that a card can comply with a rule, without thereby 'making the rule true'.

This novel task throws some interesting light on another task which Johnson-Laird *et al.* (2000) have used to argue for mental models. We did not set out to make this comparison, but our results call into question the authors' interpretation. Johnson-Laird's task, like ours, presents two conditionals related as $P \rightarrow Q$ and $\neg P \rightarrow Q$, and again subjects are told that one is true and the other false. But rather than making a card selection, subjects are simply asked a question about what follows from the conditionals about a hand of cards (not presented):

1. If there is a king in the hand, then there is an ace.
2. If there is *not* a king in the hand, then there is an ace.
Q. Is there an ace in the hand?

Well, is there? Johnson-Laird *et al.* observe that subjects conclude that there is an ace in the hand They argue that this is an inferential 'illusion', and that it is caused by subjects only considering cases in which the rules are true, as mental models theory predicts. He argues that in fact it follows that there cannot be an ace in the hand. However, this latter conclusion can only be derived from a material interpretation of the conditionals—an interpretation Johnson-Laird himself argues against elsewhere (Johnson-Laird and Byrne, in press) and is universally acknowledged to be generally hard to get people to adopt.

If, as we should expect, subjects adopt an interpretation in which the backing of the rules is about a population of hands of cards, then there certainly can be aces in the hand in question. Therefore, I would argue, Johnson-Laird's subjects, far from failing to draw a valid conclusion that there cannot be an ace, are correctly reasoning from the most reasonable interpretation of the rules that there could be an ace. If there is an 'illusion' that the subjects suffer from, then it consists of drawing the conclusion that there *must* be an ace rather than that there *might* be an ace. There are several explanations of this possible 'illusion' which should not delay us too long here. Perhaps the simplest is that subjects may construe the instruction that one rule is true and one is false as meaning that one *applies* and the other does not. If this is true, then it is another example of subjects' struggling with an inadequate vocabulary for describing the complexities of indicative semantics (see Stenning and van Lambalgen (submitted) for a fuller discussion).

But our direct interest in this task here is that, as we shall see presently, our two-rule task is actually easy compared with the classical one-rule task, invoking about 24 per cent correct competence model responses (extremely high for a more complicated version of the classical abstract task which only 3.7 per cent of the same population of subjects got right). This would be an even more startling result if Johnson-Laird *et al.* had really shown that the great majority of subjects suffer a radical inferential illusion with the same premises (albeit in a slightly different task).

This digression focuses our attention on what subjects take the domain of the conditional to be—a single case (hand of cards), four cases (cards), or indefinitely many hands or cards picked out by some unknown criterion. The comparison with Johnson-Laird's task provides yet another piece of evidence that interpretation is highly contextualized and a warning against adopting fits to simplistic competence models.

Finally, our interviews replicated Wason's original finding that it is not unusual to find a subject who recognizes that A on the back of 7 makes the rule false, but does *not* then choose the 7 card. This supports the evidence of the evaluation and construction tasks that primary conditional reasoning is not the main problem. The observation could be explained if the subject were focused on the issue of what the card says about the rule, and had an interpretation of the rule as withstanding exceptions.

Interviewing turns out to be a rich source of information. It does not provide direct access to the processes which take place in the standard experimental task, but it does provide strong evidence about which features of the task are continuing sources of confusion. The confusions that arise are at least consistent with the gross semantic differences between deontic and descriptive conditionals. The prevalent confusions about contingencies of choice between cards, and the greater facilitation of tutoring on the novel two-rule task are both consistent with the complexities of the relations between cards and sets of cards and rules (and vice versa) in the descriptive case. The tutorial dialogues do at least reveal some of the real complexities affecting performance in a task which appears all too deceptively simple the way that it is usually presented.

The depth of analysis required to decide whether a particular logical form is a reasonable one to apply *in the circumstances* is considerable. Students show some evidence of at least implicit grasp of some of these complexities. The indicative and deontic conditionals, under the most likely initial interpretation in this task, do not share the same logical form, and subjects' behaviour can be explained by recourse to a more reasonable analysis of the various forms which student subjects are likely to impose.

These observations provide *prima facie* evidence that indeed the abstract task causes difficulties related to the complexities of interpretation of the descriptive conditional. The evidence is as follows: interpretation of anaphora interacts with reasoning, but interpretation alone is not a good explanation of students' difficulties; directionality of interpretation may interact in working memory with constant-variable anaphora interpretation; the semantic complexity of the relation between card and indicative rule causes problems with contingency of choice and feedback, and can be alleviated for appreciable numbers of subjects by a change to an apparently more complex task.

Of course, it is possible to test these hypotheses by more conventional experiments (Stenning and Lambalgen, submitted). Running controlled experiments using the new two-rule task and varying instructions substantiates some of these claims. The two-rule task is substantially easier than the one-rule task, even without Socratic tutoring, as mentioned above (24 per cent completely correct). Instructions designed to remove any misunderstanding of contingencies between feedback and card-choice make the task easier (18 per cent completely correct). Separating the authority for the rule from the experimenter, and asking the subject to judge the truthfulness of that source rather than the truth of the rule also makes the task slightly easier (13 per cent completely correct). All these results are compared with a baseline of 3.7 per cent completely correct for the classical abstract task. Thus, six times as many subjects get the two-rule task completely correct, five times as many the contingency instructions, and three times as many the externalized authority task correct. There are still a lot of subjects getting these tasks 'wrong', but we have a growing list of sources of difficulty of the abstract task whose removal make the task easier, and which do not apply to the deontic task. Do these 'objective' results make the Socratic tutorial dialogue data obsolete?

Our answer is an emphatic no. The most important theoretical goal is a model of how these sources of difficulty interact with each other (and possibly with others yet to be identified) to yield the profile of performance we observe. The standard experiments help to support the transparency of the dialogue data but they cannot replace it. For example, do all these sources of difficulty add up to explain all the difference between abstract and deontic tasks? This 'addition' cannot simply be done on the conventional experimental data. We cannot tell what combinations of what difficulties what proportions of students experience. It could be that the groups of students aided by these three manipulations are distinct, in which case the arithmetic is simple and the three factors account for about half of the subjects. But it could be that all students have all problems and that the two-rule task removes all three, in which case the three factors account for only a quarter of all subjects. Or it could be that the students suffer from a selection of problems, but all problems must be overcome in order to get the task right, in which case these three problems could account for as many as all subjects' difficulties, depending on the distributions and the interactions. There is also the question of how effective these instructional manipulations are at removing problems. We have shown that they help substantial numbers of students, but we have not shown that these manipulations remove the problems for all students.

The interview data provide indirect evidence about how these problems interact. We see students making the same choices for different reasons. In the end such evidence is probably the only basis on which to build a process model which can explain how difficulties interact and how many different kinds of student taking how many trajectories through the problem space there are. We do not yet have such a model, but at least the theoretical goal points out that there are so far no explanations in the literature of the differences between the students who make the different card selections, nor, for that matter, the differences evidenced in these dialogues between students who make the *same* selections. Searching for correlations between card choices and the other individual difference measures studied earlier in this book has not yet revealed any reliable ones. This may well be because the card choices are too impoverished on their own to classify students' reasoning styles. There are too many distinct reasons for making each of the common responses for any simple correlations to emerge.

We are, of course, not the first to challenge Cosmides' account of the content dependence of conditional reasoning. We shall have more to say soon about Cheng and Holyoak's (1985) pragmatic reasoning schema account, and Sperber *et al.* (1995) have given an account in terms of relevance theory, providing more examples where non-social contract conditionals can be made easy by the right context. They used a production-line-inspector scenario comparable to Wason and Green's (1984) and similarly got good performance. Note that this scenario requires a deontic interpretation, though not a social contract one. Again this supports our claim that the different complexity of indicative-deontic semantics is what drives the data in the conventional abstract task.

Our approach is in general aligned with relevance theory's goals of subsuming conditional reasoning in this task with reasoning and communication more generally. Relevance theory is closely related to Grice's theory, and so many of the particular claims made by Sperber et al. are echoed here in what we have said about the relation between Gricean pragmatics and the data of reasoning. Our preference is to use specific semantic and pragmatic insights to make contextually specific predictions about reasoning phenomena—that students in one condition will have problems with contingencies between choice and feedback, that a task can be changed in a certain way to reduce this tendency, that an instructional variation will lead to more of another kind of responding . . . Ultimately, what is required is a model of reasoning dialogue which can say how these factors interact in real time. These specific predictions are probably consistent with relevance theory, but we remain to be convinced that relevance theory would have led us to investigate them. Relevance theory does not seem to have led to the observation that the easy cases all require deontic interpretation.

Where does all this leave content effects? We have engaged in such an in-depth analysis of one very particular task to try to give a better feel for how theories of form can develop in tandem with and interact with theories of mental processing of form and content. No very technical insight into the semantics of conditionals has been employed. The broadest outline phenomena of conditional semantics are sufficient to identify where the differences between descriptive and deontic conditionals are to be found, and to suggest how they will interact with the task's pragmatics. Form and content are relative terms. The mental process of finding an adequate form for reasoning in the content that presents itself is complex. This process of finding form is sensitive to content itself. Contentful words in the task description and rules trigger particular adoptions of formal analysis. Reasoning from that analysis produces conclusions or impasses which themselves may trigger more search for different form amid the content. The epigrammatic syllogism that began the chapter needs to be slowed down—and shown for what it is.

Where does all this leave so-called evolutionary psychology? It removes what was the founding evidence. If the abstract task is difficult because the setting interacts with the semantic complexities of descriptive rules to produce a highly ambiguous task which elicits variable responses, and the deontic task is easy because the kind of rules chosen interact with the same setting to produce a very simple reasoning task, what does all this tell us about our Pleistocene ancestors? If cheating-detectors are so poorly characterized that we cannot tell why they are not engaged by and do not achieve the abstract task, then how do they help understand our students? We are all for evolution, but it seems that a somewhat more interdisciplinary approach with a little more attention to the detail of what our student-subjects are doing is probably the best way to find out about whatever our ancestors got up to all those years ago?

According to our theory as developed in Chapter 5, what most challenges our students is understanding the subtleties of the balance of co-operative and adversarial communication in these strange laboratory situations, together with concepts required for accessing the requisite range of interpretations of representation systems. Ability to acquire a more flexible understanding of this balance, and the ability to base on it the skill of communication across conceptual, epistemic, and motivational divides may have been an important part of what our ancestors needed to live in larger groups, where communication across these divides looms large. It is almost certainly no accident that this need surfaces in education even today just at the point where students leave their family groups and go out into society. Untangling the blend of cultural and biological evolution that gave rise to us is no simple matter, but this at least looks like a departure point for an evolutionary account of how we got here, and it may even be consistent with what we know of our modern reasoning abilities. In the next chapter we shall develop this alternative to Cosmides' evolutionary scenario, but first we need to connect back the selection task to the teaching and learning of reasoning.

6.1.3   The selection task and the teaching of reasoning

How then is performance on Wason's selection task related to the phenomena of the teaching and learning of reasoning presented earlier? And to our general argument that a prominent component of human reasoning is reasoning about how to represent problems, rather than reasoning within representations of them? As a starting point, there are a number of studies which bear on the relation of form and content in learning to reason which have actually used Wason's task as a criterion of success.

One study by van der Pal (1995) concisely combines several of the topics we have covered in this book. van der Pal was concerned with the role of formality in teaching reasoning. He used Tarski's World, the precursor of Hyperproof, as a teaching environment; conditional reasoning as the topic of his teaching studies; and the selection task as his measure of success. van der Pal took the two fundamental methods of grounding a logical calculus discussed in Chapter 3—translation between the calculus and a natural language; and correspondence to diagrammatically presented 'worlds'— and studied their effects singly and in combination on students' subsequent performance in the abstract selection task. He produced a modified version of Tarski's World which used Dutch sentences (chosen for their lack of ambiguity in context) instead of those of first-order logic. He then compared three teaching conditions: teaching in Dutch only, teaching by translation between Dutch and first-order logic, and teaching using Tarski's world diagrams as a grounding for first-order logic. He used the modified programme for teaching a variety of undergraduate students broadly comparable to our subjects.

His results were quite simple on one point. Teaching conditional reasoning by the methods he studied without resort to a formalism (whether a formal calculus or a diagrammatic system) was not effective in producing gains on Wason's task. Teaching only in the students' native language had little if any benefit. Merely teaching a calculus alone was also ineffective. But teaching a correspondence between Tarski's World diagrams and a student's natural language, and teaching a correspondence between a formal language and natural language, both had large positive effects on students' selection performance. Interestingly, this improvement was most marked at a delay of several weeks—always something to cheer a teacher!

These results nicely complement those reported in Chapter 3. Just as with our results, those obtained by van der Pal show that formal teaching can be effective as long as it concentrates on the *relation* between formalism and what it formalizes. van der Pal's study makes a controlled comparison with 'informal' teaching methods and shows that they are not effective, at least in his setting. One should not be too quick to dismiss informal methods in general, but the message is that focusing on the relation between formalism and what it formalizes is the key to getting effective transfer from the teaching of formalisms. Formalisms can serve to make the familiar strange, and to help separate the information packaging that goes with co-operative communication in a natural language, from the underlying logical structure. But if the formalism is taught as a self-contained world of its own manipulations, there should be little surprise that nothing transfers. This study cannot itself tell us whether increased success at the selection task goes with more general transfer, but it does show that the task is capable of discriminating different teaching methods along the expected lines.

Readers familiar with the psychology of reasoning literature will know that there are a few prominent results showing *lack* of effects of logic teaching on reasoning ability. How are these studies to be reconciled with the results in Chapter 3 showing good generalization of logic teaching? And with van der Pal's results just reported ? A prominent example of such studies is Cheng *et al.* (1986) comparing 'pragmatic' and 'syntactic' approaches to teaching conditional reasoning as measured by performance in the selection task. This study shows the failure of real logic courses taught by real logic professors to elevate selection task performance. Of course, there is always the possibility that whatever courses are studied, the particular example courses are not well taught. But this idiosyncratic defence must be a last resort. These were real courses in prestigious institutions and are not to be dismissed so lightly. It might be that they were of a *kind* of course which is ineffective, but then we should be able to say something more general about what kind of courses transfer and which do not. In fact, as we shall argue, there are other problems with the inferences drawn.

Cheng et al. argue that human conditional reasoning with deontically interpreted rules is achieved by using **pragmatic reasoning schemas** which are more specific than the logic of the conditional (which they take to be material implication) but more general than the familiarity models proposed by earlier authors which were completely specific to particular content. The **permission** schema is an example of a pragmatic reasoning schema: *If action A is to be taken, then precondition B must be satisfied*; *Action A is to be taken only if precondition B is satisfied*; *If precondition B is not satisfied then action A cannot be taken*. If the content of a problem invokes the permission schema then all of these inference schemas are assumed to be available for reasoning.

Cheng and Holyoak (1985) had already sought and found evidence that pragmatic reasoning schemas rather than the syntactic rules of logic are used in conditional reasoning. One of the examples they studied is the postal-rule example of Johnson-Laird *et al.* 1972. The rule is 'If a letter is sealed then it has a 5p stamp on it'. This was on of the earliest rules to be shown to be highly facilitating of selection task performance. Later it was shown only to facilitate reasoning in a population of subjects who had experience of the rule as *deontic* regulation based on the idea that the sender had to pay more for sealed private letters than for unsealed junk mail. It is notable that the rule is presented indicatively, so subjects unable to recognize from the content that deontic interpretation is intended are unlikely to adopt this interpretation spontaneously. Cheng and Holyoak (1985) elicited good performance on this rule with subjects who had no experience with it, by explaining how the conditional was an example of the permission schema.

Cheng *et al.*'s (1986) methodology was to compare different teaching regimes for their effects on selection task performance in two experiments. One of their comparisons is of students who have taken real logic courses with students taught in a manner motivated by pragmatic reasoning schemas, and with controls. The logic courses chosen are described as teaching 'with an emphasis on formal rules, though using examples in lectures'. Teaching just syntactic rules, just examples, or just the logic course did not significantly change selection choices (except a minor suppression of the choice of the $\neg p$ card), but teaching both rules and examples of their application did significantly improve selection performance. One of the experiments contrasted teaching with the obligation schema (another example pragmatic reasoning schema) as opposed to teaching with the same materials but with the task described in terms of contingencies rather than obligations. Again, the pragmatic training succeeded where the other did not.

What should we make of this work and its relation to our results and those of van der Pal? Pragmatic reasoning schemas, or at least the example of obligation and permission discussed here, are deontic, and formal. They are formal in that they are general, requiring the instantiation of their variables with new content afresh for each problem. They are of course contentful in the sense that they are a formalization of the difference in content between indicative and deontic conditionals (at least this range of deontic examples). In fact, Cheng and Holyoak make an eloquent argument for a deontic logic being the basis of their subjects' reasoning, along with a case that information outside the actual wording of the rule itself contributes to what interpretation subjects make of rules. The kind of selection task rule which this training particularly facilitates is the kind where the interpretation is intended to be deontic, but where that is not very clear from the content of the rule—the 'postal rule' being the best-known example. All the explanations given above as to why deontic selection problems are easier than indicative ones apply to pragmatic reasoning schema explanations. Those explanations also make it clear why having had a logic course will not necessarily help students to settle on the intended interpretation of the selection task materials. Logic courses do not teach that material implication is the correct interpretation of natural language conditionals. All the problems with brittleness, contingencies etc. remain.

Cheng et al. present an interesting discussion of why subjects do not induce syntactic rules for manipulating material conditionals from their natural languages. They illustrate how those rules are unreliable in many natural language contexts. The examples given are cases where reversal of deontic antecedent and consequent clauses lead to anomalous interpretations, usually because of implicit problems with tense. For example, 'If a burglar breaks into your house, you should call the police', on contraposition produces the odd: 'If it is not the case you should call the police, then a burglar does not break into your house'. Although this is reversal of the clauses and an addition of two negations, it is not what a deontic logic would produce by applying *modus tollens*.

A contraposition which appropriately adjusted the tenses would be: 'If you are *not* under obligation to call the police, then a burglar *has not* broken into your house'. This may be pragmatically quaint out of context, but it does follow from the truth of the original. Therefore we can heartily endorse Cheng and Holyoak's explanation of why students do not induce the syntactic rules that Cheng et al. entertain, and the more general conclusion that the crucial process for cognitive theory is how content triggers the formalizations which it does. After all, formal logics were devised precisely so that simple inference rules could be applied universally. They had to be designed because the corresponding inference rules for natural languages are so complex. Here are the beginnings of an explanation of why teaching a formal calculus *can* help logic learning when presented in the right way by clarifying for students the structure of their language.

But Cheng *et al.*'s educational conclusions are less impeccable: 'We have shown that deductive reasoning is not likely to be improved by training on standard logic'. If training on standard logic consists in teaching these syntactic rules, and teaching that they apply across the board to natural languages at the level of sentence analysis offered, then we could even agree with this statement. And maybe many logic courses are ill-designed for the teaching of general reasoning skills. Many such courses are really aimed at enabling philosophy students to read the philosophical literature which makes use of these formalisms.

But Cheng *et al.*'s general educational claim does not stand up to the positive results of teaching reported here, and is too easily open to misinterpretation. A better summary of their and our results would be that to achieve transfer, logic teaching has to be aimed at teaching how to find form in content. The evidence of both their and our studies is that a semantic approach (whether sentential or diagrammatic) aids this process greatly. Any course that does not emphasize the tenselessness of standard logics, and the kind of tense shift phenomena in natural language illustrated above, would not be expected to get far. In fact one good reason why *modus ponens* tends to be the one formal rule for conditionals that it is easy to get students to apply correctly, is that it does not involve the clause shifting which disrupts tense and information packaging. Remember the prominence of subject-predicate reversals in driving naive logical intuitions in Chapter 5. The selection task is a particularly semantically oriented test and as we have seen involves much more than conditional reasoning. Unfortunately we do not know whether our Hyperproof students have learned to pass this test. But van der Pal's results rather strongly suggest that they may well have done.

A quite different kind of study which produced some suggestive evidence about the relation of the selection task to other scholastic performance is the study by Lehman *et al.* (1988) of the impact of different undergraduate degrees on students' reasoning. This study used Wason's selection task, along with some psychometric tests, as its measure of how much whole degree programmes improved reasoning performance. Students taking the first stages of graduate degrees in law, medicine, psychology, and chemistry were compared, both cross-sectionally and longitudinally, over 2 years. With regard to selection task performance, law, medicine, and psychology all produced large significant gains, but chemistry produced negative or insignificant gains. The authors attribute the beneficial effects of learning law, medicine, and psychology to the large component of teaching about how to apply formal rule systems (e.g. statistics, conditional reasoning, control group reasoning etc.) to situations from everyday life which were contained in these courses, but not in the chemistry course. Although chemists were taught the formal rules of statistics, they never had to apply them to situations outside the chemistry laboratory. Therefore this study provides some additional evidence that it is learning the skill of imposing form on content that improves reasoning in real-world situations. This evidence compliments our evidence that teaching logic improves general reasoning. Here we see that teaching various formalisms (notably statistics) with a heavy concentration on their application to everyday circumstances, actually improves a more narrowly logical skill—performance on the selection task.

This observation raises issues about breadth of generalization of such learning about formalisms. We do not know exactly what formalisms Lehman *et al.*'s subjects were taught, but it is unlikely that many had meantime received training in formal logic. If learning, say, statistics or experimental design and their application to the everyday world improves performance on the selection task (an apparently logical task), does not that mean that one can learn logic by learning statistics? Our evidence in Chapter 3 was that teaching logic was sufficient to teach transferable logical skills. We did not show (or argue) that teaching logic was *necessary* for producing these effects. Lehman *et al.*'s study looked at statistical-reasoning and verbal-reasoning measures alongside selection task performance and showed some correlations, but also some contrasts. What the overlap and contrasts in the cognitive effects of these different kinds of teaching of reasoning skills are is an open question. There are many things in common between logic and statistics. For one example, the imposition of a framework of cases onto problems is shared. For another example, the extensional analysis of meaning in logic has much in common with the analysis of independence in statistics. Perhaps this result should not be so surprising. There has been so much scepticism about the transfer of learning about formalisms that our empirical exploration of these matters has hardly begun.

If we accept Wason's task as a useful test of reasoning skill, these studies show that reasoning can be taught. But why should we accept it? And if we do, what is it in the task that leads to it reflecting successful learning to reason, especially if Wason's designation of 'correct' performance is questionable?

6.1.4   Content effects in logic learning

Our analysis of the many sources of complexity in the abstract selection task might give the impression that the selection task is just a laboratory curiosity, and that if it were properly explained to subjects, they would have little difficulty with it. If the task were merely such a curiosity, successful performance should not be predictive of other reasoning. There are some correlational studies of individual differences in Wason's task which show significant positive effects. Stanovich and West (2000) show that selection task performance is quite strongly correlated with other measures of scholastic aptitude. The rather rare students who choose A and 7 are also high performers on scholastic aptitude tests; their peers who choose just A, or A and 4 are less so. If the particular performance that Wason considered normative for the task is just a party trick with no functional value, why should this correlation hold?

One might try explaining it away on the belief that intelligence tests are similarly curiosities that yield these correlations for the non-cognitive reasons entertained in Chapter 3. Or one can take the task more seriously. Wason's task may well be an artificially isolated laboratory task which wrenches language from the moorings which normally anchor it for freshman undergraduates, and that may be exactly why it is such a good test of something educationally important.

When we discussed the outcomes of Hyperproof teaching in Chapter 3, syllogism learning in Chapter 4, and students' naive models of communication in Chapter 5, the focus was very much on abstract material—Ps and Qs, As and Bs—and the systems of reasoning that they entered into, rather than on how these variables were given content. Our experiments on interpretation and on reasoning actually used only As and Bs in their material. Our explanations and models of student behaviour invoked a social basis in co-operative and adversarial reasoning, but did not address the problem of how particular words contact particular content. Having looked at content effects in Wason's very particular task, we should revisit questions about how form connects to content in the earlier situations.

For example, we discussed learning as effects on strategies of reasoning within Hyperproof itself and saw the transfer of that learning to the GRE analytical subsubscale in terms of the skills of splitting into cases. These are not notably contentful skills. We also saw conventional sentential logic teaching transfer to other reasoning domains. Figure 3.9 showed that the sentential natural deduction teaching had a significant positive effect on the Blocks World reasoning of half the students (the ones who were least good at GRE analytical problems). Whereas Hyperproof's diagrammatic teaching failed to improve the scores of this subgroup of students on the highly diagrammatic Blocks World test, learning to operate with sentential calculus formulae *did* improve this performance—a surprising result. This transfer might again be explained in terms of skills of splitting into cases, which is a prominent problem in Blocks World reasoning.

But there were effects of taking the sentential logic course which we neglected. Figure 3.8 shows quite clearly that the conventional natural deduction logic course improved reasoning not only by increasing students' scores on GRE analytical subscale items, but also by improving their GRE 'logical' subscale scores, in a way that the Hyperproof course failed to match. Splitting into cases is not so prominent an issue in logical subscale problems. Even students in this population, whose scores on GRE logical problems are rather near ceiling, gain significantly from natural deduction teaching. This is a rather singular result we paid little attention to in Chapter 3, but may now be amenable to understanding in terms of content effects.

How is it that learning a sentential formalism and natural deduction proof procedures helps these students in these tasks? We should open this enquiry with a caveat. Our result does not show that just *any* conventional course would have this effect. John Etchemendy is highly committed to emphasizing the semantic relationships between formal systems and the phenomena they model, just as much when teaching sententially as diagrammatically. This may well have worked to minimise the modality effects in the study. However, our study is an existence proof—some sentential teaching can have these effects on some students. But how? What is the mechanism of transfer?

Consider the second (so-called logical) problem in Fig. 3.7—the mercury problem (repeated here for convenience):

Excessive amounts of mercury in drinking water, associated with certain types of industrial pollution, have been shown to cause Hobson's disease. Island R has an economy based entirely on subsistence level agriculture with no industry or pollution. The inhabitants of R have an unusually high incidence of Hobson's disease.

Which of the following can be validly inferred from the above statements?

(i) Mercury in the drinking water is actually perfectly safe.
(ii) Mercury in the drinking water must have sources other than industrial pollution.
(iii) Hobson's disease must have causes other than mercury in the drinking water.

- (ii) only?
- (iii) only?
- (i) or (iii) but not both?
- (ii) or (iii) or both?

What is involved in solving this problem? Let us talk through it!

Consider the three single-response alternatives in order. A first step might be to dismiss (i), but even this is not simple. We are supposed to co-operatively assume that (a) having Hobson's disease is not perfectly safe (plenty of diseases are, after all, perfectly safe), (b) that (i) means more than some relevant level of mercury which causes Hobson's disease, and (c) to notice that if both of these assumptions are correct, then (i) is inconsistent with another statement in the problem—that mercury in the drinking water causes Hobson's disease. Again we must co-operatively assume that problem statements are not supposed to be inconsistent, so we can reject (i) as not inferable. The third assumption (c) may seem outlandish until one realizes that a reader might well interpret the information about Island R in another discourse context as the results of a new study which do in fact contradict previous knowledge. It is part of understanding the GRE 'game' to understand that this is not the intended interpretation. After all this, we can dismiss alternative (i) as a conclusion. Phew!

Now the real business can begin. What about (ii)? And (iii)? Both of these statements are denials of biconditionality of conditionals given in the premises of the problem. The crux of the problem is to appreciate that either Hobson's Disease has other causes than mercury in the drinking water, *or* there are other sources of mercury than industrial pollution, *or both*. First, we should not forget that even these inferences rely on numerous co-operative assumptions—that the inhabitants of Island R do not get their drinking water from some industrial region; that they did not contract Hobson's disease while visiting Glasgow, . . . Second, there is an element of complexity introduced by the disjunction of the two possibilities. Neither of (ii) and (iii) follows by itself, because either one of them following is sufficient to resolve the impasse. In the end, assuming all these helpful things, it looks as if '(ii) or (iii) or both' is a plausible option.

The purpose of this exploration is to reveal some of the possible nooks and crannies which we may have to visit in solving such a problem. To do so reveals something of the balance between the co-operative implicit assumptions we make (whether we realize it or not) and possibilities which we adversarially test. If we do not understand that this space is there, then it is mysterious that these problems can test intelligent undergraduates' reasoning abilities. Anyone who doubts the generality of this kind of problem should sit in an exam-question vetting session. If we do not appreciate this labyrinth of assumption and refusal of assumption, we are left with the view that the problem is merely a problem of discouraging illicit conversion of conditionals. For example, it is all too easy for the expert to think of the problem premises as evidently formalizable thus:

1. $Mercury \rightarrow Hobson$

2. $Pollution \rightarrow Mercury$

3. $\neg Pollution \& Hobson$

and the response alternatives thus:[23]

i) $\neg(Mercury \rightarrow Hobson)$
ii) $\neg(Mercury \rightarrow Pollution)$
iii) $\neg(Hobson \rightarrow Mercury)$

If this formalization is available to the reasoner, then a natural explanation for a failure to solve (in fact more or less the only explanation available) is that students have a problem with applying the rule *modus tollens* in order to see that either ii) or iii) or both must be true. In fact this is quite a common explanation given for the difficulty of such

---

[23] We stick to a propositional formulation for simplicity, even though a quantification over causes would be more faithful to the surface of the problem's language—these matters rarely delay such experts for more than a second or two.

problems. According to this sort of understanding, the explanation of the improvement of reasoning stemming from the sentential logic course would be practice in applying the formal transformation of this rule—*modus tollens*. Strictly speaking (since we are in a strict phase), this is still only true if we assume a particular rule system as our proof theory. Subjects might still solve the problem using truth-tables, or a rule set which does not include *modus tollens*, perhaps in an axiom system with only one rule of inference, or an alternative proof-theory like mental models without an identifiable inference rule.

But, as we have seen, any such *formal* explanation is unlikely to cover more than a small part of the problem. In the construction and evaluation tasks, students demonstrate a quite adequate grasp of the consequence relations underlying *modus tollens* (whether or not this means that they have something we would want to call an identifiable *rule*). At a formal level, *modus tollens* is not more computationally complex than *modus ponens*. Well, perhaps there are a couple of extra squiggles, but nothing that could plausibly explain the difference in difficulty. Any explanation that does not contact the content of the problem and its relation to form is inherently unsatisfactory.

Formal explanations also make it hard to understand why solving one such problem does not teach the student how to do all the rest—quite a large proportion of the GRE 'logical' subscale problems are essentially of the same (rather trivial) form (once formalized). The problem lies in the *process* of formalization, and not in the calculation with the formalism itself. Thinking in terms of gaining an explicit grasp of the intricate integrations of adversarial and co-operative communication may be more helpful.

So how can the content explain the problem? Could the difficulty be simply in recognizing implicit assumptions that we have to make co-operatively to ensure that the conclusions follow? While this is necessary, it is not sufficient. The problem's difficulty also lies in *resisting* other implicit assumptions which we are *not* supposed to make co-operatively.

Perhaps the difficulty in recognizing the logical asymmetry of 'Mercury from pollution in drinking water causes Hobson's disease' involves content rather than just form? Assuming symmetry is just the fallacy of illicit conversion which we saw in Chapter 5 to be so prevalent. The evidence we discussed there mostly involved tendencies to convert (or fail to convert with other examples) rather abstract material, and we explained them in general terms of either lack of a grasp of the adversarial nature of the task, or problems with differentiating proposition from packaging. Here the particular content of this central causal conditional is calculated (by the test constructors) to invoke a biconditional reading—that Hobson's disease is *only* caused by mercury poisoning. Poisoning syndromes are, after all, usually the result of a single poison. Even if the same deadly effects were also caused by liquorice poisoning, that syndrome would probably be called after some toxicologist other than Hobson.

What we find is that our account in Chapter 5 in general terms (e.g. information packaging; balance of co-operative and adversarial stances) can be supplemented by particular difficulties in striking that balance caused by particular problem contents. The difficulty is a pragmatic discourse problem of finding form in content: which is not itself, of course, a formal problem.

A way of emphasizing the distinctiveness of this alternative analysis is to say that the fallacy of illicit conversion, at least in this kind of material, is a fallacy of contentful reasoning, not a mutant formal rule, nor a problem with *modus tollens*. The skill of analysing contentful passages and assigning a demarcation to what will be assumed and what tested is the skill that is involved in solving these problems. In the selection task, the tension between assuming the background rule and testing the foreground rule is an example of this same skill. Our explanation of why the conventional sentential course learning transfers to GRE logical subscale problems is also in terms of the practice of translating 'word problems' into the calculus. These skills of balancing co-operative and adversarial stances has one foot firmly embedded in the content of problems. That is why the explanation has at least some hope of success.

Notice that talking of this skill as the skill of *finding* form in content could be misleading if it gave the impression that there is a unique form waiting to be found. The skill can as well be thought of as *imposing* form on content which more adequately captures its active nature and the range of outcomes. Not that we can impose just any form on just any content. Imposing form on content is actively constructing a representation system in which to reason.

Therefore Wason's selection task may be a good test of scholastic ability because it is a severe test of students' ability to balance co-operative and adversarial elements in communication in a context where few cues to intended interpretation are given, and thus the student is forced back onto textual analysis which demands a highly objective stance toward language. Sounds just like examination questions!

The interpretation of data from Wason's task has suffered from too crude a concept of form, fostered by a lack of attention to the object versus meta-level distinction required in understanding reasoning. The selection task turns out to be all about the processes of interpretation that the subjects struggles with. We now turn to another area of reasoning in which a theory of form has been developed quite independently of any theory of logical form—analogical reasoning. Analogical reasoning is patently about finding form in content. We shall argue that relating analogical reasoning to a deduction throws new light on the empirical findings of the area. In particular, analogies are directly interpreted systems of representation. Seeing analogies as representation systems emphasizes how much of reasoning is the discovery or creation of systems to reason within—another process of interpretation.

6.2   Analogical reasoning: content + content = form

Analogical reasoning has a reputation for being vague, ill-defined, and prone to error as often as success. Shall I compare thee to a summer's day? Thee may well find the outcome uncertain enough to hesitate over an answer, were the poet only to allow enough pause. Nothing, one might think, could be farther from deductive reasoning? But I shall argue that this is a mistake born of conflating different processes involved in analogical reasoning. When these processes are distinguished, we can see the distinctions are the ones we have been arguing are necessary for deductive systems—roughly between discovery of an interpretation and operation of inference within it. Oh analogy! Shall I compare thee to deductive reasoning? Let's give it a go!

Think first of the diagrammatic systems discussed throughout this book. Are these not spatial analogies for reasoning? A thing being in a set is an analogue of a point being inside a circle. The overlap of two circles is an analogue of the intersection of two sets, and so on. As with all analogies, these analogies come along with disanalogies. For example, sets are not round. The usefulness of analogies is just that they are incomplete correspondences. If they were complete they would be quite useless for reasoning. Shall I compare thee to thyself? Better save my breath.

Not that just anything which has some similarity to something else will turn out to be a useful analogy. Useful analogies, like ladders, are ones that are extendible. The circle-as-set analogy is useful because it is extendible. The properties of sets correspond to relations between circles—intersection, union, exclusion, inclusion.[24] The analogy forms a system of relations, so that recognizing one property we can conclude about others. Euler's circles turn the analogy into a simple mechanical deductive calculator for syllogisms.

This description of analogies should be reminiscent of the definition of representation systems in Chapter 2. Representations are things which represent other things. Some of the properties of the representing thing are significant and others are not. They form systems of representation in which changes in the arrangement of the representing objects signify systematic changes in the objects which they represent . . . to recite some lines from Chapter 2. If analogies are representation systems, then should we not expect their use in reasoning to be a case of deduction? Are analogies like representation systems? Or are they *literally* representation systems? Is this an analogy? Does the analogy only hold for diagrammatic representation systems? And where are the dissimilarities between representation systems and analogies, if any?

Let us take one of the most discussed examples—the analogy of electricity to water flow. How is this analogy a representation system? Compressed into a couple of phrases, what is systematic is rather hard to see: electricity is like water. Expanding the analogy helps. An electrical circuit is like a plumbing system. Now we have wires, switches, battery, whatever, on one hand, and pipes, valves, water supply, whatever, on the other. More especially, we have potential, electrical current, and electrical resistance, on the one hand and pressure, water current, and mechanical resistance on the other. Expanding still further, we have a *class* of electrical circuits on the one hand and a *class* of plumbing systems on the other—things are beginning to look more systematic. System is just as crucial to analogy as to representation. The reason that electricity is like water is that systematic transformation between members of the class of electrical circuits are mirrored in systematic changes between members of the class of plumbing circuits.

What we have here is a *directly* interpreted representation system (in the technical sense defined in Chapter 2). Pipes represent wires, components being connected by pipes represent components being connected by wires, size of electrical potential represents size of hydrostatic pressure, etc. There are lots of Rs and *R*s but they accord with our definition of directness, and there is no abstract syntax in sight. Of course, there are many features which are insignificant, but we should be used to that by now.

This representation system is curious from the perspective of our earlier example diagrammatic systems in at least a couple of ways. First, it has an air of symmetry. Although I introduced it as an analogy of electricity to water, it is clear that once it is spelled out, it works just as well the other way around. We probably think of the water explaining the electricity because the one is more familiar and tangible than the other, but informationally the relation is symmetrical. The relation of diagram to diagrammed

---

[24] I am mathematically informed that these topological relations are really set-theoretical relations, and not topological ones at all, but I use the word descriptively.

feels much more asymmetrical. The paper-and-pencil stuff is the representation and the other stuff (hyenas and bankers) is the represented stuff, though as soon as we make the observation we might question whether the systems once defined are informationally asymmetrical. We could take the hyenas and bankers as representing the circles on the paper even if we find it hard to think of a situation in which this might have much use: pencil-and-paper is so biddable when it comes to rearrangement compared with hyenas and bankers.

The second curiosity, which causes much confusion, is that analogies are usually operated as representations, at one remove, through language. When we teach electrical circuit behaviour by analogy to hydraulics, we usually do it in words, or possibly in equations, rather than by getting out some plumbing. We use the plumbing as a representation of the electrical analogues, but only at a remove by speaking of the plumbing. Similarly, the poet uses the analogy of a summer's day by mentioning one in language, indoors, in winter. Our beloved does not have to wait 6 months for the analogy to be used. Talking about an analogy is operating one representation system through another. When analogy is grasped first hand, rather than at one remove through language, it is easier to understand why it is directly interpreted and inexpressive (in the technical sense, not the Shakespearean)—plumbing has no abstract syntax.

However, we should be a little careful here. Language is not completely uninvolved in operating diagrammatic representation systems. We do generally use Euler's circles by drawing them, even if we can with practice learn to operate them entirely through language. This latter indirect operation is the analogue of operating the plumbing analogy for electricity through language.

But there is a stronger reliance of Euler on language and it also applies to another kind of dependency of the plumbing analogy on language. Euler's circles are parasitic on language in that labellings of circles are usually required to assign them the properties they represent—A, B, and C. Even when we operate the plumbing analogy directly by getting out some copper tubes, its application depends on linguistic descriptions to convey what is significant and what is not. We have to describe the water pressure as significant just as we assigned the circles their meaning in language.

If all of this is right, then analogies are just directly interpreted representation systems, and using plumbing to reason about electricity is just another case of deduction. But of course, the psychological reader is likely to protest, that leaves untouched the interesting part of analogical reasoning—namely, how are analogies found, discovered, learned or invented? We can agree that the logical characterization of what a completely specified analogy is constitutes only the bare bones of analogy, and the interesting psychological processes are how such specifications are arrived at and then operated. But this is just what we have been arguing throughout this book about representation systems in general. Much of human reasoning is about interpreting, discovering, choosing or creating the representation systems within which to reason. What is known as analogical reasoning in the psychological literature is not a different variety of reasoning from deductive reasoning. Analogical reasoning is a name for structures and processes which contain, among other things, the operation of deductive reasoning over representation systems. Analogical reasoning usefully puts the focus on the discovery of these systems and down plays their operation.

Our epistemic situation with regard to analogies can be quite complicated and has implications for what has to be learned to operate them, and what can be learned by learning to operate them. In our analysis of representation systems like Euler's, the properties of the representations are well known to us at the outset. We do not learn anything about circles in the plane from Euler other than their correspondences to quantifiers. With analogies, the situation varies. Prior to learning elementary physics, we certainly lack much knowledge at all about the properties of electricity. This is where we stand to gain most. But we typically also lack some critical knowledge about hydrostatics. To understand fully the analogy of water to electricity we have to develop a rather sophisticated grasp of both plumbing and electricity to know exactly which properties map on to which, and so the learning can be two-way. We learn about both ends of the analogy at once, though not equally. This is reminiscent of learning to reason by learning both about Hyperproof Blocks Worlds, *and* about formulae and the relation between them.

There is some evidence that using the plumbing analogy to teach electricity is actually hampered by this lack of knowledge of hydrostatics (particularly the incompressibility of water). If mature analogies are representation systems, it is hardly surprising that candidate analogies require work to establish interpretations. The effects of learning an analogy on the language through which it is operated are also complicated. In learning about how plumbing and electricity map onto each other, we learn new terms which abstract over the correspondences. For example, 'current' has a meaning with regard to water which is transferred to 'electrical current'. These abstract terms tend to be critical in developing the mathematical languages through which we learn to operate the mature analogies.

Of course, not all analogies ever reach the stage of detailed working out of a homogeneous representation system. With the summer's day analogy for our beloved, it generally remains ill-defined exactly what correspondences are significant, just as Rembrandt's etching remained short on systematicity. But then the poet's point is not to establish a well-defined equivalence, so much as to allude to an open-ended family of possible correspondences—as the sonnet goes on to say. Multiplicity of interpretation is a hall mark of aesthetic objects.

Let us look in more detail at the *process* of discovery. Suppose we are offered a new analogy, one pulled out of the air for the purpose of illustration—cognitive science is a picnic. Here the problem is obviously to discover how to interpret the analogy. At first we cannot find any similarity. Next we find too many. Eventually we may settle on one that works, and we begin to work out just how far it extends. Try it—there is no substitute for first hand experiment. This process, which is what is, quite reasonably, meant by analogical reasoning, is certainly messy, and as prone to error as to success, if either error or success is well enough defined to recognize. In the early stages of this process we certainly do not know what is significant about picnics as representations of cognitive science. Is it that they both take place outside some institutional constraints? That they reduce people to a lower level than normal by sitting without chairs? That they dispense with the normal tools for the job? Or are fair-weather occupations? That they are not everyday sustenance? Or are popular in Britain because they are so climatically daring? Who knows?

What process does this sifting of possible significances and insignificances correspond to in the use of representation systems? What is involved when such an analogy extends? Or fails to extend? The answer to the first question is pretty clear—the corresponding process in the use of representation systems is the process of finding an interpretation. People first look at Euler's circles and most see the core of the analogy rather quickly, but many, as we have seen, take a rather longer period to work out how it extends—how to operate it as a system of reasoning. People make errors of interpretation—that is they diverge on extensions of the analogy. This is just like what we know of the process of finding analogies. This extension (analogy-finding corresponds to interpretation-of-new-representation) helps us understand both parties to the analogy better. We can distinguish between the process of finding an analogy, and what the analogy itself is—what was there all the time buried amongst a thousand other systematic or unsystematic correspondences. Its not as if we stop using analogies once we have found and understood them. A mature (wel-known and understood) analogy is a representation system; a novel analogy is a representation system waiting to be sorted out from a tangle of other systems; an unextendible correspondence between two things is just as dumb a representation system as it is a poor analogy.

The trouble with mature things is that the next thing is they die. Once usage has cleared away all the confusions with non-correspondences between analogue and analogized, the metaphor dies, and its remains are now literal truth. Is electrical current not really current because it is not liquid? Once analogies are dead (or thoroughly disinterred might be better, if this were not such an unfortunate mixture of metaphors), they are abstract relations between things which are concretely dissimilar. The analogy has become a theory. The psychological process of analogy finding is a major creative force in making new discoveries in the form of new representations, but it does not create the abstract correspondences—those were there all the time, even if we lacked expression for them. The process of finding new analogies is an important example of what has been stressed throughout this book. There are a multiplicity of representation systems always available, and choosing and creating appropriate ones is an important part of human reasoning. To think of human reasoning as the selection or construction of representations puts analogy centre stage.

How does establishing this correspondence between analogy and representation help us understand the psychology of analogical reasoning? What do we know of these processes of analogy discovery, development and deployment? The work of Gentner, Holyoak, Hofstaedter and their colleagues has taught us a great deal (see, for example, a recent collection Gentner *et al.* (2001)). Gentner's structure-mapping theory focuses on the nature of the correspondence between base and target in analogies, emphasizing the **systematicity principle**: 'a system of relations connected by higher-order constraining relations such as causal relations is more preferred in mapping than an equal number of independent matches' (Gentner *et al.* 2001, p. 176). An example from the plumbing-electrical-circuit analogy would be that the relational correspondence between increasing pressure which increased water flow, and increasing electrical potential which increases electrical current is preferred to a simple non-relational correspondence—say that both systems are often made of copper.

In a recent representative review, Kurtz *et al.*(1999) list seven desirable properties of a good analogy: structural consistency, candidate inferences, systematicity, relational focus, interactive interpretation, multiple interpretations, and cross-mapping. All these properties are phenomena discussed, sometimes under different labellings, in Chapter 2, in their application to representation systems. The authors' analysis of why systematicity is necessary to the use of analogy in reasoning is a description of how representation systems function in reasoning: 'this claim that comparison acts to promote systems of interrelated knowledge is crucial to analogy's viability as a reasoning process', (Kurtz *et al.* 1999, p. 178). We would not recognize Euler's circles as a representation of syllogistic reasoning if there were merely a correspondence between circles and properties, but no relational correspondence between inter-circle relations and inter-property relations. There would be no operations on the one which would allow inferences about the other. It is the mapping of topological relations to quantificational relations which makes it *systematic*, and makes it a representation system.

However, Kurtz *et al.* see analogy as occupying a midway position on the strong-weak and strict-loose dimensions along which they classify reasoning. They argue that although analogy is knowledge intensive (making it a 'strong' form of reasoning), it employs relatively well-specified processing mechanisms which are relatively independent of other cognitive processes (making it more like 'weak' deductive reasoning methods). The authors are led to claim that 'because analogy is not a deductive mechanism, analogy is not guaranteed to be correct' (Kurtz *et al.* 1999, p. 177). Seeing analogies as representation systems allows a more structured approach to this comparison (itself an application of the systematicity principle?). When we structure analogy by distinguishing analogy finding from analogy operation, it emerges that operating mature analogies just *is* deductive reasoning. Finding them is not analogous to reasoning within deductive systems, but rather to learning interpretations for deductive systems.

This insight reflects back onto the base of our comparison and serves to remind us that actual instances of deductive reasoning are also embedded in the processes of finding the relevant interpretation for the language or diagram of the problem specification—a major theme throughout this book. When analogical reasoning proves unreliable it is is because a well-organised correspondence (interpretation) has not yet been found; or because insignificant features of the ground have been used instead of significant ones; or alternative competing correspondences have been employed at different points in the reasoning. Competing correspondences are just what ambiguities or equivocations in deductive arguments are.

This reconceptualization of the relation of analogy to deduction is completely compatible with the empirical conclusions made by Kurtz *et al.* from their very different starting point. They note that the structure-mapping framework for analogy is necessary for grounding theories of reasoning by categories and by similarity, and that reasoning by deductive rules can be seen as a case of analogy. They even quote Wittgenstein's arguments about rule-following, arguments that we are about to revisit in the next section, as evidence for the need for similarity in applying rules to instances. They go on to propose an explanation of the content effects in Wason's selection task as the result of the support of contentful analogy for rule application. In our terms, this would be support from knowledge of content for guiding selection of interpretation or formal analysis. As such, it is an explanation complementary to our own.

Kurtz *et al.* focus on the psychological processes which implement reasoning whereas we have focused on the characterization of what is computed. They review claims in the psychological literature that implementational processes can be divided into **association**-based and **rule**-based processes (e.g. Sloman 1996). While it may well be that such a division of implementations exists, we agree with Kurtz *et al.* that a psychological understanding requires a more structured approach than simply identifying functional processes with these implementations. For one thing, learning can shift the implementations of processes from one category to another. Once a representation has been found for a problem which reduces the problem to triviality, reasoning may well be based on association, but the processes which establish the system and fit it to the problem may be slow, laborious, and based on systematic representation.

Kurtz *et al.* argue that, when structural alignment is seen as underlying both object-based similarity matching and relation-based analogical matching, 'there is a graceful learning continuum from a fully concrete mapping, in which objects transparently match their intended correspondents, to an analogical mapping in which a relational structure is imported to a new domain with no support from (or even with conflict) from the object matches, to a fully abstract mapping in which the base domain contains variables, the target contains objects, and the mapping qualifies as rule application' (Kurtz *et al.*, p. 190).

Our assimilation of analogy operation to the operation of directly interpreted representation systems serves to clarify the distinction between similarity based and analogical reasoning. Considerable confusion is evident, for example, across the psychological literature on classification. Similarity relations are necessarily founded on a classification of objects in a property space. Similarity is a relation between things only relative to such a space. Humans are notoriously flexible in their adoption of different spaces in different contexts, producing different similarity ratings for the same pairs of objects. Psychologically, we may be aware of similarity without being aware of the underlying classification (or even the properties it employs), so similarity may be phenomenologically prior, but similarity is nevertheless relative to such implicit classification. Psychology implicitly recognizes this point sometimes in its terminology of 'features' and 'properties'. Features are detected by our sensors and, weighed together, lead to judgements of category membership. But the properties that belong to entities in virtue of their category membership are not on the same logical level as the features that contribute to category judgements. The latter are meta-level judgements about category membership. Feature-space may define a similarity relation, and our phenomenal access to that similarity relation may interfere with our inferences about classification at the level of categories, but the similarity space defined at the category level is not the same similarity space.

This illustrates how the psychological literature requires a distinction between meta- and object-level inferences. Recognising that some thing is an X on the basis of observation is a perceptual meta-judgement, relative to the object-level deductive inference from the assumption that a thing is an X to the fact that it then must be a Y, on the ground of the generalization (again logically an assumption) that Xs are Ys. *Things* are not premisses of deductions. Nor are sightings of things premisses for deductions. Only assumed propositions about them are premisses. It may be that the perceptual meta-process can also be modelled in a logical system, but if it is modelled, then it is in a different system of inferences than the system of resulting categorizations.

A helpful institutionalization of this distinction between features and properties which dramatizes it for illustrative purposes, is the distinction in biology between keys for identification, as opposed to taxonomies for inference[25] Keys provide sequences of perceptually applicable tests, on the basis of which a specimen can be classified as a member of a species: 'if it has four petals, go to 103'. Taxonomies define evolutionary relationships between categories of animal, on the basis of which all sorts of inferences about their evolution, structure, and functioning can be drawn, many of which are not perceptible properties. 'Is the specimen descended from a reptile?' is not a useful question for a key. Out in the swamp there is no way of telling except by classifying it first. Keys are designed to provide recognition algorithms suitable to specific circumstances; taxonomies to enshrine fundamental biological properties applicable across all circumstances.

Keys are good publicly institutionalized analogies for our inaccessible perceptual categorization processes. Categorisation is a generally noisy process, and is highly context sensitive. A key designed for one county may not give the right categorizations in the next, because the variety of animals requiring discrimination may be different. The answers to the questions in a key may not have any systematic taxonomic significance—animals far apart in taxonomic space (like whales and fish) will tend to be close together in key-space, and have to be discriminated on the basis of such questions as 'Does the specimen have a horizontal tail fin?' This feature has no great direct evolutionary significance, and may only separate whales and fish reliably in an environment where, for example, there are no flatfish. In contrast, the taxonomy of animals does not shift with the locality where the specimens are found. As for keys, so for perceptual judgements generally. We use all sorts of local knowledge to help cut through the surface variability of the real world to a categorization. But we choose our categories for their role in information reduction in making predictions, often about non-perceptual properties.

The analogy between biological keys and perceptual processes bears careful scrutiny. Keys operate with a set of properties that are themselves the output of visual perceptual processes: 'Does it have a horizontal tail?' Only a theory of visual perception can tell us what features we actually extract to make these judgements. Fourier analysis of visual frequencies, or whatever. These are the meta-processes relative to the object-level judgements of the key's properties, which are themselves meta-level properties in the judgements of taxonomic properties. There is a hierarchy of levels. At each level of the hierarchy, there is a property-space which defines a similarity space, but similarity at one level is not defined on the same space as similarity at another. The horizontality of the tail defines one space and mammalness defines another. This is yet another place where the psychology of reasoning needs the logical-computational distinction between object- and meta-levels.

Seeing analogies as representation systems forces us to be clearer about levels of structures and processes. Seeing analogies as representation systems may explain why analogy finding can be so hard, but also raises pointed questions about why it can be so easy in some cases. It also provides insights about how finding directly interpreted analogies can drive the development of abstract vocabularies in indirectly interpreted languages.

First, why should analogy finding often be so hard? Here our knowledge of the computational properties of representation systems is of some help. More expressive

---

[25] *Field Guide to the Western Snarks* is an example of a key: *A Treatise on the Order Snarkivora* would contain a taxonomy but not a key.

logics lead to more complex reasoning. The great change in complexity of reasoning occurs between reasoning with monadic properties and reasoning with polyadic relations. That is roughly between the syllogism (more precisely, monadic predicate logic) and first-order predicate logic. The complexity of the former is related to the number of *words* in the language fragment reasoned with; the complexity of the latter is related to the number of *things* in the domain. If analogies are correspondences between higher-level relations, usually without correspondences between monadic properties, then the search space for correspondences is seriously larger.

However, this answer brings us to the second question: Why is some analogy finding so easy? The examples which most motivate this observation are not the kind of analogies that grow into scientific theories—the electricity-as-plumbing, or atoms-as-solar-system kind—but rather the analogies which abound in literature and form a major part of how we understand each other—more the beloved-as-a-summer's-day, or the love-is-a-journey kind. These are analogies which a large part of the population can grasp rather immediately when the poet points them out, and which nevertheless constitute highly abstract relational correspondences.

An example from Gentner *et al.* (1993) will illustrate the kind of analogy finding which is so easy. The second story below is an analogy for the first and is easily judged to be so by subjects.

Base story

Karla, an old hawk, lived at the top of a tall oak tree. One afternoon, she saw a hunter on the ground with a bow and some crude arrows that had no feathers. The hunter took aim and shot at the hawk but missed. Karla knew the hunter wanted her feathers so she glided down to the hunter and offered to give him a few. The hunter was so grateful that he pledged never to shoot at a hawk again. He went off and shot deer instead.

Analogy match

Once there was a small country called Zerdia that learned to make the world's smartest computer. One day Zerdia was attacked by its warlike neighbour Gagrach. But the missiles were badly aimed and the attack failed. The Zerdian government realized that Gagrach wanted Zerdian computers so it offered to sell some computers to the country. The government of Gagrach was very pleased. It promised never to attack Zerdia again.

Here is a relatively mature if not fully formalized representation system which we can operate with ease in both directions. If we suitably distort the analogous story, as below, it still remains possible to say exactly how the structure has been distorted, as is reflected in our ability to rewrite the base story so that it matches the new distortion.

Once there was a small country called Zerdia that learned to make the world's smartest computer. Zerdia sold one of its supercomputers to its neighbour, Gagrach, so that Gagrach would promise never to attack Zerdia. But one day Zerdia was overwhelmed by a surprise attack from Gagrach. As it capitulated, the crippled government of Zerdia realized that the attacker's missiles had been guided by Zerdian supercomputers.

How is this relatively easy processing of highly abstract correspondences possible? Why is this task not like the one we face as students first confronted with understanding electricity on the basis of hydraulics? Why does this story-correspondence finding process not get lost in the intractable maze of all the possible polyadic correspondences?

The short answer is that we already know about these story correspondences, whereas we do not know about the scientific ones. This answer is both banal and startling. It is banal because we obviously do know beforehand how these stories correspond. But it becomes startling when we try to explain just what it is that we know. It is a fair bet that you have never seen either of these stories before (at least outside Gentner's papers), and that you have probably never before operated an analogy in which tail feathers corresponded to computers. The fact that mature analogies are representation systems can perhaps help us understand.

Let us start by observing how we might explain to someone who failed to see why these two stories correspond. The hunter attacks Karla but fails, and she responds with a magnanimous gesture based on her understanding of why she is the object of the attack. The hunter reciprocates this magnanimous gesture with his own. Correspondingly, Gagrach attacks Zerdia but fails, and Zerdia responds with a magnanimous gesture based on her understanding of why she is the object of the attack. Gagrach reciprocates this magnanimous gesture with its own. At this level of abstraction the stories are just the same story. This is what is significant about the interpretation of one of the stories as a representation of the other. The third story is a very close relative of both of the first two, identical in structure save for one 'mutation' of reciprocation to exploitation.

These abstractions (attack, response, magnanimous, reciprocation, exploitation, . . .), if not necessarily the words chosen here to express them, are utterly mundane concepts for all of us from early on. If we did not have these concepts then we could not get around our social world. The abstractions which specify the significances on which these representations rest are the abstractions with which we explain each other's behaviour. Narratives such as these are about actors' goals and actions, and their interactions with other's goals and actions which lead to resolutions of the congruences and conflicts involved. None of this has to suggest that there is only one possible abstract structure which could be imposed on the Karla story, nor that we would be better telling the abstract version than the original. Stories are about particular characters, goals, and resolutions even if they only make sense because they can be interpreted within our abstract systems of understanding each other's behaviour.

If we look at what is left in the abstract residue that remains when these stories' correspondences are precipitated out, then what we find is that it is the motivational and affective structure of the relations between actors and events that remains. These stories are, in the end, analogues of each other because they *feel* the same. The third story contrasts with the first two because it feels close to the opposite of the other two. This observation suggests a striking conclusion—that the basis for the abstraction involved in this kind of analogy finding is our affective structure.[26]

The idea that the understanding of abstract higher-order relations in narrative might be based on our affective responses should not be surprising. Feelings just are abstract with regard to the properties of the objects to which the same feeling can become attached. The same intense emotions can attach to shoes and ships (and probably even sealing wax), given the right circumstances for these things to become affectively significant (perhaps the smell of the hot wax on the newly sealed and significant document can establish a Proustian significance for sealing wax). Although feelings are themselves so particular, through their intentional structure they classify things in highly abstract

---

[26]I will use the term affective structure to cover a wide range of motivational-emotional phenomena. Including the term 'structure' is intended as a reminder that affective states and dispositions have complex intentional structure.

ways.

At present the structure-mapping processes embodied in the various theories of analogy rely on exact, or hand-encoded, matching of the relations which are to be matched. The hand-encoding relies on the affective insight of the hand that encodes. As an illustration, suppose that we take the Karla story and reverse the affective polarity of some of the actions and events, while nevertheless preserving the 'factual' correspondences. My intuition is that the analogy is destroyed, or at the very least, well buried.

Once there was a small country called Zerdia that learned to make the world's smartest computer. One day the chief minister of its feeble neighbour Gagrach challenged Zerdia to a national tournament of Trivial Pursuits. Gagrach lost badly and a gloom descended. The Zerdian government realized that Gagrach needed Zerdian computers to help its team's memory, and so it offered to sell it some. The government of Gagrach was very pleased. It promised, in the future, to only challenge other countries to Trivial Pursuits.

My (highly fallible) intuition is that this story is not a good analogue for the first one. It is a sort of joke analogy. It preserves the non-affective correspondences between the actors and their motivations and actions pretty well, in the following sense. Gagrach attempted and failed to do something to Zerdia, which responds with a magnanimous gesture based on her understanding of why it is the object of the action. Gagrach reciprocates this magnanimous gesture with its own.

The Karla story can similarly be affectively transformed in a way that would produce an accurate analogue of the affectively transformed Zerdia story?

Karla, an old hawk, lived at the top of an old oak tree. One afternoon, she saw a clown on the ground with a bow and some crude arrows that had no feathers. The clown tried to tickle Karla with his arrows, but it did not work very well. Karla saw that the clown needed her feathers, so she offered to give him a few. The clown was so grateful that he promised never to tickle hawks again. He went off to tickle deer instead.

These two 'affective transformations' (the invasion-to-Trivial-Pursuits and the shoot-to-tickle transformations *do* seem to me to be good analogues of each other—they are the same 'joke analogy'. No doubt experimental investigation would show that the affective transformations are still at least somewhat analogous. My only claim is that the affective correspondence does play a significant role in aiding the perception of abstract correspondence.

Of course, the hard part in designing and assessing these transformations is to factor the 'facts' from the feelings. Although all the causal and goal—subgoal relations correspond appropriately, there is enough affective ambiguity about challenges to Trivial Pursuits or threats of tickling that it is not quite clear whether the final acts are magnanimous? But these problems reinforce the main point. The correspondences show signs of breaking down exactly where facts shade off into motivations and feelings. The correspondences or lack of them rest on the affective structure of the stories. The existing simulations of analogy finding rely on the hand-coding of these affective relations, but the theories do not fully acknowledge that that is what is going on. Our proposal offers a refinement, not a refutation.

We propose that perceiving the analogies between such stories is relatively easy because it is based on our pre-existing understanding of intentional social behaviour and its affective consequences and that, unlike the novel scientific analogies, these concepts predate our encounter with particular stories. Affect can be a source of abstraction just because similar feelings can attach to highly dissimilar objects. Analogies can be processed top-down in terms of these pre-existing abstractions as well as being pursued bottom-up where the abstraction is yet to be made.

Another benefit that has come out of this pursuit of the idea that analogies are representation systems is the observation that we (literate adults) already have a meta-language for talking about the underlying system on which these correspondences ride. When we wrote out the abstract 'essence' which is shared between the analogous Karla and Zerdia stories we did so in the abstract concepts of this meta-language—goal—subgoal structure, belief-desire-intention structure, temporal structure, causal structure, etc. The existence of this meta-language tells us that the grasp of these structures predates the encounter with these stories. It is an open question when this meta-language and meta-conceptualization comes in development.

Teaching literature is substantially about making explicit such correspondences, and providing abstractions for talking about them. The process of doing that provides us with an explicit language for discussing our understanding of each other. This is another case of education being about the externalization, formalization and representation of previously implicit knowledge.

Presently, in discussing word-meaning, we shall observe that these abstractions about intentional action are the elements of what has come to be called the 'theory of mind'. Whether the implementation of these abilities is a theory or a simulation or some combination is an issue we take up in the next chapter where we shall see whether casting analogy as the operation of direct systems through indirect ones can throw any light on these matters.

6.3 Word meaning and logical semantics—abstract psychology or abstract sociology?

Our third approach to issues of form and content is through questions about word meaning, another obvious general ground where form meets content. Here logical semantics has been presented as a failed theory of something which it is not a theory of at all—how language is implemented in the mind. We propose an alternative interpretation of logical semantics as a highly abstract criterion for the alignment of interpretations in fully contextualized communication. In the remainder of this chapter we prepare the ground by rejecting the criticisms of logical semantics. In the next chapter we develop a positive model of logic's role in such a theory—what we will call the argument model of comunication.

As we saw in Chapter 2, extensional semantics specifies a property as the set of elements which have the property, and a predicate's meaning as being given by the property it denotes—the predicate's **extension**. Therefore predications are true just in case the thing denoted by the term they are predicated of falls in the extension set of the corresponding property. *John is tall* is true just in case whatever is denoted by 'John' when the sentence is used, is a member of the extension set of 'tall', as that set is fixed in the context of utterance. We might dub this approach to meaning the 'extensionalist stance'. In Chapter 5 we saw that this stance was an important component of what is to be learned in elementary logic. We propose that this semantics be thought of as an abstract criterion of alignment of interpretations. Roughly, defining the meaning of a predicate as given by the set of things in the current domain of which the predicate is true sets a criterion for aligning communicative partners' interpretation of the predicate. If they would sort things the same way, this much of their interpretation is aligned. If not, not. Exactly how they might decide whether they would sort the same way is a complex issue. Certainly they would not generally achieve confidence by actually sorting. This is a criterion, not an algorithm for achieving its goal.

Psychologists, notably Rosch and her successors, have criticized logical semantics as an inadequate account of the psychological implementation of concepts—though one should remember that a psychological theory was explicitly *not* what the authors of extensional semantics supposed themselves to be creating. Rosch's arguments were that concepts have more psychological structure than sets. We pervasively structure concepts in terms of the typicality of exemplars. Collies are more typical dogs than are pekingese. The colour of blood is nearer to focal red than is the colour of red bricks or red hair. An industry of experimental investigation has told us quite a bit about the psychology of judgements of category membership.

On the basis of such data, it has been proposed that our judgements of categories are implemented in terms of prototype models. The idea is that we store a reference prototype and judge category membership by some measure of deviation from that prototype. Some of the most compelling evidence for such mechanisms is the abstraction of prototypes which are never actually encountered in the dataset of exemplars. Rightly, questions have been raised about how distinct prototype theories really are from classical necessary-and-sufficient-condition theories. In order to compare 'distance' from a prototype one needs some feature space. Our discussion earlier in this chapter suggested that there is a confusion of levels involved here also. The logical level of the features that contribute to our judgements of category memberships of specimens have to be distinguished from the logical level of the property inferences that we make on the basis of categorizations.

But the overriding point here is that these are issues of indifference to logical semantics. Its concept of an extension is to be thought of as something that results, in the limit, from the interpretation being as it is. Mental implementation is just a different, if important, question.

The data from the laboratory lend some support to the separation of the phenomena that the traditional view of logical semantics implies. For example, it turns out that subjects in the laboratory treat 4 as a more typical even number than 14. This discovery warns us against assuming that the phenomena of typicality and the fine-grain psychological structure of concepts that can be measured in the laboratory speak directly to the concerns of extensional semantics. The evenness of numbers is crisply defined if anything is, and yet our reactions to classifications of them also show gradations.

If these psychological issues are not directly problematical for extensional semantics, there are related issues which are more purely semantic problems. For example, most natural concepts, unlike sets, do not have sharp boundaries, an issue that has troubled philosophers since they first contemplated a heap of sand, or Greek equivalents of adjectives such as 'tall' and 'red'. Where in a theory of language, communication, and reasoning should we resolve this conflict between the sharpness of set boundaries and the gradedness of much human behaviour with concepts, categories, and word meanings?

If extensionalist semantics is not a theory of the mental implementation of representation systems, how is it to be integrated with the cognitive theory of mental implementation that we still need? In the remainder of this chapter we shall look at two arguments against the relevance of logical semantics to natural languages, both based on the idea that extensionalism is a failed theory of the psychological implementation of language. One is the 'cognitive semantics' argument that cognition can provide an alternative foundation for language. The other is Wittgenstein's famous argument about the meaning of 'game' which has been widely cited by psychologists in support of their construal of theories of the mental representation of categories.

We look at these arguments with an eye to providing an alternative picture of the role of logical semantics in accounts of word meaning. That picture treats extensional semantics as a highly abstract social criterion of alignment of interpretations in adversarial communication, and will be developed in the final chapter. This alternative picture suggests a quite different role for psychological theory—namely providing an account of the *implementation* of language in the mind and in society.

Cognitive semantics sets out to use a theory of mental implementation of language as a base on which to found an alternative theory of what concepts are and where they come from. I will argue that the cognitive semantics programme, if it is construed this way, fails. Mental implementation cannot provide the foundations of semantics, and logical semantics, far from being a theory of mental implementation, should be construed as an abstract social criterion for successful communication. Semantics is essentially social because communication is first and foremost a social phenomenon.

6.3.1 Cognitive semantics

Cognitive semantics seeks to found linguistic meanings on the nature of human perceptual and conceptual structure. An example of perceptual grounding of categorization, in a forerunner of cognitive semantics, is the work of Berlin and Kay (1969) on colour terminologies across languages. Their careful work tells us much about why languages have the colour terms they have, and the part that human perceptual mechanisms play in their determination. But Berlin and Kay do not try to present their work as a challenge to formal semantics. An example of conceptual grounding, is Lakoff's work on conceptual structures that cut across domains, and how these determine word meaning and patterns of inference. Such treatments of metaphor and other figurative language have played a central role in cognitive semantics. Lakoff believes that his evidence rejects logical accounts.

For example, in a seminal paper in a collection on metaphor (Lakoff 1993) he lays out the central idea in the following terms. The new study of metaphor, he claims, has been put on an entirely different footing by cognitive linguistics. Logical semantics can be identified with the traditional theoretical assumptions that everyday language is literal, that all subject matter can be comprehended literally, without metaphor, that only literal language can be contingently true or false, that all definitions given in the lexicon are literal, and that concepts used in the grammar of a language are literal. Literal language is identified with what can be analysed by logical semantics.

Lakoff goes on to claim that in the work of cognitive semantics, in contrast, huge systems of everyday metaphors have been discovered that structure our conceptual system, including most of our abstract concepts. These systems lie behind much everyday language. This discovery has destroyed the traditional figural-literal distinction, since the term 'literal' carries with it all the false assumptions just listed.

Having wrought this devastation on the traditional view, Lakoff goes on to acknowledge that although the old literal-figurative distinction is dead, one can make a different kind of literal-figurative distinction: those concepts which are not comprehended via conceptual metaphor might be called 'literal'. A sentence like 'The balloon went up' is not metaphorical. But as soon as we get away from concrete physical experience and start talking about abstractions or emotions, metaphorical understanding is the norm. (Lakoff 1993, pps. 204–5). I confess that the interpretation of 'The balloon went up' which first came to mind involved the rhetoric of Lakoff's argument—balloons are a regular trope of the debating hall—which makes the sentence a good example of what I take him to mean by conventional conceptual metaphor.

In contrast with Lakoff, I assume that logical semantics applies to both literal and figurative language, but it applies at the fully contextualized level, after figurative interpretation has been made. It remains quite agnostic about whether human implementations of language process literal language through figural means, or vice versa, or neither of the above, interesting though these questions are. The thrust of Lakoff's argument is that our conceptual system is structured by abstractions which cross domains, and that these mappings have mainly been studied under the heading of figurative language. I fully agree with Lakoff that these mappings are extremely important in understanding language and our conceptual system.

My concern here is not to argue for the literalness of everyday language. I do not believe that because figurative language was mainly studied by rhetoricians and literary critics, that they believed that mundane language did not use metaphors. But this is a historical issue that need not detain us here. Our focus is on the issue about how the abstractions underlying figurative language relate to logical semantics. I doubt that the literal-figurative distinction can be coherently drawn in any theory that offers a single-level analysis of the lexicon (see the remarks on Moravcsik's theory below). But once we separate the level of full contextualisation of language in use from the abstract level of words as represented in the lexicon, one can see metaphors, and especially extended analogies, as utterances which set up novel representations and their interpretations. This was the argument of the previous section. Many of the phenomena which have rightly interested psychologists like Rosch and the cognitive linguists like Lakoff, about the gradedness of concepts and their overarching field properties, are to be interpreted at the most abstract level of the lexicon. This is just not the level at which logical semantics applies.

Vagueness, for example, is felt as a problem if a precise meaning for a vague term has to be fixed across contexts. Defining how many grains make a heap is then truly problematical. Within a context of argument, heap may either be clear enough (if our needs are sufficiently coarse grained—puns hopefully forgiven) or may be obviously not worth clarifying (if we are engaged in fine distinctions), but if the latter, we give up the word and reach for something else. Extensional semantics is exactly the theory of meaning that separates off the issue of commonalities of meaning across contexts. It eschews claims that words must have extensions defined in every possible context. In many contexts it just is not useful to give 'heap' an interpretation.

Much of the psychological implementation of language resides in the processes which get us from the words to their fully contextualized interpretation. But cognitive semantics wants to see the psychological processes of interpretation as replacing the semantic foundations. Therefore, my main concern here is to argue against Lakoff's notion that abstract language must be understood through metaphor, and specifically that abstraction originates by metaphorical extension from concrete spatial domains.

Part of my grounds are general philosophical grounds. Empiricists (and Lakoff is here following an old empiricist tradition) are fond of this deduction of abstractions from concrete spatial language. In the late eighteenth century, Kant was already rather clear about the error of their ways. If we did not have fundamental abstract concepts such as category, property, time, state, change, and causality (and fundamental affective categories such as good, bad, and beautiful), there is no way that any amount of experience of space (or metaphor) would give them to us. We require them to have the experiences from which we gain knowledge. We may not have an explicit grasp of many of these concepts, and our grasp may shift from context to context, but we must be assumed to have some implicit grasp.

But these general philosophical arguments are only part of my grounds. I believe Lakoff's particular examples show something close to the opposite of what he concludes. I will consider two in some detail. First, Lakoff (1993, p.212) argues that the foundation of classical categories and their logic (the syllogism) is the spatial metaphor of containment. Second, he argues (Lakoff 1993, p. 206) that the LOVE-IS-A-JOURNEY metaphor is a case where we understand an abstract emotional relation in terms of a concrete spatial metaphor.

Let us consider classical categories first. According to Lakoff, our patterns of reasoning for classical categories (e.g. syllogistic logic) are derived from our knowledge that if X is in container A, and A is in container B, then X is in container B. 'This is not true by virtue of any logical deduction, but by virtue of the topological properties of containers'. He even provides an Euler diagram to illustrate his point. Therefore classical categories are, according to Lakoff, understood metaphorically: 'Something can be *in* or *out* of a category, it can be *put into* a category, or *removed from* a category. The logic of classical categories is the logic of containers'.

In the light of Chapter 4, I can hardly disagree that there is an interesting correspondence between spatial containment and category inclusion, nor that, for at least some students, this correspondence can play an important role in improving their explicit grasp of the concept of category. But none of this assumes that our fundamental grasp of categories is derived from our grasp of the topology of containment.

For a start, the logic of spatial containment is not at all simply related to the logic of categories. We cannot, *pace* Lakoff, remove elephants from the category of animals, nor even the more portable mouse. They are rather firmly stuck there in our conceptual system. So firmly that if we do succeed in removing them, we in fact change the category of animals—it becomes a different category (animal-*sans*-mouse, perhaps), whether with a different name or not. Once we start to take Lakoff literally, as surely theories are intended to be taken, problems multiply. Our mouse is contained in the category animal, and our mouse's breakfast is contained in our mouse, but the breakfast is not an animal (our mouse being vegetarian), even if the breakfast is on the way to becoming part of one (the mouse). Animals are, after all, containers. We can understand the complex correspondences and non-correspondences between categories and containers because we have a fairly firm, if largely implicit, grasp of both concepts, and of the parts that correspond and those that do not.

It is one thing to suppose that in teaching logic (i.e. in bringing into explicit awareness the logic of our natural languages) that diagrams of containment can play an important role for some students. It is quite another to suppose that our (largely implicit) concept of category rests fundamentally on our spatial concepts. Not that I would want to claim that the derivation is in the opposite direction. At least at a cognitive level, there may be good reason to take space as a fundamental category, along with the category of 'category' and the other usual suspects. Nature's implementation of language in the mind does not need parsimony in the way that mathematicians do. My objection is a narrow objection to the empiricist claim of the priority of space.

Now for the LOVE-IS-A-JOURNEY metaphor. Lakoff asks us to imagine a love relationship described as follows: 'Our relationship has hit a *dead-end street*'. He points out how extensible this metaphor is: the relationship can be described as *stalled*; it can *keep going the way it has been*, or *turn back*; the participants can observe *how far they have come, on a long bumpy road, spinning our wheels, at a crossroads*, if not completely *off the track, on the rocks*, and *not going anywhere, before going our separate ways*. Lakoff rightly believes that this kind of evidence can be taken to establish an abstract mapping between loves and journeys. He proposes that 'metaphor is not just a matter of language but of thought and reason'. He concludes that if metaphor were just a matter of language, then we would expect each of these different linguistic expressions to be different metaphors.

But who could possibly assume that the relevant characterization of language could fail to include some characterization of thought and reason? At least of linguistic thought and reasoning? And if our linguistic conceptualizations are part of our language, why should that automatically mean that they must be sliced up into isolated lexical entries, without any inferential apparatus to connect the many sentences that implement different parts of the extended mapping? Certainly no conception of language that takes logical semantics seriously. The whole framework of logical semantics is set up to provide an inferential apparatus for expressing relations between the many terms of conceptual fields in what are called 'logical theories'.

But aside from these general objections to Lakoff's presuppositions, which seem unexceptional if familiar, let us look a little harder at the details of what we are being asked to buy. On the basis of an abstract mapping evidenced on the observations quoted above, Lakoff claims that it follows that we understand the abstract emotional phenomenon of love by mapping it onto the concrete spatial phenomenon of a journey. But look at the mapping. The mapping offered applies to love, sure enough, but it also applies to more or less any experiential domain. None of the quoted phrases would be incomprehensible in descriptions of a business meeting, a funeral, a lecture, or a war. The real cognitive ground of the mapping is more abstract than both love and travel. Is the cognitive ground spatial?

Are journeys concrete spatial phenomena? Journeys, at least in the sense operative in Lakoff's metaphor, are primarily experiences. One way of seeing this more clearly is to realize that the metaphor assumes that we are talking of token journey-occasions. This ambiguity in 'journey' is apparent in the observation that in the spatial sense we make the same journey repeatedly, but in the experiential sense we make the same journey only once.

One sees this contrast in the interpretation of examples such as: 'if love is a journey, then Fred is a commuter'. This is not most plausibly interpreted to mean that Fred is faithful because he dependably has the same experience. It more plausibly means that he's feckless because he keeps mechanically going through the same motions with different people, presumably with rather little excitement each time. We infer that the relationship is with different people, because, as an experience, one cannot be sure of making the same journey twice. Therefore it is not the spatial sense of journey but the experiential sense of journey which is actually operative. If anything, journeys in this sense are primarily *temporal* phenomena rather than primarily spatial ones. Instantaneous changes of place are certainly not journeys. Even the etymology of the word is from a temporal source meaning a day's work.

Therefore this 'spatial metaphor for love' is not a metaphor for love specifically, since it works for just about any temporally extended experience, and not spatial since it is a mapping of one kind of temporally extended experience onto other kinds of experience, some of which are spatial and some not. Far from space being fundamental here, space is rather tangentially involved.

What do we conclude about cognitive semantics? Not I think that metaphor is unimportant, or that it is primarily a lexical phenomenon. We can agree with Lakoff there. What we should conclude is that the attempt to lay semantic foundations on top of cognitive implementations does not work. We definitely need theories about how cognitive structure determines what categories we can use and how we compute with them in our mental processes, but we cannot get such theories to work if we simultaneously try to make them do the foundational work of defining what categories and word meanings are.

But before leaving love, notice an interesting feature of Lakoff's example. The source of the compelling nature of the correspondences between loves and journeys is not that one is spatial, but it *is* that as experiences, loves and journeys (and business meetings and other temporally extended experiences) can share what we have been calling affective structure. The basis of the correspondence is the *feelings* that all domains of temporally extended experience can share. This observation will be repeated when we look at Wittgenstein's argument about games. This is another indication that developing a theory of the psychological implementation of language will require an account of the relations between affect and cognition.

6.3.2 Wittgenstein's argument and the concept of game

66. Consider for example the proceedings that we call 'games'. I mean board-games, card-games, ball-games, Olympic games and so on. What is common to them all?—Don't say: 'there must be something common, or they would not be called "games" '—but *look and see* whether there is anything common to all.—For if you look at them you will not see something that is common to *all*, but similarities, relationships, and a whole series of them at that. To repeat: don't think, but look!—Look for example at board-games with their multifarious relationships. Now pass to card-games; here you find many correspondences with the first group, but many common features drop out, and others appear. When we pass next to ball-games, much that is common is retained, but much lost.—Are they all 'amusing'? Compare chess with noughts and crosses. Or is there always winning and losing, or competition between players? Think of patience. In ball-games there is winning and losing; but when a child throws the ball against a wall and catches it again, this feature has disappeared . . . And the result of this examination is: we see a complicated network of similarities overlapping and criss-crossing: sometimes overall similarities, sometimes similarities

of detail. (Wittgenstein 1958, (3rd Edn.) pp. 31–2)

The main purpose of Wittgenstein's argument is to to establish that the meaning of a word is not a psychological entity. His argument that there is no necessary and sufficient set of properties which define games, no 'essence' in common between all the exemplars of a property like 'game', was, above all, an argument against essences as mental meanings. For Wittgenstein, a language is constituted by a set of social coordinations. Ramscar and Hahn (1998) are right to reject the interpretation of Wittgenstein by some cognitive psychologists who, following Rosch's arguments for more mental structure, claim that Wittgenstein wanted to replace mental representation in terms of of essences, by mental representation in terms of family resemblances (or prototypes, or templates or theories, or whatever other kind of mental representational apparatus). If categories were not mentally constituted by necessary and sufficient conditions for Wittgenstein, they certainly were not constituted by mental prototypes or some other mental structure. It was not that the mental apparatus was wrong in detail. It was that no *mental* apparatus could fulfil the function of being the foundation of meaning—a stony ground for cognitive semantics.

Exegesis of Wittgenstein is not our prime concern, but I should preface discussion of the argument with some words of warning about anachronistic interpretation. Our interpretation of extensionalist semantics is of a piece with Wittgenstein's argument in that it rejects the idea that logical semantics is a theory of the cognitive implementation of word meanings. It is true that in his late work which concerns us here, Wittgenstein was antagonistic towards logical semantics, but it was a different interpretation of logical semantics than the one proposed here. Nor do I think that Wittgenstein would have rejected the idea that people must have mental implementations of word meanings in order to use language. His objection was to the idea that word meanings are *constituted* by their mental representations. I believe that my modest construal of logical semantics is thoroughly in the spirit of Wittgenstein's argument. But in the end, I am not concerned with the exegetical point. Predicting what Wittgenstein would make of modern musings is a mug's game. The objective here is to construct a theory of how cognitive and social aspects of word-meaning can be integrated, and Wittgenstein's argument is a useful departure point.

Although the social conclusion of Wittgenstein's argument is conducive to our argument that extensional semantics provides a criterion of social agreement, I do not think that Wittgenstein's argument is sound. Its conclusion, or at least this aspect of its conclusion, may be true, but the premises seem at least in need of examination. When they are re-examined, they continue to support the social foundations of meaning, but suggest somewhat different conclusions about the content of word-meaning, and some different ways of thinking about how concepts are mentally implemented.

Wittgenstein's examples of games are intended to throw doubt on the idea that there could be any commonality between all games. But on reflection, the properties discussed seem strange candidates for commonalities—the details of apparatus, the number of players, whether there are rules, winners or losers, and so on. Surely these properties are at the wrong level of abstraction to expect to find essences? It is rather akin to looking for what is common between all pairs of objects at the level of the properties of the single objects themselves?

What happens when we look at a more promising level of abstraction? Wittgenstein's example word, 'game', when analysed at a level which defines the kind of thing games are, and the kinds of thing which are most closely comparable but are non-games, actually appears to be a rather good example of a word with a highly coherent though abstract meaning. A game is defined in *Webster's Dictionary* as *an activity engaged in for diversion or amusement*. Therefore one thing that all games have in common is that they are activities.[27] So Wittgenstein's premiss is false—there is at least one thing that all games (in this sense) share—they are activities. His own word in the passage above was 'proceedings'.

This one thing will not be enough for a basis of the meaning of 'game' because it helps determine the *genus* but not the *species*. However, his actual claim is that there is nothing in common—not that there is nothing in common and possessed by nothing else.

But perhaps that is to quibble? What are the properties that all games have that differentiate them from other activities? 'Diversion' and 'amusement' are pretty perfunctory pointers in conceptual space. Wittgenstein himself, in the quote above, asks us to entertain the idea that it is amusement that is in common between games, and to reject the idea by contrasting the different kinds of amusement involved in a serious game like chess or a trivial pursuit like noughts and crosses. But if chess and noughts and crosses are both amusing they surely share a property even if they exemplify it in rather different ways? We return below to the issue of amusement.

The real problem is not that different games are different kinds of diversion and amusement, but that diversion and amusement will not serve to differentiate games adequately from other activities which we engage in for diversion and amusement but which we do not call games, and from other near-games which are nevertheless non-games. On the other hand, we have more space than *Webster's Dictionary* in which to pursue a finer differentiation. What is involved in doing that? If games are activities, what are their neighbours in conceptual space and what lives opposite?

The situation in English is complicated by the existence of the verb 'play' alongside the noun 'game'. My intuition at least is that play is conceptually more primitive than game. Let us start with play. Probably the fundamental opposition is between work and play. Work is *not* something we could define as being engaged in for diversion or amusement (even though we may well do so on occasion, and even if there are some individuals who inveterately do so). Work is an activity that we engage in for some end rather than for diversion from ends. This contrast is surely one of the fundamental contrasts which structure the meaning of 'game', however complex the actual relations may be. Professional games are obvious paradoxical cases, though ones which in the end support the contrast.

Work is one of the defining conceptual contrasts with play. It is not the only one. There are others which are more subtle. 'Ritual' and 'art' are contrasting neighbours, rather closer in conceptual space to 'game'. Rituals are activities which share with games their contrast with work. Rituals are not engaged in to achieve mundane ends—at least not by working. If a farmer irrigates by ritual he does not thereby irrigate by labour—so instrumentality is involved as well as motivation. Some of the same paradoxes attend rituals as attend games. A priest may be working as well as worshiping, just as a

---

[27] It is true that there is a sense of game which means the paraphernalia employed in some games—the Monopoly set—which are not activities, but this is merely a different, though metonymically related, sense

professional sportsman can be both working and playing. But rituals are differentiated from games (as well as from work) in terms of their ends—their purpose is not diversion or amusement, even if they might incidentally achieve these ends on occasion.

Even closer to games are artistic activities. Music is an activity, often engaged in for diversion or amusement, yet it is not an activity which is called a game. The same goes for other artistic activities. Just as the ritual is engaged in for spiritual ends, the artistic activity is engaged in for aesthetic ends. Both are contrasted with work's ends, and with games' lack of ends other than diversion from other ends.

Certainly there are lots of conundrums in developing such an account of games but the exceptions tend to reinforce the generalizations that such an analysis provides. Complexity of surface manifestation is what we should expect of any fundamental abstract concept. For present purposes, we do not need this sketch to be right in detail, or to constitute the only account of the semantic space, though I think that we would question an adult's grasp of the meaning of game if he or she did not understand the relevance of these contrasts. All we need here is to argue that the work of describing what is in common between games is a work of ethnography in our culture. No doubt there are already serious attempts at what can hardly be more than burlesqued here. The argument is merely that such analysis can uncover the differentia for the species game—properties that games do have in common, and which set them off from near-games that are non-games. There might even be competing accounts of the contrasts by which we fix the concept of game, but if there are then there will be contrasting usages (and senses) in the language. Neither our culture nor our conceptual system, nor our language has to be globally consistent or monolithic.

The fact that I cannot point out or provide any well-honed general account of games might be seen to provide a knockdown argument against my objection to Wittgenstein's premiss. We English speakers know what *game* means, and I cannot provide an abstract specification, so that just proves Wittgenstein's point. Even if I were to be able to offer a lucid and complete ethnographic analysis, someone might still object that since the analysis is new, and the word has been with us for a long time, the analysis cannot give the meaning of the word.

These objections are salutary reminders that we need to be clear about just what is required of an account of what is in common among games (or any other category). An algorithm for recognizing games is too high a demand—even the most essence-laden natural-kind term ('gold' or 'human') does not come with such a recognition algorithm as part of its meaning. For one thing, the algorithm would have to yield different delineations in different contexts. At Wittgenstein's lexical level of question, there cannot be an algorithm for recognizing games. Moravcsik (1998) provides an insightful account of just why full specification can only be achieved in context in his analysis of what constitutes a game of baseball, a much more specific question than Wittgenstein's, but one which Moravcsik shows to be still radically unspecified out of context. If we witness some people engaged in what looks like a prima facie game of baseball there are a hundred questions of detail that can become relevant to answering whether what we saw was a game: Was the distance between the bases just right? Were they practising rather than playing? Was it one of the games in the published schedule? etc. Each of these questions will change its significance from context to context, because our interpretation of 'game' shifts from context to context. Algorithms, even where they are specifiable, are specifiable only at the fully contextualized level. Algorithms are not what Wittgenstein was asking for, I think.

Therefore, the account of game in terms of contrasts with work, ritual and other highly general categories of the purposes of human activity is not intended to provide an algorithm for recognizing games, or a criterion for deciding the difficult cases in demarcation disputes about the extensions of the term in context. At the top level of abstraction all that can be done is to provide the dimensions which structure the concept. Nevertheless, at that level there is a highly abstract but rather coherent core to the concept.

The only novel point in the argument is that it is odd that the outlines of a reply to Wittgenstein's question have not been formulated at this level of analysis. What comes out of this reply is that there are highly coherent if abstract properties that set the activities that are games off from other activities. These properties are what gives inertia to the meaning of 'game' as it travels from context to context, discourse to discourse, argument to argument. But these are not the properties that are found deciding particular sortings along the boundaries of its extension in particular contexts. Since different ones will be operative in different discourse, their adjudications about the very same events may classify them as games in one discourse and non-games in another. At this fine-grain level, the necessary and sufficient conditions vary from context to context. Our interpretation of extensional semantics makes it a totally local account of meaning, which is wholly sympathetic to Wittgenstein's emphasis on contextual sensitivities.

We saw a case of the need for these two levels of interpretation earlier in this chapter when we discussed the problems of deciding the domain of interpretation for the rules in Wason's selection task, and noted the variable balance between emphasis on the backing for generalizations and on their application to particular cases. If a conditional is backed by a generalization it is likely to be treated as resistant to exceptions; if it is merely a partial description of a case then it may be treated truth-functionally. The former emphasis is of a more synoptic level and the latter of a more contextualized one.

This renovated argument should, I think, be seen as merely vindicating Wittgenstein's general conclusions. If the contemporary logical semantics of Wittgenstein's time implicitly claimed that extensional semantics rested on a mental essence, Wittgenstein was right to attack. Our interpretation of logical semantics as applying at the fully contextualized level of discourse, sidesteps this objection. But I think that something new is contributed by exploring what it is like to give an account of the concept of game at a plausible level of abstraction. Taking a very local view of the interpretation of representation systems (here discourse fragments, but equally diagrams, or whatever) leaves accounts of the synoptic lexical level of word meaning as accounts of mental and social implementation. How does the mind and society have to be structured for us to be able to speak languages and negotiate interpretations for them in context? This is surely what cognitive semantics ought to be about, and indeed *is* in the hands of some adherents.

This brings us to our postponed second question: How is the meaning of a word like 'game' mentally implemented? Can our re-examination of Wittgenstein's argument throw any light in this question? Suppose that our sketch of an analysis of the contrasting concepts that anchor 'game' (work, play, ritual, art, etc.) is acceptable in outline if not in detail. What then follows about what we must know to be able to use the word? About its cognitive implementation? Here, 'game' is a particularly insightful choice of example. 'Game' is a word that stands for a rather psychologically primitive concept. However complicated the full ethnographical ramifications of the concept may be, children acquire enough grasp of it to enable them to use the word in at least some range of contexts at a rather early age. Unlike the words that come up in the dictionary definition of 'game' ('activity', 'diversion', 'engage', 'amusement', ...), children acquire some grasp of 'game' early on. What is so intriguing about the example is that the concept is rather abstract, but also conceptually rather primitive and early acquired. Perhaps we should disappear down the burrow of innateness? We can surely do better than that?

Some authors (Gopnik and Wellman 1994) have suggested on the basis of observation similar to these, that children must have *theories* as their mental foundations for words. With 'game' this would amount to something like our sketch above of an ethnography of 'game'. Such claims have rightly been criticised by philosophers of science on the grounds that whatever children do have as a mental foundation for word meanings, it is not much like what we know of scientific theories, and scientific theories are our paradigmatic if not our only examples of theories. If that is not what is meant by theory then we do not have much grasp of what is. I agree that the explicit grasp of the web of meanings which characterize 'game' is a late and never completed achievement, witness my current struggles. And implicit theories are consistently oxymoronic. What the 'theory theory' is right about is that grasp of word meaning is something that ramifies through our mental make-up—it is not a point-to-point correspondence between a sound and an isolated meaning. But theories are not the only entities that can spread the load.

What is left for the child's mental foundation for use of the word game? My answer would be that the obvious foundation is affective. The core of the child's first grasp of 'game' is an affective understanding of the difference between play and other activities—play is fun. Play is when children are able to decide what goes. Perhaps all the very young child has is a combination of this affective understanding, and some of the superficial details (the props of play, taking turns, make-believe, etc.) which are involved in whatever few specific exemplars the child has already encountered.

This too, I think, would have been fine by Wittgenstein. In his memorable phrase, a game is a form of life. Without the capacity to experience affective commonalities between the activities the child calls games, nothing on earth would help the child to use the word. In fact there are children who do not play (some autistic children among others), and do not appear to have the concept of play. They are considered by psychiatrists as having an abnormality in their affective make-up. A definition of game in terms of perceptual features, even if such were available, would be of little help to such a child acquiring the concept, if he or she did not have suitably structured feelings. I am not suggesting that there is no cognitive component to the child's understanding of 'game', but that there is an irreducibly affective component, and the affective component is particularly important in understanding the implementation of the abstractness of the meaning.

'Game' is fascinating because the core of its meaning is affectively primitive. Young mammals engage in play (though non-humans probably do not engage in games). Play is set off from non-play by certain signals that it is not 'serious'. Probably the most widespread form of play is play-fighting—fighting but not fighting. Play-fighting serves to learn the real thing. The signals that set play-fighting off from fighting are essential for the preservation of the peace. Even the beginnings of a physiological story of how this mammalian behaviour pattern is implemented could perhaps be told. Even if such an account lost all the fine detail, it should serve to remind us that if we were not constructed this way, then we would not have the word 'game' for the concept we use it for. But 'game' is not a name for these physiological arrangements. Game takes its meaning from our classification of activities which is distantly based on these arrangements. Our affective structure implements this aspect of our language. It is perhaps particularly fitting that Wittgenstein's example should be of one of the precursors of representational behaviour—behaviour that stands for something other than itself (Bateson 1972).

What does Wittgenstein's example tell us generally about word meanings and specifically about logical semantics? The most important moral is that the lexicon-level of word meaning and the fully contextualized use of words in specific circumstances of communication (such as a specific arguments), are two distinct levels of analysis. Any theory which does not distinguish these levels cannot hope to do justice to word-meaning or language use—or to the relation between form and content. Without its affective core fitting our affective constitution, we could not extend the word to each new situation. But when we examine the actual occurrences of words in discourse, with all the contextual determination that applies, then what we see is a level of meaning which is only indirectly connected to that core. If we reject a particular apparent episode of some players hitting a leather-covered ball and running around what look like bases as a game of baseball on the grounds that the bases were an inch too close (or because it accidentally took place on the wrong day in the season's calendar), then we should not expect our synoptic ethnographical map of our culture's purposes for activities to reflect this particular call.

Moravcsik's theory of lexical meaning proposes the necessity of this multilevel structure. At the top level of word meaning is the classification of games as activities, along with more detailed but nevertheless abstract information about the metaphysical categories of its meaning. But at the bottom level (which Moravcsik presents as a level incorporating pragmatic factors) the particularities that may adhere to the word are quite distinct. It is at this lower level, of detail, that Wittgenstein's claims about the lack of common properties makes sense. And we may thoroughly agree with him that there is nothing necessary and sufficient in common between all the things that would be classified as games across all such contextualized uses—that is just what extensional semantics captures so well.

Moravcsik draws somewhat different conclusions from his theory with regard to logical semantics. He concludes that extensional semantics cannot give an account of the top lexical level of the meaning of words of natural languages. I conclude that extensional semantics is naturally construed as applying to the meaning of words at the fully contextualized level, after the operations of figurative and pragmatic levels of interpretation. These two conclusions are complementary.

On the account we have proposed in this section, logical semantics is a (highly abstract) criterion of alignment of interpretations in fully contextualized communication. This reappraisal of extensionalism as a criterion of alignment leads to a better articulated view of the chain of interpretation that goes on between a word's lexical meaning and its fully contextualized meaning. Criticisms of logical semantics mostly turn out to be applications of the criteria appropriate for contextualized communication to questions about general lexical meanings. Cognitive semantics attempts to give accounts of the commonality between contextual uses, and therefore addresses the higher level of lexical meaning as a cognitive theory of mental implementation should. But it should not be seen as giving a foundational account of meaning in context, nor as conflicting with the foundational account given by logical semantics.

When we acknowledge that logical semantics provides an abstract criterion of alignment of interpretation, this casts issues of mental implementation of language in a new light. One important source of the mental anchoring of abstract vocabulary is in our affective lives. Loves and games both illustrate this point. We can begin learning the all-important abstract but primitive vocabulary of natural languages because our feelings are structured the way they are. Only later, if at all, can we articulate the ethnography behind the distinctions on which the meanings of these words rest. Ethnographic analysis can be seen as a demonstration of the systematic nature of our affective responses, but language use is implemented in these responses whether or not the analysis is ever forthcoming. Language is a form of life given content by affect.

Our investigations into the relation between form and content have used three disparate areas: conditional reasoning in the selection task, analogical reasoning, and word meaning. Nevertheless, the three areas serve to ground similar arguments. The first illustrated how much more goes into an interpretation than the gross form of the sentence interpreted: deciding on the domain of interpretation, the likely backing of the rule, the social position of the speaker, the demands of making sense of all the task constraints, the complexity of the reasoning that results from different interpretations, the balance of co-operative and adversarial stances, and so on. All these issues involve content in the assignment of form in the iterative processes of interpretation. The literature can be encapsulated as showing that conditionals interpreted with deontic force lead to simple reasoning in the selection task; conditionals interpreted with descriptive force lead to complex reasoning in the same task. Different subjects experience different balances of component problems, but this differential semantic and pragmatic complexity explains the observations. Affective responses may play a significant role in how we reason about cheating on social contracts, but if so it appears to play similar roles in our assessments of whether our communicative partners are telling the truth or lying.

The second area, analogical reasoning, also illustrates how much goes into the processes of interpretation of novel representation systems. The process of establishing an analogy is the process of finding an interpretation for a directly interpreted representation system, operated at one remove through language. This insight explains why analogies in general can be so hard to establish even when some ingredients of the necessary abstract correspondences are available at the outset—the sheer number of possible relational mappings is intractable unless clues are available to limit possible correspondences. The same insight can also explain why, for the well-developed representations we have of the intentional basis of each other's behaviour, fitting a new narrative onto the already available abstractions can be relatively simple. An important source of at least some of the abstractions involved in these readily available mappings is based on affective relations because motivations are a major component of intentional structure. Seeing analogies as direct representations means that analogy finding can be seen as the creation or selection of representations.

The third area, word meaning, illustrates in a different way how much representational work goes on in the gap between synoptic lexical meaning and fully contextualized extensions. Trying to make a cognitive theory of concepts out of extensional semantics is doomed to failure, just as trying to seek a foundation for meaning in the mental implementation of concepts is also doomed. A cognitive semantics should provide a theory of how the process of interpretation that gets from lexicon to extension is implemented in minds. An essential ingredient of this implementation is our implicit affective responses to things. Again, affect is a source of abstraction in the mental implementation of concepts. Again, much of reasoning turns out to consist of the processes of developing a suitable interpretation in a context.

Adopting this radically contextualized reading of logical semantics in fact makes natural and artificial languages far closer together semantically than the more conventional view that logical semantics is about lexicon-level meaning. After all, formal languages are radically contextually sensitive because their Ps and Qs are reinterpreted and the borders of their domains are redrawn in each new circumstance, just as we have argued that natural languages are. The fact that, in natural languages, there are common origins for contextualized meanings at a higher lexical level just makes natural languages appear to the casual observer as if they are universally interpreted. What goes for language is even more evidently true of diagrammatic representations.

On this view, much of a cognitive theory of representation is about how content operates in the process of finding or imposing form. In the next chapter we turn to the issue of mental implementation and develop a speculative account of how affect and form are related in the business of representation.

7 Individual, community, and system: human implementation of representations

At the beginning of this book, we started with semantic contrasts between diagrammatic and linguistic systems, and then looked at the incorporation of formalisms of both types into students' minds. Having seen that incorporation had systematic impacts, we asked what students' minds were like before teaching, and how incorporating formalisms built on what was already there, changed the students' grasp of public discourses. Formalisms internalized made pre-existing intuitions explicit, but not without modifying those intuitions. Armed with new intuitions and explicit expressions for them, students now engaged in different public discourses, notably in problem solving. The picture that has been building up relates individuals and communities through representation systems.

A distinctive feature of the approach adopted throughout this book is that in each investigation we have started from semantic considerations about systems of representation, and delayed issues about how systems are implemented in minds. Publicly available representations are first characterized as systems of significance. Only then are issues about a user adopting and reasoning with an interpretation of a system introduced. This is a distinctive methodological choice, but we believe an important one in the current state of theory. Mixing up questions about what a system is like with questions about how it comes to be interpreted that way, and what mental processes are involved in reasoning about and within it, leads to little but confusion.

Taking this stance towards representations that describes them first as relations between representation and represented, as a prelude to asking how a user interprets, constructs, or negotiates them, reverses the developmental and evolutionary sequences and postpones questions about how they develop in individual ontogeny, in communities, and in each discourse of use.

Of course delay in payment increases debt. We owe the reader at least an outline account of how systems are implemented in minds before we finish. That is the main business of this chapter. What we have in mind as a theory of implementation are some rather abstract conceptual schemas for the several ways in which individuals, communities, and representation systems interact in communication and reasoning. This conceptual schematic is highly speculative, and could not have been developed bottom up by the kind of experimental approach pursued so far. But this schematic underlies all the particular investigations that have been presented here. Our only claim is that it posits novel relations between cognition and affect, and between individuals and communities, and can perhaps serve as a foundation for future empirical investigation. Certainly some such schematic view is needed, and many conventional offerings are defective. One thing we can be certain of, and that is that the appropriateness of the schematic view will determine the success of subsequent empirical investigations.

As will perhaps have been obvious since the last chapter, we seek a much more intimate relation between cognition and affect than has generally been accepted. Programmatically we want to see emotions, and affective structure more generally, as *implementing* systems in individuals, and in communities. This image is intended to displace ideas that cognition and emotion are parallel processes or forces, and even the more acceptable idea that affect is the engine of cognition. Affect is not only the engine but also what implements the structures.

The best we can hope at this stage is that this image focuses attention on some neglected aspects of relations between cognition and emotion. One of these novelties is that representations and systems of representation are themselves objects of affective experience. We shall presently try to motivate this observation and make a preliminary exploration of some of its manifestations, explanations, and consequences for mental implementation. But first, we need to draw together and generalize what has largely remained implicit so far about how we take logical systems to relate to behaviour.

We begin by looking at two sources of confusion about applying formal systems to reasoning behaviour. When things start happening in minds in real-time, the neatly distinguished theoretical components—systems, interpretations, and implementations—become intercalated in complex mental and social processes. A great deal of the confusion about the relation between formal systems and computational implementations of them in people comes just from the idea that their idealized transformations map straightforwardly onto real-time processes. The other great source of confusion is the belief that rationality demands acceptance of derivations from systems.

Having observed these two errors, we propose a general model which synthesises our specific analyses of form and content in the last chapter—an, albeit abstract, account of how theories of communication and reasoning can be founded on logical models of representation systems. This is, in effect, the revival of an older tradition in the interpretation of logic as providing an abstract criterion of alignment of interpretations in argument. We dub this model the 'argument' model of communication and defend it from some common but, we believe, misguided complaints. This traditional model of logic as an abstract theory of adversarial communication underlies all the treatments of cognitive phenomena in this book. If we have been able to make detailed explanations of students' diagrammatic reasoning, or logic learning, or naive logical intuitions, or behaviour in Wason's task, it is because this general model of the relations between systems and people provides an adequate conceptual framework.

The argument model of communication couples affective and cognitive phenomena of communication, and raises acute questions about the instrumentality of system in behaviour. Here we distinguish two stances. The one that has provided much of the subject matter for this book is what we shall call the 'system-as-technology' stance in which people learn to use a system as a cognitive tool, and in learning they incorporate the system into themselves. This stance is to be distinguished from the 'system-as-nature' stance in which a system is an analysis of some pre-existing behavioural system. This stance has frequently been our theorists' stance towards our subjects' behaviour. These two stances need to be accommodated to each other and integrated into theories of the human mind, its development and evolution. The system-as-technology stance gives a clear sense to the instrumentality of system, at the expense of raising questions of origin. How far back do the incorporations go? Where does the human ability for incorporating systems as technologies come from? The system-as-nature stance presents itself as a solution to questions of origin (even if only by begging the question), but pays the price by raising questions about instrumentality. What part, if any, does system play in determining behaviour? Perhaps system is only a theorists' fiction?

These are evolutionary questions. Where does our capacity for incorporating 'formalisms' into our minds' originate? What is its relation to the capacity for language? Here our distinction between direct and indirect representation systems may throw new light on old questions about the co-evolution of syntactic and semantic components of language. But the problem is not merely of the origin of representation systems, but also of their intentional use—what we have touched on at several points as the theory of mind. Again our approach to representations is suggestive of new questions. There has been extensive argument whether our intentional capacities are currently implemented by a theory-of-mind or by simulations of our own and others' minds? But what are the critical properties of simulations for this question? How do simulation and theory interact? And how do affect and cognition figure in these processes? Here, we explore the implications of our distinction between direct and indirect representations and the casting of analogical reasoning as the operation of direct systems through indirect ones.

The argument model of communication is essentially social, but is equally applicable to communication *within* the individual as between individuals. This observation leads to new conceptualizations of the relations between individuals and their communities. Vygotsky's model of the internalization of public systems of representation provides a psychological starting point but needs elaboration to accommodate the externalization or articulation of private thoughts and feelings. Seeing internal debate as analogous to public argument, and public argument as a model of communication across misalignments, gives us a way of understanding the process whereby feelings and attitudes are articulated in language and other representations. Affect is not merely an external motivator for knowledge seeking, but is much more intimately involved in the product of learning. But how can affect be a source of knowledge without itself determining knowledge?

Knowledge is a peculiarly human value. Its pursuit takes up a high proportion of human calories. This proportion is extraordinarily high at birth, declining throughout life. Knowledge has its physical instrumentalities but it also has powerful social instrumentalities defining groups and social structures within groups. Little wonder that representations evoke powerful emotions quite beside what emotions their referents evoke themselves. Knowledge also has its own distinctive economics. These obvious but little observed facts are key to understanding the relation between individuals, systems of representation, and their communities of users. How can we bridge the divide between the cognitive approach we have taken here, to sociological and anthropological treatments of communication and reasoning? Often social and cognitive approaches to communication are simply taken as incompatible, or parallel but unrelated investigations.

We end with three brief exploratory studies of the relation between cognition, emotion, and society—each highly speculative but perhaps suggestive. The first is a look at rational choice theory in the context of Damasio's studies of brain damaged patients. The second returns to Cosmides' evolutionary claims and inverts her evolutionary account of the relation between communication and exchange by seeing reasoning implemented in affective structure, and by reconsidering the economics of information. The third looks at an example of anthropological and sociological treatments of affective attitudes to representations.

7.1   Applying systems to behaviour—please mind the gap!

This section sets out to motivate a different relation between representation systems and their individual users. Throughout Chapter 6 we argued that much of the work of reasoning was imposing form on content, using content as cues to form. System is much farther from data (both for theorist and for subject) than has been allowed in the psychology of reasoning.

What are the general effects of knowledge, belief and attitude on judgements of an argument's validity? This was one of the earliest preoccupations of the experimental study of reasoning. Early researchers observed what are usually called **belief-bias** effects in reasoning. These are content effects which arise from prior beliefs about premises or conclusions. A classic observation is that subjects are more likely to accept a conclusion as valid which they already believe strongly than one which they either disbelieve or have no opinion about, where the logical structure of the argument remains constant (Wilkins 1928).

Belief bias is observed with a wide range of kinds of belief but the early literature concentrated on emotionally loaded beliefs. Two classical studies of syllogisms about Russians and Bolsheviks date from two periods when attitudes to Russia were prominent in public awareness in the West. The first (Morgan and Morton 1944) must have collected data contemporary with the siege of Stalingrad when more than a million Russians gave their lives to the defeat of the Nazi armies in the turning point of the Second World War. The second (Henle and Michael 1956) was conducted at the height of the Cold War, when Soviet Russia had been reassessed (if not yet named) as the evil empire.

Both studies show belief bias effects with syllogisms such as: *All Russians regiment people, Some Russians are Bolsheviks*, therefore *All Bolsheviks regiment people* (this example drawn from the later study). There being no logically valid conclusion, anti-Russian reasoners are observed to be more likely to endorse the invalid conclusion than are their colleagues with neutral attitudes to Russia. Unfortunately, no group with positive attitudes could be found in the later study, and its belief-bias effects are correspondingly smaller than the earlier one, lacking a full range of attitude contrast.

This kind of observation, often repeated, leads to interpretations which are sometimes called the tug-of-war model of the relation between reason and emotion. Reason pulls one way and passion the other, ranged as similar forces only differing in direction. Here we seek to replace this model with a different one, but first we ask some questions about its relation to the data offered in support of the tug-of-war.

The first thing to say is that it takes a firm and unwavering grasp of the distinction between validity and truth even to explain why belief bias should be seen as a bias at all. Outside logic class and the psychological laboratory, when we are asked to assess arguments, this generally means to assess their conclusions, rather than to assess them as formal patterns of validity or invalidity. We generally want the bottom line. Vernacular English simply does not insist on the technical logical distinction. If I believe or disbelieve very strongly that all Russians regiment people then I may not be lead to change my assessment of that conclusion very much by being given the premises of the syllogism above. My prior beliefs about the battle of Stalingrad, or the evil empire, or whatever, may quite sensibly dominate my choice. There is nothing irrational about this. Why should I rationally be moved in my opinions by pieces of information of unknown origin typed on a sheet of paper and given to me by some strange psychologist?

As we have had cause to reflect, students (and some of their professors) unsurprisingly do not have a firm unwavering grasp of the distinction between truth and validity. The instructions of the experiments barely even make the task clear to someone who has the distinction, let alone one who has never thought about it explicitly. However, subjects in these and other experiments are not *simply* choosing the truth value they already hold for the conclusions. Even in these materials there are many propositions that subjects may have no beliefs about. They are influenced at least somewhat by the materials as arguments. But then we know that it is most unlikely that all the subjects are doing the same thing as each other, or even the same thing from trial to trial. If some of the subjects are sometimes treating the task as to say what they think of the truth value of the conclusions, then that will generate the observed 'belief bias'.

The second thing to say is that when the literature is surveyed more carefully, belief bias turns out to be dominated by effects in responding to syllogisms *without* valid conclusions (like the example above). Specifically, subjects are much better at detecting invalidity of conclusions when given highly unbelievable examples. In one study by Evans *et al.* (1983) only 10 per cent of subjects accepted invalid conclusions that they disbelieved, whereas they accepted 71 per cent of believed invalid conclusions—the effect of belief accounts for a 60 per cent shift. But with valid syllogisms the shift was only from 56 per cent to 89 per cent i.e. 33 per cent. The belief bias effect doubles with invalid syllogisms. This shows that there is something more than merely judging how likely it is that conclusions are true: at least some subjects have at least some grasp that they are asked to judge a relation between premises and conclusion. But there is still plenty of scope. They could be judging whether the truth of the premises would make the conclusion more or less likely (see the remarks in Chapter 5 about this interpretation of Newstead's questions).

Besides these effects of prior beliefs ascertained by screening prior to the reasoning task, there are also content effects of information introduced by the experimenter during reasoning episodes. These have some importance for how we think of logic being embedded in the reasoning process. For example, Byrne (1989) found that when presented with the following conditional premise and its antecedent as a second premise, subjects typically conclude the consequent:

If Fred has an essay, Fred is in the library
Fred has an essay

Fred is in the library

Modus ponens is one proof-theoretic mechanism that achieves such inferences. All is looking good for the straightforward view of the role of logic (and more specifically the role of *modus ponens*) in reasoning, argues Byrne, until we *add* a new premise:

If Fred has an essay, Fred is in the library
Fred has an essay

If the library is open, then Fred is in the library
_____

?

Byrne observes that subjects now refused to draw the same inference. So much is data—this is what is observed in experiment. Byrne draws the theoretical inference that the subjects are now thereby rejecting the rule *modus ponensmodus ponens*.

Were it true this would be serious, since the consequence relation underlying this rule is about the only constant ingredient of every logic that has ever been proposed for modelling inferences. Strictly speaking we should not worry about the rule—that is the particular proof rule used for computing conclusions. There are logics which do not have this rule as such, but only because they have some other mechanism for modelling the consequence relations involved—axioms, other rules, other connectives, defaults etc. etc. But we should definitely worry about the consequence relation—the fact that the new argument pattern is not judged to be valid, if there were any evidence that that was what was going on.

It is difficult to overestimate the gulf of misunderstanding between psychologist and logician here. Examples like Byrne's are routinely the material of introductory logic courses and are explained by observing that the subjects, given the third premiss, knowingly or unknowingly, abandon the first one. The subjects no longer reason from the premiss 'If Fred has an essay he is in the library' which they now (possibly implicitly) hold to be false. Instead a boundary condition (see, for example, the discussion of ravens in Chapter 6), previously implicit, is made explicit and the premiss is reinterpreted to mean something like, 'If Fred has an essay, *and* the library is open, Fred is in the library'. This shift of meaning is a classical case of equivocation as discussed in Chapter 5, 155.

A modern way of modelling such changes in assumption is the use of non-monotonic logics which, although they contain *modus ponens* as a rule, do not use it to model either of these inferences. In fact such changes in assumption are not logical processes under a classical understanding and one might reject the idea that these non-monotonic logics are logics in the narrow sense. The issue of whether or exactly how to model such changes is complex and technical. But the technical details are not what is at issue. The very last thing a logician is likely to say is that the reasoner has abandoned *modus ponens* (or better the consequence relation underlying *modus ponens*). That would be rather like a physicist abandoning the law of the conservation of energy on the grounds that the rope broke on the pulley system under study. Modifying premisses or their interpretation during reasoning is about the lowest-level kind of event in explaining mismatches to accounts of reasoning.

Psychologists sometimes express irritation that logicians can *know* that this pattern of argument is valid: how can they know that? Byrne operationalizes the pattern and shows that subjects stop accepting it. It must be false! This is a manifestation of some very odd views about the relation between formal theory and empirical investigation. Formal theories do not settle empirical questions but they anchor our concepts. Logicians can be very confident about this particular claim because it is a core conceptual truth. If the consequence relation exploited by *modus ponens* isn't a valid inference within the systems it appears in, then we have little idea what might be. *Modus ponens* just is a logical concept. If psychologists want to make use of the concept, they need to understand it and its embedding in the field of other logical concepts that give it meaning. Part of understanding logic is understanding how the data of argument can be fitted to formal theories. Besides, since mental models theory is just another logical proof theory, it needs the same kinds of conceptual distinctions itself. There is no point in struggling against the conceptual anchoring of one's own concepts.

Reasoning is not a linear process which is committed to a fixed set of premises until it is forced to accept a derived conclusion. In the last section we saw evidence of the complexities of interaction between interpretation and reasoning in the selection task—complexities that focused on anaphora, the reversibility of cards, and the logical reversibility of biconditional interpretations of a single simple grammatical structure. We saw reasoners choose interpretations because they simplified reasoning. For understanding logic's role in communication, nothing is more important than understanding the interactive cycling of interpretation and reasoning—meta- and object-level stances. The effect of a derivation on reasoning can perfectly well be rejection of a premise. If new premises turn up that conflict with old ones, various things can happen many of which will withdraw earlier inferences. In the selection task task literature, effects have been classified as content effects which can be analysed as formal differences between indicatives and deontics. Here, an effect is described as formal (rejection of *modus ponens*) which is more plausibly due to a low-level change of content induced by a new premiss.

The interactive nature of real psychological processes of interpretation, reasoning and communication is what most needs our attention in solving the philosophers' conundrums about the incompatibility of wide content, causal psychological explanations, and computational theories of mind. Computational processes operate by virtue of formal properties of representations, but they also have to sustain interpretations which connect them to wide content. Our computations yield contentful conclusions according to these interpretations, and can be tested, more or less directly according to circumstances, against the world. In sensorimotor loops, the iterations of interpretation, computation, action, and re-interpretation may take place on the timescale of milleseconds. In many of the reasoning processes that concern us here, the cycling is much slower and the tests of interpretation against results are far more indirect. Nevertheless, neglecting the necessarily interactive nature of interpretation and reasoning is the main source of psychologists' rejection of formal conceptualization of reasoning. For example, our complaint about theory in Chapter 4 was that it was either a formal theory just like the rest (in fact more or less the same formal theory), or that it mixed formal and interpretational components in a way that left us without an account of either.

Thus the gap between formal system and behaviour is wider than often assumed. Wider in the sense that we may adopt a full range of attitudes to the content of formalizations, and wider in the sense that the formal models are not process models but static mappings. A pervasive misunderstanding about the part that analyses of form play in understanding reasoning is the misconception that the process of reasoning is linear: *contentful problem–formalization–computation–translation back–contentful answer.* We dub this picture of logic's role in reasoning the 'pipeline' model. Our first aim is to get rid of this model in favour of a highly interactive one. If we persist in thinking in terms of plumbing, then a refinery with its host of tangled loops feeding back products into earlier stages of processing would be a better model than the pipeline that brings the oil.

Theories of form must be seen as abstract mappings of sets of premises onto conclusions. These theories do not say that we should believe valid conclusions. They only say that *if* we believe premises, we *do* in fact thereby believe valid conclusions. The conclusions are already contained within the premises, whether we noticed or not. Noticing what premises contain may be reason enough to reject them—as a can of worms, perhaps.

Theories of form do not even tell us which premises to change when we derive an inconsistency from the assumptions—merely that at least one assumption has to go. According to theories of form, there must be much more to reasoning than form. An important implication of the fact that consequence relations between premises and conclusions have this timeless and directionless character is that when we build process models on top of theories of form, we have to knit the pipeline into a refinery.

Another source of confusion is the easy dichotomy between the rational and the emotive which surfaces in all sorts of places in cognitive science. This easy dichotomy tells us that logic might be suitable for explaining reasoning about neat, well-defined and supposedly rational subject matter like that of mathematics and the physical sciences, but particularly ill-suited to characterizing phenomena of our emotive lives which are seldom neat or well defined—saviours of the Western world and evil empires. The study of deductive reasoning in the psychology laboratory began with observations of subjects' inability or disinclination to insulate their reasoning from their strongly held beliefs and attitudes, and lead, through study of tasks such as Wason's, to the conclusion that logic was unsuited to a role in explaining reasoning as it happened in contentful everyday life.

This typecasting of logic is perhaps understandable in the light of the dominance of technical work on the foundations of mathematics in the last century's far-reaching developments. But in a larger historical context it should be seen as gross miscasting. Logic began as an educational practice for the improvement of communication in circumstances where communication is fraught and concepts murky—the discourse of political and legal argument. Logic maintained its place in the educational curriculum on the strength of belief in this role, warranted or not, for a long period of Western history. This is the construal of logic we are attempting to update as the argument model of communication. .

Thus, if these are the pitfalls of misunderstanding the relation of logical models to behaviour, what are the positive benefits? How was logic traditionally supposed to structure the processes of argument? Logic was supposed to have a rather modest but fundamental role to play in understanding communication across emotive and conceptual divides. It certainly was not supposed to fulfill the role of oracle—the provision of authority for definitive resolutions. In fact what logic does is isolate issues of authority, and this is critical to its functioning in adversarial communication. In co-operative communication, it is generally the case that the parties agree who knows what, and therefore acknowledge asymmetrical patterns of authority with regard to the topics at hand. When being told a story, truth or fiction, we accept the authority of the teller for the information told. We may or may not believe it, but we behave as if we do believe it for the purposes of the discourse.

In contrast, in a dispute, parties assert inconsistent views (or views they at least believe to be inconsistent) and neither party can merely assume authority to get their premises accepted. Logic does not provide 'third-party' authority. The only authority logic has to offer is for *patterns of communication*, and these abstract patterns are rarely at issue between the parties, outside, perhaps, discussion of the foundations of mathematics . . . or logic.

Therefore logic's fundamental distinction between assuming premises and deriving conclusions is what structures the authority relations of discourse. A theorem is represented by a string of premises on the left-hand side of the 'turnstile' ($\vdash$) and the target conclusion on the right: $P, Q, R \vdash S$. The proof is a filling in of the gap between turnstile and conclusion with intermediate conclusions. In logical terms, a story (or more generally, a piece of co-operative exposition in which one party accepts the other's authority) consists of a sequence of introduced premises—the discourse of the left-hand side of the logical turnstile. A proof consists of the sequence of derivations—the discourse of the right-hand side.

The authority relations on the two sides of the turnstile are quite different. As far as logic is concerned, we can write *any* sequence of premises on the left—to do so is merely to choose what assumptions to reason from. If we are engaged in communication with another party, then agreeing these assumptions can be done in many ways. One party can acknowledge the other's superior knowledge or authority, and merely accept the premises (at least for the sake of the argument). But if there is dispute about the premises, then this approach will not work. The point is that for derivation to proceed there must be agreement about the premises, and agreement is achieved by whatever non-logical structure and processes of authority the participants can muster.

Once on the right-hand side, and engaged in derivation, then authority is ceded by all parties to the rules of inference. Any move must be sanctioned by a formal rule, and the formal rules are sanctioned by the semantic structure of the representation system, not by any superior social authority. On the left of the turnstile, it may be perfectly germane to appeal to an authority for the introduction of a premiss. If Aristotle thought that this was a useful argument to explore, then that may be reason enough—he had good taste. But once we pass through the turnstile to the right, such authority is irrelevant. Only the form of the inferences matters. Aristotle could make mistakes too.

Unlike real turnstiles, logical ones do not block return. The results of reasoning may lead us to change the premises if we come to dislike them, and then we are back on the left and back with its authority arrangements, needing to agree about what we are going to reason about. We return to interpretation of these patterns of authority when we consider the emergence of proof.

According the argument model, it is this process of iterative development of shared assumptions and interpretations which constitutes communication. What logic on this model *was* supposed to provide were some criteria for deciding when a debate was satisfactorily formulated, and some heuristic rules of procedure for facilitating the approach closer to such a state of formulation. We might even call it *formalization* as long as we remember to take a sufficiently broad view of formalism. The role of logic might be described as something like this. The parties to a disagreement come with strongly held and externally motivated beliefs, opinions, and goals with regard to some topic—whether the meeting should support a motion, whether a proposition should be made law, whether the accused is guilty, or whatever. Logic sets the criteria for well-aligned interpretations of the language involved. The parties must attempt to identify a set of mutually agreed premises, and to show how their conclusions follow validly from the truth of these premises. Each setting (court, parliament, etc.) typically has a considerable body of extra-logical rules and procedures developed for allowing the pursuit of this abstract logical goal. The procedural rules were known as **dialectics** in traditional rhetorical theory. There is much more to reasoning and communication than logic, but the much more is arranged around logical fundamentals.

This is, of course, no mean criterion that logic sets. The first thing that should be clear is that the parties at the outset usually do not know what the basis of their disagreement is, at least to the degree of refinement that rational debate demands. Or they may be able to identify their disagreement—that the accused is guilty or not, say—but not know the grounds of this disagreement. They may, for example, not know whether they agree that the accused pulled the trigger. The basis of the defence might be that someone else pulled the trigger, or that the pulling was accidental, or that the accused believed the bullet to be blank, or that he was out of town, or that he was out of his mind. Similarly, the defence may not know whether the prosecution agrees that he was not there (but believes that he hired the hit man), or agrees that he believed that the bullet was blank (but that he intended death to ensue from shock, knowing that the deceased had a weak heart), or whatever. The parties need to find out what they agree on, and what they disagree on—they need to negotiate premises and their interpretation.

In cases of political debate, the unknowns may be more conceptual than is typical in the criminal legal case, at least in the lower court. Debates about campaign contributions may centre on freedom of expression, or on bribery and corruption. Even when the former category is agreed to be the issue, opponents of curtailing campaign contributions may claim the right to pay for advertisements as free speech, whereas its supporters may argue that money is used to close off the freedom of expression of political opponents with less cash. So they may agree on what is the higher issue, but disagree on the implications. However sure we may be that we disagree (perhaps we observe that we are growling at each other?), we rarely have a precise characterization of the underlying grounds of our disagreement before we have engaged in argument. Grounds of agreement and disagreement have to be identified. Communication really is necessary. Even in these highly adversarial situations, a species of co-operation is also required.

Interestingly some legal processes have rather explicitly institutionalized demarcations between a stage of the process for identifying *issues* where disagreement lies (a stage called 'pleadings') and reasoning from the now agreed premises to a resolution of issues (called 'trial'). In terms of our plumbing metaphor, this distinction can be seen as an attempt to achieve something at least partially pipeline like, precisely because the processes of argument, left to themselves, are so notoriously non-linear. The legal purpose of the demarcation is to prevent endless cycling caused by the introduction of new issues i.e. to close off a legal filibuster. This demarcation is an institutional reflection of the logical distinction between assumptions and derivations. Pleadings establishes shared assumptions: trial conducts derivations from them. Arguments do take place at pleadings, but they are meta-arguments about admissibility, not object-level arguments about what follows.

Of course, the contrast in social authority arrangements between the left-hand and right-hand sides of the turnstile sketched above are a huge simplification as an account of courts and parliaments and argument in general. In court, for example, the prosecution and defence will not necessarily pause to agree their premises. What they are really interested in is that judge or jury *believe* their chosen premises, and disbelieve the other party's where they conflict. The manoeuvring is about credibility, and the manoeuvring is anything but co-operative. There is an important extra channel of communication between each party and the court.

By the same token, the adversarial communication of the right-hand side may be socially co-operative. We may agree to collaborate on checking a proof for mistakes by seeking counter-examples. The discourse is still logically adversarial in the technical sense that it seeks counter-examples and for ways of resolving conflicts.

Not surprisingly, 'argument', 'debate', and 'adversarial' tend to summon up images of arid contention and *lack* of communication. The formal discourse of courtroom and parliament often straightjackets participants into binary oppositions. For example, recent research on cultural styles of thinking by Nisbett *et al.* (in press) might be construed as evidence that Westerners adopt something like the argument model whereas Orientals seek consensus and avoid polarisation. *If* this is a good characterization of real differences, then, at the level of abstraction that concerns us here, both styles could be incorporated within the argument-based model of communication proposed here. Seeking consensus requires exploration of differences of opinion, and that is what the model emphasizes.

So, at the theoretical level, the distinction between the discourses of right- and left-hand sides still stands. The processes which determine what premises reasoning proceeds from are quite different from the processes of derivation of conclusions from premises. Logic has little to say about the processes that choose assumptions; its focus is the derivations from them and therefore on the consequence relations between premises and conclusions. But to understand communication on a logical basis we have to embrace the processes of both sides.

Therefore, the argument model of communication proposes that communication is the process of constructing the sequence of interpretations. In the sense in which languages include their interpretations, this process is literally the process of constructing a mutual language. This process is the process by which we learn from communication. Logic itself only provides a definition of an abstract criterion for having a mutually shared interpretation—a definition of the ideal goal. The whole process of argument is seen as highly interactive, progressing through a sequence of interpretations held by one or both parties, and its ideal product is a mutually shared interpretation of a language fragment.

In the last chapter we saw that if we take communication as the process of evolution of understandings of terms during an extended argument, we obtain a quite different picture of extensional theories of meaning. It might be summarized by saying that ex-tensionalism views lexical meaning in context as essentially protean—the extensions of the same predicate may vary from interpretation to interpretation in logically ineffable ways, and the interpretation changes dynamically as an argument proceeds. The object-level inferential apparatus that logic specifies is only taken to operate *within* any fixed interpretation in this dynamic sequence. It operates uniformly for every such fixed inter-pretation. But it does not specify the non-logical processes which govern the dynamics of the trajectory from interpretation to interpretation—how we realize which term is causing trouble between us, or what steps we take to actually resolve it. On this view, the synoptic role of logical semantics is merely to set a criterion at the limit for what has to be fixed to fix an interpretation—what we called abstract sociology.

For our current purposes, what is essential about this foundation for a theory of communication is that it is essentially social, and essentially about the articulation of emotions. It is social because of the different social arrangements that govern exposition and derivation—the discourses that operate on either side of the turnstile. It is essentially about the articulation of emotions because it is about how the parties to communication seek to find a language to express (and perhaps resolve) their differences.

Let us review some of the objections routinely brought against this model of logic's role in communication. A common objection to this casting of logic in the drama of argument is that legal or political argument never comes down to the level of examining the structure of deductions. Outside logic journals, the validity of deductions is rarely at issue. Even inside professional mathematics, argument rarely gets down to the level of detail of logic's electron microscope. But surely this is exactly what we would expect on this casting of logic. Logic successfully provides the criteria of adequate agreement and this is witnessed by the fact that disagreement about deductions does not break out. Whenever disagreement about what follows seems to be about to break out, the parties realize that instead there is disagreement about what is being assumed, the meaning of a word, the decomposition of a concept, the relevance of a topic, the admissibility of evidence, the priority of a statute, etc., etc. All that logic offers is criteria for the assurance that our representation systems are sound.

In the nineteenth and early twentieth century, before a good grasp of the distinction between meta-level and object-level phenomena had been achieved, philosophers were puzzled by where logic's authority for patterns of argument came from? Why, for example, is *modus ponens* a valid inference rule? The consequence was an appearance that logic was the ultimate authority in debate—an authority above both parties. One still sees vestiges of this stance in rejections of logic as the tool of the ruling classes or gender. With an understanding of the metalogical properties of systems of representation, this illusion disappears. Soundness is a desirable property of communication and reasoning systems for peculiarly mundane reasons. Soundness is the property that assures the user that reasoning begun from true premises will not yield false conclusions. In unsound systems generally, any conclusion may be reached from any set of premises. Soundness is a constitutive condition on what we mean by communication and reasoning.

With understanding of this meta-stance comes our modern proliferation of logics. From the nineteenth-century notion of a single logic laying down the laws of reasoning, logic has moved to being the representational supermarket: 'Tell me what reasoning you want to model, and I'll find you a nice system for it' is the spirit of the age.

Another misapprehension is that this view supposes that the conclusion of an argument is a truth of logic. 'The defendant is guilty' does not follow deductively from the axioms of any logic. If it follows, it follows from assumptions of the case as hammered out in court: he did pull the trigger, he did intend death, he did know what he was doing, and *if* he did all these things, *then* he is guilty as charged under Law X. The requisite conditional that bridges the inference is typically a legal premiss, not a logical axiom. When these conditionals are laws, they are legal laws, not laws of logic. In logic these observations are encompassed in the distinction between a logic and a non-logical *theory* couched within it—between logical principles and principles of what are picturesquely called the 'special sciences'. Logic is an account of how domain general and domain specific knowledge interacts—just what is lacking from many accounts of 'modularity'. If putting logic at the top of the hierarchy of generality offends, then we could perfectly well accept that logic is itself a special theory—the abstract theory of representation and communication systems. Logic is highly general in that it is about all representation systems; logic is highly specific in that it is about representation systems. This perhaps reduces any residual imperialism.

Notice that this approach has important conceptual implications for the modularity of reasoning. Basing one's theory of reasoning on logic is usually taken to assume that reasoning is domain general. But logic in the view developed here is precisely a theory of the domain dependence of reasoning or, perhaps better, a theory of the interactions between domain-general features of representation systems and domain-specific knowledge encoded in them. This is another area in which the recent logical concentration on mathematics has distorted common interpretations. In the development of logic as a foundation for mathematics, the issue of what mathematical truths could be derived *solely* from logical truths was the issue. It was eventually resolved when it was shown that mathematics requires special domains for its interpretation. But the demarcation of logic from mathematics is not the issue at stake for cognitive theories of reasoning. Domain specific reasoning still requires logic, but it is logic operating on encodings of domain-specific information.

Another common objection to the role for logic sketched here is that a logical basis for argument leads us to expect that argument will terminate in agreement. Leibniz' fond vision of replacing war with logical calculation nicely encapsulates this view. But we should dismiss this objection on the current casting of logic as a criterion for establishing a mutual language in communication. In Leibniz' day, it was believed that logic could decide all sorts of matters which we nowadays recognize as empirical issues. This imperialist picture of logic is not the one we would want to return to. We do not have to reach agreement for communication to have succeeded. If, at the end of an argument, we know more about the structure of our opponents' assumptions and conclusions, then we shall have succeeded in communicating, but we may well be further apart in our views than we were at the outset. We may have discovered that our views are more irreconcilable than we first thought. We might decide to go to war!

We might try to rescue a remnant of Leibniz' optimism with a claim that on average, better mutual understanding will tend to make it more likely that war–war, the alternative to jaw–jaw, is seen to be unprofitable. But such a rescue would have to be based on more than logic, even if the exercise of logic might play a useful role in clarifying the many opaque concepts that are involved.

Analogously, it might be objected that logic cannot assure us that we shall be any nearer to the truth at the end of debate than we were at the beginning, nor that the 'right' side will win. These claims are correct, but not objections. Logical skill in the formulation of arguments can as well be used to deflect the argument from the important conclusion by motivating a change to false premises, as to hasten us to belief in the truth. Argument in the asylum is likely only to lead to lunacy. All this can be accepted without leading us to reject the conclusion that logic provides some rather weak but foundational criteria for the conduct of communication.

Logic gives us ways of exploring relations between sets of assumptions and conclusions. A useful picture here is to think of logic as developing islands of coherence—sets of assumptions and their implications—set in a sea beneath which most of the logical relations between assumptions are submerged. The relations between these islands and any shore generally remains unclear. Sometimes causeways are built between islands, but it is unwise to see the goal as the drainage of the sea.

This point that logic is agnostic about the truth of assumptions and premisses often gets lost. An antidote to the idea that logic is primarily a matter of modelling beliefs is to think of logic as providing techniques for exploring *fictional* worlds. Such worlds are characterized by sets of assumptions which are internally coherent, but bear an unspecified and complicated relation to the real world. Logic just as naturally provides underpinning for drama and imagination, as for mathematics or physics.

It is cognitively interesting that the explicit technical grasp of this point in logic appears to be very recent. Hodges has recently claimed that no logical account of suppositional reasoning predates the invention of natural deduction by Jaśkowski and Gentzen in the 1930s, after Łukasiewicz had called attention to this kind of reasoning in 1926.[28] Hodges' claim is striking. An initial response is often that *reductio ad absurdum* arguments are both old and examples of suppositional reasoning. But Hodges points out that these are examples that support the generalization. Earlier formalizations of *reductio ad absurdum* which might be construed as suppositional reasoning in fact treat it as system-internal reasoning from conditional premisses: *if P then Q, if P then* $\neg Q \vdash \neg P$. It cannot be a coincidence that the explicit understanding of suppositional reasoning arrived just when the metalogical results of the early 1930s achieved an understanding of the necessity of distinguishing object and meta-level reasoning.

Finally, it is often objected that logic provides a mechanical account of argument, and that the data of argument clearly establish that no such mechanical process is in progress. Argument is endless. Again one can accept the conclusion and reject the premiss. Logic has done more than any other discipline to clarify the fundamental nature and limits of mechanical accounts of reasoning. Its results show that a mechanical account of reasoning is not generally attainable. Logic has proved, under plausible assumptions, that there can be no mechanical algorithms for testing whether arbitrary conclusions follow from given premisses, in most logical systems of sufficient expressiveness to be of much use in formalizing arguments—the first-order predicate calculus of Chapter 3, for example. Logic has even proved that there are true but unprovable propositions contained in simple formalizations of, for example, elementary number theory. It is not that Leibniz's dream was right about mathematics but wrong about war. Leibniz' dream is unattainable for mathematics.

Logic has thus shown how much more to argument there is than logic. The relevant theorems of metalogic are beyond the scope of this book, but they are the technical development that most changed the philosophical outlook of twentieth-century logic, and can potentially defuse the conflict between logical and psychological accounts of reasoning. When seeking to recover a traditional view of the role of logic in argument, we should be careful to leave behind the attitudes of traditional logic that this technical revolution has laid to rest.

Much of this case for recasting logic consists of showing that logic does not make the assumptions that the opponent ascribes to it. The opponents' final riposte is likely to be that if that is all there is to the theory, then there is nothing left of the theory—what

---

[28]Lecture to Cognitive Science Society Annual Conference, Edinburgh, August 2001

remains can do no useful work. We should be careful not to confuse insufficiency with dispensability. If logic is not the whole of reasoning that does not mean that it is no part. If we accept that the theory has a modest role, where should we look for evidence that this modest role is indispensable?

One kind of reply to this complaint that the unpretentious model of logic's role is too weak to be useful, has already been made throughout this book—the provision of examples of empirical investigation of reasoning grounded on logical analysis. Chapter 3 presented observations that learning logic *can* improve general reasoning; Chapter 4 argued, with regard to psychological theories of the syllogism, that their purported differences could not be distinguished in the data offered, but could potentially be understood in terms of directness and indirectness of their semantics. That chapter also showed that the same kinds of processes and individual differences in learning found with Hyperproof occur when learning syllogistic reasoning. Chapter 5 asked what it could mean to *learn* to reason and resolved the paradox in terms of the explicitness of grasp of alternative kinds of discourse, and of information packaging. Again empirical observations guided by elementary logical analysis showed that measuring students interpretation could predict their subsequent reasoning. The last chapter opened with a demonstration that formal analyses of language can guide the investigation and explanation of what subjects do in reasoning with conditionals in the selection task, and how content interacts with form in affecting that reasoning.

But notice that these roles are not the ones that logic has been expected by psychologists to fulfill. Logic's contribution here is not a set of widgets for reasoning—a mechanism. Our analysis of the mechanisms underlying learning from Hyperproof was couched in terms of strategies for deploying different kinds of representation. In the narrow sense, these are theorem-prover, not logic. Students were observed to tune their strategies of reasoning in logically interpretable ways. Students learn about representations and skills for their use, and they learn the difference between validity and truth, object and meta-levels, and so on. In studying naive logical intuitions, logic functioned to distinguish kinds of discourse and models of communication—not by providing some mechanism for reasoning. In analysing content effects in conditional reasoning, logical semantics provides an analysis of the differences between deontic and indicative conditionals which told us where to look for differences in reasoning behaviour in Wason's very particular task. These places to look ranged from expectations about contingencies between card choices to the social psychology of the experiment. In reappraising the component processes of analogical reasoning, logical semantics provided a criterion for distinguishing reasoning about systems during their discovery or construction, as opposed to reasoning within mature systems of representation. Above all this model of logic's role in understanding cognitive phenomena suggests that logic will come to prominence whenever we have to explain people's behaviour in negotiating interpretations during communication and reasoning.

But these small forays into empirical investigation are only one kind of answer to the question of what logic can do for cognition in its newly modest clothes. Another kind of reply entirely to the objection that our modest view leaves logic harmless but useless, is to develop the general implications of the model for how representation systems are implemented in minds and societies. On this score, we noted that the model is both inherently cognitive and inherently social. The two sides of the turnstile are distinguished by their different social arrangements for authority for discourse moves. Yet the consequence relations between premises and conclusions are the stuff of cognition if anything is. Notice also that on this model, the processes of reasoning and communication are distinguished into meta and object-level processes, and that those levels interact throughout. Notice finally that the model conceptualizes communication as an inherently affective phenomenon; its paradigm case is the resolution of dispute, where dispute calls into question the alignment of interpretations.

How can these logical foundations of communication help us understand the instrumentalities of system in behaviour? First we need to acknowledge two contrasting involvements of systems in behaviour.

7.2 Implementation: logic as nature or logic as technology

So here is the tension that we have to resolve. If logic is a mere abstract analysis and has to be implemented in some mechanism before it provides any causal account of mental process, then what use is the conceptual map which logic provides? If people only compute *as if* they were obeying some system, then how does systemic analysis achieve mental analysis? Stones fall *as if* they were obeying physical laws, but representations of the laws are not instrumental in their behaviour. Perhaps people are just like stones are to physical laws in this regard with respect to systems of representation.

This is a question which requires an answer if the whole programme of this book is to be carried through. If we have no answers, then we either conclude that logic is irrelevant to understanding behaviour because it is not causally involved, or we could opt for a simple causal role in which logic is a natural mechanism the laws of thought.

Answers we had better have, but we absolutely should not expect *one* answer. Taking our more abstract view of logic opens a large space between system and implementation. Logics can be implemented in many different ways. They can be implemented in different physical substrates, but much more importantly, implementations differ in all sorts of much more cognitively substantial ways. Implementations may cross individuals as well as happening within a single individual. As is obvious from the construction of engineered systems, if it was not obvious before, there are many levels of system and implementation. Biology being what it is, we should expect different solutions to be found to different problems, and moreover we should expect them to be reused whenever they become appropriate to some new task.

The research programme described in this book started by looking at the learning of formalisms and its impact on subsequent reasoning. Here are the kinds of cases which are the most direct evidence for instrumental involvement of system in behaviour. We observed people *learning* to use systems and observed the way that that changed what they could subsequently do. Students learn say a graphical representation system and can then be shown to reason in a different way. We have good grounds for saying that they have now incorporated some implementation of the system at some level.

To put it baldly, learning is the most direct evidence of instrumentality. This does not presuppose some behaviourist theory of learning, or that learning requires no prior mental structure, or that we should be able to find some logical rule system encoded in students' synapses. It merely means that observing the internalization of a new representation system and its impact on reasoning is the most direct kind of observation we can make of the instrumentality of representation systems in the mind.

Of course the immediate response tends to be that by narrowing the field to such cases to purchase a strong view of the system's instrumentality, we have paid the price of narrowing the system's causal powers back to the logic classroom. 'Sure when we learn first-order predicate calculus and it changes what we can do, logic is instrumental in behaviour. But that's the only time, and it only applies to a handful of the population, and it can only possibly apply since the first half of the twentieth century because first order predicate logic was not taught to anyone before that.' But our argument will be that this extreme end of the dimension is a good place to start in seeking generalizations about the internalizations of representations.

We have presented some of the evidence that the impact of learning formalisms in logic class is much wider than merely learning the formal system itself. And by starting with this extreme example, we have been able to raise a series of questions about this model of the instrumentality of representations which has much broader implications. For example, we have shown that understanding what happens during such system incorporation demands an understanding of what was there before incorporation. The formalization is formalization of knowledge which was already implicit before.

Learning representations for things is not confined to the logic classroom. Much of formal education can be viewed as learning representation systems—learning to write, learning to understand literature, and learning mathematics are perhaps the three central examples. Here we learn representation systems and they change what we can do. They are instrumental in our subsequent cognition. We (along with whatever paper and pencils and computers we continue to use) implement these systems, however partially or approximately.

For a convenient name for this relation between representations and their instrumentality in behaviour we shall call it the system-as-technology model. It contrasts with a model which sees logic as a theoretician's account of a mechanism that has been incorporated into us through evolution without any direct causal involvement of representations of the logical system itself. This latter kind of relation we shall call the system-as-nature relation.

First, it is important not to see these views of logic's relation to behaviour as necessarily in global competition with each other. They may compete to explain the appearance of some particular behaviour, but they are not once-and-for-all world views. We can perfectly well see logic as a theorist's tool for analysing behaviour which is assumed to be evolved without any recourse to learning representations, in some cases, while simultaneously seeing representation systems as technology incorporated by learning in other cases. Historically, one perspective or the other has dominated one or another discipline at different periods.

When mathematical logic was invented before the turn of the twentieth-century, it was seen as a technology for reasoning, necessary because natural language was deemed to be so hopelessly messy and confused a system for doing any serious work on the foundations of mathematics or science. By the middle of the twentieth-century, Montague was claiming that English *is* a formal language, and a particular logic was a characterization of a natural phenomenon (natural language). Both of these views could in principle be correct—they are claims about different behaviours. I am not proposing to replace one view (the currently most popular system-as-nature view in cognitive science) with another (the system-as-technology view). I want to distinguish them because I believe that the truth requires an integration of the two.

The hard case for understanding the consequences of this contrast in perspectives is, of course, natural language. The contrast makes it clear that natural language is not one unitary set of capacities. At the technology end of the spectrum, consider the impact of learning to write one's mother tongue. Literacy has rather considerable impacts on people's language itself as well as on their mental constitution, even if that impact cannot easily be separated from the impact of living in a literate culture. How differently Scribner's schooled and unschooled subjects respond to the same verbal problem? One might argue in a similar vein about the learning that goes on in school in so-called 'English' class (for English speaking students—'first-language class' in general). We learn to do many of the things we can do with our native language as a result of formal education—representation and reasoning being no small part. Here is strong evidence for the systems-as-technologies view of the instrumentality of system in behaviour, though it is culture-specific evidence. Not all humans are like this, nor are they like this all the time.

But what about learning to talk? Here is a set of external (acoustic) representation systems which are incorporated into behaviour and have profound effects on our mental constitutions. Is the abstract system which we acquire arrived at on the system-as-technology model or on the system-as-nature model? Is spoken language a cultural artifact or a natural phenomenon? Is natural language natural? Was language an invention or an adaptation?

The battlelines are already drawn up. But I would like to sue for peace. Both answers can perfectly well be correct, though they cannot simply be munged together. We need to pay rather careful attention to what level of abstraction we intend when we talk of a representation system. Technologies depend for their adoption upon the nature of the adoptee (and the cultural context). Not just any technology can be incorporated into our behavioural repertoire, and even if one can be incorporated, its behavioural consequences depend intimately on what is there already, and what social circumstances we find ourselves in. Incorporation is not a matter of writing on a *tabula rasa*, or the mere imprinting of habits through repetition. Our model of acquisition that explains how representations can be incorporated as mental technologies needs to be thoroughly cognitive.

Nor does the idea that representation systems are inventions mean that we could have invented just any systems we pleased. We do not ascribe this arbitrariness to any other kind of invention. One-wheeled cars, for example, just do not get invented. Unsound representation systems are pretty much like one-wheeled cars: they neither stand up nor catch on. Why should we believe that invention means freedom from mathematical, physical, biological or social constraint? What an insult to inventors and their cultures! Try telling an Edison or a Watt that they operate free from constraints in making inventions. No one believes that biological adaptations are unconstrained.

Natural language behaviour—speaking and understanding—makes a pretty strong case that there is *some* causal involvement of an internalization of a representational system in behaviour. Natural language just is, among other things, a representational activity, and is internalized. Human beings have an ability to incorporate suitable novel representation systems into their mental makeup. Other species do not. Does this mean that they have an innate 'cognitive technology incorporation' faculty? Is this the 'nature' that we have which permits culture? Is this the innate biological basis for culture?

I first want to argue that innateness and acquiredness are not the interesting issue here. The issue of innateness (or acquiredness) is, in fact, the reddest of herrings. Even if a complete correct universal grammar were found in the DNA or the neurons or whatever bit of the body,[29] the only interesting question would be *how* this code was instrumental in behaviour, or whether, for that matter, it was 'junk' DNA. Merely discovering it would not decide whether language was innate (or acquired). In actual fact, of course, we could not tell whether any sequence was such an encoding until we did have an account of how it was expressed—expressed in the environment of the developing phenotype.

In an age where we understand perfectly that the heritability quotient of a gene is a function of the environment in which the phenotype develops, including the metabolic effects of all the other genes (e.g. Waddington's (1957) classical work on *Drosophila*), it is incredible that this dispute can still go on in the social sciences without reference to relevant biological theory. Even supposing we were to find universal grammar encoded in our DNA (never forgetting its copyright declaration), we would be no nearer understanding how language performance comes to be expressed in whatever environments, or to what extent the expression of the relevant abilities in phenotypes are dependent on learned (or innate) behaviours (whatever they may be). At this level of specification, these questions are meaningless. They are nineteenth-century relics that have survived the scientific developments that refined them out of a job, preserved in the discourse by dimly felt ideological needs.

One might understand appeals to innateness as statements about idealizations adopted for the purposes of getting work done—drawing a line in the sand and admitting that past this line, mental origins are unknown, or unexamined in the current effort. Appeals to modularity work in rather similar ways, as declarations that interactions with other mental structures are outside the scope of the current work. To make progress we have to focus. But inevitably, both innateness and modularity are translated into claims of insight. Their proponents claim they make real contributions because they strike a blow against generalized theories of computation or learning, but we have seen that these theories are straw men. Logic is not a theory that reasoning is homogeneous or learned by rote. In fact it is a good basis for developing highly modular theories of processing. But merely claiming modularity with explaining interaction is vacuous.

The scientific need is for some account of the functionalities involved, and how the selection pressures of human prehistory were maintained to give a continuous account of the evolution of our facility with the incorporation of new representation systems such as spoken natural languages, writing systems, graphical systems, music, and mathematics. One of this book's arguments has been that even thinking of natural languages as unitary systems of representation makes it impossible to do justice to human semantic capacities. Natural languages may be highly syntactically homogeneous (within themselves) but they are highly semantically heterogeneous (within themselves). Natural languages are indefinitely large sets of related interpretations of interlocking fragments of highly specialized representation systems. Their semantic apparatus has to be considered at a

---

[29] We can even imagine it is complete with publisher's copyright symbol: 'God reserves all rights of reproduction by whatever means ...'

completely contextualized level in order to see many of its generalities. Before we could even start looking for some genetic representation we need to know how to describe the phenotype, and the available descriptions are controversial.

There is also the issue of the interpretation of the use of representation systems as intentional entities. Possession of semantic and syntactic components of a natural language (the competence to generate and parse linguistic objects) is not itself sufficient to allow the use of language for communication.

The semantic, the syntactic, and the pragmatic apparatus of natural languages are three candidates for functional elements of human representational abilities. Leaving aside the pragmatics for a moment, the result of this contrast between the homogeneity of the syntactic structure and the heterogeneity of semantic structure is that they present different problems to an evolutionary account. It may be plausible that the ability for syntactic processing is based on a relatively functionally modular biological innovation. It is less plausible at this level of description that human semantic abilities are based on a single modular computational innovation. Think for example of the mental apparatus required to detect and control the higher-level relational correspondences in analogical reasoning (and other directly interpreted representation systems); the ability to interpret an operation transforming one representation into another as corresponding to a transformation of one represented situation into its correspondent (the essentials of system); the ability to distinguish types and tokens of representations; the ability to understand correspondence remote in time and place; the requirement of an episodic memory for understanding the semantics of temporal reference . . . The computational implementations of these disparate abilities seem likely to be highly heterogeneous.

This contrast between the homogeneity of syntactic abilities and the heterogeneity of semantic abilities cuts rather the other way when the goal is to explain continuity of selection pressure. Most of the many abilities that make up our semantic competence can perhaps be seen as plausibly making a piecemeal contribution to biological fitness, precisely because they are rather a heterogeneous set of abilities. This is why we can sometimes find precursors to them in a range of species. But the syntactic component of language really does look rather monolithic. Sequential processing of abstractly categorized token representations is easier to think of as a computational module, but it is correspondingly hard to give a continuous account of its contribution to fitness.

One problem then is to understand how both syntactic and semantic capacities could come together in evolutionary history. Natural language without syntactic structure is not natural language: natural language without structured contextualized semantics is not natural language. Whatever fitness is conferred by speaking natural languages is conferred by their combination, even if they each conferred other fitnesses before their combination.

It has been argued recently that language was the product of sexual selection, as if this freed us from the obligation of functional analysis. Sexual selection is still natural selection, however distinctive the functional fitnesses involved may be. There is a relatively simple story about how the peacock's tail got the way it is, because it is a relatively simple device with a relatively simple function. But for sexual selection to explain language, we need to understand how language functions in mate selection— on just which of its myriad dimensions is it so impressive to potential partners, and what structure and functions did it have, and how did it come to have them before it 'got bigger'. Quite besides the quaintness of the idea that language originated in the male, and the observation that the larger 'tail' appears to have developed on the wrong gender for this explanation. But at least this proposal helps to understand that the selection pressures that maintained the component capacities required for language may have been rather disparate before they were welded together into representational competence.

Syntax might be the pattern on the peacock's tail. But it would still have to be selected under the pressure of, say, some social advantage in complex structured ritual which initially had no recursive connection to our proto-semantic abilities to construe operations on things as referring to changes in arrangements of other things in systems of representation. Only subsequently might syntax and semantic components ever have become linked. That is to say, the selection pressure for syntax might have been some success at phatic rather than ideational communication.[30] An example of usefulness is the proposal that chatter is a more efficient phatic mechanism than grooming when social groups grow larger. Perhaps proto-chatter as a replacement for grooming is not selected for its recursiveness, but is recursive incidentally.[31] Perhaps chatter does not initially need a propositional semantics?

Where does this leave us in our search for the instrumentality of representation systems in behaviour, its development, and its evolution? Systems can operate as technologies used by participants, or as tools for analysts. Human beings have adaptations for incorporating representation systems into their cognitive make-up, and incorporation turns us into potential analysts. Human language and the communication based on it is at least one important adaptation which enables system-as-technology incorporation, but is itself a candidate case for a technology incorporated. Being an indirectly interpreted set of systems of representation (or capacity for creating indirect systems), natural language has a syntax and a semantics and it is explaining how these two components could evolve and integrate which is such a hard task for an evolutionary account. Selection pressures might have been initially different for the two components but at some point the two have to begin working together.

One proposal suggested by our analysis of direct and indirect systems of representation is that interactions between the two kinds of system might play a critical role at certain points in both ontogeny and phylogeny of representational capacities. It is this interactionist thesis which I will explore now. It points to questions about the relation between direct and indirect systems of representation in our capacities for understanding each other as intentional beings.

The theory presented in Chapter 2 about the contrast between sentential and diagrammatic semantics is offered as a small piece of the process of developing articulate functional descriptions of human semantic abilities. Direct diagrammatic semantics is formally structured but not syntactically structured. This immediately raises the question of whether human diagrammatic abilities arose before, after or concurrently with human language abilities. Historically, the kind of diagrams we have found it convenient to study here, for the purpose of developing a theory of the semantic contrast, are extremely

---

[30] Phatic communication is communication that creates or maintains social groupings.

[31] I am reminded of the molluscs which display wonderful complex recursive patterns in vivid colour on their shells, although these patterns remain entirely invisible throughout the molluscs' lives, covered by dull grey mantle. The recursiveness of the patterns is a consequence of the growth patterns controlled by the same genes.

recent—eighteenth-century in particular, probably classical Greek more generally. But the essential elements of their semantics can be found in maps and schematic pictures, and the human use of maps and pictures appears to be rather ancient. However, oral language is biologically primitive and perhaps much older. Does it therefore necessarily mean that the kind of diagrammatic semantics we studied here, and the abilities that implement it, played no role in the evolution of the semantics of natural languages?

One of the contributions of a semantic approach to these questions is to differentiate dimensions on which representations differ. Directness sets diagrams off from natural language, but not diagrams alone. Analogies are also directly interpreted but systematic representations, as argued in Chapter 6. So are simulations, as argued in Chapter2. The ability to perceive and operate analogies is a competence with directly interpreted representation systems. In discussing analogy we noted that human analogical reasoning is distinctive because it is direct representation operated through indirect representation— natural language. Here might be a model for the co-evolution of the two parts of human representational distinctiveness—syntax and semantics. Here might be a model for how the technology incorporation faculty arose in evolution. Let us explore this idea further.

Tomasello and Call (1997) review the evidence of the evolutionary course of human cognition. Primates are set off from their ancestors in having at least the beginnings of analogical abilities (e.g. the ability to form relational categories based on transitivity). Human cognition is in turn set off from primate cognition generally by the acquisition of the categories of intentionality in the social domain and causality in the physical domain. All these developments are seen as driven primarily by the demands of social life in groups of increasing size and complexity.

What is involved in humans understanding each other as intentional entities? This question has received its most sustained discussion in connection with the so-called theory of mind (Premack and Woodruff 1978; Leslie 1987). Not surprisingly, the proposals of the 'theory theory' crop up in various guises across cognition. We encountered them in discussions of word-meaning. They have been applied to psychological explanations of autism, characterizing the relation between scientific and folk psychology (Goldman 1993), and in many other places. The theory theory is sometimes thought of as a specification, or even an explanation, of human intentional capacities, but I take it here to be a name for a problem. Human beings treat each other as intentional entities. They understand and predict each other's behaviour (and their own) in terms of what is sometimes rather restrictively called 'belief-desire' psychology—more generally in terms of mental attitudes. They treat each other as if they had minds, and the perceptions and inferences required to do this are rather different from the perceptions and inferences required for dealing with objects that do not have minds.

The problem is to specify what these abilities are, and to explain how they are implemented, how they develop, and how they evolved. Note that our 'theory of mind capacities' are not defined initially as representational or linguistic or communicative capacities. So one might ask how a specification or even an explanation of these capacities will help us with our problem of understanding how people incorporate formalisms (in our broad sense) into their mental make-up and reasoning capacities. Within our theory of communication based on argument, I hope the answer is obvious (and perhaps the question even a little odd). Persons are things which can adopt alternative interpretations of representations and can negotiate towards common interpretations. This ability may not be necessarily a linguistic ability, it is a communicative ability and does require an intentional understanding of communicative partners. As I hope I have established, it centrally involves reasoning, both at the object level within systems and at the meta-level about alternative interpretations of systems.

As we shall argue presently, seeing argument as the paradigm of communication allows us to conceptualize communication *within* ourselves. In the current context this reminds us that such thinking requires intentional interpretation of our own internal representations. An obvious example is that once a creature has an episodic memory, it has the problem of interpreting retrievals of representations from that memory. 'Is this a representation of something that happened? Something I wished had happened? I expected to happen? Something I planned to do? . . . ' Interestingly these internal representations require deontic interpretation.

Perhaps the most concrete instantiations of what is distinctive about reasoning about minds are the tasks used to investigate the development of normal and autistic children e.g. Perner's *et al.*(1987) false-belief task. A child shares with a doll some information about where an object starts off. The doll then goes off-stage and the object is moved to another hidden location. The doll re-enters and the child is asked where the doll will look for the object. Before the critical point in development (about 3.5 years) the child says that the doll will look where the child knows the object is; after that watershed, the child predicts that the doll will look where the doll falsely believes the object is. Autistic children tend to continue failing this task after normal children, or even children of comparable intelligence, pass it. [32] More complicated iterated false belief tasks catch less severely autistic children and still can differentiate them from controls.

There are many questions about what ability is being measured here. For example, Petersen and Riggs (1999) show that failure on the false-belief tasks are highly correlated with failure on inferentially closely related counterfactual tasks. The child observes the doll move the hidden object from the cupboard to the refrigerator in the course of baking a cake, and is then asked where the object would be if the doll had not baked a cake. Failure to place it in the cupboard is failure at counterfactual reasoning about what *would* have been the case. So how are we to characterize what failure is going on here—lack of ability to reason about beliefs (especially false beliefs), or lack of ability to reason counterfactually? False-belief tasks involve a kind of counterfactual reasoning, though counterfactual reasoning is a much broader category than false-belief reasoning. I cite this as a typical example of the problems of specifying *what* is involved in the capacities which are required by theory-of-mind tasks. Another example would be Russell's (1997) proposal that autists' problems with these tasks are related to 'executive function' problems. Or Happé's (1994) ideas about 'central coherence'.

These alternative proposals are sometimes seen as proposals to 'explain away' the 'theory of mind'. But that is only a sensible interpretation if the theory of mind is taken to be an *explanation*—roughly that we have an innate module based on an implementation of a theory that performs theory-of-mind inferences and it starts operating at this age. If one takes theory of mind to be a useful label for a problem, then these proposals are specifications and proto-explanations of what develops when children cross this watershed and become able to take the 'intentional stance'. They are explanations that

---

[32] One might wonder how the autistic child, who is deemed to have problems with entertaining phantasies, is nevertheless supposed to be able to imaginatively construe the doll's participation in this experiment.

may reduce our tendency to see the abilities as neatly modular, or innate, but then so much the better, since modularity and innateness should not be seen as any more than explanatory debts to be discharged when we can say something more about development and interactions.

Simultaneously with psychological investigations of developmental theory of mind tasks, there has been extensive philosophical discussion of alternative ways of explaining how people do the reasoning that is involved in treating each other (and themselves) as intentional entities. This debate has been between 'theory' and 'simulation' theorists (Carruthers and Smith 1996).

Nichols *et al.* (1995) provide a useful illustration of the contrast. If we seek to predict what will happen when say a tailplaneless aircraft takes to the air, we may apply a theory of aerodynamics made up of principles about angles of attack of aerofoils, lift, laminar flow, stalling, etc. or we may place a model of our proposed plane, alike in suitable respects, in a wind-tunnel which simulates flight, and observe what happens. Whereas a theory of aerodynamics requires explicit principles, a simulation can achieve its ends without explicit principled knowledge. That is to say, somewhat principled knowledge about how the simulation corresponds to the real thing may be required (e.g. shape is relevant but colour is not) but this knowledge falls far short of the detailed theoretical principles of aeronautics.

Applied to our reasoning about humans as intentional entities, simulation is the idea is that we can reason about others by setting some parameters in the mechanism we use to make our own decisions about how to behave in possible circumstances, and then 'let the mechanism run' and interpret its output as predictions about what someone else would do with those parameters. The supposition is that we have a simulation mechanism which we can use for making our own decisions, and that it must 'run off line' when we plan what to do (i.e. we can plan without executing), so it can be run off-line when predicting what someone else will do. Let us leave aside the questions about whether such 'internal' reasoning is based on external observations of others, or vice versa.

None of this supposes that our reasoning will be infallible. At the simplest level we may not have the information we need to set the simulation well. More fundamentally, we may be different from the person we are trying to predict (or even from ourselves at the time we later carry out our plan) in ways which the available parameters do not allow us to vary. Perhaps we do not have, say, a 'gender switch' on our simulation device (or we have one, but it only models the other gender rather poorly) and so we make systematic mistakes about predicting across gender. Or in predicting what we would do after changing genders . . .

Some theorists have criticized this account using empirical evidence that we cannot actually predict what we would do ourselves, let alone how others will behave. Psychology would be a simpler business if we could! For example, Nichols *et al.* show that subjects routinely fail to predict how they and others will perform in social psychological experiments (e.g. the Langer effect that subjects value a lottery ticket chosen themselves above one randomly assigned to them). But this is surely too harsh a demand of simulations. Things get into the social psychological literature pretty much only if they are counter-intuitive effects. It may well be that the mechanism we use to predict what we shall do is better at predicting what we feel we *ought* to do according to some normative ideas about behaviour than what we shall actually do, and it may be that conflict between these intuitive predictions and behaviour is exactly what gets a phenomenon into social psychology journals. Nichols and Stich might reply that whatever our mechanisms are that decide what to do, they actually do work right down to the detail of what actually happens *ex hypothesi*. But that does not mean that we can or must use the whole system when we plan, or that we have only one level of detail at which we can run simulations. It all depends how much of our mechanisms we do (or can) 'take off line' and run when we are thinking, and whether the outputs of our simulator are interpreted through our theoretical knowledge to some extent. Similarly, we should assume that simulations can be affected by learning. For example, our models of other-gender behaviour at least sometimes improve with experience. This whole area of interactions (or lack of them) between learning from principles as opposed to learning experientially is what is studied in the 'implicit learning' literature as well as the literature on social modelling.

These arguments are reviewed here to make the idea of simulation (or theory) vivid for our discussion. As is to be expected of wide-ranging debates about fundamental capacities by theorists with contrasting theoretical concerns, participants in this debate give quite different characterizations of both simulations and theories in pursuing their different but related explanatory aims. Theories and simulations are taken by some, but not all, participants to contrast on the following dimensions.

- An explicitness dimension: theories are bodies of explicit principles whereas simulations may rely on tacit correspondences.
- An encapsulation dimension: theories may be taken to be encapsulations of knowledge in modules which process independently of other theories, whereas knowledge embodied in simulations is not thereby partitioned.
- A cognitive penetrability dimension: processing based on theories is assumed to be penetrable by knowledge relating to that being processed, whereas simulations are supposed to be cognitively impenetrable or uninfluenced by relevant knowledge except as it can be incorporated into inputs and outputs to the simulation.
- A personal-subpersonal level distinction: both theories and simulations may be thought of at both levels—as consciously accessible personal knowledge, or as inaccessible parts of our subpersonal computational machinery.
- A propositional-affective dimension: theories operate on representations of propositions about behaviour whereas the operation of simulations may include feelings and affective attitudes that we have as we simulate the workings of our predictions.
- In Chapter 2, I added an expressiveness dimension: simulations are, like analogies, inexpressive and therefore directly interpreted whereas theories are expressive and indirectly interpreted.

Different authors place different emphases on these dimensions for their different theoretical purposes, and it is clear that usage is directly conflicting in some cases. For many philosophers, their concern is with problems of grounding symbols in content—wide or narrow—whereas cognitive scientists are more concerned with theories or simulations as implementations of cognitive functions. Indeed some of the participants to the debate do not see this as primarily an empirical issue at all (Heal 1996). The philosophically controversial nature of what theories are is a further complicating factor. Are theories to be construed on the deductive-nomological model—as sets of sentences under an interpretation, with inference rules—or do they also include the tacit knowledge and the real-world procedures and techniques which underpin their founding observations?

Perhaps they must even incorporate features of the social organisation of their users which are preconditions for theoretical discourse. Many of the issues that arise about the nature of scientific theories are the very issues that arise in deciding whether implemented theories might be the psychological mechanism underlying our understanding of each other's mental processes. Our cognitive implementations of scientific theories may even be partly simulations.

If theories are subpersonal-level pieces of machinery, what does it mean to say that they are principled or explicit? And if modules can communicate with each other (as they must to some degree), then how much encapsulation is required for a capacity to count as an encapsulated theory? Encapsulation and impenetrability might appear to be the same property, but one is defined at the level of knowledge and the other at the level of implementation. If simulations can be iterated allowing inputs of knowledge to penetrate and influence the outcome, and simulations could themselves be based on mechanisms which are computational implementations of theories, then what is at stake any more?

Consider an analogy that is sometimes used to motivate the plausibility of a theory of mind as a mental mechanism—the analogy of our core-language capabilities as being implemented as a 'theory of grammar' module. Our knowledge of our native language is highly systematic, yet prior to some energetic education we cannot articulate its principles and this is taken as motivating the idea that our knowledge of our language is implemented as an encapsulated theory-of-grammar module which is a computational implementation of the grammar of our language. Grammars (in the linguists' sense) really are like deductive-nomological theories, perhaps?

We might ask whether this analogy actually motivates the plausibility of theory-implementations, or of simulation-implementations? The best current theories of the implementations of our language capacities do not contain anything much like grammars (at least deductive nomological rule-based grammars). They certainly operate in ways which give rise to principled linguistic behaviour, but their computational guts are in hot dispute.

This motivating example can at least point up the question of what behaviour we are talking about. There are at least two kinds of ability which such a 'grammar module' might be held to explain: our routine use of our native language is the obvious one, but our intuitions and judgements about our language's structure are another. Whether the 'grammar-theory' module underlying natural language use is implemented in terms of rules or not, when we non-linguists use the module to make grammatical judgements we use it in simulation mode. When we are asked say whether a certain string is a sentence, or what it would mean, we input the sentence to 'our grammar module' along with some inferred parameters about context of utterance, and then inspect its outputs—parses, structures, meanings etc. Issuing grammaticality judgements is a distinct skill from talking, subject to different kinds of errors. Our errors of judgement can frequently be put down to failing to search adequately the space of possible contexts for the candidate sentence, and thus setting the input parameters right. We realize too late that the string we rejected was exactly what we would say in some context we had not thought about. If we had conscious access to rules of grammar, we presumably would not have to paramaterize to context. So it is crucial to remember what capacities we are trying to predict when we decide whether those capacities are based on simulations or on theories. We return later to the intriguing observation that such implicit knowledge of language structure is experienced as *feelings* about representations. That is as grammatical *intuitions*.

To return to the implementations underlying our theory-of-mind capacities, this two-level structure of language behaviour is very suggestive. Perhaps our 'theory-of-mind' implementation (whether it is a simulation or a theory) is used in one way in our 'routine' intentional behaviour, and a rather different way when we are asked to make reflective judgements. The false belief task is a reflective judgement, at least for four-year-olds.

One might be tempted to give up the idea that any empirical differences can be found between simulations and theories as components of our mental processing. Legislation about others' use of the terms simulation and theory is hardly a useful way forward.

What I think we can contribute from our particular perspective is to emphasize dimensions that have been relatively neglected and may be relatively suitable for empirical investigation. Emphasizing the inexpressiveness and the possible involvement of affective experiences in simulation, I will argue that simulations are promising candidates for important roles in the development of some of our evolutionarily novel capacities for representation, and that this interpretation provides a further example in which affect plays an important role in implementing cognition. On this interpretation, one can still believe that we *also* have theories (suitably interpreted) about minds, and that interactions between our principled theories and our available simulations are an important locus for explanations in cognition. In fact this interaction is precisely one approach to explaining what happens as we internalize formalisms.

On the expressiveness dimension, simulations are importantly inexpressive representations in two ways. As argued in Chapter 2, simulations are temporally inexpressive, being unable to represent partial orderings of events. They are also typically inexpressive in their representation of their inputs and outputs. The model aeroplane in the wind tunnel and the maps of temperatures, humidities, pressures, and wind speeds that are the parameters for starting weather simulations are direct representations of what they are simulating. The same goes for the outputs.

Of course its much harder to say what the inputs to our simulations of behaviour are like, but if our concept of simulation is to mean anything, then our simulations of others' intentionality will not accept arbitrary abstractions over sets of parameters. This specificity of simulations predicts that we need to have some kinds of information about individuals and their motivations before we can start thinking about what they are likely to do, whether or not those kinds of information are predictive. This is quite a good abstract description of the conclusions that social psychologists have drawn about our predictions of others' behaviour and the basis for social stereotyping.

We cannot even watch sets of dots moving suitably on a blank screen without ascribing them definitive intentional and causal relations, much less observe other people without ascribing determinate motivational and causal analyses of their behaviour at some level of granularity. This inexpressiveness is of course considerably more complicated to specify than temporal inexpressiveness, but is no less real for that. So I would expect simulations of behaviour to be incapable of taking as input certain kinds of abstractions about feelings, motivations and causes. This seems to me the most neglected dimension that can help to distinguish simulations from theories.

The last dimension (propositional versus affective involvement) is particular to theories/simulations of minds, behaviour and experience. While theories might be able to predict what will be true descriptions of feelings, they will not themselves enact those feelings. In contrast, predicting what we (or someone else) will feel in situation X by simulation may involve us experiencing that situation perhaps at some pale level of vividness. This assumption of course treads close to issues about the fundamental possibility of the computational simulation of mind, but we do not need to settle those issues here. We could believe in strong artificial intelligence, and believe that it is possible in principle to give a computational account of mind 'all the way down' but still draw a distinction between how theories of emotion are implemented and how simulations of emotion are implemented. One could even believe that we have both, perhaps one as implementation for routine monitoring and the other for reflective inference.

But there is an empirical problem with determining the role of emotional experiences in theory-of-mind inferences. It is obviously too quick to say that theory theories will predict that emotional experiences will not occur during episodes of predicting others' behaviour. We might have a real pencil-paper-and-equations model of mind (imagine yourself as a theorist who finally cracks psychology), and some application of it involving lengthy calculation may lead us to predict some absolutely ghastly experience for an episode's protagonist. At this point we may feel empathy. The empathy was not an implementation of any part of the calculation, but a result of the calculation's prediction. The outputs of the theoretical calculation are fed into our own experiential mechanisms. This is the corresponding difficulty to the possibility of our theories of mind being applied to the outputs of simulations. Once the mind is hybrid, psychology becomes much more difficult. And the mind is hybrid. No one said psychology was easy.

Having said that this will necessarily be a complicating issue for empirical attempts to discriminate between theories and simulations, I do not think that it means that the issue cannot be refined into a real empirical issue. In principle there is a difference between when emotional reaction happens, and whether it is instrumental in our reasoning.

Thus I pin my hopes for empirically analysing what parts simulations and theories play in our theory-of-mind capacities on their modes of abstraction and on their differential involvement of affective states. On the former issue, directly interpreted simulations will have to achieve what abstractions they achieve despite their information enforcements, through the employment of what we have termed abstraction tricks. An illustration of this line of analysis is provided by Petersen and Riggs (1999), who present what they interpret as a hybrid model of some theory-of-mind tasks, but which might be interpreted as a simulation-plus-abstraction-tricks model. This model combines model-like representations of worlds with notations carrying information about how models are related to other models through modifications.

What about the involvement of affective processes in our theory-of-mind inferences? Our capacities for narrative analogizing discussed in the last chapter are rather closely related to our capacities for theory of mind reasoning. Being able to see the Zerdia-and-Gagrach story as an analogue of the Karla-the-hawk-and-the-hunter story requires us to abstract away from the details of the structure of the intentional relations that is the narrative. We argued there that affective commonality is an important part of the basis for the abstraction involved. Our *gedanken* experiment with Gentner's story of the hawk and the hunter (versus the clown) was an illustration. If our affective transformation of the Karla story with the clown replacing the hunter really degrades the similarity of the structure of the two stories, then that would provide some suggestive evidence that affective response is instrumental in whatever mechanisms perform theory-of-mind reasoning.

We also argued in the previous chapter that analogies are direct representations operated through language, an indirect representation system. The analogical component of our understanding of narrative might be implemented as a directly interpreted simulation process crucially dependent on affective similarities between analogue narratives. But as we observed there, the operation of the direct simulation through the indirectly interpreted language can generate, in development, something more akin to a true theoretical grasp of intentionality. Operating analogies through language gives rise to an abstract vocabulary for describing the shared schematics of analogous narratives, and these schematics are composed of true abstract principles relating the new vocabulary items—the origin of theory. Theory can then play a role in changing how our simulations run. Here is a case where the operation of a direct system of representation (a simulation) through an indirect system of representation (a natural language) plausibly plays a role in generating a theory of intentional behaviour in development.

This example is a process in development. What about the evolutionary process? Why should the possession of narrative analogizing capacities resting on affectively based simulations play any role in generating theory-like abstractions and indirectly interpreted systems such as languages in evolution? Direct and indirect systems cannot work in consort before indirect systems exist. However, the social interactions which are the raw material of narrative analogy are temporally extended, hierarchically organized and sometimes recursive; and their elements require to be analysed as token exemplars of types of action. The tokens and types are not listable in the way that syntactic categories are, so 'story grammars' are not grammars in any technical sense, but nevertheless the ability to enact and to understand the structure of social interaction seems by far the most plausible precursor for the evolution of the computational implementations required for syntax. Donald's (1991) proposal of the part played by mimesis as the origin of language is one development of related ideas.

Versions of these developmental and evolutionary issues about our capacities for intentionally interpreted communications have so far been explored in most detail in attempts to understand the psychological basis of autism. Autists have deficiencies in their interpersonal relations and in their communicative abilities—their treatment of other persons and themselves as intentional entities. If one thinks of the theory-of-mind as a computational module then autists might be crudely characterized as lacking this theory-of-mind module (or having an impaired or delayed module). Behind this prevalent idea there seems to be an implicit evolutionary equation of the form: primate + theory of mind module = human. A second equation relates autists to humans: human - theory of mind module = autist. Solving these simultaneous equations yields the inference that autists should be like primates.

But nothing could be less like autistic behaviour than the machiavellian chimpanzee, a hyper-social creature. It may be worth considering an alternative equation. The alternative is that autistic behaviour represents a taking to extremes of the innovations that turned primates into humans. Autism is pathological, and presumably pathological relative to any ancestral stage. But there is the very interesting possibility that it may represent the 'sickle-celled anaemia' of human differentiation—a double dose of a capacity which is evolutionarily novel, maintained in the population because of the usefulness of the single dose we see in 'normals'. I do not intend the genetic analogy to suggest the basis is necessarily genetic (even less that it is a single allele): we need first to understand the functional dynamics.

What does this novel equation suggest might be the nature of the innovation? If we accept Tomasello's characterisation of chimpanzees as having an intentional understanding of their conspecifics' goals but not of their epistemic states, then we must think of human evolution as a move in the direction of 'depersonalising' intentional analysis. The truth of a proposition emerges as an invariant from the multiplicity of possible individual motivations it might be involved in. Of course the normal human achieves this extraction of the invariant without losing track of its primitive linkage to individuals' intentional behaviour. Our suggestion is that autists may take this distinctively human trait to pathological extremes. On this speculation, the autist is to be thought of more as holy fool than pre-human primate.

Autism comes in a range of severities continuous with the 'normal' range of cognitive styles. One empirical way into these issues may be through the study of learning styles in normal individuals. It is a fascinating possibility that the styles described in earlier chapters, characterized as favouring learning from directly or indirectly interpreted systems because of their different treatments of authority-for-knowledge, may be strategies in balancing focus on the propositional and the interpersonal.

Where does all this speculation leave the theory of mind? As a crucial label for a problem to be solved, this approach certainly supports the importance of the theory of mind. As a computational explanation it casts some doubt. Hobson (1993) has been the most eloquent advocate for the need to go deeper in our psychological explanations of our capacities for intentional inferences than this acceptance of a module as explanation. Hobson seeks to explain our theory-of-mind capacities as arising in development from the affective structuring of interpersonal relations, and autism as a deficiency in this development of interpersonal relations. Or more accurately, Hobson argues that we must reassess our conventional factoring of cognitive and affective aspects of these processes. In my terms, he sees cognition as resting on what are essentially affective implementations in early development.

Very briefly, Hobson builds on earlier accounts of normal development, particularly those of Werner and Kaplan (1984) and Vygotsky (1978) an argument that the capacity for symbolization develops from the affective-cognitive dynamics of early intersubjectivity between infant and mother. In differentiating himself from both things and other people, the infant has to come to appreciate that others can have different representations/feelings about the same object than he does himself. Hobson diagnoses autists' primary deficiency as a deficiency in the rewardingness of intersubjectivity, rather than a deficiency in the cognitive capacities for meta-representational inference. He is content that the former gives rise to the latter (or whatever is the right account of the developed system) in the course of normal development. But for the autist who appears to lack motivation for establishing intersubjectivity, the experiences on which normal development feeds its construction of a theory (or simulation) of mind never occur, or are delayed.

Hobson invokes Bruner's (1983) illustrations of how turn-taking games provide the scaffolding for the development of multi-word utterances structured by a given-new dichotomy, i.e. the development of the information packaging structures which develop into the grammatical structures of indirectly interpreted representation systems (language), only to require unpacking in logic class. However, note again that this is development, not evolution. Many autists are not in fact so much impaired in their developmental course for the acquisition of grammar—phonology, syntax, semantics. Their abnormalities are focused on the interpersonal pragmatics of communication—the use of language, not its structure. Ontogeny cannot in general recapitulate evolution.[33] Even if the development of our theory-of-mind capacities for intersubjectivity and interpersonal communication played an instrumental role in the evolution of our syntactic capabilities, autistic development does not provide evidence that our current capacities for processing structured language develop from those theory-of-mind capacities, however dependent our abilities to use language for interpersonal communication is on our theory-of-mind capacities. But neither does the fact that our modern capacities for structured and indirectly interpreted language are largely independent of our developing interpersonal communication capacities mean that those capacities were not instrumental in the origins of language. At the present point of understanding, we do not know. But this still seems one of the more promising avenues of exploration.

The idea that the emergent coupling between direct and indirect systems may have been a driving force in the evolutionary development of our theory-of-mind capacities can be illustrated on a social scale in historical episodes of cultural 'cognitive' development. What the use of diagrams in close coupling with language does seem to have precipitated in historical time is the explicit discovery of the discourse of proof. Netz (1999) has argued eloquently that it was a particular combination of the use of diagrams and specialized languages in the study of geometry in classical Greece that gave us the first institutionalization of a discourse of mathematical proof. For example, the eradication of variably resolvable anaphors from the language of geometric proof was both required and enabled by the labelling of diagrams. It is not until (a peculiarly restricted fragment of) natural language emerges through this combination with diagrams, in a discourse of demonstration, that proto-formal language precipitates out. A relatively formal language is of great advantage in stipulating patterns of valid inference. Geometry appears to have played a central role in the discovery of the discourse of pure deduction, and arguably still plays an important part in the ontogenetic grasp of this concept. Recent changes in the Anglo-Saxon mathematical curriculum that have removed geometry from the syllabus may have lead to an impoverished grasp of the concept of proof.

Chapter 5 argued that gaining an explicit grasp of this novel discourse of proof is still a major part of our modern educational process. It is still seen as a major policy problem in mathematics education that not enough students gain a proper understanding of this discourse. If this analysis is right, then what the invention of the formal technology achieves is not just a formalization of part of a pre-existing natural language (though it does that), but also a creation of new practices within the culture—the practice of justification by proof, and the explicit formalization of the differences between the authority arrangements on either side of the turnstile.

If proof is important, why was the interaction of direct and indirect representation systems instrumental in its cultural discovery, and what were its repercussions (or at

---

[33] As biologists discovered from exploring recapitulationist theory, if ontogeny generally recapitulated phylogeny, *Homo Sapiens* would have gone through a phylogenetic stage of being a solely milk-eating creature incapable of independent locomotion.

least accompaniments) in other cultural developments? We would propose an answer based on our analysis of the contrasts in learning styles developed in Chapter 4. Proof by diagrammatic construction makes the semantics *available*; accompanying sentential proof institutionalizes line-by-line justification. It takes the combination of the two for the process to be seen as more than 'a means for arriving at the empirically obvious' to quote a report of a prevalent student misconception (Strom *et al.* 2001, p. 735). Our empirical finding was of individual differences in emphasis of the roles that different sources of authority-for-knowledge played in learning from diagrams and language. Perhaps culturally too, both kinds of learning style have to be accommodated in cultural practices of justification.

It is perhaps no accident that classical Greece also saw the development of new kinds of legal and political discourse of justification, combined with the explicit development of theories of communication based on logic, and their use in education. There have been arguments that Greece was not so unique, and that ancient China also saw the development of the concept of proof in mathematics (Chemla 1992). Whether we accept those arguments or not, uniqueness is not what is important for our purposes. What is important is that in particular cultural circumstances particular couplings of direct and indirect representational systems seem to play instrumental roles in changing human reasoning abilities and practices. These incidents may be models for earlier stages in the evolutionary process. They may of course be misleading models but at present they are the best we have. Their contribution is that they do allow detailed functional analysis of the cognitive as well as the social changes that occurred. A promising place to look for an account of the evolution of the human faculty for incorporating formalisms is in the co-evolution of the use of direct and indirect representation systems.

One of the reasons that it is so hard to become clear about how the two perspectives of system-as-technology and system-as-nature fit together in explaining evolution and development, is that 'natural language' is a different thing depending on which of the two perspectives it is viewed from. From the natural perspective it is a highly circumscribed core of phonetic-phonological-syntactic abilities abstracted from any particular content and from any context of use. From the cultural perspective it is a family of representation systems and their interpretations, implemented in mental and social structures. Neither of these perspectives is the true perspective—they are just perspectives on a phenomenon, more or less useful for different kinds of enquiry. Both are completely necessary for our enquiry and so we have to work towards a co-ordination. When, from the natural perspective, it is claimed that all human beings (save for a few abnormal cases) develop a full language competence, and this is evidence of its innateness, we must remember that this core competence is a wonderful but circumscribed set of abilities, largely defined without reference to any semantic content, let alone interpersonal communicative skills, and that we have little idea what 'innate' might mean beyond negative characterizations in terms of 'not learned by rote'. When, from a cultural perspective, it is claimed that language is a family of representation systems acquired through a lifetime's hard cognitive labour in social and physical interaction with the world, that is not to say that its construction does not rest on the language apparatus narrowly construed. Innateness really is the reddest of herrings and modularity the least well defined of computational properties in these discussions.

In summary, the instrumentalities of systems in behaviour is complex because systems can be participants' technologies in reasoning, or theorists' tools in describing nature, and both at different stages in development and in evolution. Humans are peculiar in being able to incorporate systems into their constitutions and thereby change themselves. The capacity for natural language is one candidate component of the innovation which enables this incorporation, but in trying to understand how language itself might have evolved we are faced with the problem of understanding how our syntactic and semantic capacities might have arisen and become integrated with the necessary intentional interpretative capacities for human communication.

Another essential component of our 'technology-incorporation facility' is the capacity for perceiving and constructing narrative analogies—abstract correspondences and contrasts between different sequences of purposive behaviour. This capacity is at the heart of our ability to treat each other as intentional entities—what has been labelled the theory of mind. Analogies are direct systems of representation which are now customarily operated through language, an indirect system. But if we think of narrative analogy capacity originally being operated directly, then perhaps we have a path for the evolution of the development of the indirect systems of natural languages.

We might suppose that the original implementations of narrative analogy were simulations of our own and others' intentional behaviour, and that these simulations were both inexpressive and implemented to an extent on shared affective structure. But because the subject matter of narrative analogy is the hierarchically organized plans of human interaction classified into abstract categories and played out in sequence, this subject matter has the properties of the syntactic objects of natural language. Our proposal is that this was the arena for the development in evolution of the indirect operation of directly interpreted representations of human behaviour.

The abnormal developmental path of autistic children can be interpreted as an illustration of a failure in development of a process which is related to the evolutionary process by which our distinctive representational capacities originated. But our speculation is that autism might be a not the lack of a module but rather the hyperdevelopment of the strategy which made the break between primate and human. On this interpretation of autism (and conjecture about language evolution), the affective status of intersubjectivity is what drives cognitive development of our capacities to understand each other intentionally, and the implementations of these capacities were originally affectively based simulations. In us modern humans the operation of principle and simulation are intimately intercalated in our intentional capacities. The interactions of direct and indirect systems of representation are a fruitful place to search for the evolutionary engines of our representational capacities.

The argument model of communication outlined in the previous section provides a thoroughly intentional model of communication. Successful communication is the achievement of interpretations of a language shared between two parties. But as far as the discussion so far has gone, the internal implementations (e.g. theories and simulations) might be purely the underpinnings of the conduct of *public* debate and communication. It is true that some accounts of simulation come with an assumption that our treatment of other people as having 'other minds' is an inference from our experiences of our own minds. But even if this is true in development, it does not have to be true in evolution. We turn now to consider communication with ourselves, and what it can tell us about relations between cognition and emotion.

7.3   System turned inwards

Taking the system-as-technology stance towards explaining the instrumentality of representation systems and its ramifications throughout cognition changes how we conceptualize relations between individuals and their communities, and between affect and knowledge.

What goes for communication in public debate applies equally well to internal debate within an individual. Individuals are not homogeneous or consistent bodies of belief, knowledge, supposition, or interest. There are many topics on which we do not 'know our own minds'. Internal debate starts, just as we observed public debate does, from a felt tension between two assumptions, both of which are perhaps attractive: 'Free speech is a bedrock of a decent society: unlimited campaign contributions are a form of legalized corruption.' Of course, these feelings necessarily have to receive form to be expressed here, on the page, but internally they may be more incohate—an approval of images of the maverick on the hustings being a thorn in some special interest's flesh; a distaste for images of lobbyists with plain brown envelopes ... Just as with public debate, we debate with ourselves to understand more about the structure of our beliefs, desires and possibilities for feeling and action.

Our proposal about the epistemology of debate, both public and private, is that participants' access to the affective and to the propositional structure of debate are at least sometimes, at least partially, independent of each other. There are always indefinitely many propositional articulations of felt conflict. Some are more affectively successful than others in resolving our feelings about an issue. It is not that our feelings must be accounted for by some single articulated structure of propositions hidden somewhere in our make-up which drives our affective experiences, gradually unfolding itself as debate proceeds. Many contingent happenings and negotiations may determine what articulation we reach if we reach one at all, and the process of articulation routinely changes the feelings that are involved. The proposal is that both affective structure and propositional structure play instrumental roles in this process of articulation.

At the outset, our conflicting feelings about campaign contributions are not necessarily propositionally connected. The sentences quoted in the example are two islands set in a sea without exposed connections. 'Sure free speech is a good thing, and sure unlimited campaign contributions are a bad thing. So what?' says the sceptical voice who does not share our feeling of conflict. Of course the feeling of conflict may be misguided (and the sceptic right). This is what we mean by saying that we cannot articulate a relation. Seeking to understand a propositional basis of the feeling of conflict, or to satisfy ourselves that the felt connection is spurious, is what debate sets out to achieve.

This example is typical of public debate and may not achieve much recognition as an example of internal debate with those not much interested in political argument. But the same considerations apply to the most incohate and mundane experiences of conflicting feelings about personal relations. We like something about Fred and we find something else about him difficult. That in itself is unlikely to spark much internal debate. But perhaps we concurrently experience the feeling that the two aspects of Fred are one and the same—that it is the same thing which we both like and dislike.

Perhaps we simultaneously find the very same action of Fred's both admirable and despicable. Perhaps our admiration is a rather secret one, but nevertheless leaves us uncomfortable. Now soliloquy ensues as we debate with ourselves how we can resolve the felt inconsistency. We want to know *why* we feel like this? This internal debate will reach for a conceptual framework which can articulate our feelings.

What kinds of resolutions can we achieve? Well, we may decide that it was a lot of fuss about not much—the fire goes out of the debate without any resolution. The two descriptions of the action are no longer felt to conflict. We end up agreeing with the sceptical voice. Or we may succeed in understanding something about ourselves (or Fred, or campaign contributions) which resolves the felt inconsistency in our attitudes or his behaviour. Our refined way of thinking may resolve the conflict by explaining to us the origins of the conflict: or may reassure us that the conflict was more apparent than real. Or we may just be left still feeling conflict without successful articulation. Just as with public debate, the logical model does not guarantee success or denigrate failure. It does not even tell us what to do in the face of contradiction. We have to change the assumptions, but that is, in itself, hardly much constraint. We may be quite right to hold that we are still in internal conflict and that none of the formulations that we have been able to find adequately articulate the issue. Perhaps there is no resolution. Life, with its conundrums, goes on.

This model of internal communication emphasizes parallels between internal and external discourse. We are internally no more a monolithic, homogeneous and consistent body of desire, knowledge, and belief, than we and our interlocutors are a monolithic, homogeneous, and consistent *community* of shared desire, knowledge, and belief. In this role, in both public and private arenas, logic sets a criterion for alignment of interpretations, but the process of communication is constituted by the sequence of interpretations we go through in search of resolution. Assumptions change; words change their meaning. These changes change our feelings in a reverberative process. Logic provides the framework for articulating conflict. Feelings drive our choice of response to inconsistency, and logic comments on the new round of assumption and rerepresentation.

So, we propose, logic plays fundamentally the same role in our internal debates as it does in public. If logic provides a framework for understanding adversarial public communication, it also gives us a way of conceptualizing part of our internal affective lives as communication between conflicting systems of belief, imagination, and desire. It plays the same role in private that it plays in public: demanding that implicit assumptions be brought to explicitness. Here is a theory of communication that stands some chance of explaining why we bother to communicate with ourselves and how that is possible. Talking to oneself is perhaps the first sign of affective and cognitive health? On the 'code model' of communication it is unclear why we should even try.

The most important consequence of this view that private debate is fully parallel to public debate is that our feelings become a source of knowledge, and not just about our own bodies and minds. Not oracles of truth, but nevertheless, indispensable sources of knowledge. However incohate the raw affective material may be, logic's demands of consistency, operating on the expressions that are related to conflicting feeling, can lead us to articulate our feelings in context. Far from being a force of the same kind as our passions, but one pointed in an opposing direction, our reason becomes the instrument of access to the implications of our affective states as well as to those of others. Articulation can be important for public communication, but it is just as important for internal communications that are the basis of belief and subsequent action.

This has not been the standard model of the relation between reason and the emotions. It gives credence to what remains mystifying on the conventional account—that our internal senses and feelings can be sources of knowledge about more than our minds and bodies. Here we are, the product of billions of years of evolution, with unimaginable quantities of information encoded in our DNA and the product of years of intensive experience of our world encoded in our synapses. Yet our dominant epistemology has been that knowledge arises from encoding the information which arrives between eye-blinks from our senses tuned to the external world. Rationalists may credit us with the odd innate idea, usually of a mathematical nature, but little attention has been paid by epistemology to our inner feelings and senses as sources of knowledge.

Why should this be? Feelings are notoriously labile yet lability has hardly been taken to be grounds for the dismissal of other foundations for knowledge. What could be more labile than the sensory impressions of vision, audition, taste, smell—the external senses? Yet these are assumed to be our main source of knowledge. It is routinely accepted by researchers in external perception that their chief goal is the explanation of how we have a relatively stable experience of our world derived from wildly variable immediate sensory impressions. Why not the same for affect and our internal senses and feelings as sources of knowledge?

Some of our internal feelings are, it is true, quite labile, but others are rather persistent. We are pretty much defined by our long-term attachments and revulsions. If *these* feelings were completely unstable from second to second—if we could extract no stable sense from them—we would be in the same kind of serious trouble as if we could extract no stable world from our external sensory impressions. Just as with our external senses, what we particularly notice are the changes which are significant, picked out against a background of continual but relatively insignificant variation, all correlated with features of the external world. Understanding how our feelings can play a part in our gaining knowledge would seem a high priority if we are to understand how affect and cognition relate in reasoning and communication.

The traffic between emotions and articulations of them in language or some other representation system is two way. We have so far presented the example of an implicit experienced conflict between feelings seeking a consistent articulation in language or other representation. But traffic in the other direction also occurs. Paradox is the discernment of a formal inconsistency in representations not previously felt, which leads to an engagement of the emotions in thinking. It is pointed out to us that we believe a set of assumptions, and, by hypothesis, we have harboured these assumptions quite contentedly without feeling any conflict (or maybe even connection) between them. It is then pointed out that a contradiction is derivable from the assumptions, and if the derivation is compelling, we immediately experience affective conflict. How can we possibly believe *that*? How can we possibly reject any of the premises?[34]

Some care is essential here to distinguish different degrees of claim about the relation

---

[34] If this is too philosophical an example to resonate, then a simpler one is where a redescription of our routine behaviour suddenly makes it ethically or aesthetically unacceptable to us—perhaps the Sunday roast is redescribed as cadaver.

between affect and knowledge. The weaker position is that while affective states may drive the process of seeking knowledge, they play no part in informing the outcome. Ambition may motivate scientists to make discoveries, but ambition is not a source of the knowledge that those discoveries represent. A stronger position is that what I have been calling our affective structure does play some part in determining not just *that* we seek knowledge, or even just *where* we seek knowledge, but also in the nature of the knowledge that results from these processes. I want to argue for the second stronger point of view.

To be clear at the outset, I do not propose that wishing makes it so. I need a relation between affect and knowledge which lies somewhere between the idea that affect motivates the search for knowledge (which of course it may), and the false idea that affect determines what is true.

The basis of my belief is that such a middle ground is to be found in the model of the learning of formalisms which has been emerging in this book. Students start with implicit knowledge of some domain—say their mother tongue and communication with it. This knowledge is expressed not only in performance of the skills involved, but also in intuitions—grammatical or logical intuitions, or intuitions of word meaning being obvious examples. That is, we *feel* that such and such is grammatically correct, or logically follows, or is a case of 'game', but in many cases we cannot articulate why.

This intuitive knowledge is sufficient to practice communication in a variety of contexts, but is not accompanied by explicit knowledge of what it is that is known, and may not be sufficient for us to ascribe knowledge in many contexts. An explicit theory of the domain is then taught perhaps through the teaching of an interpretation for a novel formalism. This formalism encompasses some intuitions and demolishes others. After such learning we have changed intuitions, some of them about different objects and concepts, and we now have explicit knowledge of things we only had intuitions about before. Furthermore, we can develop skills of operating this knowledge in contexts previously closed to us. My speculative proposal is that we could not do any of this without the requisite affective structure at the outset, and that what we have learned remains implemented in a new affective structure after learning. This process gives meaning to the claim that our affective structure is a source of knowledge.

These intuitions and feelings are not just general motivational factors but highly specific feelings about representations in contexts which may be indefinitely subtly classified. It might be objected that talk of logical intuitions as feelings alongside feelings about non-representational things is just a pun. I hope to persuade this is not mere pun. Naive logical intuitions have the epistemological hallmarks of affective states—they are implicit and beyond articulation, and they have some sorts of valence, however pale. It might be objected that there is much more to these intuitions than mere affect. We can only agree: we interpret affect broadly. Our affective structure is not merely a few unstructured feelings. Our feelings are highly differentiated intentional states including all their references to their objects, but nevertheless they are indubitably affective. Aesthetic feelings may be a more useful model for these feelings than generalized emotions about some situation such as rage or ecstasy about an event. Why should this relation between affect and knowledge arise? How can it arise?

This puzzling relation between affect and knowledge at least satisfies the requirement that it occupies a middle ground between motivating learning and determining truth. Affective structure is instrumental in determining what we learn, and how we subsequently deploy it, but not in determining what is true. It is instrumental in determining what we learn both as a precondition for learning and because it is what comes to implement the new capacities which constitute our learning.

Let us explore this involvement of affect in learning further. Notice that in this discussion of the roles of affect in communication there has been a slide from the particular to the general. We started by observing that argument originates with felt tension between particular positions. Here the feelings are feelings about particular topics of agreement and disagreement. We ended by talking about the role of affective structure in the implementation of systems of representations, as evidenced by our representational intuitions. I believe that this elision reflects a uniquely human phenomenon whereby affect skips levels, moving from attachment to particular referents, to attachment to representations and features of systems of representation. We return to develop this idea further in the next section, but first some comparisons with other learning theories might help to make this model of affective-cognitive interactions in representational behaviour more vivid.

Among psychologists, it is Vygotsky (1962, 1978) who most famously explored the relationship between public and mental representations. According to Vygotsky, the two arenas are related in that the discourse of the mental arena originates in the internalization of public representations—especially natural language.

How does this picture apply to our observations of the processes involved in learning formalizations? Does Vygotsky's picture of the internalization of public language fit the internalizations of predicate calculus or the syllogisms of Chapters 3 and 4? In gross outline, Vygotsky's picture fits rather well. Students taught a formalism do internalize it and that internalization changes what they can do in reasoning, both cognitively and socially. Vygotsky was concerned with the internalization of early spoken language, and to some extent with the later learning of a written formalism for spoken language, rather than with late tertiary acquisition of logical formalism. But there are distinct parallels even at such different stages of development.

On the other hand, our results perhaps enrich the available observations. Most prominently, our findings are that although students' gross reasoning performance benefited from internalizing logic, subgroups of students internalized something different in response to teaching with different representation systems—diagrams or calculi and their combinations. If the idea of *internalization* is taken too literally as some sort of wholesale incorporation, then it becomes surprising that one representation system would not be internalized as well as another, or that two students internalizing the same formalism should change so differently. Internalization sometimes seems to be thought of (though obviously not by Vygotsky) on the model of installing a new language in a computer. There may be usefulnesses in this metaphor, but one disanalogy is definitely that such installations are rather indifferent to what was there before. From this point of view a better computer analogy would be the building of one system 'on top of' another—implementing a high-level language on top of a lower-level one, for example. This metaphor leaves us in no doubt that the underlying language will continue to have substantial effects on the behaviour of the higher level system it implements. Moreover, it is possible that these effects will be complexly structured. A given underlying language may not make everything in the higher language fast or slow, but rather the underlying language may betray itself in the profile of things that are done quickly or slowly in the higher level language. There are good scientific and political reasons why Vygotsky was not primarily interested in individual differences, but nevertheless they can enrich his theory.

A nice empirical illustration of the argument model of communication, and Vygotsky's ideas applied to the internalization of debate, is provided by Chi's work on the self-explanation effect (Chi 2001; Chi *et al.*, in press). Chi has shown that students' asking themselves questions and providing explanations while reading conceptually rich text is an important part of the learning process. Students who do this learn more than ones who do not, and students can even be taught to self-explain with the increases in learning that indicate that self-explanation is instrumentally related to learning outcome. The particular insight of Chi's work is that not just any question-asking, or any self-explaining facilitates learning. Self-explanation arises at places in the text where there is explicit or implicit *conflict* between the students' existing conceptual model and the statements in the text. Just talking to oneself is probably not so helpful unless the talk is organized around felt conflicts. Articulating felt conflicts is beneficial for learning.

A comparison with another contemporary learning theory may perhaps provide another useful anchor. Anderson's (1996) ACT-R cognitive architecture presents the most developed current theory about the acquisition of cognitive skills in conceptual learning. For our purposes it is interesting that the theory has been applied to the learning of elementary formal systems—examples are geometry and the LISP programming language. Anderson's theory focuses on the interactions of declarative and procedural knowledge in conceptual learning: knowledge starts off in the declarative form, as it is found in textbooks, say, and becomes implemented in the skills of inference required for reasoning in the domain. One could view ACT-R as analysing just how complicated this process of internalization is. But it is a distinctive feature of Anderson's system that it does not give an account of the role of prior language (or diagrams, or any other external representation system) in learning. Knowledge arises by the internalization of the textbook's axioms, but the theory does not yet give an account of how the process depends on the intuitions which are the prior implicit knowledge of the domain. It does not give an account of how implicit knowledge is externalized through achieving a formalization. It is an intriguing question what addition this would entail.

So the argument model of communication can explain why we talk to ourselves and how affect can be the source of knowledge in learning. The need for aligning interpretations even between internal representation systems is what makes the internal case parallel to the public case. Here is a theory of communication that can explain why we have to treat each other and ourselves as intentional entities to speak natural languages or to be able to incorporate new formalisms and representation systems into our mental make-up. One human peculiarity is the jumping of levels of affect from referent to representation, a jump whereby we have feelings and intuitions about representations, and these feelings and intuitions are instrumental in conceptual learning.

7.4 The implementation of systems in affective structure

This chapter began with the question of how systems of representation come to be implemented in human beings and social groups in the course of learning, development and evolution. Without implementation, system is not causally instrumental. we noted that systems were, at one time or another, technologies incorporated into the mind or theorists' tools applied to 'natural' phenomena, and that there is a dynamic through time between the two relations. We sought a schematic account for relating systems to individuals and groups, and gave this in terms of the internalization of public systems within the individual, and the externalization by the articulation of feeling.

But this account emphasizes the question of where our capacity for formalism incorporation originate. Our speculation about evolutionary paths was that our capacities for narrative analogy provide a starting point for understanding the intentional stance and our symbolizing capacities. The operation of direct systems for modelling social behaviour might have given rise to their operation through indirect systems. In Hobson's theory of modern development, the affective dynamics of interpersonal communication are the ontogenetic origins of our capacity for symbolization. Without those dynamics, our now evolved capacities for language structure are never engaged by an intentional system for their deployment.

These theoretical speculations about the centrality of affect in evolution and ontogeny raise the question of what the relation between affect and cognition in the modern mind would be like if these speculations are useful, at least in outline.

One place to start to observe the emotional life of representations is where it is most rarefied and encapsulated—our aesthetic responses to high art. The objects of aesthetic emotions are commonly, though not invariably, representations—statues, paintings, poems, novels, plays. One advantage for present purposes of the field of self-consciously aesthetic discourse is that here it is evident that the emotions that attach to representations are not simply emotions about the objects represented. A Cezanne painting of a bowl of fruit engenders emotions which we do not have about bowls of fruit. That is not to say that the objects depicted are irrelevant to the emotions, nor that aesthetic reactions are merely emotions, or are entirely different from non-aesthetic emotions, or are invariably about representations. But it does mean that some aesthetic reactions to representations are affective reactions to the *relations* between representation and represented thing.

Human beings are not only weird animals who construct systems of representation, but also still weirder ones who have emotions about what they have constructed. A whole realm of emotional experience arises which has no direct analogue in the affective lives of other animals, though the emotions found there do generally bear some correspondence to their basic counterparts. Experience of beauty in a work of art is the same generic emotion as the experience of beauty in a person, a thing, or an act. Experience of suspense in a novel is the same generic experience as the experience of suspense in real life. There may be special properties of aesthetic emotions, but nevertheless these general correspondences exist and they are an important part of what endows art with its significance. Mostly, what is special about aesthetic emotions is not the feelings but their objects—which are often representations.

This peculiar affective relation to representations is not just to the relation between single representations and their corresponding represented objects, but also to representations as *systems* of representation. As we noted in Chapter 2, system arises because operations on one representation transform it into another, and there is a corresponding transformation between what each of these representations stand for. In that earlier discussion we observed that it was quite *unlikely* that aesthetic objects such as Rembrandt's etching belonged to a single homogeneously interpreted system like the Euler diagrams and other examples we sought to explore. In fact, we were tempted by the idea that the aesthetic significance of such objects was somehow associated exactly with their involvement in multiple possible interpretative systems. So this affective relation to system is not to a single system of representation. But it is still a relation to systems. Our responses to paintings, novels, and plays are bound up in expectations, some fulfilled and some flouted, and expectations are functions of systems.

Representational activities other than high art are just as prone to powerful aesthetic responses—mathematics and science being prime examples. Nor are aesthetic emotions limited to high culture, though they may perhaps be most easily identified there because our recognition of them is institutionalized in practices of criticism. Affective aesthetic responses also attach to the utterly mundane—the thought well expressed, the clumsy gesture, the elegant diagram, the ugly word, or the haphazard book.

Because 'aesthetic' is often reserved for high art, and yet emotions whose objects are representations are not exclusive to art, we need to coin a term for this wider class of emotions. We shall call them the 'epistemic' emotions: affective attitudes towards knowledge, belief, and their representation. A paradigm example of an epistemic emotion is the range of affective attitudes and states engendered by understanding something. Understanding is a highly affectively charged business.

Here again, just as with narrowly aesthetic emotions, it is important to distinguish emotions that must be understood in terms of the relation between the representations involved and their referents, from ones that might be understood simply in terms of the referents themselves (the bowl of fruit as opposed to the painting). I may experience intense satisfaction from managing to prove that the sum of the angles of a triangle is 180°, while remaining utterly indifferent about the *fact* that the sum is 180. If the fact were what was exciting, I would be excited when I came to believe the theorem rather than when I succeeding in proving it.

One vivid source of epistemic emotion is when things 'hang together'. The examples can be much more vernacular than slave boy geometry. We can experience emotions when assembling the most mundane conjunctions of information makes something comprehensible—somebody's behaviour perhaps. Equally, loss of knowledge or understanding can be a source of emotion, typically though not necessarily negative. Usually forgetting is a source of regret, which can be deep. Again the driver of the emotional response may be its referent (forgetting where we put the key can be regretted because of what we cannot open) but it may equally well be something much more intangible (when we can no longer vividly recall some defining incident, or lose some understanding of a concept we thought we had mastered).

Why should the human animal have emotions about representations? Perhaps none of this is the least bit surprising when we consider how much human effort the pursuit of knowledge consumes. Well before our developed societies invested at current levels in science, technology, and the arts, people spent considerable proportions of their efforts in learning of one sort or another, perhaps most explicitly in learning the folklore and religion of their cultures. Knowledge is power, and power is useful in all sorts of prosaic ways.

What perhaps lends their defining characteristics to our epistemic emotions is that it is in the nature of knowledge that the instrumentalities of any piece of knowledge are hard to predict. A small piece of knowledge can invoke the coherence (or incoherence) of large bodies of other knowledge, and this can have widespread effects on distant instrumentalities. That Church Street is first left after High Street is perhaps as bland a fact as can be found when we learn it, but when driving the getaway car 20 years later, it can be the source of intense relief, recrimination, or remorse.

This indirectness perhaps explains our satisfactions in understanding, even in cases where the particular understanding does not seem to be instrumentally rewarding. At even one further remove, our emotions about, say, the coherence of representation systems of trivial facts may derive from the importance of the formally equivalent coherence of instrumentally important systems—trivial pursuits as models for passionate pursuits. Perhaps the most indirect emotions of all are witnessed in the passions aroused by gambling for matchsticks, where even the object of desire is represented by some totally arbitrary 'currency'. The example betrays interpersonal relations as an important source of emotions about representations.

If either explanation is sufficient, they are nevertheless cognitively slanted sorts of explanation. Human societies impose strong epistemic obligations on their members who must know their conventions high and low—from the language to the law, from table manners to ethical and aesthetic norms. And conventions are only the generalities. Cultures demand knowledge of the particularities of their geography and history to say nothing of the knowledge and mutual memory required for sustaining social relations between individuals. The man who mistook his wife for a hat was no doubt in less trouble than the one who mistook her for someone else's. Our knowledge plays a very large part in determining what social groups and subgroups we belong to, and our status within them. Were *you* there when *it* happened? If not you may not belong to the group of us who were. Learning something is simultaneously learning that some proposition is true, or some skill at performing some task, *and* becoming a member of a group of adepts defined by the resultant cognitive change. Needless to say, social affiliations are sources of intense affective significance—perhaps the most basic and intense of all human affective relations.

The cognitive and social phenomena of epistemic emotion are inseparable. They both tend to lead to the spreading of affect from the specifics of emotionally loaded content to the generalities of representational form, i.e. from object-level attitudes to referents to meta-level attitudes to properties of representations and their systems. Coherence, consistency, efficacy in reasoning, breadth of coverage—these are all properties of systems of representations, and our feelings about them are not to be explained away in terms of the shoes and ships the representations represent. While propositions may be abstract mathematical functions from possible worlds to truth values, the mental implementation of their representations can be a matter of huge value, and therefore of huge affective significance. In the previous section we proposed that affect played a distinctive role in bringing about the evolution of human representational capacities. We now argue that the end result is that emotions transfer in complex and indirect ways from objects to their representations.

If there are reasons why representations should be objects of emotion for human beings, what kind of evidence is there about how these relations are mediated and how they work in practice? Three examples will illustrate how thinking of our affective structure as implementing reasoning may help to the causal instrumentality of representation systems.

7.4.1 The emotions as implementations of rational choice theory

Helpfully for our purposes, there has recently been a debate about rationality and the emotions in reasoning, inspired by neurological findings. Several authors, notably Damasio (1994), have attacked the tug-of-war model as a basis for understanding the relation between emotion and cognition. Damasio portrays the effect of emotion on cognition in generally positive terms. On the basis of some celebrated neurological cases, he identifies a syndrome of brain damage which leads to the attenuation of affective reactions, combined with subtle but significant deficits of reasoning. He interprets these two observations as showing that, far from interfering with reasoning, affect is essential for its guidance.

For example, Damasio first noticed that a group of his neurological patients showed little emotional reaction when discussing the tragic effects of their brain injuries on their own lives. They were quite able to discuss the complex details of their histories, but did so like a colleague discussing another patient. Their reasoning seemed not to be impaired but rather emotionally decontextualized. For example, he describes a patient entering into a half hour long cost-benefit analysis of a choice between two dates for his next appointment, but responding with complete indifference when finally interrupted and politely informed which date it would have to be. The effort put into reasoning is not related to the importance of the outcome.

After much investigation using standard reasoning tasks which failed to find any cognitive impairment, Damasio succeeded in characterizing one cognitive deficit of these patients as a tendency to discount the future in making risky decisions in uncertainty. He developed a laboratory gambling paradigm which was capable of distinguishing patients from suitable controls in the laboratory. They failed to anticipate the bad consequences of their rash behaviour. This deficit seems an intuitively good fit to Damasio's descriptions of the predicaments that these patients get into in their everyday lives.

Damasio interprets these and other data to show that real-world reasoning, as distinct from the solution of laboratory puzzles, needs affect for effective control. This positive contribution of affect is exemplified by cases of affective tie-breaking preventing procrastination, and improved focus on the important issues. He cites an example of a patient having to decide whether to enter into a lucrative business deal with the arch enemy of the patient's best friend. Whereas an affectively healthy individual is alerted to the main issue immediately by a 'gut feeling' about the social consequences for friendship, the patient enters into a lengthy and inconclusive cost-benefit analysis of the details of the many factors involved.

Damasio appeals to the operation of gut feelings or, as he rebrands them, 'somatic markers', and supposes that these feelings can effectively guide decision because they are structured and controlled by past reinforcement. In the earlier example of the decision about dealing with the patient's best friend's enemy, a gut feeling concentrates attention onto the deleterious consequences for friendship so that the cognitive reasoning mechanisms reject solutions down this path. If we accept Damasio's interpretation of his evidence, how should we conceptualize this positive contribution of affect to rational reasoning in normal subjects?

Rational choice theory provides the usual departure point. Rational choice theory accounts for motivations in reasoning through utilities. Individuals are assumed to make the decisions that maximize their expected utilities. So if we have an exclusive set of choices, together with the subjective probabilities of their outcomes, and we know their respective costs and benefits, we choose whichever maximizes the combination of costs and benefits. What could be simpler, or less controversial? Here is the other great formal framework for human reasoning and decision, after logic.

Controversy about rational choice theory enters in many ways, an important one in our context being that it is far from clear what kinds of things utilities can be and whether they obey the kind of arithmetic that the equations require of them.

Reasoning enters into the equation chiefly because reasoning is required to make the calculations. Calculating the probabilities and utilities is itself a cost. It is not hard to show that trivially simple decisions might involve astronomical calculation costs if the relevant probabilities and utilities were to be calculated via the equations of the theory. Spending a year deciding which action will save a penny is palpably irrational, unless of course the occupation of calculation is so pleasurable and the year is affordable.

Faced with such cases, it is usually more rational to toss a (perhaps suitably loaded) coin than to continue in calculation. In this book we have emphasized that an important part of reasoning is deciding how to represent the problem to minimize object-level calculation, and so this meta-reasoning will also have to be accounted in the costs of calculation, adding its own extra layer of complexity. Knowing when to stop looking for a better representation and get on with object-level calculation is yet another hard computational problem with its own costs and benefits and problems about 'stopping rules'.

Needless to say, an important source of the complications of calculation are the interdependencies of human actions on other humans' actions. The Prisoners' Dilemma is perhaps the classical illustration of the interdependence of action on mutual belief. If we trust our colleague in crime, then we can minimize mutual cost, but only provided that she trusts us.

An even more radical source of problems for the nature of utilities is attitudes to the calculation process itself. Suppose that an agent has a strong distaste for conceiving a certain kind of decision in terms of certain kinds of calculation of utilities. Should this aversion be regarded as a disutility to be weighed in her equation? This may seem highly academic until we realize that this appears to be a central feature of the most important kinds of life decisions for many of us. One often quoted instance of the application of rational choice theory is Darwin's report in his autobiography that he took his decision to marry by noting down the pros and cons and adding up the costs and benefits. We can be confident that this process remained private at the time, rather than being done in consultation with his future spouse. Is it necessarily irrational that we feel that such decisions should not be taken exclusively on the basis of the kinds of costs and benefits that can be publicly articulated in the terms required by the rational choice equations?

Of course, one might take the system-as-nature stance and argue that mate-selection mechanisms in animals (Darwin having demonstrated that he was one himself) have come to implement rational choice theory, or some approximation to it, through the processes of evolution, although the part played by Darwin's pencil and paper may be hard to incorporate under this account. But one cannot take the system-as-technology stance towards the application of rational choice theory without incorporating the extra complication that agents have powerful and not necessarily irrational utilities attached to the way in which agents (including themselves) take decisions. Trust is a critical issue in taking socially interactive decisions, and trust is notoriously hard to explain on a rational choice account. Trust is generally not fostered by public calculation as to whether to be trustworthy.

Rational choice theory can either be taken as a bland mathematical framework for relating probabilities and utilities of whatsoever kinds of things are taken to be desirable, or the theory can bring with it a lot of utilitarian philosophical baggage which prescribes what ought to be counted as desirable, and especially the desirability of its countability. The former approach is obviously the only scientifically sustainable one. Furthermore, rational choice theory, like logic, can be taken as a theorists' tool for describing nature, or as a technology for participants' decisions. Treated as a highly abstract formal framework embodying conceptual truth, rational choice theory can play the important role of driving empirical study of behaviour. Under what conditions and at what level of description, and with what ontology of utilities, does people's behaviour fit the equations? Much of the value of such theories is to show just where the theory is inapplicable, and why it breaks down there. Taken this way, asserting that rational choice theory is true, is on a par with saying that arithmetic is true.

If we take rational choice theory at its promised word that it is merely a neutral mathematical framework, and interpret the theory as a theorist's tool for describing nature, then there is an interesting way of describing Damasio's patient whom we left pondering the business deal with his best friend's worst enemy, and more generally, of describing an important role of emotion within rational choice models of reasoning. Above and beyond accounting reasoning as itself a cost (and therefore something attracting negative utility), and the values (either positive or negative) of experiencing emotions themselves, emotion might be thought of as what *implements* at least part of individuals' utility functions. Affectively intact reasoners, unlike Damasio's patients, know immediately that the decisive issue is whether any monetary reward can outweigh the consequences for friendship. Whatever their resolution of this issue, this is where their emotional response focuses their attention. In the case of someone who immediately decides that no possible monetary reward could compensate for the probable damage to their friendship, the emotional response simply prunes out a large part of the search space involved in the calculation. This is the part of the search space that Damasio's subject fails to prune.

To think of emotions as implementing utility functions is to propose that theory is not faced by a tug-of-war between calculation and emotion, but instead that the emotional reaction *is* the calculation. In an organism with multiple and often conflicting goals (perhaps to become rich and stay friends as well as to eat, stay warm and reproduce), a major problem is the synoptic control of its goal-direction through time, in accordance with its long-term knowledge of the large-scale landscape of its utilities. The typical examples of rational choice theory are, with regard to this larger landscape, microtactical.

For a rational choice theorist to complain that this shift in thinking leaves the implementation radically heterogeneous—composed of a combination of consciously directed cognitive problem-solving processes and implicit emotional responses—is just to smuggle back in some of that philosophical baggage that was supposed to be left at the door. If rational choice theory is a bland mathematical framework, it is well above the level of having anything to say about its mental implementation. Its equations may conjure up images of cool arithmetical calculations, but this is just gratuitous phenomenology. In computational terms, on this account, the emotions are part of the theorem-prover that guides search in the calculation of costs and benefits. One might doubt that it is possible for affective structure to implement the necessary calculations, but as long as we think of affect as implementing calculations, then what we would expect is for them to implement approximations. There might exist some riskless way of doing the deal with the friend's worst enemy to make a profit, put the enemy out of business, and strengthen the friendship, but if so, it is the needle that remains hidden in most affectively healthy decision-makers' search-space haystacks.

The standing of rational choice theory is analogous with the standing of logic as a formal theory of behaviour. Applying the framework requires that the formalism is applied to the contentful situation, and this requires making a distinction between object-level and meta-level processes. Once this line is drawn, the framework applies. But when we entertain participants using the framework as a technology, the object-level—meta-level line is always prone to being redrawn during, and as a result of, the outcomes of object-level computation. When the line is redrawn, and valuations of what were previously meta-processes have to be included within the system, then the results of the object-level calculations change. Shifts of the meta-object boundary are often associated with emotional responses perhaps precisely because they happen when we become aware of the significance of our framing of our problem.

I hope that this example helps to motivate the idea that emotional reactions can be seen as implementations of reasoning processes. However, these examples are still ones where emotion is operating as an implementation of a utility function and thereby guiding reasoning (the theorem-prover). The core of reasoning (the representation system) might still be thought of as a separate cognitive process. But our earlier examples were of a still more intimate integration of affective structure into cognitive processes: the affective basis of narrative analogy; and for word-meaning generalization. These examples were brought to propose that the underlying processes of reasoning themselves had some affective basis.

7.4.2 Feelings as implementations of deductive reasoning

Here we shall exploit an example that we have already considered in some detail. Cosmides' and Tooby's (1992) cheating-detectors might be respecified and reconstrued in terms of a proposal for the affective implementation of conditional reasoning, and perhaps by extension deductive reasoning in general. As we pointed out in Chapter 6, we might suppose that our reasoning with both descriptive and deontic conditionals and their contrasting semantics might be implemented in the same affective knowledge about lying and cheating. In a potentially adversarial situation, when reasoning about whether a descriptive conditional is true, we might dramatize by thinking in terms of liars and this dramatization might be instrumental in episodes of our reasoning. Of course, it would not automatically be enough to get the selection task 'right' because of all the extra complexities of descriptive semantics analysed before.

Under this proposal, our conditional reasoning would still be based on our general grasp of the conditional semantics of our mother tongue, and more specifically on knowledge of the relation between descriptive and deontic semantics, which is why we can readily adapt to reasoning about permissions, obligations, prudential situations etc. when scenarios supply suitable assumptions, without supposing a different widget for each. Nor need we suppose that our ability to adopt these affective implementations of our reasoning were evolved each as separate adaptations. We would surely want to know a great deal more about how our affective systems in general functioned before attempting to carve them into separate widgets, and even if we did come to believe in separable modules, we would need to keep continuously in mind the problem of how these modules would have to communicate with each other (in how general a language, for example) in order to yield systematic behaviour. Our best guide to the interactions between domain-general and domain-specific aspects would be logic's analysis of the dependence of reasoning on assumptions.

In modern undergraduate subjects (rather than Pleistocene ones), this implementation in terms of affective understandings might exhibit itself in a stage of reasoning in which difficulty is experienced with reasoning about scenarios that do not specify enough detail to trigger these affective responses with all their attendant assumptions. For example, subjects might well not be able to reason effectively when variables such as P and Q replace contentful descriptions, or when an abstract rule about letters and vowels is not accompanied by enough information about what communication is intended (e.g. what the utterer's purpose might be). Certainly the subjects of these experiments are used to understanding utterances in terms of the truthfulness of their utterers rather than the truth values of their utterances. However, once subjects become better accustomed to the task's demands, they may become able to invoke the relevant affective schemas for the rules in more abstracted scenarios. Logic class might further refine their strategies of deployment of these affective implementations, which might by then have become fairly well hidden.

The other possibility is that the affective schemas are replaced and reasoning is implemented in purely formal symbol shuffling. We have argued against this latter alternative in general (though it is undoubtedly possible in some limited circumstances), because it leaves open all the problems of how form contacts content. Instead we opted for an account in which learning symbol shuffling helped students to train their affectively based implicit grasp of their pre-class communicative habits. That is what we mean by saying that formalisms become implemented in our affective structure.

This proposal that affect implements system in reasoning and communication fundamentally contrasts with Cosmides and Tooby's proposal that cheating-detectors implement social contractual exchange. Under the current proposal knowledge of conditional semantics, deontic-descriptive contrasts, etc. is held to be general knowledge about representations whose skilled deployment depends on the ability to engage affectively with new content. On our account, what is fundamental and general is the subjects' understanding of the difference between representations representing how things *are*, as opposed to representing how they *should* be, how we *would like* them to be, how some law says they *ought* to be, how we plan they *should* become etc. etc. i.e. the logical distinction between descriptive and deontic uses of representations. On our account, the same affective basis could underlie both descriptive and deontic reasoning.

When the relation between our affective responses and deductive reasoning is conceived in this way, the example suggests an almost opposite evolutionary account of the relation between informational exchange in communication and the contractual exchange of costs and benefits, and this alternative account provides an interesting if speculative example of the affective implementation of a system of representations. We pursue this evolutionary proposal here for what it can tell us about the roots of human reasoning and its relation to our affective and social structure in the implementation of representation systems.

Here we approach a central issue about how humans differentiated from other primates. To state it baldly, which came first, communication or 'social contractual exchange'? To follow the implications of our analysis in terms of affective implementations of reasoning, we need to re-examine the evolutionary models used in the arguments that exchange is primary. Again, these turn out to be rational choice models. Cosmides and Tooby's 'evolutionary psychology' seeks to explain communication and reasoning with conditionals, on the basis of cognitive capacities evolved for performing cost-benefit contractual exchanges. They claim the need for 'cheating-detectors' but not 'altruism detectors' to operate in the rational choice models of these transactions.

The game theoretic models for the evolution of co-operation that could be reasonably applied to the range of population structures that typified hominid hunter-gatherers require the existence of some mechanism for detecting cheaters or otherwise excluding them from the benefits of co-operation. This is because the capacity to engage in social exchange could not have been continually exploited by cheaters. But most models do not require the existence of a mechanism for detecting 'altruists'—individuals who follow the strategy of paying the required cost (thereby benefiting the other party), but not accepting from the other party the benefit to which the act entitles them. (Cosmides and Tooby 1992, p. 193)

The models in question are game-theoretic models of Prisoners' Dilemma games in which two non-communicating prisoners face a decision as to whether to co-operate with the police in return for reduced sentences. The pay-off matrix for this decision is given in Table 7.1. If both co-operate with the police they both receive a large penalty.

Table 7.1 Pay-off matrix for Prisoners' Dilemma.

Player 2	Player 1	
	Co-operate	**Compete**
Co-operate	P1: +3 P2: +3	P1: -2 P2: +5
Compete	P1: +5 P2: -2	P1: 0 P2: 0

If one does and one does not, the collaborator gets off free, but the non-collaborator receives a worse penalty. But if they both refuse to talk, they both get off with small or zero punishment for lack of evidence. With suitable adjustment of the pay-off matrix to satisfy well-understood constraints, the best *total* outcome for the pair is achieved by their staying quiet, but the best *individual* outcome is to be the lone informer. The worst total outcome (both individual and total) is for both to be informers. And yet, unable to communicate, the prisoners must trust each other to avoid this outcome.

In a single laboratory game with partners unknown to each other, players will often fail to co-operate and lose out. But once iterated play is possible, players commonly employ a tit-for-tat strategy of trusting their partner unless they were betrayed on the last trial. Iteration is necessary for the development of reliable trust. But in more realistic situations, behaviour depends on the cohesion of and relations between social groups. Thieves frequently do co-operate and maintain their silence even in single plays of such games.

Evolutionary theorists (Hamilton 1964; Maynard-Smith 1964; Axelrod and Hamilton 1981) have used Prisoners' Dilemma games to model the evolution of co-operation by modelling exchanges of goods or services on the original games of exchange of information. Cosmides and Tooby (1992) base their theories on this work. The models show that indiscriminate cheaters will always come to dominate a population of indiscriminate co-operators. Cosmides and Tooby use the term 'altruistic' for this latter kind of behaviour, arguing that evolution would have selected for cheating-detectors but not for altruism detectors, and they seek to show that undergraduate subjects cannot 'detect altruism' in an experiment (Cosmides and Tooby 1992, pp. 192–5). Concerned that their subjects might not be understanding 'altruistic', they replaced it in a replication with 'selfless'. But one might wonder whether the experimenters understand 'altruism' in its usual sense? Altruists are not people who go into shops and pay for goods they do not take away. I do not know if there is a name for inverse kleptomania in the annals of psychiatry, but I am confident that the name is not 'altruism' [35].

Let us pause to ask how well this formal model fits its desired application to the human biological phenomena at hand. First, there is the question of what mental apparatus is needed by the creatures simulated in these Prisoner's Dilemma models. For example, on iterated plays, players in a population have to remember who has co-operated and who has cheated in order to have a base for their policies. Even the vampire bats quoted as rare non-human examples of co-operative exchange beyond kin in population biology need to have a memory for past transactions of blood exchange, perceptual and memory mechanisms for individual identification etc. But to generalize co-operation and cheating beyond the exchange of a single commodity in tightly determined circumstances, in an otherwise homogeneous population, as Cosmides and Tooby acknowledge is necessary, actors would need a grasp of each other as intentional entities. They would need to be able to communicate their values.

None of this can be done by cheating-detection algorithms unless they include theory-of-mind abilities, communicative abilities, and trusted affiliations among groups. Cosmides and Tooby implicitly acknowledge a more reasonable interpretation of altruism in quoting Trivers' (1971) definition of social exchange as 'reciprocal altruism' where one partner is altruistic to the other at the point the transaction begins, and the other reciprocates at the completion. In this more plausible sense of altruism, creatures do need altruism detectors to come to develop exchange, and if undergraduate students really could not detect this kind of altruism they would not be able to negotiate exchange either.

All these factors are idealized away in the models. That may or may not be fine for Axelrod and Hamilton's (1951) purposes in modelling simple creatures' exchange of non-informational goods in homogeneous populations, but the idealization goes to the

---

[35] The *Oxford English Dictionary* gives 'devotion to the welfare of others' as the meaning of altruism.

heart of the issue of modelling the evolution of human altruism. Altruism as we need to understand it consists in submerging one's own immediate interest in the interests of some larger group. In the philosophical limit this group might contain all conspecifics, or even a wider group, but plausible evolutionary models can perfectly well start with some subgroup smaller than the whole, and perhaps radically so (two?). Evolutionary models use the concept of 'inclusive fitness theory' (or kin selection) (Maynard-Smith 1964; Hamilton 1964) to explain evolution of such traits as altruism *within* genetically related groups, but require something more than this to extend beyond them. But perhaps we should see the origins of altruism in the spread outwards from the genetically related group of capacities for trusted communication which were originally selected by kin-selection.

All applications of rational choice models of exchange require the existence of trust. A simple illustration of this point, due to Basu (1983), is the paradox of paying the taxi driver. We enter into an agreement with a taxi driver to take us to B. When we get to B, we pay him. But why? Well, a first application of rational choice theory might claim that it is because we fear the costs involved in the fuss that he will make if we do not pay. But then why do we believe that he will not make a fuss, with all the same costs, after we have paid him? And why, for that matter, did he take us to B without prior payment? No calculations based on the single transaction can explain why we do in fact pay, or why he trusted us to pay. Even attempts to introduce explanations in terms of laws and sanctions for disobeying them do not go very far. The costs to society of policing small transactions is out of all proportion. The law would not work if most people did not obey it thoughtlessly most of the time, and that because of the mutual benefits of being able to forget it, rather than the calculative benefits taken transaction by transaction. Only larger considerations about the value of living in an orderly community stand any chance of success, and these demand the explanation of trust and social co-ordination through communication. Adam Smith (1786) made explicit reference to this dependence of trade on language in *The Wealth of Nations*. (Paragraphs 1 and 2 of Book I chapter II).

Applying the Prisoner's Dilemma to understanding the evolution of human altruism requires that the models are augmented with accounts of the community structures involved, and the trust they involve. This need reveals another really fundamental issue that is glossed over in this modelling—the slide from the Prisoner's Dilemma's *informational* exchange to the exchange of non-informational goods and services. The exchange of information has rather different properties from the exchange of conventional goods and services. The cost of supplying information once garnered (its replication cost) is generally small, and the benefits of information to the receiver are, as just argued in the previous section, indefinitely indirect and unpredictable. As discussed above, knowing one's way around is extremely valuable, but its particular instrumentalities are various and unpredictable. The costs to the information provider of supplying otherwise unavailable information are highly context specific, both to the kind of information involved and the nature of the partner in exchange. Giving away street directions, for example, only leads to competition costs in rather special situations.

Each of these factors makes information exchange difficult to model in rational choice frameworks. Testimony to just how hard it is to get information to behave like non-informational benefits in rational choice models of economic behaviour is the outpourings of recent work on the 'knowledge economy'. Although the knowledge economy (in the economist's sense) is a recent arrival (if it has arrived at all), in evolution it is arguable that the knowledge economy (in the sense of the evolution of communication between intentional entities) preceded the widespread exchange of non-informational goods. What we need is an explanation of how perhaps genetically related groups came to be able to operate an 'information economy', and then how it could spread beyond into larger groups. Our proposal is that some affective basis of trust (i.e. a basis prior to calculation) is required to get informational exchange to work, and we speculate that this is able to emerge in the development of communication because of the peculiar 'economics' of information. In particular, we speculate that it is interactions between knowledge and social affiliation of subgroups that played an evolutionary role in applying selection pressure towards communication within groups larger than genetically related units.

The data seem to fit this theoretical conclusion. In evolutionary terms, economic exchange as conceived of in rational choice theory (the exchange of varied goods and benefits according to a value system) arose when human beings began to participate in widespread exchange of goods and services between genetically non-related individuals, probably about 10000 years ago (Mithen 2000). It might be argued that specific divisions of labour predate this development— perhaps stone axe exchange for the spoils of hunting? But if so, and if this developed before trusted communication through intentionally interpreted representations, then it would not constitute the capacity for understanding social contracts (just as vampire bats do not understand social contracts).

So if we ask what had to come first, the cognitive and affective capacities for communication and the trust of communication, or the apparatus for the large scale social exchange of goods and services, the answer must be the former needed to proceed the latter. The exchange of information in trusted communication is more fundamental to understanding human evolution (at least the species differentiation of humans from their ancestors) than the exchange of non-informational costs and benefits. Explaining the evolution of the latter will not provide a bridge to explaining the former because the rational choice models used specifically stand in need of founding on trusted communication.

How could trusted communication develop and how does an account rest on the affective implementation of cognition? Let us look more deeply at the Prisoners' Dilemma and what it tells us about communication and trust. The irony, of course, is that the prisoners' situation is one of *non-communication*. But the prisoners' situation is all about community, or more accurately two communities and their relations— the police and the criminal underworld. In laboratory experiments in which subjects and experimenters lack differentiation of broader interest, where subject-pairs do not know each other and where there are no long-term consequences beyond accumulation of points in a game, subjects frequently fail to co-operate on the non-iterated Prisoners' Dilemma. But when more realistically, police and suspects come from two well-differentiated social groups with strong identity and conflicting interests, it is common for pairs of 'subjects' to achieve co-ordination on single play games.

It was Schelling (1960) who first elucidated the importance of the Prisoner's Dilemma for understanding real social co-ordinations ranging from union negotiations to meeting a friend at the station. The application of games theory to the prisoners incommunicado reveals the hinterland of mutual knowledge and affiliation required for communication in general—remember Wittgenstein's forms of life. Lewis (1969) went on to analyse convention, a crucial foundation for intentionally interpreted representation systems, on the basis of these insights about the necessity of shared knowledge. If altruism (as opposed to random giving away of benefits) is to be modeled on the Prisoners' Dilemma, then affiliation into groups within which altruism is practised, and outwith which it is not, is one of the first demands we should make of any modelling of altruism's emergence and spread beyond genetically related groups in evolution.

As we observed above, the modern situation is clear enough. Human beings form social affiliations on the basis of mutual knowledge and belief. Every epistemic effect of communication also has phatic consequences, however slight. Every phatic effect of communication depends on some epistemic consequence, however trivial. Our proposal is that it is precisely the linkage of phatic and propositional effects of communication, and the nature of knowledge exchange, that drove the development of human communication and the treatment of each other as epistemic and not just instrumental agents.

If we were *only* socially obliged to be truthful where false-saying constituted violation of a contract for instrumental social exchange (of information), then we would not be coherent communicative partners. The condemnation of false-saying is universalized well beyond the violation of pseudo-contractual exchanges. It is considered malicious to give false information to people simply because we do not owe them anything. Again, the reason is the indirectness of the instrumentality of knowledge and the necessity of being able to apply the principle of charity in interpretation once representations have to be interpreted.

So rational choice models developed in more realistic ways can provide useful frameworks for demonstrating how much more than rational choice is involved in understanding the development of trusted communication as a necessary basis for subsequent developments of social contractual exchange. Human evolution somehow had to get from an animal which had considerable capacity for understanding the motivations of its conspecifics in carrying out complex intentional behaviour to an animal that had the capacity to treat its conspecifics as epistemic agents, each with their own knowledge and beliefs, each with their own social affiliations. The particular economics of informational exchange suggests that the most powerful selection pressures for this leap would operate especially for the exchange of information which is of low cost to the provider (both replication and competition cost) and of great but indirect and unpredictable instrumental value to the receiver, and where the distant instrumental value is accompanied by powerful immediate phatic value.

These speculations suggest a further one—that the capacity to treat each other as epistemic agents in communication may have evolved initially in the mother-child relationship where altruism is most secured by genetic forces. The human infant must expend more energy acquiring knowledge with more distant instrumentality than any other organism. The infant's immediate motivations are more plausibly phatic than propositional. Some immediate pay-off is needed to sustain this effort. Perhaps this shift to the phatic value of representations is what leads to a jump in levels of the object of our affections and lead to the affective implementation of representations.

Perhaps these epistemic capacities emerged in mother-infant interactions and travelled down the ontogenetic sequence towards the adult through neoteny, spreading out beyond the genetically related group only gradually and under the pressure of coordinating larger communities. The increasing gap between mother and infant cognition must have been one of the most powerful selection pressures in human prehistory for the ability to communicate across epistemic misalignments of interpretation—forces which also argue for a major role for *changes* in the relation between affect and cognition in the evolutionary dynamics. Human infants are primates born prematurely. The evolutionary advantage of premature birth is presumably that the external environment can play an earlier role in the maturation of a still plastic nervous system. But there are very significant downsides—a very long period of biological helplessness which has to be compensated by heavy parental investment in protection and enculturation. Here is a source of selection pressure (chiefly on mothers) for the skill of interpreting communications from substantially different other minds. Something needs to feed the baby's appetite for representations of knowledge with such distant instrumentality, and the mother's appetite for supplying. Linking knowledge to affect through its phatic consequences seems to have been the solution.

It is one thing to reveal the benefits that adaptations would have had, but another to explain how they could have come about. We do not pretend that this sketch does that. Hobson's theories of the relation between interindividual affect and the development of symbolism are perhaps the best illustration we have of the kind of explanation required. At least this sketch suggests very different places to look for evolutionary routes.

An alternative picture emerges of the prolonged dependence of human infants driving a need for communicative skills within the genetically related unit, just as that prolonged dependence enables and requires the development of more complex social groups, eventually leading to the division of labour and the economic behaviour dependent on trust of genetically unrelated and even unfamiliar individuals. The ability to detect cheating on exchange contracts is usefully seen as a small and not particularly differentiated generalization of the development of communicative abilities, however important its ramifications may have been for economic behaviour. The ability to communicate across misalignments of belief, knowledge, goals and desires is the ability to articulate feelings in externalized public representations, and to resolve differences of feelings through construction of new articulations of them.

Several key proposals emerge from this speculation. Thinking in terms of computation offers the idea that the relation between affect and cognition is that the former implements the latter. In that implementation, the source of abstraction over the details of each context is the commonality of affective structure across situations. The economics of informational exchange are central to understanding the selection pressures. The Prisoner's Dilemma has the value of illustrating how social factors of group delineation may play their part in achieving 'cognitive' calculation of group and individual benefit. It is not a matter of choosing between logic and the involvement of affect in reasoning.

This evolutionary sketch is better supported by the narrow evidence of the selection task and interpretation of the rational choice models, but it is little more that a guide for empirical investigation. The best hope we have of discovering what happened all that time ago is to work towards better articulated functional characterizations of what our modern subjects are doing, and that demands the application of what is known about reasoning from all the disciplines concerned.

7.4.3   Representation and affect in social symbolism

Anthropologists have done as much as any discipline to establish some of the relations between society, emotion and representation. A classic example is Douglas's (1966) analysis of the concepts of pollution and taboo of primitive societies. Following Durkheim's analysis of religion as a projection of society onto nature (if not his distinction between religion and magic), Douglas argued that social anomalies are expressed as symbolic anomalies. For example, most famously, unclean categories of animals are those which are anomalies in the reigning taxonomy. The abominations of Leviticus—the unclean fauna that shall not be eaten—are the animals that are atypical of their categories— violations of the community's conceptual scheme: fish that do not have scales; cloven footed creatures that do not chew the cud; land animals with creepy kinds of locomotory habits ... It is as if the authors of Leviticus had read Eleanor Rosch on typicality being the foundation of categories. The relations of representational anomaly and ambiguity express what is affectively significant in a society's conceptual scheme. Here is another phenomenon consisting in emotions about systems of representation.

But Douglas goes beyond demonstrating a simple static alignment of social symbolism and cognitive structure, and confronts an old question about primitive religion. Why is it that what is generally abominated may become sacralized in some specific religious contexts? To take but one example, Douglas observes that the pangolin is as anomalous for the Lele as it is possible for an animal to be: 'It is scaly like a fish but climbs trees. It is more like an egg-laying lizard than a mammal but it suckles its young. And most significant of all, unlike all other small mammals, its young are born singly.' But, Douglas continues, 'instead of being abhorred, the Pangolin is eaten in solemn ceremony by its initiates who are thereby enabled to minister fertility to their kind.'

Douglas's first observation is that not just any polluting thing can become a sacred thing in some other context. But her general explanation for the ambivalence towards anomaly is that representation schemes, just like social structures, are not monolithic, or static, or enduringly satisfactory. What is pollution in one symbolic scheme gives rise to the innovations which create new systems of representation. Disorder is dirty, but dirt is fertile—it can lead to new order. Social dynamics project a moving picture of our changing conceptual schemes.

The main difference between primitive cultures and ourselves in this respect is that because primitive cultures are relatively undifferentiated by structural divisions of labour, and because almost everything in a primitive culture is within the scope of religion, the symbolism derived from representational anomaly almost always has social and religious significance. In our societies heavily differentiated by secularization, representational anomaly is, as Douglas documents, no less widely felt, but much less often has religious or social significance. The miscegenation of interdisciplinary research and the attendant passions it precipitates are perhaps a good example of the operation of the same mechanisms of representational anomaly in a sphere closer to home.

Douglas illustrates the pervasiveness of our feelings of pollution and taboo with examples of domestic tidiness/untidiness, but notes that for us, in contrast with the undifferentiated primitive society, ideas of defilement are secular matters of hygiene and aesthetics: 'If we can abstract pathogenicity and hygiene from our notion of dirt we are left with the old definition of dirt—matter out of place'. Being out of place is dependent on some representational scheme of what it is to be in place.

In thinking of the symbolic schemes of even primitive societies as subject to a dynamic of representation and re-representation, Douglas contrasts two attitudes to ritual representations. One stresses the performance of outer ritual; the other the experience of inner meaning and its direct translation into conduct. She defends primitive religion against earlier anthropologists' tendencies to dismiss any rite with enough symbols to be observed as an indication that it was an empty ritual without religious content. She reads her predecessor's claims as the venting of Protestant prejudice against religious symbolism and observes that 'as with society, so with religion, external form is the condition of its existence'.

Our interest in these two attitudes towards symbolism is in what light they can throw on matters closer to home and the study of the internalization of formalisms. What has the anthropologist's interest in the projections of the structure of primitive society onto nature via symbolism got to do with the goings on in logic classroom? Anthropologists have felt deeply the need to reconcile the sophistication of the religious thought of primitive societies with the apparent cognitive limitations of their members as measured by standardised tests. Levy-Bruhl (1922) is perhaps the best-known example in his attempts to understand why the kind of deductive reasoning which has been our focus is not easily elicited from the members of primitive societies.

Douglas defends Levy-Bruhl against his accusers who see him as a crude ethnocentrist. She sees his error as one of psychologizing rather than sociologizing his explanation. The complexity of Dogon cosmology is quite incompatible with the idea that the Dogon are simple-minded. Douglas describes Levy-Bruhl's insight: 'He insisted that their [the Dogon's] alleged dislike of discursive reasoning is not due to intellectual incapacity but to highly selective standards of relevance which produce in them insuperable indifference to matters bearing no relation to those that interest them' (Douglas 1966, p. 76) [36] Remember Scribner's unschooled syllogizer who refused to abandon social norms that insist that comment on character requires first-hand knowledge.

What does interest the Dogon? Douglas argues that the interests of primitive societies never range far from the religious. In these societies where 'the technical problems have been more or less settled for generations past, the live issue is how to organize other people and oneself in relation to them; how to control turbulent youth, how to soothe disgruntled neighbours, how to gain one's rights, how to prevent usurpation of authority, or how to justify it.' (Douglas 1966, p. 92). She argues that these people's cosmologies are what Durkheim saw them as—projections of the social onto nature—not metaphysical theories about the physical universe. Needless to say, what is projected is primarily what is affectively charged.

The Greek achievement of differentiating political and legal from religious debate, and of making debate an object of theoretical study by logicians, produced an awareness of language as a medium of thought—a theory of communication, but a theory with its origins firmly rooted in the earlier modes of symbolic projection. An expansion of interests became both possible and necessary. A number of studies in the history and philosophy of science suggest that our highly differentiated intellectual activities nevertheless bear the marks of their origins in primitive symbolic projections onto nature. Bloor (1981), in particular, has studied one incident in the development of nineteenth-century mathematics in these terms. Bloor analyses the controversy between

[36] Logic teachers amongst readers might experience some twinge of recognition?

Hamilton and Peacock about their respective philosophical understandings of algebra. This incident is an example of the projection of social categories onto nature, but it is of particular relevance here because the dimension of controversy between the parties was the use of imagery in mathematics.

Sir William Rowan Hamilton was the Irish discoverer of quaternions, a representation and algebra of complex numbers. George Peacock was the champion of a group of Cambridge mathematicians, the Analytical Society, responsible for adopting and developing the French style of symbolic algebra in Britain. Hamilton's discovery of quaternions was achieved by considering several geometrical interpretations of complex numbers. The resulting algebraic system dropped the principle of commutativity for multiplication by i, the imaginary component. Hamilton believed passionately that his geometrical and semantic way of thinking about the formalism was the true essence of algebra—what he called, with a Kantian inspiration, a science of pure time.

In contrast, Peacock regarded algebraic symbolism as an uninterpreted calculus. Any interpretation that was offered might show that the truths of algebra held sway over other dominions (geometry, for example) but algebraic truth owed nothing to the existence or non-existence of these interpretations.

In modern terms, Hamilton was an intuitionist and Peacock a formalist. There is a suggestive analogy between this distinction and the contrast between reasoning with and without diagrams. Directly interpreted diagrams ensure the existence of physical interpretation for formalism; sentential calculi do not. Hamilton and Peacock make a fascinating study just because they agreed about so many of the aims, procedures, methods, and technicalities of their subject, but disagreed so vehemently about its philosophical foundations.

Bloor sets out to show that these metaphysical differences are correlated with differences in social attitudes about authority for knowledge. He traces Hamilton's communications with Coleridge and evidence from Carlyle's writings about the social employments of Coleridge's 'idealist' philosophy. The idealist aesthetic and metaphysic was against the utilitarian ethic of the industrial revolution which threatened the existing social hierarchy and broke down the organic solidarity of pre-industrial society in favour of the mechanical solidarity of the industrial order.

Bloor shows that Hamilton's and Peacock's views on religion, professional politics, and politics proper, also contrast in ways which correspond to the contrast in their mathematical philosophies. Hamilton was high church (albeit protestant), for obedience in religion, a (moderate) political conservative, and against the contemporary professionalization of mathematics. Peacock was an evangelical founder of the Analytical Society, for the following of conscience in religion, politics, and mathematics, and for the professionalization of mathematics. Bloor explicitly offers his study as an example of Douglas's projection of social structure and interests onto 'nature'—mathematical nature in this case. Irish and English academia of the eighteenth-century are a far cry from the primitive societies of Douglas's examples. But, Bloor argues, the same kinds of projection occur within niches of the highly differentiated societies of the developed world.

Bloor's study cannot serve here as more than one tantalizing example, but it is potentially an instructive one. It offers the possibility that deep-seated temperamental differences between people can be understood fundamentally as epistemic emotions about the origins of authority for knowledge. These differences can then be seen as expressing themselves in social, political, religious and intellectual spheres, but in each sphere there would be an underlying epistemological account in terms of differences in where individuals seek authority for knowledge: whether, as in Peacock's case, they look to the authority of their social group and its projection onto the rules of professional procedure; or whether, as in Hamilton's case, they look outside the social group for their ultimate authority for correspondence to the world.

Bloor's interest in his account lies in the expression of social interests in intellectual forms. That analysis is at a different level than our interest here in the relation between social attitudes and representational preferences. From our point of view it is less important whether social interests determine theoretical choice, or whether it is simply a correlation that the same epistemic temperamental trait is expressed in each sphere. What is an exciting prospect is that it might be possible to give some coherent account of an individual's attitudes across all these spheres, and that this account could serve as the basis for understanding how individuals of different temperaments learn in different social contexts. Formalism and intuitionism could be seen as attitudes to the origins of authority for knowledge right across the board. But formalism and intuitionism would now no longer be seen as purely cognitive beliefs, but through the link between phatic and propositional communication, they are now seen as contrasting attitudes to the origins of knowledge. Such an account provides a speculative way of understanding links between our affective and our intellectual lives.

Our logic students learning better from diagrams or from sentential presentation are, on this account showing where they seek authority for logical knowledge. Do they learn well from diagrams when the direct semantics make available to them correspondences between representation and subject matter and reveals the meta-properties of the reasoning system? Do they learn well from sentential presentations when those presentations enforce the justification at each successive step by rules agreed within their community? Social groups are composed of members with varied learning styles, and it is social groups which develop knowledge through the interactions between their varied kinds of component individuals.

It is a commonplace to contrast computational models of cognition within individuals with distributed models of cognitive processes implemented in groups of people. This contrast sometimes implicitly comes with an assumption that the latter are non-computational processes. For some reason, it is felt that describing a far-flung system of parts, some of which are human beings, as a 'computer' violates some intuition that computational processes have to be located inside boxes or heads. If so, this is an intuition that violates the most fundamental nature of computation. Computational systems just are made up of diverse components, and their processes cannot be localized within any subpart smaller than the whole system.

As promised, this has been a speculative chapter. The relations between cognition and emotion are many and multifarious. Our argument is that the relation of system to implementation is a candidate that has been little explored and yet one that is obviously necessary if we are to have a serious computational theory of mind—one that can account for relations between individuals information systems and societies. Systems unimplemented remain abstract objects.

Getting rid of the idea that a logical analysis of information systems is an alternative to psychology rather than a foundation has been a major goal throughout this book. Getting rid of the destructive idea that they are alternatives opens up a broad space of possible integrations, a few of which have been explored here. Our original question about which picture is worth which thousand words leads, naturally I hope, to a quite different theoretical and empirical program for future investigation.

References

Amarel, S. (1968). On representations of problems of reasoning about actions. *Machine Intelligence* (ed. Michie, D.), Vol. 3, pp. 131–71. Edinburgh University Press.

Amarel, S. (1969). Problem solving and decision making by computer: an overview. *Cognition: a multiple view* (ed. Paul A. Garvin). Spartan Books, New York.

Anderson, J. R. (1996). *The architecture of cognition.* Lawrence Erlbaum, Mahwah, N.J.

Axelrod, R. and Hamilton, W. D. (1981). The evolution of cooperation. *Science*, **211**, 1390–6.

Barwise, J. and Etchemendy, J. (1995). Heterogeneous logic. *Diagrammatic reasoning: cognitive and computational perspectives* (ed. B. Chandrasekaran, N. H. Narayanan and J. Glasgow), 211–34. MIT Press Cambridge, MA.

Barwise, J. and Etchemendy, J. (1994). *Hyperproof.* CSLI Publications, Stanford, CA.

Basu, K. (1983). On why we do not try to walk off without paying after a taxi-ride. *Economic & Political Weekly*, **18**, 2011–12.

Bateson, G. (1972). *Steps to an ecology of mind.* Chandler, San Francisco.

Berger, J. (1972). *Ways of seeing.* BBC Publications, London.

Bergman, M. Moore, J., and Nelson, J. (1990). *The Logic Book*, McGraw-Hill, NY.

Berkeley, G. (1709). *An essay towards a new theory of vision.* Rhames, Dublin.

Berkeley, G. (1710). *The principles of human knowledge.* Penguin, Harmondsworth (1988).

Berlin, B. and Kay, P. (1969). *Basic color terms: their universality and evolution.* University of California Press, CA.

Bird, O. (1984). *Syllogistic and its extensions.* New Jersey: Prentice Hall.

Block, N. (1981). *Imagery.* MIT Press, Cambridge, MA.

Bloor, D. (1981). Hamilton and Peacock on the essence of algebra. *Social history of nineteenth century mathematics* (ed. H. Mehrtens, H. Bos, and I. Schneider), Birkhauser, Basel.

Bruner, J. (1983). *Child's talk.* Oxford University Press.

Byrne, R. (1989). Suppressing valid inferences with conditionals. *Cognition*, **31**, 61–83.

Carruthers, P. and Smith, P. K. (1996). *Theories of theories of mind.* Cambridge University Press.

Castelfranchi, C. (1992). No more cooperation, please! In search of the social structure of verbal interaction. *A. I. and Cognitive Science Perspectives on Communication* (ed. A. Ortony, J. Slack, and O. Stock). Springer, Heidelberg.

Chandrasekaran, B., N. H. Narayanan and Glasgow, J. (ed.) (1995). *Diagrammatic reasoning: computational and cognitive perspectives on problem solving with diagrams.* MIT Press, Cambridge, MA.

Chapman, I. and Chapman, J. (1959). Atmosphere effect re-examined. *Journal of Experimental Psychology* **58**, 220–6.

Chemla, K. (1992). Resonance entre demonstration et procedure: remarques sur le commentaire de Lui Hui (III siecle) aux *Neuf chapitres sur les procedures mathematiques (I siecle)*. *Extreme Orient—Extreme Occident*, **14**, 91–129.

Cheng, P. , Holyoak, K., Nisbett, R. E., and Oliver, L. (1986). Pragmatic versus syntactic approaches to training deductive reasoning. *Cognitive Psychology*, **18**, 293–328.

Cheng, P. and Holyoak, K. (1985). Pragmatic reasoning schemas. *Cognitive Psychology*, **17**, 391–416.

Chi, M. (in press). Self-explaining expository texts: the dual processes of generating inferences and repairing mental models. *Advances in Instructional Psychology* (ed. R. Glaser). Erlbaum, Mahwah, NJ.

Chi, M. T., Siler, S., Jeong, H. Yamauchi, T., and Hausmann, R. (2001). Learning from human tutoring. *Cognitive Science*, **25**, 471–533.

Clarke, J. (1993). Cognitive style and computer assisted learning: problems and a possible solution. *Association for Learning Technology Journal*, **1**, 47–59.

Collins, A. and Quillian, M. (1969). Retrieval time for semantic memory. *Journal of Verbal Learning and Verbal Behaviour*, **8**, 240–7.

Copi, I. (1978). *Introduction to logic* (5th edn.) Macmillan NY.

Cosmides, L. (1989). The logic of social exchange: has natural selection shaped how humans reason? Studies with the Wason selection task. *Cognition*, **31**, 187–276.

Cosmides, L. and Tooby, J. (1992). Cognitive adaptations for social exchange. *The adapted mind: evolutionary psychology and the generation of culture*. (ed. J. Barkow, Cosmides, L., and Tooby, J.), pp. 163–228. Oxford University Press, NY.

Cox, R., Stenning, K., and Oberlander, J. (1995). The effect of graphical and sentential logic teaching on spontaneous external representation. *Cognitive Studies: Bulletin of the Japanese Cognitive Science Society*, **2**, 56–75.

Cronbach, L. and Snow, R. (1977). *Aptitudes and instructional methods: a handbook for research on interactions*. Irvington, NY.

Damasio, A. R. (1994). *Descartes' error: emotion, reason and the human brain*. Putnam, NY.

Donald, M. (1991). *Origins of the modern mind: three stages in the evolution of culture and cognition*. Harvard University Press: Cambridge, MA.

Dodgson, C. (1896). *Symbolic Logic*. Reprinted as Book III in *Lewis Carroll's Symbolic Logic* (ed. W. W. Bartley). Harvester Press, Hassocks, Sussex. (1977)

Douglas, M. (1966). *Purity and Danger: an analysis of the concepts of pollution and taboo*. Routledge, London.

Ekstrom, R. B., French, J. W., and Harmon, H. H. (1976). *Manual for kit of factor referenced cognitive tests*. Educational Testing Service, Princeton, NJ.

Erickson, J. (1975). A set analysis theory of behaviour in formal syllogistic reasoning tasks. *Information processing and cognition: the Loyola Symposium* (ed. Robert L. Solso). Erlbaum, Hillsdale, NJ.

Euler, L. (1772). *Lettres a une princesse d'Allemagne*, Vol. 2: *Sur divers sujets de physique et de philosophie*. Letters pp. 102–8.

Evans, J., Barston, J., and Pollard, P. (1983). On the conflict between logic and belief in syllogistic reasoning. *Memory and Cognition*, **11**, 295–306.

Ford, N. (1984). Learning styles and strategies of postgraduate students. *British Journal of Educational Technology*, **16**, 65–79.

Ford, M. (1995) Two modes of mental representation and problem solution in syllogistic reasoning. *Cognition*, **54**, 1–71.

Galton, F. (1883). *Inquiries into human faculty and its development*. Macmillan, London.

Gebauer, G. and Laming, D (1997). Rational choices in Wason's selection task. *Psychological Research*, **60**, 284–93.

Gentner, D., Holyoak, K., and Kokinov, B. (eds.) (2001). *The analogical mind*. MIT Press, Cambridge, MA.

Gentner, D., Rattermann, M. J., and Forbus, K. (1993). The roles of similarity in transfer: separating retrievability and inferential soundness. *Cognitive Psychology*, **25**, 524–75.

Gigerenzer, G. and Hug, K. (1992). Domain-specific reasoning: social contracts, cheating, and perspective change. *Cognition*, **43**, 127–71.

Goldman, A. (1989). Interpretation pscyhologised. *Mind and Language*, **4**, 161–85.

Goldman, A. (1993). The psychology of folk psychology. *Behavioural and Brain Sciences*, **16**, 15–28.

Goodman, N. (1968). *The languages of art: an approach to a theory of symbols*. Bobbs-Merrill, Indianapolis, IN.

Goodman, N. (1954). *Fact, fiction and forecast*. London University Press.

Gopnik, A. and Wellman, H. (1994). The theory theory. *Mapping the mind*. (ed. Hirschfeld, L. and Gelman, S.). Cambridge University Press.

Grice, H. P. (1975). Logic and conversation. *Syntax and Semantics* Vol. 3: *Speech acts* (ed. P. Cole and J. Morgan), Academic Press, London.

Hamilton, W. D. (1964). The genetical evolution of social behaviour. Parts I, II. *Journal of Theoretical Biology*, **7**, 1–52.

Happé, F. (1994). *Autism: an introduction to psychological theory*. University College London Press.

Heal, J. (1994). Simulation vs. theory-theory: what is at issue? *Proceedings of the British Academy*, **83**, 129–44.

Heal, J. (1996). Simulation and cognitive penetrability. *Mind & Language*, **11**, 44–67.

Henle, M. and Michael, M. (1956). The influence of attitudes on syllogistic reasoning. *Journal of Social Psychology*, **44**, 115–27.

Hobson, R.P. (1991). Against the theory of mind. *British Journal of Developmental Psychology*, **9**, 33–51.

Hobson, R.P. (1993). *Autism and the development of mind*. Lawrence Erlbaum Associates.

Jamnik, M. (2001). *Reasoning with diagrams*. University of Chicago Press, IL.

Johnson-Laird, P. and Wason, P. (1970). A theoretical analysis of insight into a reasoning task. *Cognitive Psychology*, **1**, 134–48.

Johnson-Laird, P. (1983). *Mental models*. Cambridge University Press.

Johnson-Laird, P. Legrenzi, P., Girotto, V., and Legrenzi, M. (2000). Illusions in reasoning about consistency. *Science*, **288**, 531–2.

Johnson-Laird, P. and Steedman, M. (1978). The psychology of syllogisms. *Cognitive Psychology*, **10**, 64–99.

Johnson-Laird, P., Byrne, R., and Tabossi, P. (1989). Reasoning by model: the case of multiple quantification. *Psychological Review*, **96**, 658–73.

Kurtz, K., Gentner, D., and Gunn, J. (1999). Reasoning. *Cognitive science: the handbook of perception and cognition* (2nd edn.) (ed. Rumelhart, D. and Bly, B.), pp. 145–200. Academic Press, San Diego, CA.

Lakatos, I. (1976). *Proofs and refutations: the logic of mathematical discovery.* Cambridge University Press.

Lakoff, G. (1993). The contemporary theory of metaphor. *Metaphor and thought* (2nd edn.) (ed. A. Ortony), pp. 202–51. Cambridge University Press.

Lear, J. (1980). *Aristotle and logical theory.* Cambridge University Press.

Leevers, H. J. and Harris, P. L. (2000). Counterfactual syllogistic reasoning in normal four-year-olds, children with learning disabilities, and children with autism. *Journal of Experimental Child Psychology*, **76**, 64–87.

Lehman, D. Lempert, R., and Nisbett, R. (1988). The effects of graduate training on reasoning: formal discipline and thinking about everyday life events. *American Psychologist*, **43**, 431–42.

Leslie, A. (1987). Pretence and representation: the origins of a 'theory of mind'. *Psychological Review*, **94**, 412–26.

Levesque, H. (1988). Logic and the complexity of reasoning. *Journal of Philosophical Logic*, **17**, 355–89.

Levy-Bruhl, L. (1922). *La mentalité primitive*. Paris.

Lewis, D. (1969). *Convention: a philosophical study*. Harvard University Press: Cambridge, MA.

Lohman, D. and Kyllonen, P. (1983). Individual differences in solution strategy on spatial tasks. *Individual differences in Cognition*, (Vol. 1) (ed. R. Dillon and R. Schmeck), pp. 105–35. Academic Press, NY.

Manktelow, K., Fairley, N., Kilpatrick, S., and Over, D. (1999). Pragmatics and strategies for practical reasoning. *Deductive reasoning and strategies* (ed. G. De Vooght, G. D'Ydewalle, W. Schaeken, and A. Vandiernedonck). Erlbaum, Mawah, NJ.

Manktelow, K. and Over, D. (1990). *Inference and understanding: a philosophical perspective*. Routledge, London.

Maynard-Smith, J. (1964). Group selection and kin selection. *Nature*, **201**, 1145–7.

Miller, G. A. (1967). *The psychology of communication*. Basic Book, New York.

Mithen, S. (2000). Mind, brain and material culture: an archeological perspective. *Evolution and the human mind: modularity, language and meta-cognition* (ed. Carruthers, P. and Chamberlin, A.). Cambridge University Press.

Monaghan, P. and Stenning, K. (1998). Effects of representational modality and thinking style on learning to solve reasoning problems. *Proceedings of 20th Annual Meeting of the Cognitive Science Society*, pp. 716–21. Lawrence Erlbaum Associates, Maweh, NJ.

Monaghan, P., Stenning, K., Oberlander, J., and Sönstrod, C. (1999). Integrating psychometric and computational approaches to individual differences in multimodal reasoning. *Proceedings of the 21st Meeting of the Cognitive Science Society*, pp. 405–10. Lawrence Erlbaum Associates, Maweh, NJ.

Montague, R. (1974). English as a formal language. *Formal philosophy: selected papers of Richard Montague* (ed. R. Thomason). pp. 108–221. Yale University Press, New Haven, CN.

Moravcsik, J. M. (1998). *Meaning, creativity and the partial inscrutability of the human mind*. CSLI Publications, Stanford, CA.

Morgan, J. J. and Morton, J. T. (1944). The distortion of syllogistic reasoning by personal convictions. *Journal of Social Psychology*, **20**, 39–59.

Netz, R. (1999). *The shaping of deduction in Greek mathematics*. Cambridge University Press.

Newell, A. (1973). You can't play twenty questions with nature and win. *Visual Information Processing*. Academic Press, New York.

Newell, A. and Simon, H. (1972). *Human problem solving*. Prentice-Hall, Englewood Cliffs, NJ.

Newstead, S. (1989). Interpretational errors in syllogistic reasoning. *Journal of Memory and Language*, **28**, 78–91.

Newstead, S. (1995). Gricean implicatures and syllogistic reasoning. *Journal of Memory and Language*, **34**, 644–64.

Nichols, S., Stich, S., Leslie, A. (1995). Choice effects and the ineffectiveness of simulation: Response. *Mind and Language*, **10**, 437–45.

Nisbett, R. E., Peng, K., Choi, I., and Norenzayan, A. (in press). Culture and systems of thought: holistic vs. analytic cognition. *Psychological Review*.

Oberlander J., Monaghan, P., Cox R., Stenning, K., and Tobin, R. (1999*a*). Unnatural language discourse: an empirical study of multimodal proof styles. *Journal of Logic, Language, and Information*, **8**, 363–84.

Pask, G. (1975). *Conversation, cognition, and learning: a cybernetic theory and methodology*. Elsevier, Amsterdam.

Peacocke, C. (1994). Content, computation and externalism. *Mind and Language*, **9**, 303–35.

Perner, J., Leekham, S., and Wimmer, H. (1987). Three-year olds' difficulty with false belief: the case for a conceptual deficit. *British Journal of Developmental Psychology*, **5**, 125–37.

Peterson, D. M. and Riggs, K. J. (1999). Adaptive modelling and mindreading. *Mind and Language*, **14**, 80–112.

Premack, D. and Woodruff, G. (1978). Does the chimpanzee have a theory of mind? *Brain and Behavioural Sciences*, **1**, 515–26.

Ramscar, M. and Hahn, U. (1998). What family resemblances are not: the continuing relevance of Wittgenstein to the study of concepts and categories. *Proceedings of the 20th Annual Conference of the Cognitive Science Society*, pp. 865–70. Lawrence Erlbaum Associates.

Rips, L. (1994). *The Psychology of proof*. MIT Press, Cambridge, MA.

Russell, J. (ed.) (1997). *Autism as an executive disorder*. Oxford University Press.

Schelling, T. (1960). *The strategy of conflict*. Oxford University Press.

Schubert, L. (1976). Extending the expressive power of semantic networks. *Artificial Intelligence*, **7**, 163–98.

Scotto di Luzio, P. (2000). Formality and logical systems. *Theory and application of diagrams: lecture notes in artificial intelligence 1889* (ed. M. Anderson, P. Cheng, and V. Haarslev), pp. 117–31. Springer Verlag, Berlin.

Scribner, S. (1977). Modes of thinking and ways of speaking: culture and logic reconsidered. *Discourse production and comprehension* (ed. R. Freedle), Erlbaum, Hillsdale, NJ. Reprinted in: *Mind and social practice: selected writings of Sylvia Scribner* (ed. E. Tobach, R. Joffe-Falmange, M. Parlee, L. Martin, and A. Scribner) (1997). Cambridge University Press (1997).

Scribner, S. and Cole, M. (1981). *The Psychology of literacy*. Harvard University Press, Cambridge, MA.

Sells, S. (1936). The atmosphere effect: an experimental study of reasoning. *Archives of Psychology*, **29**, 3–72.

Shimojima, A. (1999). The graphic linguistic distinction. *Artificial Intelligence Review*, **13**, 313–35.

Shin, S. (2002). *Iconicity in logical systems*. MIT Press, Cambridge, MA.

Sloman, A. (1996). The empirical case for two systems of reasoning. *Psychological Bulletin*, **11**, 3–22.

Smith, A. (1786) *An inquiry into the nature and causes of the wealth of nations*. (4th edn.). Strahan & Cadell, London.

Snow, R. (1980). Aptitude processes. *Aptitude learning and instruction* Vol. 1: *Cognitive process analyses of aptitude* (ed. R. Snow, P-A Frederico, and W. Montague). Erlbaum, Hillsdale, NJ.

Sowa, J. F. (1984). *Conceptual structures: information processing in mind and machine*. Addison Wesley, Reading, MA.

Sperber, D. and Wilson, D. (1995). *Relevance: communication and cognition* (2nd edn.). Blackwell, Oxford.

Sperber, D., Cara, F., and Girotto, V. (1995). Relevance theory explains the selection task. *Cognition*, **57**, 31–95.

Stanovich, K. and West, R. (2000). Individual differences in reasoning: implications for the rationality debate? *Behavioural and Brain Sciences*, **23**, 645–726.

Stenning, K. (1978). Anaphora as an approach to pragmatics. *Linguistic theory and psychological reality* (ed. M. Halle, J. Bresnan, and G. A. Miller). MIT Press, Cambridge, pp. 162–200.

Stenning, K. (1992). Distinguishing conceptual and empirical issues about mental models. *Models in the Mind* (ed. Y. Rogers, A. Rutherford, and P. Bibby), pp. 29–48. Academic Press, New York.

Stenning, K. and Oberlander, J. (1995). A cognitive theory of graphical and linguistic reasoning: logic and implementation. *Cognitive Science*, **19**, 97–140.

Stenning, K. (1996). Embedding logic in communication: lessons from the logic classroom. *Logic and Argumentation* (ed. J. van Benthem, F. H. van Eemeren, R. Grootendorst, and F. Veltman), pp. 227–40. North Holland, Amsterdam.

Stenning, K. (1997). Distinguishing semantic from processing explanations of the usability of representations: applying expressiveness analysis to animation. *Proceedings of Intelligent Multi-Modal Interface Workshop*. (ed. J. Lee). AAAI Press. http://www.aaai.org/Press/Books/Lee/

Stenning, K. (1999*a*). Representation and conceptualisation in educational communication. In van Someren, M., Reimann, P., Boshuizen, E., and de Jong, T. (eds.) *Learning with multiple representations*, pp. 321–334. Kluwer.

Stenning, K. (1999*b*). The cognitive consequences of modality assignment for educational communication: the picture in logic. *Learning and Instruction*, **9**, 391–410.

Stenning, K. (2000). Distinctions with differences: comparing criteria for distinguishing diagrammatic from sentential systems. *Theory and application of diagrams: lecture notes in artificial intelligence 1889.* (ed. M. Anderson, P. Cheng, and V. Haarslev), pp. 132–48. Springer Verlag, Berlin.

Stenning, K. and Cox, R. (submitted). Rethinking deductive tasks: relating interpretation and reasoning through individual differences.

Stenning, K. and Monaghan, P. (2000). Cooperative vs. adversarial communication: contextual embedding vs. disengagement. Commentary on 'Individual differences in reasoning: implications for the rationality debate?' by Stanovich, K. E. and West, R. F. *Behavioral and Brain Sciences*, **23**, 696–7.

Stenning, K. and Oberlander, J. (1994). Spatial inclusion as an analogy for set membership: a case study of analogy at work. *Analogical connections.* (ed. K. Holyoak and J. Barnden), pp. 446–86. Erlbaum, Hillsdale, NJ.

Stenning, K., Cox, R., and Oberlander, J. (1995*a*). Contrasting the cognitive effects of graphical and sentential logic teaching: reasoning, representation and individual differences. *Language and Cognitive Processes*, **10**, 333–54.

Stenning, K. and Tobin, R. (1997). Assigning information to modalities: comparing graphical treatments of the syllogism. *Logic, action and cognition: essays in philosophical logic.* (ed. E. Ejerhed and S. Lindstrom), pp. 211–28. Kluwer, Dordrecht.

Stenning, K., Cox, R., and Oberlander, J. (1995*b*). Attitudes to logical independence: traits in quantifier interpretation. Proceedings of Seventeenth Meeting of the Cognitive Science Society, Pittsburgh 1995. pp. 742–7.

Stenning, K., Inder, R., and Neilson, I. (1995). Applying semantic concepts to the media assignment problem in multi-media communication. *Diagrammatic reasoning: computational and cognitive perspectives on problem solving with diagrams* (ed. B. Chandrasekaran, N. H. Narayanan, and J. Glasgow), pp. 303–38. MIT Press, Cambridge, MA.

Stenning, K. and van Lambalgen, M. (submitted). *A little logic goes a long way: basing experiment on semantic theory in the cognitive science of conditional reasoning.*

Stenning, K. and van Lambalgen, M. (2001). Semantics as a foundation for psychology: a case study of Wason's selection task. *Journal of Logic, Language and Information*, **10**, 273–317.

Stenning, K. and Yule, P. (1997). Image and language in human reasoning: a syllogistic illustration. *Cognitive Psychology*, **34**, 109–59.

Stenning, K., Yule P., and Cox, R. (1996). Quantifier interpretation and syllogistic reasoning. *Proceedings of the Cognitive Science Conference* (ed. G. W. Cottrell), pp. 678–83. Lawrence Erlbaum Associates, Mahwah, NJ.

Stenning, K., Greeno, J., Hall, R., Sommerfeld, M., and Wiebe, M. (2002). Coordinating mathematical with biological multiplication: conceptual learning as the development of heterogeneous reasoning systems. *The Role of Communication in Learning to Model* (ed. P. Brna, M. Baker, K. Stenning, and A. Tiberghien). Lawrence Erlbaum Associates, Maweh, NJ.

Sternberg, R. J. (1985). *Human abilities: an information-processing approach.* W. H. Freeman, New York.

Strom, D., Kemeny, V., Lehrer, R., and Forman, E. (2001). Visualising the emergent structure of children's mathematical argument. *Cognitive Science*, **25**, 733–73.

Tomasello, M. and Call, J. (1997). *Primate cognition*. Oxford University Press.

Trivers, R. (1971). The evolution of reciprocal altruism. *Quarterly Review of Biology*, **46**, 35–57.

van der Pal, J. (1995). The balance of situated action and formal instruction for learning conditional reasoning. PhD Thesis, Twente University. ISBN 90-9008710-9.

Vygotsky, L. (1962). *Thought and language*. MIT Press, Cambridge, MA.

Vygotsky, L. (1978). *Mind in Society* (ed. M. Cole, V. John-Steiner, S. Scribner, and E. Souberman). Harvard University Press, Cambridge, MA.

Waddington, C. H. (1957). *The strategy of the genes: a discussion of some aspects of theoretical biology*. Allen and Unwin, London.

Wason, P. (1968). Reasoning about a rule. *Quarterly Journal of Experimental Psychology*, **20**, 273–81.

Wason, P. and Green, D. (1984). Reasoning and mental representation. *Quarterly Journal of Experimental Psychology*, **36A**, 598–611.

Werner, H. and Kaplan, B. (1984). *Symbol formation*. Lawrence Erlbaum Associates, Hillsdale.

Whitley, K. N. (1997). Visual programming languages and the empirical evidence for and against. *Journal of Visual Languages and Computing*, **8**, 109–42.

Witkin, H. A., Oltman, P. K., Raskin, E., and Karp, S. A. (1971). *A Manual for the Embedded Figures Test*. Consulting Psychologists Press, Palo Alto, CA.

Wittgenstein, L. (1967). *Philosophical Investigations* (3rd edn.) (translated G. E. M. Anscombe). Blackwell, Oxford.

Subject index

Author index